THE DESTINY OF MAN

"It is sad not to see any good in goodness"—GOGOL
(*from a note-book for* 1846)

NICOLAS BERDYAEV

FREEDOM AND THE SPIRIT
THE ORIGIN OF RUSSIAN COMMUNISM
THE MEANING OF HISTORY
SLAVERY AND FREEDOM
SPIRIT AND REALITY
SOLITUDE AND SOCIETY

NICOLAS BERDYAEV

The Destiny of Man

HYPERION PRESS, INC.
Westport, Connecticut

Published in 1954 by G. Bles, London
Hyperion reprint edition 1979 1986
Library of Congress Catalog Number 78-14100
ISBN 0-88355-775-4
Printed in the United States of America

Library of Congress Cataloging in Publication Data
Berdiaev, Nikolai Aleksandrovich, 1874-1948.
   The destiny of man.   .

   Translation of O naznachenii cheloveka.
   Reprint of the 4th ed. published in 1954 by G. Bles,
London.
   Includes bibliographical references.
   1. Ethics   2. Christian ethics—Orthodox Eastern
authors. 3. Man. 4. Eschatology. 5. Philosophy and
religion. I. Title.
[B4238.B43023 1979]   241   78-14100
ISBN 0-88355-775-4

Contents

PART I

PRINCIPLES

CHAPTER

PAGE

I. THE PROBLEM OF ETHICAL KNOWLEDGE - - - - 1

1. Philosophy, science and religion.—2. Subject and object. Objectification in knowledge.—3. The task of ethics.—4. The fundamental problem of ethics. The criterion of good and evil.

II. THE ORIGIN OF GOOD AND EVIL - - - - - 23

1. God and man.—2. The Fall. The origin of good and evil.

III. MAN - - - - - - - - - - 45

1. The problems of philosophical anthropology. Types of anthropological theory.—2. Personalism. Personality and individuality. Personality and society.—3. Sex. The masculine and the feminine.— 4. The conscious and the unconscious.—5. Freedom of will and ethics.

PART II

MORALITY ON THIS SIDE OF GOOD AND EVIL

I. THE ETHICS OF LAW - - - - - - - - 84

1. The dualism of good and evil.—2. The primitive moral consciousness.—3. The social character of the law.—4. Normative ethics. Pharisaism.

II. THE ETHICS OF REDEMPTION - - - - - - 103

1. The good under grace.—2. The morality of the Gospel and the morality of the Scribes and Pharisees.—3. The Christian attitude to the sinful and the wicked.—4. The Christian morality as the morality of strength.—5. Suffering. Asceticism. Love.—6. The Gospel message of the Kingdom of God.

III. THE ETHICS OF CREATIVENESS - - - - - - 126

1. The nature of creativeness.—2. The creatively individual character of moral acts.—3. The part of imagination in the moral life. The ethics of energy.

v

Contents

CHAPTER   PAGE

IV. CONCRETE PROBLEMS OF ETHICS - - - - -   154

1. The tragic and paradoxical character of the moral life.—2. On truth and falsehood.—3. Conscience and freedom: The critique of pure conscience.—4. Fear, terror and anguish. The dull and the commonplace. Phantasms.—5. Love and compassion.—6. The state, revolution and war.—7. The social question, labour and technical progress.—8. Sex, marriage and love.—9. Human ideals. The doctrine of gifts.—10. Symbolism and realism in ethics.

PART III

OF THE LAST THINGS. ESCHATOLOGICAL ETHICS

I. DEATH AND IMMORTALITY - - - - - - - - 249

II. HELL - - - - - - - - - - 266

III. PARADISE. BEYOND GOOD AND EVIL - - - - 284

CHAPTER ONE

The Problem of Ethical Knowledge

I. PHILOSOPHY, SCIENCE AND RELIGION

I DO not intend to begin, in accordance with the German tradition, with an epistemological justification. I want to begin with an epistemological accusation, or, rather, with an accusation against epistemology. Epistemology is an expression of doubt in the power and the validity of philosophical knowledge. It implies a division which undermines the possibility of knowledge. Thinkers who devote themselves to epistemology seldom arrive at ontology. The path they follow is not one which leads to reality. The most creative modern philosophers, such as Bergson, M. Scheler and Heidegger, are little concerned with epistemology. Man has lost the power of knowing real being, has lost access to reality and been reduced to studying knowledge. And so in his pursuit of knowledge he is faced throughout with knowledge and not with being. But one cannot arrive at being—one can only start with it. In using the term "being" I am not referring to any particular system of ontology, such as that of St. Thomas Aquinas, which is prior to a critical theory of knowledge. I do not believe that it is at all possible to return to a pre-critical, dogmatic metaphysic. All I mean is that we must turn to reality itself, to actual life, and overcome the duality which undermines the value of cognitive activity. It was inevitable that philosophical knowledge should pass through this duality and critical reflection; such was the path of philosophy in Europe. It was its inner dramatic destiny. The critical theory itself, claiming as it does to be independent of the concrete facts of life, was an expression of European life and culture. It was a higher and more subtle form of European "enlightenment" which claims to be universal. Kant continued the work of the ancient and the Anglo-French rationalistic philosophy, but he considerably deepened the conception of enlightenment. Reason seeks to possess itself, to recognize its limits and possibilities. It limits itself in Kant and expands to infinity in Hegel.[1] The dogmatic ontology of the Greek and the mediaeval philosophy could not resist the critique of reason, and it is impossible to return to the pre-critical forms of philosophizing. Even modern Thomism, which refuses to

[1] This is rightly pointed out by Kroner in his book, *Von Kant bis Hegel*.

recognize Descartes and indeed the whole of modern philosophy, is nevertheless bound to be neo-Thomism and to pass through critical reflection. The point is that the critique of knowledge, the reflection of reason upon itself, is not the abstract theory which it claims to be, but a living experience. However strongly knowledge may contrast itself with life and doubt the possibility of knowing life, it is itself a part of life ; it is generated by life and reflects its destinies. The same thing is true of epistemological thought. It is an experience of life, and such experience cannot be simply annulled : it can only be lived through and superseded by another, a fuller experience which will necessarily include the first as a part of itself. The opposition between knowledge and existence, regarded as an object standing over against the knowing subject, is not primary but secondary, and is a result of reflection. The primary fact is that knowledge itself is a reality and takes place in reality. One of the worst assumptions of epistemology is that knowledge is concerned with objects which lie outside it and must somehow be reflected and expressed in it. But if we rise to a spiritual conception of knowledge, we shall see that knowledge is an act in and through which something happens to reality. Reality is illumined through knowledge. It is not a case of someone or something cognizing being as a separate and independent object : being cognizes itself, and through this cognition expands and is lit up from within. It is only at the second stage that we find the object of knowledge as a *Gegenstand*.[1] A cleavage takes place in reality, and in knowledge it expresses itself as objectivization.

In saying that being is primary I am referring not to being which has already been rationalized and shaped by categories of reason, but to " first life " prior to all rationalization, to being which is still dark, though this darkness signifies nothing evil. Only a reality which has already been modified and rationalized by acts of knowing can stand over against the knowing subject. " First life " does not confront him as an object, for originally he is submerged in it. The severance between knowledge and reality is the fatal result of rationalism which has not been thought out to the end. It denies that the act of knowing is an existential act. But if reality stands over against knowledge, there can be no inner connection between the two, and knowledge does not form part of reality. Hence, knowledge is not *something*, but is *about something*. The knower does not take his knowledge seriously. The world of real ideas ceases to exist for

---

[1] N. Hartmann in his book, *Metaphysik der Erkenntniss*, arrives at the conclusion that the knowing subject is a part of reality and that reason is plunged into the dark sphere of the trans-intelligible which transcends it, but in which it is immanent.

him, and he is left only with ideas about the real ; there is no God but only various ideas about God which he investigates ; there is no real good and evil but only different ideas about good and evil, and so on. At the time when knowledge was part of being and took place within it, the knower could himself be known. Plato, Plotinus, St. Augustine, Pascal, Jacob Boehme and others were both knowers and subject-matter of knowledge—and of very interesting knowledge, too. But a modern knower who places himself outside reality cannot be known, since only reality can be the subject-matter of knowledge. He refuses to form part of reality and does not want his knowing to be a living, existential act.

This degraded position of philosophical knowledge coincides with the stage at which philosophy wants to be a science and finds itself in slavish dependence upon natural sciences. Philosophy is filled with black envy of positive science, so prosperous and successful. This envy leads to no good and results in a loss of dignity both for philosophy and the philosophers. Scientific philosophy renounces wisdom (Husserl) and regards this as a gain and an achievement. There is something tragic in the fate of philosophic knowledge. It is very difficult for philosophy to vindicate its freedom and independence, which have always been threatened on different sides. Philosophy, in the past dependent upon religion, is at present dependent upon science. It is for ever menaced with being enslaved either by religion or by science, and it is hard for it to retain its own place and pursue its own way. Indeed the kind of independence which it does defend must be recognized as mistaken. The claim of philosophy to be independent of life and to separate itself from it is a false claim, and as a matter of fact can never be realized. The knower's religious faith and religious life are bound to influence his philosophy ; he cannot forget them in his cognitive activity. Nor can he forget his scientific knowledge. But the fact of a philosopher having religious faith and scientific knowledge is certainly not a disadvantage ; the trouble only begins when religion and science become an external authority for his thought. Both religion and science may enrich philosophical knowledge from within, but they must not dominate it from without. Philosophy has been expected to conform either to theology or to science and even to mathematical physics. Only at brief intervals has philosophy been able to breathe the air of freedom. Emancipating itself from the crushing power of theology it fell into still worse slavery, to autocratic and despotic science.

But to say that philosophy must not be enslaved by foreign elements does not imply that it is self-contained and detached from life. If a philosopher believes in the religious revelation his thought is bound to be nurtured by it. The revelation, however, is for him not an external authority but an inner fact, a philosophical experience. Revelation is present in philosophical knowledge as a light from within. Philosophical knowledge is essentially human and always contains an element of free-dom. It is not revelation, but man's free cognitive reaction to revelation. If a thinker is a Christian and believes in Christ he is not in the least bound to make his philosophy conform to the Orthodox or Catholic or Protes-tant theology ; but he may acquire the mind of Christ and this will make his philosophy different from that of non-Christian thinkers. Revelation cannot force upon philosophy any theories or ideal constructions, but it may give it facts and experiences which enrich knowledge. If philosophy is to be at all possible it must be free ; it brooks no constraint. In every act of knowledge it freely faces truth and cannot put up with obstacles or barriers. Philosophy is led to its conclusions by the cognitive process itself; unlike theology it cannot have the results of knowledge forced upon it from without. This does not mean, however, that philosophy is autonomous in the sense of being self-centred and self-sufficient. Auto-nomy is a misconception and is by no means the same thing as freedom. Philosophy is a part of life ; spiritual experience lies at the basis of philoso-phical knowledge ; a philosopher must be in touch with the primary source of life and derive his cognitive experience from it. Knowledge means consecration into the mystery of being and of life. It is a light which springs from being and within it. Knowledge cannot create being out of itself, out of the idea, as Hegel thought. Religious revelation means that being reveals itself to the knower. He cannot be blind and deaf to it and affirm the autonomy of philosophical knowledge in spite of that which is revealed to him.

It is the tragedy of philosophy that having freed itself from the higher realm of religion and revelation it falls into a worse dependence upon the lower realm of positive science and scientific experience. Philosophy loses its birthright and all proof of its ancient lineage. Its autonomy has been but of short duration ; so-called scientific philosophy is certainly not autonomous. Science was once born of philosophy and grew out of it, but the child rose against its mother. No one denies that philosophy must reckon with the growth of sciences and take their results into consideration. But this does not mean that it must subordinate itself to particular sciences in its highest contemplations or try to imitate them, tempted by their striking outward success. Philosophy is knowledge, but it is impossible to identify it with scientific knowledge. Philosophy is *sui generis* and cannot be reduced to science or to religion. It is a special domain of

4

spiritual culture, different from, but standing in complex and intimate relations with, science and religion. The principles of philosophy do not depend upon the results and achievements of science. Philosophy cannot wait for the discoveries of science. Science is in a perpetual flux ; its theories and hypotheses frequently change and become out of date ; it continually makes new discoveries. During the last thirty years there has been a revolution in physics which has radically changed its fundamental principles.[1] But can it be said that Plato's theory of Ideas has been superseded by the scientific discoveries of the nineteenth and twentieth centuries? It is far more stable than they are, far more eternal, for it is more concerned with that which is eternal. Hegel's philosophy of nature is out of date and, indeed, never was his strong point ; but his logic, ontology and dialectic have not been in the least affected by the growth of natural sciences. It would be absurd to say that Jacob Boehme's doctrine of the *Ungrund* or of Sophia are disproved by modern mathematical sciences. It is clear that we have to do here with quite different and incommensurable objects. The world is revealed to philosophy in a different way than it is to science, and the philosophical way of knowing is different. Sciences are concerned with abstract, partial realities, they do not see the world as a whole or grasp its meaning. The claim of mathematical physics to be an ontology, discovering as it were things in themselves and not empirical events, is ridiculous. It is precisely mathematical physics, the most perfect of sciences, which is farthest away from the mysteries of being, for these mysteries are revealed only in and through man, in spiritual life and spiritual experience.[2] In spite of Husserl, who does his utmost to make philosophy a pure science and eliminate from it all element of wisdom, philosophy always has been and will be wisdom. The end of wisdom is the end of philosophy. Philosophy is the love of wisdom and the unfolding of wisdom in man, a creative effort to break through to the meaning of existence. Philosophy is neither religious faith nor science—it is itself. It is bound to wage a painful struggle for its rights, which are always called into doubt. Sometimes it puts itself above religion, as it does with Hegel, and then it exceeds its bounds. It was born in the struggle of the awakening thought against traditional popular beliefs. Freedom is the very breath of life to it. But even when the

[1] See e.g. Eddington's *The nature of the physical world.*

[2] Heidegger in his *Sein und Zeit*, the most remarkable philosophical book of recent years, bases the whole of his ontology upon the knowledge of human existence. Being as Care (*Sorge*) reveals itself in man only. The French philosophy of science in Meyerson, Brunswig and others follows a different line of thought.

philosophical thought of Greece separated itself from and opposed itself to the popular religion, it preserved its connection with the higher religious life of Greece, with the mysteries and Orphism. We see this in Heraclitus, Pythagoras and Plato. Philosophy, which is truly significant and is more than a mere play of the intellect, is always based upon spiritual and moral experience. Intuitive insight is only vouchsafed to thinkers whose entire spirit is intent upon knowledge. How, then, are we to understand the relation between science and philosophy, to distinguish their respective domains and to co-ordinate them? It is not sufficient to define philosophy as the theory of principles or as the most generalized knowledge about the world or even as the theory about the nature of being. The chief characteristic which distinguishes philosophic from scientific knowledge is that philosophy knows being in and through man and finds in man the solution of the problem of meaning, while science knows being as it were apart from man and outside him. Therefore for philosophy being is spirit and for science being is nature. This distinction between spirit and nature has, of course, nothing to do with the distinction between the psychical and the physical.[1] In the end philosophy inevitably becomes the philosophy of the spirit, and only in that aspect is it independent of science. Philosophic anthropology must be the basic philosophic discipline : it is the central part of the philosophy of the spirit. It is essentially different from the sciences which study man—biology, sociology or psychology. The difference lies in the fact that philosophy studies man in and through man and regards him as belonging to the kingdom of the spirit, while science studies man as a part of the kingdom of nature, i.e. as an object. Philosophy must not deal with objects, for nothing must be objectified for it. The fundamental characteristic of the philosophy of the spirit is that for it there is no object of knowledge. To know man in and through man means not to make him into an object. Meaning is revealed to me only when I am in myself, i.e. in the spirit, and when thinghood, external objectivity, does not exist for me. Nothing that is an object for me has meaning. There can only be meaning in that which is in me and with me, i.e. in the spiritual world. The only way radically to distinguish between philosophy and science is to admit that philosophy is unobjectified knowledge, knowledge of the spirit as it is in itself and not as objectified in nature, i.e. knowledge of meaning and participation in meaning. Science and scientific foresight give man power and security, but they can also devastate his consciousness and sever him from reality. Indeed it might be said that science is based upon the alienation of man from reality and of

[1] See my book, *The Philosophy of the Free Spirit.*

reality from man.[1] The knower is outside reality, and the reality he knows is external to him. Everything becomes an object, i.e. foreign to man and opposed to him. The world of philosophic ideas ceases to be my world, revealing itself in me, and becomes an objective world standing over against me as something alien to me. This is why works on the history of philosophy are an instance of scientific and not of philosophical knowledge. History of philosophy can only be philosophic and not merely scientific if the world of ideas be the knower's own inner world, known in and through his own consciousness. I can know philosophically my own ideas alone, making Plato's or Hegel's ideas my own, i.e. knowing them from within and not from without—knowing them in the spirit instead of objectifying them. This is the fundamental principle of all philosophy that has its roots in reality. There is nothing subjective about it, for subjectivity is merely the correlative of objectivity. An excellent monograph on Plato and Aristotle, on St. Thomas Aquinas and Descartes, or on Kant and Hegel may be of great value to philosophy, but it will not be philosophy. There can be no philosophy about other people's ideas or about the world of ideas considered from without. Philosophy can only be about one's own ideas, about the spirit, about man in and for himself; in other words, it must be an intellectual expression of the philosopher's own destiny. The historical method which overloads memory and objectifies ideas, regarding them entirely from outside, is as fatal to philosophy as subjective idealism or naturalism. The spiritual devastation that results from these three ways of approaching philosophy is truly terrible. They result in a relativism which is made absolute. This is how the creative power of knowledge is destroyed and the discovery of meaning becomes impossible. It is enslavement of philosophy by science—scientific terrorism.

Philosophy sees the world from the point of view of man, while science sees the world apart from man. To free philosophy from all anthropological ideas would be to destroy it. Naturalism also sees the world from the point of view of man, but it does so secretly and will not admit it. It is not true that being, interpreted objectively, has primacy over man ; on the contrary, man has primacy over being, since being is revealed only in and through man. And it is only in man that spirit is revealed. The conception of being which is not spirit, and is " without " and not " within ", results in the tyranny of naturalism. Philosophy easily becomes abstract

[1] The view worked out by Meyerson in his *De l'explication dans les sciences* concerning the ontological character of science seems to me mistaken. Science is pragmatic.

and loses touch with the sources of life. This happens whenever it seeks knowledge outside man instead of in and through him. Man has his roots in life—in "first life"—and is given revelations concerning its mysteries. It is only at those depths that philosophy comes into contact with religion, but it does so freely and from within. Philosophy is based upon the assumption that the world is part of man, and not *vice versa*. If man were merely a small and fragmentary part of the world, the audacious idea of knowledge could never have occurred to him. This truth is implicit in science, too, but it is foreign to scientific method. Knowledge of reality in and through man has nothing to do with subjective idealism, which, on the contrary, confines man to the objectified world of nature. Considered psychologically man is but a fragmentary part of the world. It is not subjective idealism but transcendental anthropologism which is meant here. It is strange to forget that I, the knower, the philosopher, am a human being. Transcendental man is the presupposition of philosophy, and to ignore this means either nothing at all or the death of philosophical knowledge. Man is an existent, he has being and is a part of being, but *being is conformable to man,* and this is why I can discover in it meaning which is commensurable with me and my understanding. In so far as Husserl's phenomenological method is intended to do away with the human element in knowledge it must be pronounced invalid, in spite of its merits in other respects. It has led to excellent results in anthropology, ethics, ontology (M. Scheler, N. Hartmann, Heidegger), and has brought philosophy out of the *cul-de-sac* in which the Neo-Kantian theory of knowledge landed it. But Husserl's phenomenology is connected with a particular form of Platonism, with the conception, namely, of an ideal non-human realm—and this is its weakness. Knowledge does not consist in man's passively receiving into himself the objects of knowledge—ideal, non-human entities (*Wesenheiten*) ; it implies man's spiritual creative activity. The meaning of things is revealed not through their entering into man who is passive in relation to them, but through man's creative activity reaching out to meaning beyond an unmeaning world. There is no meaning in the solid, concrete world of objects. Meaning is only revealed in man's activity and implies that reality is conformable to man. Non-human ideal being is meaningless. Meaning is in the spirit and not in things or in nature. Being is conformable to man inasmuch as it is spiritual. In spite of its passive and non-human character Husserl's method is valuable because it is directed upon being and not upon constructions of thought. Man's creativeness does not mean that he construes a world of his own. Meaning is to be found not in the object which enters the mind and not in the subject who construes a mental world, but in the spiritual world which is neither objective nor subjective but is pure activity and spiritual dynamics. The process of knowledge is a real event, and meaning is revealed in it actively, i.e. the darkness of being becomes light. Knowledge *is* spiritual life and a part of the reality which is being known.

2. SUBJECT AND OBJECT. OBJECTIFICATION IN KNOWLEDGE

German epistemologists always talk about the subject and the object, the subjective and the objective. Knowledge for them is objectification. The knowing subject is not an existent ; he is an epistemological and not an ontological entity ; he is the bearer of ideal logical forms which are not human at all and whose connection with man is incomprehensible. Concrete reality disappears and is replaced by the " subject and object ". The knower is not a self, not a concrete particular person, but an epistemological subject which is not human and does not exist but is outside existence and stands over against it. And that which he knows is not an existent either, but an object correlative to him and specially constructed for knowledge. Existence slips away both from the subject and the object. The very opposition of the two does away with existence. Objectification destroys life and being. If knowledge is objectification it can never reach its goal. This is the tragedy of knowledge which many philosophers have clearly recognized and formulated as follows : existence is irrational and individual, but we can only know the rational and the general.[1] The object proves to be utterly alien to the subject and opposed to it. They are logically correlative and cannot be separated one from the other, and yet they are for ever opposed to each other. If " Plato " or " early Christianity " or " German mysticism " become an object of knowledge for me, I cannot understand them or discover any meaning in them. To objectify is to destroy meaning ; in order to understand meaning, one must enter into it, and this communion is not objectification.[2] This is perfectly clear in the so-called " spiritual sciences ", where objectification invariably means the end of true knowledge. With the " natural sciences " the case is somewhat different, but I am not concerned with that at the moment.

[1] This is particularly insisted on by Windelband's and Rickert's school of thought.

[2] That which Lévy Bruhl regards as characteristic of primitive mentality—communion with the content known, participation in it—is, as a matter of fact, true knowledge of reality. See his remarkable book, *Les fonctions mentales dans les sociétés inférieures*.

The fundamental problem of epistemology is to determine who the knower is and whether he belongs to the realm of existence: its business is to find a new and deeper meaning in the inevitable presupposition that knowledge is a human activity. Kant and the idealists maintain that man is not the knower—for if he were, knowledge would be relative, and the world is not that which is known, for if it were, we should be committed to naïve realism. Theories of knowledge which date back to Kant substitute for the problem of man and of his power to know reality the problem of transcendental consciousness, of the epistemological subject, world-spirit or divine reason. Or, if they are not concerned with transcendental consciousness, they study the psychological contents of consciousness. But neither the transcendental self nor the series of psychic events is *man*. Epistemology refuses to study man as a knower and abandons him to psychology or sociology. And yet the fundamental question of knowledge is that of the relation between transcendental consciousness or the epistemological subject and man as a concrete and living personality. Kant's services to epistemology are invaluable, but he has not solved its problems ; he has not really answered the challenge of scepticism or relativism. The *a priori* forms which are supposed to vindicate the validity of knowledge have no direct relation to the concrete man who is the knower. Transcendental consciousness may have perfectly firm and secure grounds for knowledge, but then man's consciousness is not transcendental : it consists of mental events and is therefore doomed to be relative. Kant does not show how the transcendental consciousness gains possession of the psychical or how the latter can rise to the transcendental level. As a concrete living being struggling with the stupendous task of knowledge I derive little comfort from the fact that there is a transcendental unity of consciousness with its *a priori* forms, and that in that super-human realm scepticism and relativism are defeated from all eternity. What is important to me is that they should be defeated on the human level, by the concrete man and not by the epistemological subject. I want myself to have knowledge, instead of leaving it to the epistemological subject or to world-reason ; I want knowledge as a creative activity of man. The theory of knowledge must become a philosophical anthropology and concern itself with man and not with the transcendental ego. But it must study man from the spiritual and ontological point of view and not from the point of view of psychology or sociology. It is no consolation to me to know that there exists a Universal Reason, if I do not understand what connection it has with my human reason. Nor is it any use to have theories about God which fail to teach of the effects of His grace upon man and the world. I ask, then, what grace or light does transcendental consciousness or the world-spirit throw upon man as a living, concrete personality? How are the permanence and validity of knowledge manifested not in the superhuman realm, but in the individual man? This is the fundamental question. Neither Kant nor Hegel has given a satisfactory answer to it. According to Hegel it is not man who is the knower, but the world-reason or world-spirit, or, in the last resort, the Deity Itself. True, the self-consciousness and self-knowledge of the Deity are achieved in and through man—but what comfort is it to me? The theory that in man the Deity comes to know Itself and that the world-spirit attains its highest development in philosophy might appear highly gratifying to man's pride and his sense of dignity ; but it leaves him no independence whatever. Man is merely a function of the world-spirit, the world-reason or the Deity, merely a means or an instrument for the realization of ends that are not human at all. Nor does Husserl's " ideal being " save us from relativism and scepticism. Philosophy is saved from man, but man is not saved from it. According to Husserl, in order to know an object we must renounce everything human, become entirely passive and make it possible for the object to speak within us. In the act of cognition man must cease to exist. Knowledge takes place in the realm of ideal logical being and not in the human realm. There is more truth in the view of St. Thomas Aquinas, for although he belittles man, including him among the lower intellects, he does concern himself with the question of human knowledge.

The essential and fundamental problem is the problem of man—of his knowledge, his freedom, his creativeness. Man is the key to the mystery of knowledge and of existence. He is the enigmatic being which, though a part of nature, cannot be explained in terms of nature and through which alone it is possible to penetrate into the heart of being. Man is the bearer of meaning, although he is a fallen creature in whom meaning is distorted. But fall can only be from a height, and the very fall of man is a token of his greatness. Even in his fallen state he retains the mark of his high origin and remains capable of a higher life and of knowledge which rises above the meaningless world of things. Philosophy is bound to centre round man—there are ontological grounds for this. Man cannot be left out of knowledge, but he must be raised from the physical and the psychical to the spiritual level. The gulf between transcendental consciousness, the epistemological subject, the ideal logical being and the concrete living man makes knowledge impossible. I, a man, want to know reality, and the knowledge which may be attained in non-human realms is nothing to me. I, the knower, abide in reality from the very first and am an inalienable part of it. I know reality in and through myself, as man. Only an existent can know existence. If knowledge were not existence to begin with it could never get at existence. Knowledge takes place in being and is an event within being, a change in it. Both the knower and the knowledge are real. Knowledge is a light within being. It therefore has a cosmogonic character. When philosophers seek intuition, they seek knowledge which is not objectified but is communion with being, penetration into its depths. Intuition may be understood in an active sense and not merely passively as by Husserl or Bergson. Knowledge does not mean that being enters into the knower who is outside being. If the knower is a part of being, knowledge is active and means a change in being. Knowledge is spiritual activity. Objectification in knowledge implies that the knower and the known are mutually alien. It results in knowledge ceasing to be " something " and becoming merely " about something ". To be " about something " means to be an object of knowledge. The knowing subject confronted with being that has been thus objectified can no longer be " something ", but is excluded from being. When knowledge is " about something ", the question as to its ontological reality and value cannot be properly asked. When ideas are approached from a historical or psychological point of view, there is no point in asking whether the world to which those ideas refer is real. Has the world in which the thought of Plotinus dwelt any reality? What is essential to knowledge is that we should know God Himself and not ideas about God, i.e. that we should know the spirit and in the spirit. But this is utterly impossible if there be objectification. In this respect there is an essential difference between natural sciences and sciences of the spirit. In natural sciences objectification does not destroy the object of knowledge, since nature, which these sciences study, is itself the result of objectification. In making its discoveries physics deals with the actual real objects and not with their reflections in the human mind. In natural sciences objectification means finding the real object. They do not result in the same devastation as do the historical or the psychological inquiries into the spirit. In the realm of the spirit objectification means destruction of the reality which we seek to know, for that reality is not an object. Natural sciences are justified if only by their practical results which could not have been attained had the sciences no relation to reality.

Philosophy and " the humanities " lead to no practical results. Knowledge of the spirit—of the spirit itself and not of human thoughts and mental states—cannot be objectified. In philosophy, which is knowledge of the spirit, there must be an inner kinship between the knower and the known. There must be creative spiritual experience and a recognition of the reality of the spirit. Knowledge of truth is communion with truth and life in it; knowledge of righteousness is communion with righteousness and life in it. Knowledge of the spirit is "something" and not "about something". But the psychological and the historical treatment of philosophy involve objectification, and therefore the reality of the spirit disappears. Consciousness presupposes the subject-object relation; hence philosophical knowledge which transcends objectification and relativity is rooted in subconsciousness and rises to super-consciousness. Ethics occupies a very important, indeed a central place among spiritual sciences. Ethical knowledge can least of all be objectified and be "about something", about an object standing over against me as something alien to me. If the moral reality which I wish to know be thus objectified, it disappears completely. It is impossible to posit a value as an object of knowledge without making a valuation, i.e. without making a creative spiritual act. Theoretical and practical reason are in this case indivisible: knowledge of value cannot be separated from valuation, i.e. from life in the world of values. Moral life is not an event in nature and cannot be discovered among the series of such events. Moral life presupposes freedom; a moral valuation is always a free act. Freedom can never be found solely in the known, but must be present in the knower as the very basis of his being.

The phenomenological method goes further than the psychological and the historical and seeks to arrive at that which truly is. It requires keen insight into reality capable of penetrating to the meaning of phenomena. It may be useful in ethics, as can be seen from the work of M. Scheler and N. Hartmann; and yet phenomenology cannot provide a basis for ethics, for it does not take into account man as a knower. It assumes that we can take up a cognitive attitude enabling an object to enter our consciousness. A systematic application of the phenomenological method would always make an intuitive description of an object possible; but the point is that ethical objects cannot be described in this way at all. They are only revealed to the person who performs creative acts of valuation. The person cognizing an ethical object cannot be in a passive state and simply receive that object into his mind. If he did, the object would disappear. N. Hartmann could write his *Ethik*—a remarkable book in many respects —only because he was engaged in a moral struggle and performed creative spiritual acts. His morally-grounded atheism is an expression of that struggle. M. Scheler in his *Der Formalismus in der Ethik und die materiele*

Wertethik makes discoveries in moral knowledge only because he is engaged in defending the value of personality. The adherents of the phenomenological method do not remain true to it and this is why they achieve results that have ethical and ontological value. But Husserl who is faithful to the method he has invented has not made any discoveries by means of it. The mystery of knowledge is that in the act of knowing the knower transcends the object of knowledge. Knowledge always means transcendence of the object and creative possession of it. Knowledge must be a source of light and shed it over reality. Hence reality is enriched by knowledge. Moral knowledge inevitably strives to better reality. This does not mean, of course, that the knower must think of himself as being on a high moral level ; it simply means that he must have moral experience and through it obtain light for himself, even though it be a single ray.

There is something profoundly tragic in knowledge thus understood. Knowledge of God is difficult and in a sense impossible. We must inevitably arrive at negative results in theology and recognize that the positive method is vain and fruitless. God cannot be an object of knowledge because in the act of knowing man cannot rise above God. In moral knowledge we not merely receive moral truth into our minds, reflecting it as in a mirror—we also create it, building up the world of values. We cannot, however, create God : we can only be united to Him, serve Him with our creative activity, answer His call. Knowledge requires great daring. It means victory over ancient, primeval terror. Fear makes the search for truth and the knowledge of it impossible. Knowledge implies fearlessness. Those who stand in awe of traditional moral ideas and valuations, which always have a social origin, are incapable of creative moral knowledge. Conquest of fear is a spiritual cognitive act. This does not imply, of course, that the experience of fear is not lived through ; on the contrary, it may be deeply felt, as was the case with Kierkegaard, for instance.[1] But the creative achievement of knowledge is victory over fear. The task of ethics is not to draw up a list of traditional moral norms, but to have the daring to make creative valuations.

And it must also be said of knowledge that it is bitter, and there is no escaping that bitterness. Those who love only the sweet are incapable of knowledge. Knowledge can bestow upon us moments of joy and of highest elation, but the fruits of knowledge are bitter. In our world-aeon knowledge means exile from Eden, the loss of paradisaical bliss. Particularly bitter is moral knowledge, the knowledge of good and evil. But the

[1] See Kierkegaard, *Der Begriff der Angst*. *Angst* with him means " terror " rather than " fear ".

bitterness is due to the fallen state of the world, and in no way undermines the value of knowledge. The origin of the distinction between good and evil will be discussed further on, but in defining the nature of ethical knowledge it must be said that the very distinction between good and evil is a bitter distinction, the bitterest thing in the world. Dostoevsky says " that devilish good and evil cost us too dearly ".[1] Knowledge means fearlessness and victory over fear ; it is bitter and means acceptance of bitterness. Moral knowledge is the most bitter and the most fearless of all for in it sin and evil are revealed to us along with the meaning and value of life. There is a deadly pain in the very distinction of good and evil, of the valuable and the worthless. We cannot rest in the thought that that distinction is ultimate. The longing for God in the human heart springs from the fact that we cannot bear to be faced for ever with the distinction between good and evil and the bitterness of choice.

Ethics occupies a central place in philosophy because it is concerned with sin, with the origin of good and evil and with moral valuations. And since these problems have a universal significance, the sphere of ethics is wider than is generally supposed. It deals with meaning and value and its province is the world in which the distinction between good and evil is drawn, valuations are made and meaning is sought.

3. THE TASK OF ETHICS

Abstract *a priori* systems of ethics have little value. The basis of ethics is moral experience, which, indeed, is the basis of philosophy as a whole. A dialectic which does not rest upon any moral experience is simply an intellectual game. Plato's philosophy was inspired by moral motives, the quest for the highest good. Hegel's dialectic was an expression of genuine moral experience. But *a priori* principles in ethics really imply the rejection of moral experience ; Kant denies moral experience in theory, though, like every true philosopher, he has had it in life. Ethics cannot be merely a theoretical philosophical discipline, for it is also a moral and spiritual activity. It was that for Plato, Spinoza, Fichte and others. Ethical knowledge has a morally liberating significance. It is the final stage of the philosophy of the spirit, the harvest of a philosophical life. Christian ethics is often indentified with the doctrine of the means of salvation ; but ethics cannot be merely a soteriology, it is also a theory of values, of man's creative activity. Man is a creative being as well as a being seeking salvation.

[1] This is the main theme of L. Shestov's writings.

I should like to work out a system of ethics which is not tyrannical, i.e. not normative. All normative theories of ethics are tyrannical. My book is an attempt to give a concrete presentation of human life, its meaning, aims and values. Such a presentation inevitably has man for its centre. Ethics must be both theoretical and practical, i.e. it must call for the moral reformation of life and a revaluation of values as well as for their acceptance. And this implies that ethics is bound to contain a prophetic element. It must be a revelation of a clear conscience, unclouded by social conventions ; it must be a *critique of pure conscience*. Ethics is axiology, the theory of meaning and values. But meaning and values are not passively given, they are created. The theory of values is rooted in the highest value, which is a power radiating gracious regenerating energy. Ethics teaches about value as a force, as the highest good and the source of all power ; in this sense it is ontology as well as axiology. This is why it cannot be merely normative, for a norm as such is powerless. Ethics is concerned not with abstract, impotent norms and laws, but with real moral forces and qualities which have power. N. Hartmann's *Ethik*, the most interesting modern work on the subject, seems to me to be logically unfounded, for his ideal values are, as it were, suspended in a vacuum. He has no explanation to give of the origin of man's freedom, nor of his power to realize values in the world. Man is for him the mediator between the world of permanent ideal values and the meaningless natural world. Through his freedom man must introduce into the world purposes and value borrowed from the timeless ideal realm. Such a conception of the moral life is utterly unintelligible. In postulating atheism as the morally necessary condition of man's freedom in realizing values N. Hartmann is bound to admit the impotence of values and of goodness, or, in other words, to end in normative idealism. He thinks it an advantage that value is not based upon any ontological reality.

But N. Hartmann is right in widening the domain of ethics and including in it relations to every kind of value, whether it be cognitive or aesthetic. Man's relations to truth and to beauty unquestionably have a moral character. We have a moral duty towards truth and beauty. A cognitive or an artistic activity is not in itself moral, but our attitude towards it implies a moral activity. Ethics embraces everything that is connected with human freedom, i.e. with freely made distinctions and valuations. A free moral act may refer not only to what is generally called " moral life ", but to man's spiritual life as a whole and to all its values. Ethics is knowledge of the spirit and not of nature, and is concerned with manifestations of spiritual freedom and not of natural necessity. The spiritual world is known in a different way from the natural. Ethics has a scientific aspect, it draws upon the material provided by the history of culture, sociology, mythology, mental pathology, etc. But it is a philosophical discipline and has all the characteristics of philosophical as distinct from scientific knowledge. Ethics is bound to be prophetic, and, what is even more important, it is bound to be personal. The present book deliberately presents a personal view, for it springs from life and not from abstractions.

4. THE FUNDAMENTAL PROBLEM OF ETHICS : THE CRITERION OF GOOD AND EVIL

The fundamental problem of ethics is that of the criterion of good and evil, of the genesis of morality and the origin of moral distinctions and valuations. It is a very different question from the one asked by evolutionists who inquire into the origin and development of moral ideas. It is an infinitely deeper question. How does the distinction itself come about? how can the good be the criterion of it, when the good comes to be only after the distinction has been made? The highest value lies beyond good and evil. The force of the question is not often seen ; as a rule, ethics is entirely on this side of good and evil, and the good is not a problem for it. Nietzsche did see the full force of it. He said that the will to truth is the death of morality. It is the business of ethics both to provide a basis for morality and to show up its falsity. The paradoxality of the problem lies in the fact that the good is called into doubt and the question is asked whether it is not really evil. Gogol has given a masterly expression to the paradox in the words used as an epigraph to the present book : " It is sad not to see any good in goodness." But in asking the question " is the ' good ' good? " I still remain in the realm of yea and nay, of distinction and valuation. Suppose I say that the good is not good, that it is evil, that we must say " no " to it. That will mean that I make a valuation of the " good ", and distinguish it from something which I oppose to it and which lies beyond this " good " and this " evil ". If I regard that which is " beyond good and evil " as higher than that which is " on this side of good and evil ", I distinguish between the higher and the lower, I condemn, I appraise, I draw comparisons. And, of course, Nietzsche was a moralist, though he denied it. " Beyond good and evil " he discovered either a higher morality, thus remaining still bound by moral determinations, or the same evil as on " this side ", exemplified, for instance, by the figure of Caesar Borgia. In either case he failed to break away from the distinction between good and evil. And so did the Hottentot who defined good and evil by saying, " It is good if I steal somebody else's wife and bad if my wife is stolen from me ". That Hottentot was a moralist—and there are many like him among us. The old good is replaced by the new good, values are revalued, but none of these changes take us beyond good and evil. Even if we say that the distinction and valuation are themselves an evil, we are still wholly within their power. " Beyond " there should be neither good nor evil—but we are always up against one or the other. We shall reach a more satisfactory result when we grasp that our valuations relating to good and evil are symbolic and not real. " Good " and " evil ", the " moral " and the " immoral ", the " high " and the " low " do not express any real existent, but are merely symbols—not arbitrary or conventional symbols, however, but reasonable and inevitable. In its inmost being reality is neither good nor evil, neither moral nor immoral, but it is symbolized in this way in accordance with the categories of this world. The world is not the ultimate reality but only a phase of it—a phase in which being is alienated from itself and everything is expressed by symbols. The spatial symbols of " high " and " low " may express absolute truths of the moral and spiritual order. That which in reality is not separate assumes in our fallen world the form of division. In reality there is neither " high " nor " low ", but the symbol of " height " does give us some insight into the nature of reality. The same thing is true of the generic symbols of " father " and " son " which express the truths of religious revelation. " Father ", " son ", " birth " are words borrowed from our earthly life, but they are used, rightly and inevitably, to express the truth about the Divine life. God as Being-in-itself is neither " father " nor " son " and no birth takes place in Him ; and yet something expressed by those symbols has an absolute significance. Only in pure mysticism and spirituality is symbolism overcome and we are plunged into " first life ". Our ethics is symbolic and so are all its distinctions and valuations. The problem is how to pass from symbols to reality. All that lies " on this side of good and evil " is symbolic ; only that which is " beyond good and evil " is real. The symbolism of " good " and " evil " is not artificial, accidental, or " wrong " ; it tells us about absolute, about the ultimate reality, but does so " darkly ", reflecting it, as it were, in the mirror of the world.

The very existence of moral life with its distinctions and valuations presupposes freedom. Hence ethics is a philosophy of freedom. The traditional scholastic doctrine of free will does not touch on the real problem of freedom. That doctrine was invented in order to find a culprit, someone who could be held responsible and so vindicate the idea of punishment in this life and in eternity. The doctrine of free will was modelled to suit a normative, legalistic morality. It implies that man is confronted with the choice between good and evil, and may or may not fulfil the law or norm imposed upon him. Man will be justified if he chooses the good and fulfils the law, and condemned if he chooses evil and fails to fulfil the law. In spite of a certain confusion of thought, there is profound truth in Luther's rebellion against justification by works connected with free will.[1] It is paradoxical that so-called " free will " should be the source of man's enslavement. Man is enslaved by the necessity to choose between that which is forced upon him and carrying out the law under fear of penalities. He proves to be least free in that which is connected with his " free will ". Yet freedom may be understood not merely as the possibility given to man of fulfilling the law and justifying himself by good works due to his free will, but as man's creative energy resulting in the production of values. Freedom may lead man to evil ; it is tragic in character and does not come under any pedagogical or morally legalistic categories. Freedom is the essential condition of moral life—freedom in evil as well as in good. There can be no moral life without freedom in evil, and this renders moral life a tragedy and makes ethics a philosophy of tragedy. Legalistic, normative ethics, for which freedom is merely the condition of fulfilling the moral law, leaves out of account the tragic aspect of moral life. Tragedy is an essential element of morality and a fundamental ethical category. It is the tragic that leads us to the depths and heights, beyond good and evil in the normative sense. The tragic springs from freedom and is neither " good " nor " evil " in the sense in which these terms are usually defined in ethics, yet ethics must inquire into it. Ethics has to deal both with the tragic and the paradoxical. Moral life is made up of paradoxes in which good and evil are intertwined. They cannot be solved rationally, but have to be lived through to the end. The tragic and paradoxical character of ethics is due to the fact that its fundamental problem is not that of the moral norm or of the good, but of the relation between the Divine and the human freedom.

Ethics is not only bound up with sociology, but dominated by sociology. This is not the result of the nineteenth and twentieth century positivism or of the work of Auguste Comte and Durkheim. It is due to the tyranny which social life and social norms exercise over the moral life of man throughout the world. The terrorism of the social unit, the power of society over the individual, is to be found almost everywhere in history

[1] See Luther's *De servo arbiterio*, the most remarkable of his works.

and dates back to primitive community. Even Christianity has not been able to free man from it entirely. When Westermarck wrote his *Origin and Development of Moral Ideas* from the scientific and positivist point of view he wrote a book on sociology and not on ethics. Moral ideas have a social origin and develop in accordance with social laws laid down by the community. Ethics, customs are investigated by social sciences. The social origin of moral consciousness is affirmed not only by positivists who reject all metaphysics ; it is upheld by metaphysicians, since sociality is a metaphysical category. This is what Heidegger means by *Das Man*.[1] It is *das Man*, the social whole, the common life of everyday that reigns in the fallen sinful world. Society plays an enormous part in moral conscious-ness, and it is the difficult task of philosophical ethics to distinguish between the spiritual and the social elements in moral life and to reveal *the pure conscience*. The ethical problem must be freed from social terrorism. The social element is so important to the moral life that people often ascribe a moral character to facts of purely social origin, to social manners and cus-toms. But in its essence the moral is independent of the social. A purely moral fact does not depend upon society, or depends upon it only in so far as society itself is moral. Moral life is rooted in the spiritual world, and social relations are merely a projection of it. The moral is the ex-planation of the social and not *vice versa*. Moral life is not merely personal, it is also social. But the purity of moral consciousness is permanently vitiated by what I call the " herd " element in social life.

The nineteenth and twentieth century systems of ethics which take society to be the source of moral valuations and distinctions and affirm the social character of good and evil are obviously involved in a vicious circle. Society cannot be the supreme value and the final end of human life. Even if it were possible to prove that the distinction between good and evil had a social origin, this would throw no light on the nature of moral valuation. The object of philosophical ethics is to know not the origin and development of ideas about good and evil, but good and evil as such. What matters to it is the ontological nature of good and evil, and not man's ideas about them. The modern mind is so demoralized by the historical and the psychological methods of approaching the subject that it finds it difficult to distinguish the problem of the good as such from that of human ideas about the good, beginning with the Hottentot morality and ending with Kant and Comte. The ideas about good and evil embodied in manners and morals depend upon society, but good and

[1] See his *Sein und Zeit*. If we observe the distinction drawn by Tönnies between *Geselschaft* and *Gemeinschaft*, it is to *Geselschaft* that I am referring.

evil in themselves do not depend upon it ; on the contrary, social institutions depend upon the ultimate nature of good and evil. It may be objected that my knowledge of the good is only my idea which forms part of the general body of opinion about it. This is the usual argument of relativism. My ideas about the good may be mistaken and in that sense they are relative. But it would be meaningless to form ideas about a good which did not exist, just as it would be meaningless to have knowledge which did not refer to any reality. Moral valuations inevitably presuppose a moral realism and imply that the good exists and is not merely my idea. And it is utterly impossible to substitute society for the good. Durkheim tried to put society in the place of God, but this is the most monstrous form of idolatry.[1] Society itself stands in need of moral valuation and presupposes the distinction between good and evil. Social utilitarianism has been completely exploded and need not be discussed here. To be consistent, a sociological theory of morality ought, following Durkheim, to recognize society as God, and not as a natural and historical part of a world plunged in sin.

It is indisputable that man is a social being, but he is also a spiritual being. He belongs to two worlds. It is only as a spiritual being that man can know the good as such. As a social being he knows only the changing conceptions about the good. A sociology which denies that man is a spiritual being, deriving his valuations from the spiritual world, is not a science but a false philosophy and even a false religion. It is only as a being which rises above the stream of the naturally historical and psychical life that man can make valuations and see goodness, truth and beauty. This means not that ethics must disregard the social aspect of life, but that social life must be grounded in morality, and not morality in social life.

Nor can ethics depend upon biology, which, like sociology, claims to be a philosophy of life. A biological philosophy tries to establish a criterion of good and evil and to base moral valuations upon the principle of the " maximum of life ". " Life " is the highest good and the supreme value ; everything that increases " life " is good, and everything that decreases it and leads to death and non-being is evil. We ought to work for the utmost possible increase of life. Such a philosophy is different from any form of hedonism. A rich and full life is a good and a value even if it brings with it suffering and not happiness. The greatest representative of this view was Nietzsche, a bitter enemy of hedonism and utilitarianism. Klagess is another thinker who opposes the vital principle to the spiritual.

---

[1] See his *Les formes élémentaires de la vie religieuse*. Durkheim does seek for a reality corresponding to the religious ideas and finds it in the community.

It is certainly indisputable that the good is life and that the final end is the fullness of life. But the trouble is that it is too general a truth. "Life" cannot be a criterion of value because it is all-embracing. Everything is life and life is everything. Qualitative distinctions and valuations have to be made within life. "The maximum of life" cannot be the criterion, for it is a quantitative and not a qualitative conception. We are thus involved in a vicious circle. Life may be low and lofty, good and evil, beautiful and hideous. How are we to judge it? The biological criterion of the maximum of life can certainly not serve as a moral criterion. In order to have value and be a blessing life must have meaning. But meaning cannot be derived from the mere process of life, from its quantitative maximum; it must lie in that which is beyond and above life. Valuation from the point of view of meaning always presupposes rising above that which is valued. We are compelled to admit that there is such a thing as true life in contradistinction to the false and fallen life. Life can reach a higher level not through quantitative increase, but through ascending towards something higher than itself. And this means that life may be interpreted spiritually as well as biologically. But a spiritual interpretation presupposes the existence of the Divine as well as of the human life. Spiritual life always implies something higher than itself towards which it is ascending. The supreme value and the highest good is not life as such, but spiritual life rising up to God—not the quantity, but the quality of life. Spiritual life is not in the least opposed to, or destructive of, mental and physical life; it transfers the mental and the physical to a higher plane, imparts a higher quality to them and raises them towards the heights, towards that which is beyond life, beyond nature, beyond being. "Life" may become for us the symbol of the highest value and the highest good, but these are in their turn but symbols of true being, and being itself is but a symbol of the final mystery. Ethics is thus confronted with infinity, and consequently a great deal of it is problematic. The normative ethics is blind to this. The problem of ethics is connected with the mystery of man. Ethics must be the theory of the destiny and vocation of man, and must inquire in the first instance into the nature of man, his origin and his goal.

CHAPTER TWO

The Origin of Good and Evil

I. GOD AND MAN

THE question of the distinction between good and evil and of its origin cannot be solved apart from the prior question as to the relation between God and man, between the Divine and the human freedom, or between grace and freedom. The feud between the Creator and the creature which overshadows our whole existence concerns evil and its origin. And the struggle against the Creator is waged not only by those who distort with evil the image of the created world, but also by those who suffer from the evil in it. The ethical problem presupposes a theodicy, without which there can be no ethics. If there is a distinction between good and evil, and if evil exists, God must be justified, since the justification of God is the solution of the problem of evil. If there were no evil and no distinction between good and evil, there could be no ethics and no theodicy. Putting it paradoxically it may be said that ethics judges not only man, but God also. The good as well as the wicked rebel against God, for they cannot reconcile themselves to the existence of evil. Atheism may spring from good motives and not solely from evil ones.[1] The wicked hate God because He prevents them from doing evil, and the good are ready to hate Him for not preventing the wicked from doing evil and for allowing the existence of evil. The very distinction between good and evil which is the result of the Fall becomes the source of atheism. Ethics springs from the same source as atheism, and this throws a sinister light upon it. The traditional doctrines of theology do not solve the painful problem of evil. The ordinary theological conception of the creation of the world and the Fall turns it all into a divine comedy, a play that God plays with Himself. One may disagree with Marcion,[2] the Gnostics and the Manichees, but one cannot help respecting them for their being so painfully conscious of the problem of evil. Evil is generally said to be due to the abuse of freedom with which God endowed His creatures. But this explanation is purely superficial. The freedom through which

[1] Proudhon is the type of man who rebels against God in the name of goodness, justice and righteousness. See his *De la justice dans la révolution et dans l'église*.
[2] See the best of Harnack's works, *Marcion*.

23

the creature succumbs to evil has been given to it by God, i.e. in the last resort is determined by God. Freedom is a fatal gift which dooms man to perdition. It is impossible to rationalize this idea and to express it in terms of positive theology. It is precisely the traditional theology that leads good men, inspired by moral motives, to atheism. The ordinary theological conception of freedom in no way saves the Creator from the responsibility for pain and evil. Freedom itself is created by God and penetrable to Him down to its very depths. In His omniscience, ascribed to Him by positive theology, God foresaw from all eternity the fatal consequences of freedom with which He endowed man. He foresaw the evil and suffering of the world which has been called into being by His will and is wholly in His power ; He foresaw everything, down to the perdition and everlasting torments of many. And yet He consented to create man and the world under those terrible conditions. This is the profound moral source of atheism. In expecting an answer to His call from man whom He endowed with freedom, God is expecting an answer from Himself. He knows the answer beforehand and is only playing with Himself. When in difficulties, positive theology falls back upon mystery and finds refuge in negative theology. But the mystery has already been over-rationalized. The logical conclusion is that God has from all eternity predetermined some to eternal salvation and others to eternal damnation.[1] Calvin's horrible doctrine has the great merit of being *a reductio ad absurdum*. He clearly says that which inevitably follows from the traditional doctrine of creation. True, predetermination itself is an impenetrable mystery, terrifying to reason and conscience, but we are led to it by rational theology. Positive theology goes too far in rationalizing the mystery and at the same time it does not go far enough, for it puts limits to knowledge and lays down prohibitions. When we pass to negative theology, we begin to breathe more freely as though coming out of a prison-house. Mystery, *docta ignorantia* have a profound significance. The whole meaning, importance and value of life are determined by the mystery behind it, by an infinity which cannot be rationalized but can only be expressed in myths and symbols. God is the infinite mystery that underlies existence—and this alone makes the pain and evil of life endurable. They would be unendurable if the world and man were self-sufficient, if there were nothing beyond, higher and deeper and more mysterious. We come to God not because rational thought demands His existence but because the world is bounded by a mystery in which rational thought ends. Consequently, all systems of positive theology are exoteric and do

[1] See Calvin : *Institution de la religion chrétienne.*

not touch upon the last things. Mystical negative theology brings us closer to the final depths. The limit to rational thought is set by a mystery and not by a taboo.

The Divine Nothing or the Absolute of the negative theology cannot be the Creator of the world. This has been made clear by German speculative mysticism. It is the burden of Eckehardt's doctrine of the *Gottheit* and of Boehme's conception of the *Ungrund*. Out of the Divine Nothing, the *Gottheit* or the *Ungrund*, the Holy Trinity, God the Creator is born. The creation of the world by God the Creator is a secondary act. From this point of view it may be said that freedom is not created by God : it is rooted in the Nothing, in the *Ungrund* from all eternity. Freedom is not determined by God ; it is part of the nothing out of which God created the world. The opposition between God the Creator and freedom is secondary : in the primeval mystery of the Divine Nothing this opposition is transcended, for both God and freedom are manifested out of the *Ungrund*. God the Creator cannot be held responsible for freedom which gave rise to evil. Man is the child of God and the child of freedom—of nothing, of non-being, το μηον. Meonic freedom consented to God's act of creation ; non-being freely accepted being. But through it man fell away from the work of God, evil and pain came into the world, and being was mixed with non-being. This is the real tragedy both of the world and of God. God longs for His " other ", His friend ; He wants him to answer the call to enter the fullness of the divine life and participate in God's creative work of conquering non-being. God does not answer His own call : the answer is from freedom which is independent of Him. God the Creator is all-powerful over being, over the created world, but He has no power over non-being, over the uncreated freedom which is impenetrable to Him. In the first act of creation God appears as the Maker of the world. But that act cannot avert the possibility of evil contained in meonic freedom. The myth of the Fall tells of this powerlessness of the creator to avert the evil resulting from freedom which He has not created. Then comes God's second act in relation to the world and to man. God appears not in the aspect of Creator but of Redeemer and Saviour, in the aspect of the suffering God who takes upon Himself the sins of the world. God in the aspect of God-the-Son descends into the abyss, into the *Ungrund*, into the depths of freedom out of which springs evil as well as every kind of good. This is the only possible interpretation of the mystery of the Incarnation—if we are not to interpret it in the juridical sense. Out of the abyss, out of the Divine Nothing is born the Trinitary God and He is confronted with meonic freedom. He creates out of nothing the world and man and expects from them an answer to His call—an answer from the depths of freedom. At first the answer was consent to creation, then it was rebellion and hostility towards God, a return to original non-being. All rebellion against God is a return to non-being which assumes the form of false, illusory being, and is a victory of non-being over the divine light. And it is only then that the nothing which is not evil becomes evil. Then comes God's second act : He descends into non-being, into the abyss of freedom that has degenerated into evil ; He manifests Himself not in power but in sacrifice. The Divine sacrifice, the Divine self-crucifixion must conquer evil meonic freedom by enlightening it from within without forcing it, without depriving the created world of freedom.

Only such an interpretation of the Divine mystery saves ethics from the danger of atheism. Let it not be said that this is pantheism. Pantheism does contain some truth, and that is the truth of negative theology. But the falsity of pantheism lies in rationalizing the mystery and translating the truth of negative theology into the language of the positive. Mysticism has a language of its own and cannot be directly translated into the language of theology. Pantheism is an instance of such mistranslation. This is why mystics are so often accused of pantheism, and for the most part unjustly.

In traditional positive theology there is always a desire to humiliate man. But the existence of evil for which the creature and not the Creator is supposed to be responsible makes such humiliation unintelligible. The responsibility for evil exalts man instead of humiliating him. It implies that he has a tremendous power of freedom capable of rising against God, of separating itself from Him, of creating hell and a godless world of its own. The idea of the Fall is at bottom a proud idea, and through it man escapes from the sense of humiliation. If man fell away from God, he must have been an exalted creature, endowed with great freedom and power. It appears, then, that the only occasion when theologians exalt man is when they speak of the Fall and of the responsibility for it. On all other occasions they belittle the creature. The very word " creature " acquires a deprecatory meaning. The creature is insignificant, impotent, pitiful, helpless, it is nothing. It is as though in creating the world God wanted to humiliate the creature and demonstrate its nothingness and helplessness. All He requires of it is blind submission, and He cruelly punishes disobedience. All this seems to imply that man is essentially sinful ; but, as a matter of fact, such a conception of the relation between God and man is simply unintelligible. The ideas of Creator and creature are symbols taken from our world. But in our world a work bears its creator's name, expresses his idea and is an embodiment of his energy. There can be no question of the work of a great artist being poor, low and insignificant simply because it is created. But the Creator of the world is the greatest of artists, and there is no reason why it should be denied that He can create something divine and lofty. True, it will be said that God's creatures have spoiled and distorted their own image. But the idea of creation and creature as such does not imply a fallen state. Theologians regard creature as low and insignificant because it is creature and not because it is fallen. The fact of the Fall proves, on the contrary, its independence, the extent of its freedom and the power of its determination to be something more than a creature. There ensues a series of insoluble paradoxes. Man's " nature " is created by God, but his " freedom " is not created, not determined by any being and is prior to all being. Being springs from freedom and not freedom from being. That which is called " the creature's nothingness " is precisely that which is uncreated in the creature—its freedom ; and the rest of its nature is created by God and therefore cannot be called " a nothing ". Neither the created nature nor the uncreated freedom belittle the creature. What belittles it is the evil that springs from freedom ; but that evil is not a constituent part of its nature for it has not been created by God. The slavery of the creature is connected with a monarchic conception of God characteristic of the lower and non-Christian forms of theism. It is the conception of an autocratic master. This is an aspect of God which precedes the Christian revelation. Christianity is not a monotheistic religion like Mahometanism, it is a trinitary religion. The trinitary conception of God rules out slavery and justifies the freedom and dignity of man. Atheism has often been simply a form of anti-theism and a protest against abstract monotheism and monarchism. The Christian Trinitary God, the God of love and sacrifice, leaves no room for atheism. The moral consciousness cannot rise against Him in the name of " the good " as it does against the abstract monotheistic God who humiliates His creatures, and endows them with freedom in order to make them responsible for the misuse of it and to punish them cruelly.

It is strange that human thought and especially theological thought has never concerned itself with God's inner life. Probably this was considered impious. The most incomprehensible part of traditional theological theories is the psychology of the Deity. These theories were always framed from the human point of view. Theology has been anthropocentric rather than theocentric, and this is particularly true with regard to the monarchic conception of God. Can God be said to have no inner life, no emotional and affective states? The static conception of God as *actus purus* having no potentiality and completely self-sufficient is a philosophical, Aristotelian, and not a biblical conception. The God of the Bible, the God of the revelation, is by no means an *actus purus* : He has affective and emotional states, dramatic developments in His inner life, inward movement—but all this is revealed exoterically. It is extraordinary how limited is the human conception of God. Men are afraid to ascribe to Him inner conflict and tragedy characteristic of all life, the longing for His " other ", for the birth of man, but have no hesitation in ascribing to Him anger, jealousy, vengeance and other affective states which, in man, are regarded as reprehensible. There is a profound gulf between the idea of perfection in man and in God. Self-satisfaction, self-sufficiency, stony immobility, pride, the demand for continual submission are qualities which the Christian religion considers vicious and sinful, though it calmly ascribes them to God. It becomes impossible to follow the Gospel injunction, " Be ye perfect as your Father in Heaven is perfect ". That which in God is regarded as a sign of perfection, in man is considered an imperfection, a sin. In accordance with the principles of negative theology God, of course, cannot be described as good or perfect, for He is above goodness or perfection, just as He is above being. He is not something but no-thing, and none of our determinations are applicable to Him. We can only think of God symbolically and mythologically. And a symbolic psychology of God is possible—not in relation to the Divine Nothing of negative theology, but in relation to God-the-Creator of positive theology. And it is utterly unthinkable to ascribe to God the Creator self-sufficiency, self-satisfaction and despotism as characteristic of His inner life. It is more worthy of God to ascribe to Him a longing for the loved one, a need for sacrificial self-surrender. People are afraid to ascribe movement to God, because movement indicates the lack of something, or the need for something which is not there. But it may equally well be said that immobility is an imperfection, for it implies a lack of the dynamic quality of life. Tragic conflict in the life of the Deity is a sign of the perfection, and not of the imperfection, of the divine life. The Christian revelation shows us God in the aspect of sacrificial love, but sacrificial love, far from suggesting self-sufficiency, implies the need for passing into its " other ". It is impossible to deny that the Christian God is first and foremost, the God of sacrificial love, and sacrifice always indicates tragedy. Dramatic movement and tragedy are born of the fullness, and not of the poverty of life. To deny tragedy in the Divine life is only possible at the cost of denying Christ, His cross and crucifixion, the sacrifice of the Son of God. This is the theology of abstract monotheism. Abstract monarchic monotheism which refuses to recognize the inner dramatism of the Divine life is a clear instance of the confusion between negative and positive theology. Creation of the world cannot be deduced from the Absolute which is perfectly self-sufficient. Creation of the world implies movement in God, it is a dramatic event in the Divine life. It is unthinkable that there should be movement in the Absolute, creating an order of being external to It. In the Absolute nothing can be thought positively, it admits of negative characteristics only. If the Absolute of negative theology be identified with the Creator of positive theology, the world proves to be accidental, unnecessary, insignificant, having no relation to the inner life of the Deity and therefore, in the last resort, meaningless. Creature has meaning and dignity only if the creation of the world be understood as the realization of the Divine Trinity within the inner life of the Absolute, as a mystery of love and freedom. For an exoteric theology the inner life of the Deity does not exist, but an esoteric theology is bound to recognize the presence of tragic conflict in God. It is what Jacob Boehme calls the theogonic process. It takes place in eternity and signifies not the birth of a previously non-existent God, but a divine mystery-play going on in the eternal hidden life of the Deity, the perpetual birth of God out of the *Ungrund*.[1]

The theogonic process and the presence of tragedy in God presuppose the existence of primeval freedom rooted in nothing, in non-being On the secondary plane, where there is the Creator and the creature, God and man, the uncreated freedom may be thought of as outside God. We may not think of being as outside God, but we may thus think of non-being. This is the only way to understand evil without making God responsible for it. The distinction between being and non-being is merged in the last mystery of the Divine Nothing. In apophatic knowledge nothing can be thought of as external to God—neither the created world nor freedom. Pantheism is true in so far as it refers to the God of apophatic theology, but it is false in so far as it translates mystical truth into the language of rationalistic positive theology.

The world and the centre of the world—man, is the creation of God through Wisdom, through Divine Ideas, and at the same time it is the child of meonic uncreated freedom, the child of fathomless non-being. The element of freedom does not come from God the Father, for it is prior to being. The tragedy in God is connected with freedom : God the Creator has absolute power over being, but not over freedom. Fathom-

---

[1] See my *Studies in Boehme* (in Russian), *Put* No. 20.

less freedom springing from non-being entered the created world, consenting to the act of creation. God the Creator has done everything to bring light into that freedom, in harmony with His great conception of creation. But without destroying freedom He could not conquer the potency of evil contained in it. This is why there is tragedy and evil in the world ; all tragedy is connected with freedom. And we can only reconcile ourselves to the tragedy of the world because God suffers in it too. God shares His creatures' destiny. He sacrifices Himself for the world and for man whom He loves and yearns for.

The conception of createdness and of creature by means of which theologians hope to solve all their difficulties is vague and ambiguous. It is impossible to work out any rational idea of the creation of the world. It is a myth and not an idea. But the myth is too often interpreted as belittling the creature. In the case of man, that which he creates is more expressive of him than that which he begets. The image of the artist and the poet is imprinted more clearly on his works than on his children. The most unintelligible part of the idea of createdness is that it is intended both to establish a gulf between man and his Creator and to make man utterly insignificant and entirely dependent upon the Creator. The conception of a created freedom is, of course, the most inadmissible of all. The world is created, man is created, but being is uncreated and is from all eternity. This implies that Divine being alone is being in the true sense of the term. By comparison with God the world is secondary ; by comparison with ontology, cosmology is secondary. The world is either the creation of Being which is identical with God or a state of Being, a certain aeon in its destinies. In the first case the fundamental characteristic of the world is its createdness. It is created out of nothing, and its nothingness springs from that source and not from God. But the conception of createdness throws no light upon the " nothing " out of which the world is created. If that " nothing " is primeval uncreated meonic freedom, we are faced with an unfathomable mystery ; yet in seeking to penetrate into it we attain results that have more meaning and are less insulting to man than the conclusions of traditional theology. But the mystery can only be approached through myth and not through logical ideas. Perhaps the most important point with regard to the idea of creation is to make clear the meaning of tragedy, for it is the tragic that leads us beyond the confines of the world and brings us nearer to the mystery. There may be two conceptions of tragedy.

Pre-Christian tragedy is the hopeless misery and suffering of the innocent. It is the tragedy of fate. It is based upon the interpretation of cosmic life as completely self-contained. There is no supercosmic God to whom the innocent sufferer can appeal. The world is full of gods, but the gods do not rise above the cycle of cosmic life and are themselves subject to the higher power of fate, *Μοῖρα*. The only way out is through aesthetic reconciliation, through feeling the beauty of hopeless suffering. This is the *amor fati*, and is a unique, primary category. But is all tragedy that of fate, or is a Christian tragedy possible?[1] Traditional theology is afraid of the very idea of it, though it is curious that the religion of the Cross should deny tragedy. As distinct from the ancient tragedy of fate, the Christian tragedy is that of freedom and reveals the primary source of the tragic as such. Fate is secondary and is found in a finite world separated from the first source of being. Fate is the child of freedom, and so is necessity. Freedom is primary. Christian consciousness overcomes fate in the classical sense of the word and frees the human spirit from the power of the world and of cosmic forces. But Christianity reveals freedom which is the primary source of tragedy. It reveals tragedy in the Divine life itself. God Himself, the Only Begotten Son, suffers and is crucified, an innocent sufferer. The tragedy of freedom shows that there is a struggle between the conflicting principles which lie deeper than the distinction between good and evil. Fate is the child of freedom—this means that freedom itself is fatal. Christianity does not believe in the power of blind fate, for it reveals to us Meaning which transcends the world and rules it, and to which appeal can be made against the pain, the suffering, the "fatal" happenings of life. But it transfers tragedy to a greater depth, to freedom which is prior to being and deeper than it. Fate is bound up with meonic freedom, with primeval darkness, the *Ungrund*.

Three principles are active in the world : Providence, i.e. the super-cosmic God ; freedom, i.e. the human spirit ; and fate or destiny, i.e. nature, the solidified, hardened outcome of the dark meonic freedom. The interaction between these three principles constitutes the complexity of the cosmic and the human life. Christianity, too, has to recognize the element of fate, but it does not regard it as supreme and unconquerable. Tragedy means a conflict between polarities, but it need not necessarily be a conflict between good and evil, the divine and the diabolical. True depths of tragedy become apparent when two equally divine principles come into conflict. The whole of my book is devoted to describing conflicts of that type. The greatest tragedy is suffering caused by the good and not by evil, and consists in our being unable to justify life in terms of

[1] See Hans Ehrenberg, *Tragödie und Kreuz* I Band. *Die Tragödie unter dem Olymp.* II Band *Die Tragödie unter dem Kreuz.*

the distinction between good and evil. Tragedy existed before the distinction was made and will go on existing after the distinction has been transcended. The most tragic situations in life are conflicts between values which are equally noble and lofty. And this implies that tragedy exists within the Divine life itself. The appearance of evil and of the diabolical is something secondary.

The new ethics must be knowledge not only of good and evil, but also of the tragic which is constantly present in moral experience and complicates all our moral judgments. The paradoxality of moral life is connected with the presence in it of the tragic element which cannot be subsumed under the ordinary categories of good and evil. The tragic is not a result of evil, but is morally guiltless. The Golgotha is the supreme tragedy just because the Crucified is absolutely sinless and innocent. It is impossible to moralize about tragedy, for it lies beyond good and evil. The tragedy of freedom is overcome by the tragedy of the cross. Death is conquered by death. Judgments which are on this side of good and evil fail to penetrate to the final depths. Man's moral consciousness is blunted both by evil and by spurious, perverted good. Moral purification and regeneration always mean acquiring the unspoilt, virginal power of moral judgment. The paradoxical, tragic and complex character of moral life lies in the fact that not only evil and the wicked are bad, but that good and the good may be bad also. " The good " may be evil because they believe in an evil " good ". Evil is so to speak the retribution for spurious good. And this is where tragedy begins. The good who create a hell and relegate the wicked to it are an instance of tragedy. This is deeper than the ordinary distinction between good and evil.

God created man in His own image and likeness, i.e. made him a creator too, calling him to free spontaneous activity and not to formal obedience to His power. Free creativeness is the creature's answer to the great call of its Creator. Man's creative work is the fulfilment of the Creator's secret will. But creativeness by its very nature is creation out of nothing, i.e. out of meonic freedom which is prior to the world itself. This element of freedom springing from the pre-existential abyss is present in every creative act of man, in artistic conception and inspiration. In contradistinction to God man needs matter for his creativeness : a sculptor needs marble from which to make the statue ; but it is not of matter borrowed from the world that creativeness is born. The element of primeval freedom, the " freedom of nothing ", always penetrates into the artistic conception. The answer to God's call comes from the depths of that freedom. It is curious that theologians fail to recognize the presence of freedom in artistic creation, and only think of it with reference to the Fall, guilt and punishment. This is the weakness of theological theories which renders them unable to justify man's creative activity and provide a basis for it. The nature of that activity can only be understood by contrasting creation with procreation : one springs from freedom, and the other from the womb of nature. Birth means a separation and redistribution of forces that are already in existence, rather than the making of something that has never existed before. The progenitor puts forth a part of his matter, his nature. The absolutely new arises through creativeness alone, i.e. through freedom which has its roots in non-being. *Creation means transition from non-being to being through a free act.* Evolutionism does not really admit the possibility of creativeness, for it does not recognize freedom and knows only necessity ; procreation and redistribution are the only changes it allows. It is remarkable that theological theories often coincide with the naturalistic in denying creativeness. Primeval meonic freedom can alone provide an explanation of creativeness as well as of evil.

Theology established the distinction between birth and creation for the sake of interpreting the inner life of the Holy Trinity and the creation of the world. The Son is eternally born of the Father, but the world is created by God and not born of God. Birth implies a unity of nature, consubstantiality—ὁμοούσια, while creation means similarity, ὁμοιούιασ, with difference in nature. But birth and creation have different significance in God and in the world. In the world birth always means severance and movement along the line of bad infinity, while in God it does not imply any severance. On the other hand creativeness in the world means the making of something entirely new without any division or lapse into the bad infinity. In the world there is a greater bond between a creator and his work than between parent and child. Birth means pain and suffering as a consequence of the evil disruption of the world. Creation means conformity to the idea of man and to the vocation bestowed upon him by God.

The origin of the world and of man becomes intelligible to us only in the light of Christ. The dogma of Christ—the new Adam, is not merely a dogma of salvation, and the coming of Christ means more than redemption from sin. Apart from Christ and the Trinitary principle the creation of the world cannot be understood. It cannot be deduced from a monarchic conception of God. Creation of the world can only be interpreted in the light of the mystery of the Holy Trinity. The Lamb is slain from the foundation of the world. The Divine sacrifice forms part of the plan of creation from the first. Redemption is a second stage in the world history, a new relation of God to His creature, a fuller, higher, and more perfect revelation of the Deity as sacrificial love, i.e. a new moment in the development of the world and of man. The problem of creativeness is first and foremost the problem of freedom, and freedom of the creature becomes completely intelligible to us only through the God-Man, i.e. through the revelation of the sacrificial aspect of God. Pantheism is false if only because it is bound to deny freedom. But dualistic theism denies it, too, or admits it solely for the sake of man's moral responsibility. Gnostic and Manichean dualism also denies freedom, for it finds the source of evil in an evil god or in matter. It must be admitted that in the antinomies of the Creator and the creature freedom appears as a paradox which cannot be subsumed under any category. A monistic or a dualistic interpretation of the relation between the Creator and the creature equally lead to a denial of freedom. Man is not free if he is merely a manifestation of God, a part of the Deity ; he is not free if he has been endowed with freedom by God the Creator, but has nothing divine in himself ; nor is he free if evil has its source in an evil god, in matter upon which he is dependent. All these points of view prove dangerous to man's freedom. The Christian dogma of grace was an attempt to save freedom. Man is not free if God stands to him in the relation of a Creator, but he is free if God's relation to him is that of giving him grace. Man is not forced by grace : he receives or rejects it freely. But the doctrine of grace has undergone a change which brought it into conflict with freedom. If grace acts upon man independently of his freedom we get the doctrine of predestination. The only possible way out is to admit that freedom is uncreated and has its roots in non-being.

The more refined forms of atheism, such, for instance, as we find in N. Hartmann, are based upon the idea that human freedom and creativeness of values are incompatable with the existence of God. If God exists, man is not free and cannot create values. N. Hartmann's contention is false, but the problem with which he is struggling is a very real one. It is difficult to reconcile the idea of human freedom with the idea of God's existence, and it is equally difficult to recognize freedom if God does not exist. N. Hartmann's ideal values, abstract and impotent, are of no help in this connection. It is unintelligible how man can have freedom if he is merely a part of nature. The paradoxical solution of the problem is that freedom, without which creativeness and moral life are impossible, comes neither from God nor from the created nature. In other words, freedom is uncreated and at the same time it is not divine. The recognition of divine freedom does not in any way solve the question of human freedom.

The relationship between grace and freedom is equally paradoxical. So far from diminishing, forcing or destroying freedom, grace seeks to increase it and raise it to a higher level. The paradoxicality of the problem of freedom and grace is reflected in the disputes between St. Augustine and Pelagius, the Jansenists and the Jesuits, in Luther's teaching of the slavery of the will and Calvin's doctrine of predestination. Human freedom as such is powerless to turn man to God, to conquer sin, to vanquish its own abysmal darkness and rise above its own destiny. Pelagius failed to understand this. On the other hand, grace comes from God and not from man, and does not mean that man turns to God and conquers evil and darkness ; it is not man's answer to God. Failure to see this was the mistake of Calvin and the Jansenists. The impotence of human freedom and the superhuman nature of grace create an insoluble paradox. The answer to it is contained in the mystery of Christ the God-Man, but that mystery cannot be rationalized, In trying to rationalize it theology makes it meaningless. Only in Christ the God-Man does the paradox of the relation between the Creator and the creature find its solution. That is the essence of Christianity. Creator and creature, grace and freedom present an insoluble problem, a tragic conflict, a paradox. The coming of Christ is the answer to it. Such is the theological and anthropological problem which is logically prior to ethics. It throws light on the Fall and on the origin of good and evil. Philosophical ethics must inquire not only into the distinctions and valuations on this side of good and evil, but also into the origin of the distinction between good and evil. The problem of the Fall is the fundamental problem of moral philosophy, and without reference to it there can be no ethics. Moral distinctions are the result of the Fall.

2. THE FALL. THE ORIGIN OF GOOD AND EVIL

Christianity has adopted the myth of the Fall and of the Garden of Eden ; thinkers who have given up Christianity and do not want a religious basis for ethics reject it. But the problem of ethics cannot even be formulated unless it be admitted that the distinction between good and evil had an origin in time and had been preceded by a state of being " beyond " or " prior to " good and evil. " Good " and " evil " are correlative and in a sense it may be said that good comes into being at the same time as evil and disappears together with it. This is the fundamental paradox of ethics. Paradise is the state of being in which there is no valuation or distinction. It might be said that the world proceeds from an original absence of discrimination between good and evil to a sharp dis-

35

tinction between them and then, enriched by that experience, ends by
not distinguishing them any more.

The memory of a lost paradise, of a Golden Age, is very deep in man,
together with a sense of guilt and sin and a dream of regaining the Kingdom of Heaven which sometimes assumes the form of a Utopia or an
earthly paradise. The Kingdom of God is thought of as " beyond good
and evil ". The good which is realized in this sinful world is always
based upon distinction and separation from evil. When the " good "
men triumph they destroy the " wicked " and finally relegate them to
hell. The triumph of a " good " based upon valuations and distinctions is
certainly not paradise or Kingdom of God. The Kingdom of God cannot
be conceived moralistically : it is on the other side of the distinction. It
is the Fall that made moralists of us. We are faced with a profound
enigma : how could man have renounced paradise which he recalls so
longingly in our world-aeon? How could he have fallen away from it?
Paradise appears to us as the blissful life in which the cosmos was in man,
and man was in God. The exile of man from paradise means that man
fell away from God, and the cosmos fell away from man. Paradise was a
life of bliss, but was it the fullness of life? were all the possibilities realized
in it? The Bible story has an exoteric character. It expresses in symbols
events in the spiritual world, but a deeper interpretation of those symbols
is essential. Not everything was revealed to man in paradise, and ignorance was the condition of the life in it. It was the realm of the unconscious. Man's freedom was not as yet unfolded, it had not expressed itself
or taken part in creation. When the world was created, meonic freedom,
which springs from non-being, was temporarily hidden, but it could not
be destroyed. It remained in the subsoil of the paradisaical life and was
bound to manifest itself. Man rejected the bliss and wholeness of Eden
and chose the pain and tragedy of cosmic life in order to explore his destiny
to its inmost depths. This was the birth of consciousness with its painful
dividedness.[1] In falling away from the harmony of paradise and from
unity with God, man began to make distinctions and valuations, tasted
the fruit of the tree of knowledge and found himself on this side of good
and evil. The prohibition was a warning that the fruits of the tree of
knowledge were bitter and deadly. Knowledge was born out of freedom, out of the dark recesses of the irrational. Man preferred death and
the bitterness of discrimination to the blissful and innocent life of ignorance. He could have fed on the fruits of the tree of life and lived for ever

[1] Thinkers like Klagess would like us to return to the original paradisaical unconsciousness.

the life of unconscious, vegetative bliss. In the innocent life of paradise in which man was nurtured by the tree of life and shunned the tree of knowledge, the relation between the Creator and the creature was limited to the aspect of God as the Father. The Divine Trinity was not revealed in paradise, and the Son did not manifest Himself in the aspect of infinite love and sacrifice. God was merely a sustaining power. The myth of the Garden of Eden seems to imply that only God the Father was present— or, indeed, not even God the Father, for there can be no Father without the Son, but God as creative force. The paradox of Christian consciousness is that Christ could not have appeared in the life of paradise. True, it may be said that God the Word was present in it, but the Word was not incarnate as man and had not made the sacrifice of love. Life in the Garden of Eden was lived entirely under the Old Testament categories and did not exemplify the Divine Tri-Unity. If man had remained in the passive state of paradisaical innocence and unconsciousness, i.e. if he had remained at the stage of the divinely natural life, he would not have known Christ or attained deification.

The origin of the knowledge of good and evil has two essentially different aspects, and this leads to a paradox. It is possible to interpret the knowledge of good and evil as the Fall.[1] When I know good and evil, when I make distinctions and valuations, I lose my innocence and wholeness, fall away from God and am exiled from paradise. Knowledge is the loss of paradise. Sin is the attempt to know good and evil. But another interpretation is possible. Knowledge in itself is not a sin and does not mean falling away from God. Knowledge is good and means discovery of meaning. But plucking the fruit of the tree of knowledge indicates an evil and godless experience of life, an attempt on the part of man to return to the darkness of non-being, a refusal to give a creative answer to God's call and resistance to the act of creation. Yet knowledge connected with this act is a manifestation of the principle of wisdom in man, a transition to a higher consciousness and a higher state of existence. It is equally wrong and contradictory to say that the knowledge of good and evil is good and to say that it is evil. Our terms and categories are inapplicable to that which lies beyond the state of being which has given rise to those terms and categories.

Is it a good thing that the distinction between good and evil has arisen? Is good—good, and evil—evil? We are bound to give a paradoxical answer to this question : it is bad that the distinction between good and evil has arisen, but it is good to make the distinction, once it has arisen ;

[1] L. Shestov does this ; see his book, *Na vesah Iova* (*On the Scales of Job*).

it is bad to have gone through the experience of evil, but it is good to know good and evil as a result of that experience. When Nietzsche substituted for the distinction between good and evil the distinction between the fine and the low, he thought he was replacing moral and cognitive categories by natural and elemental, i.e. by paradisaical categories. But it was an Eden after the Fall, Nietzsche cannot find his way to paradise. "Beyond good and evil", i.e. in paradise, there ought to be neither good nor evil in our sense of these terms, but with Nietzsche evil remains. Man has chosen the knowledge of good and evil through experience, and he must follow that painful path to the end ; he cannot expect to find Paradise half-way. The myth of the lost paradise symbolizes the genesis of consciousness in the development of the spirit.

Paradise is the unconscious wholeness of nature, the realm of instinct. There is in it no division between subject and object, no reflection, no painful conflict of consciousness with the unconscious. That conflict, which, according to Freud and his school, gives rise to every kind of neurosis and psychosis, is a product of civilization. When Klagess speaks of the birth of consciousness, intellect and spirit as decadence and disease, he is expressing in scientific and philosophic language the ancient myth of the lost paradise. But he interprets the idea of paradise in naturalistic terms and believes that it can exist in a fallen world. When Bergson contrasts instinct with intellect he, too, has in mind the paradise which man has lost through the Fall. The same idea underlies L. Shestov's struggle against the rational and the good. Consciousness which involves dividedness and loss of wholeness appears to be the result of the Fall. We are faced with the fundamental question : is consciousness an indication of man's fallen state? The fruits of the tree of knowledge have proved bitter, and that bitterness has been transferred to the very birth of consciousness. Consciousness is born in pain and suffering. Consciousness *is* pain, and loss of consciousness appears to us as the cessation of pain. Dostoevsky says that suffering is the only cause of consciousness. Consciousness involves a painful division. From its very nature it can never embrace the whole of our being, which includes the realm of the subconscious and the superconscious. As modern psychology has shown, consciousness is hampered by the subconscious and closed to the superconscious. The very existence of consciousness involves limits and distinctions which cause pain. In our aeon, in the fallen world, consciousness is bound to be pain and suffering. This is why man is so eager to lose himself in ecstasy or intoxication, whether it be of the higher or of the lower kind. Distinctions and valuations made by consciousness always cause pain.

The Origin of Good and Evil

After the Fall the forces of meonic pre-existential chaos were let loose, and the image of man could only be preserved through the formation of a clear-cut, limited consciousness. The unconscious was no longer paradisaical, a dark void was formed in it, and consciousness was needed to safeguard man from the yawning abyss below. But consciousness also shuts man off from the superconscious, divine reality and prevents intuitive contemplation of God. And in seeking to break through to superconsciousness, to the abyss above, man often falls into the subconscious—the abyss below. In our sinful world consciousness means loss of paradise. But paradise is not completely lost. Its reflections and memories still linger in us. Through dividedness, pain and suffering man ascends to wholeness, unattainable for consciousness, to regeneration and bliss in God. Through the experience of evil he reaches the highest good. Hegel speaks of the " unhappy consciousness " which implies division and for which God is transcendent ; but this is true of consciousness as such.[1] Unhappy consciousness can only be overcome through super-consciousness.

There are three stages in the development of the spirit : the original paradisaical wholeness, pre-conscious wholeness which has not had the experience of thought and of freedom ; division, reflection, valuation, freedom of choice, and, finally, superconscious wholeness and completeness that comes after freedom, reflection and valuation. Those stages cannot, of course, be understood merely chronologically—they express an ideal successiveness. Elemental passion, natural force, is the *Ungrund*, the freedom that is prior to consciousness, reason, goodness, truth, valuation and choice. Good and evil arise later. The final completeness and wholeness include all the experience that has been lived through—the experience of good and evil, of division and valuation, of pain and suffering. Morality inevitably involves pain. There can be no bliss in " the good "—there can only be bliss " beyond good and evil ".

The origin of good and evil is expressed by a myth, and ethics is bound to have a mythological basis. Both at the beginning and the end ethics comes upon a realm which lies beyond good and evil : the life of paradise and the life of the Kingdom of God, the preconscious and the superconscious state. It is only the " unhappy " consciousness with its dividedness, reflection, pain and suffering that is on " this side " of good and evil. And the most difficult question of all is what is the nature of the " good " before the distinction between good and evil has arisen and after it has ceased to be? Is there " good " in paradise and in the Kingdom of God?

[1] See an excellent book by Jean Wahl, *Le malheur de la conscience dans la philosophie de Hegel.*

This is the essential metaphysical problem of ethics which is seldom considered.

Ethics should be the theory of good and evil, and not of the norms of the good. The problem of evil is as important for ethics as the problem of the good. Traditional theodicy does not really solve the problem of evil. If Satan is entirely subordinate to God and is the instrument of Divine Providence, if God makes use of him for His own good ends, evil does not really exist. This is an entirely optimistic theory. Evil exists in man only, but in the universe as a whole there is nothing but good. In Leibniz's theodicy evil does not exist. In *Faust*, in the " Prologue in Heaven ", the theme of which is borrowed from the book of Job, Goethe speaks of God allowing evil for good purposes, for the sake of trying us. This is really the orthodox point of view. Evil as well as good is in God's hands and depends upon Him. But this inevitably leads to the conclusion that evil is necessary for the sake of the good.

The problem of evil is paradoxical for our consciousness, though rational theology refuses to admit this. The paradox is that either evil depends upon God and is needed for the sake of the good, or it does not depend upon God, and God is powerless before it—and in that case the good is not the supreme ontological force. The paradox springs from the fact that we apply categories of good and evil, i.e. categories engendered by the Fall, to Divine being which is beyond good and evil. The doctrine of original sin, with which ethics begins, has a very different meaning from the one usually ascribed to it. The myth of the Fall does not humiliate man, but extols him to wonderful heights. Modern psychology of the unconscious discovering in man a terrible underworld of darkness and showing the low character of his loftiest states certainly does humiliate man and trample him into mud. But the doctrine of the Fall throws a different light upon the underworld that surges up in man, upon the criminal instincts in his subconscious. If man is a fallen creature and if he fell in virtue of freedom inherent in him from the first, it shows that he is a lofty being, a free spirit. Awareness of original sin both humbles and exalts man. Man fell from a height and he can rise to it again. In the consciousness of original sin there is nothing humiliating to man as there is in believing that he has his origin in mud and is essentially a nonentity. The myth of the Fall is a myth of man's greatness. But theologians are apt to regard original sin as a kind of hereditary disease. Thus understood it has nothing to do with the idea of personal responsibility.

Just because we carry original sin within us and live in a fallen world doomed to move within the categories of good and evil, our thought is riddled with insoluble paradoxes. If we think deeply and consistently we are compelled both to identify evil with non-being and to admit its positive significance. Evil is a return to non-being, a rejection of the world, and at the same time it has a positive significance because it calls forth as a reaction against itself the supreme creative power of the good. Freedom of evil is a good thing and without it there could be no freedom of the good, i.e. the good itself could not exist. The possibility of evil is the condition of the good. A forcible suppression or destruction of evil would be a great evil. And good easily turns into evil. God's toleration of evil is a paradox which is not sufficiently dwelt upon. God tolerates evil, allows evil for the sake of the good of freedom. Toleration of evil is a part of God's providential plan. With the insight of genius Jacob Boehme perceived that every principle presupposes for its manifestation its opposite, a principle that wars against it. Light presupposes darkness. Light shines in darkness. The rational does not exist apart from the irrational, and yet the irrational can never be finally rationalized. Light shineth in darkness and darkness comprehendeth it not, and yet light presupposes the infinity of darkness.

It may paradoxically be said that the development of the spirit is connected with sin, with the loss of paradisaical innocence, and at the same time it presupposes a heroic struggle against sin. Kierkegaard says that fear, which he regards as a very important religious phenomenon, is connected with the awakening of spirit.[1] The less spirit there is, the less suffering. But fear is a consequence of the Fall. So long as there is sin, there is bound to be fear—fear of God, fear of His judgment. And yet fear must be overcome, for perfect love casteth out fear. The genesis of spirit, of consciousness, of valuation and distinction inspires us with unreasoning and groundless fear—fear of the mystery of the divine life from which man has fallen away. Exile from paradise provokes terror which may increase with man's spiritual growth. The world of Greek paganism was not at all a Paradise as some would like to paint it. There was incredible fear and terror in it which was never conquered. Man sought to escape from that terror by extinguishing consciousness and returning to the realm of the unconscious. But this is not the way to regain lost paradise. The knowledge of good and evil has poisoned man. He cannot break through to paradise that lies beyond the painful distinction between good and evil, and the suffering connected therewith. Man's fear of God is his fear of himself, of the yawning abyss of non-being in his own nature.

Such are the problems and paradoxes of good and evil. We come at

[1] See Kierkegaard, *Der Begriff der Angst.*

every step upon insuperable difficulties and contradictions. We become slaves now of evil and now of good. The good become " wicked ", " the wicked ", when menaced with destruction, appeal to " the Good ". Those are the evil fruits of the knowledge of good and evil. Moral tragedy lies first and foremost in the fact that " good " cannot conquer " evil ". Normative ethics cannot get beyond this fact. The purpose of life is perpetual creativeness, and not obedience to laws and norms. But " good " knows of no other way of overcoming " evil " than through law and norm.

There are men who suffer acutely from the problem of evil and pain. This is true of Marcion, of some of the Gnostics and Manichees, of Jacob Boehme and Dostoevsky. Thinkers who are particularly sensitive to the problem of evil may seem to be moralists *par excellence*, but this requires some explanation. Moralists may be utterly indifferent to the problem of evil and remain perfectly complacent and content with their norms and laws, believing that " good " is always in the right with regard to the very fact of the existence of " evil ". Even hell may appear to a moralist as the triumph of the Good, for the main problem for him is the justification of the Good and not the existence of evil. Marcion and the Gnostics failed to understand freedom and this accounts for their erroneous belief that the world was created by an evil god, Demiourgos. They taught that evil had its roots in material nature which was not created by the God of goodness. Marcion did not understand that the evil world has been created not by God but by sin, and sin springs from freedom and not from an evil God or from matter. Hence came his wrong interpretation of the biblical story of the creation of the world. But there is something essentially noble in the way Marcion and other Gnostics suffered from the problem of evil.[1] There is great depth and nobility in the teaching of Boehme, for whom the problem of evil is connected with *Ungrund*—freedom.[2]

The sting of the problem is not in the actual existence of evil, but in the difficulty of justifying the good in the face of evil. Do not the good and goodness help to crystallize and to perpetuate evil? The fatal question is whether the good is really good, but the very wording of it is paradoxical. Nietzsche understood the poignancy of the question, but completely failed to grasp the attitude of Christianity towards it. The absolute originality of the Christian teaching lies, in the first place, in the fact that for it the sun rises equally on the evil and on the good, that the first shall

[1] See Harnack's remarkable book on Marcion : *Das Evangelium vom Fremden Gott.*
[2] See my studies in Boehme (in Russian) in No. 20 of *Put* and A. Koyré's *La philosophie de Jacob Boehme.*

be last and the last first, and that the law of righteousness does not necessarily save, and thus the good becomes problematical. Christian thought is deeply concerned with the relation between God and freedom, between God and goodness, between freedom and value. Is God limited by the moral good and subordinated to it? Is He free in relation to it? Does God will the good, or is the good that which God wills? Duns Scotus defended God's freedom in an extreme form. In answering a wrongly formulated question as to the relation between God and the good he worked out a conception of God that likens Him to a tyrannical Eastern potentate. Ockham went still further. In truth, however, such a question cannot be asked : it is equally wrong to say that God is bound to will the good and that the good is that which God wills. We cannot judge of God from our side of the distinction between good and evil. If theodicy passes judgment on God from the point of view of the good that has come into being after the Fall, it is on a wrong track. Theodicy should seek to justify God by accounting for the origin of the distinction between good and evil.

It is obvious that God is " beyond good and evil ", for on " this side " of it is our fallen world and certainly not God. God is above good. And there cannot be in Him any evil that is on this side of the distinction. When we ask whether God is free to will evil we apply to Him the categories of our fallen world. One can only think of the subject in terms of negative theology. God certainly is not bound by the moral good and is not dependent upon it. He *is* the Good as an absolute force. But we have at once to add that He is above good, for the category of goodness is not applicable to Him. It is impossible to pass judgment on God, for He is' the source of all the values by reference to which we judge. God reveals Himself to us as the source of values, as infinite love. Theodicy can judge God only in the light of what God has revealed to us about Himself. It defends God against human conceptions of Him, against human slander.

The problem of the relation between freedom and values is even more troublesome. It may be said that man in his freedom is confronted with ideal norms or values which he has to realize ; his failure to do so is an evil. This is the usual point of view. Man is free to realize the good or the values which stand above him as for ever laid down by God, forming an ideal normative world, but he is not free to create the good, to produce values. The scholastic conception of free will comes precisely to this, that man can and must fulfil the law of goodness, and if he fails to do so, it is his own fault and he is punished. This choice between good and evil is forced upon him from without. Freedom of will is not a source of creativeness, but of responsibility and possible punishment. This purely normative conception has been specially worked out for legal purposes. True freedom, however, consists not in fulfilling the law, but in creating new realities and values. As a free being man is not merely a servant of the moral law, but a creator of new values. Man is called upon to create the good and not only to fulfil it. Creative freedom gives rise to values. As a free being, a free spirit, man is called to be the creator of new values. The world of values is not a changeless ideal realm rising above man and freedom ; it is constantly undergoing change and being created afresh. Man is free in relation to moral values, not merely in the sense that he is free to realize or not to realize them. Similarly, in relation to God man is free not merely in the sense that he can turn towards God or away from Him, can fulfil or not fulfil His will. Man is free in the sense of being able to co-operate with God, to create the good and produce new values.

Hence a system of ethics is needed which interprets moral life as a creative activity. There are no superhuman or non-human ideal values, changeless and eternal. Creative gifts and values are dynamic, and through them the creation of the world is going on. The new ethics rooted in Christianity must go beyond the conception of ideal norms. Platonism cannot be the basis of a creative morality. The teleological point of view must be transcended also. The fundamental question is to determine not the purpose, whether immanent or imposed upon us from without, which our moral life ought to subserve, but the source of the creative energy which is realized in our life. The teleological point of view enslaves man as a creative being. N. Hartmann thinks that a teleological interpretation of the natural world, according to which a higher purpose is being realized in it, is incompatible with freedom and moral life. But it may equally well be said that Hartmann's conception of ideal values which man must freely realize in the world is incompatible with freedom and moral life. That, too, is a teleological conception, though of a different type. In truth, purpose is posited in and through a free creative act, values are created by man. The first question, therefore, is to determine what is man, whence he comes and what is his goal. These are problems of philosophical anthropology which have as yet been scarcely worked out. N. Hartmann's philosophy does not explain what man is and what is the origin of his freedom. Ethics brings us up against two conceptions of life : one is duration in time, " bad infinity ", endless longing and torment— the other is eternity, divine infinity, victory over time. It is a mistake to imagine that creativeness leads to bad infinity. Creative activity may bring us into eternity, and eternity may be creative and dynamic.

CHAPTER THREE

Man

I. THE PROBLEMS OF PHILOSOPHICAL ANTHROPOLOGY.
TYPES OF ANTHROPOLOGICAL THEORY

MAX SCHELER, who is more interested than other philosophers in the problem of anthropology, says : " *Zu keiner Zeit der Geschichte der Mensch sich so problematisch geworden ist, wie in der Gegenwart.*"[1] This means that the time has come to formulate a philosophical anthropology which has not existed in the past. Man has begun to feel uneasy about himself. Psychology, biology and sociology have not solved the problem of man. Man has been approached from various points of view and studied in parts. The name of anthropology is applied to a science which throws least light upon man as such. And yet a philosophical anthropology must be the basis of ethics ; indeed, the problem of man is fundamental for philosophy as a whole. The ancient Greeks understood that man can only begin to philosophize through knowing himself. The key to reality is to be found in man.

The analysis of knowledge shows that man is quite a special kind of being, not on a par with other realities. Man is not a fragmentary part of the world but contains the whole riddle of the universe and the solution of it. The fact that man as an object of knowledge is at the same time the knower has an anthropological as well as an epistemological significance. I have already said in the first chapter that we cannot substitute for the problem of man the problem of the epistemological subject or the transcendental consciousness, or the problem of the psychical consciousness, or of the spirit, or of ideal values and ideas of goodness, truth, beauty, etc. Man is neither the epistemological subject, nor the " soul " of psychology, nor a spirit, nor an ideal value of ethics, logics or aesthetics. All spheres of being intersect in man. Philosophy must get rid of psychologism, but it cannot get rid of man. Philosophy must be consciously and not instinctively anthropological.

Man is a profound riddle to himself, for he bears witness to the existence of a higher world. The superhuman principle is a constituent element of man's nature. Man is discontented with himself and capable of out-

[1] See his *Die Stellung der Menschen im Kosmos.*

45

growing himself. The very fact of the existence of man is a break in the natural world and proves that nature cannot be self-sufficient but rests upon a supernatural reality. As an entity belonging to two worlds and capable of outgrowing himself man is a self-contradictory and paradoxical being, combining opposite poles within himself. With equal justice he may be said to be base and lofty, weak and strong, free and slavish. The enigmatic and contradictory nature of man is due not only to the fact that he is a fallen creature—an earthly being preserving memories of heaven and reflections of a heavenly light ; a still deeper reason for it is that man is the child of God and of non-being, of meonic freedom. His roots are in heaven, in God, and also in nethermost depths. Man is not merely a product of the natural world, although he lives in it and participates in the processes of nature. He is dependent upon his natural environment and at the same time he humanizes it and introduces a new principle into it.[1] Man's creative activity has significance for the whole world and indicates a new stage of cosmic life. Man is a new departure in nature.

The problem of man is utterly insoluble if man be considered merely as a part of nature and correlative to it. He can only be interpreted through his relation to God ; he can only be understood through the higher and not through the lower. Consequently, it is only the religious consciousness that has really tried to grapple with the problem of man. All theological doctrines deal with it. There exists no philosophical anthropology in the true sense of the term, but there has always been a religious anthropology. The Christian teaching is that man is a being created by God in His image and likeness, free, but through his freedom fallen away from God, and in his fallen and sinful state receiving from God grace that saves and regenerates him.

The conception of man is slightly different in the Catholic, the Protestant and the Orthodox theology. According to the Catholic view man has been created as a natural being, lacking in the supernatural gifts of the contemplation of God and communion with Him ; the supernatural gifts were bestowed upon him by a special act of grace.[2] Through the Fall man lost precisely those supernatural gifts, but as a natural being he suffered comparatively little damage. Such a view does not do justice to the Divine image and likeness in man and may lead to a purely naturalistic interpretation of human nature. The naturalistic element is very strong in the teaching of St. Thomas Aquinas, who tends to regard man as a non-spiritual being. According to the classical Protestant conception, the

[1] See Edouard Le Roy, *Les origines humaines et l'Evolution de l'Intelligence.*
[2] See Bainval, *Naturel et surnaturel.*

46

Fall has completely ruined and distorted human nature, darkened man's reason, deprived him of freedom and made all his life completely dependent upon grace. From such a point of view human nature can never be hallowed and transfigured, so that naturalism is victorious once more, though, so to speak, from another end. The Orthodox view of man has been but little worked out, but the central point in it is the doctrine of the Divine image and likeness in man—the doctrine, i.e. that man has been created as a spiritual being. The Godlike and spiritual life of man is not destroyed but merely damaged by the Fall, and the image of God in man is dimmed. This point of view is the very opposite of naturalism. Christian anthropology teaches not only of the Old Adam but also of the New Adam, of Christ the God-Man, and is therefore a divinely human anthropology. Its central idea is that of the God-Man. Man is a being created by God, fallen away from God and receiving grace from God—this is the essence of Christian anthropology. It takes a humble view of man as creature and makes more of the idea of sin than of the Divine image and likeness. But Christian thought does face the problem of man and clearly sees what a paradoxical being man is, and in this respect it is infinitely superior to all philosophic theories of man. Man is a tragic being, and the tragic element in him makes him ill-adapted to the world in which he lives. Man is in conflict not only with the world but with himself. His tragedy is, as we have seen, not merely a struggle between good and evil but something still deeper—a conflict between values which are equally good. Man is a being who humanizes nature ; but he also humanizes the idea of God, and through this humanizes himself.

M. Scheler has established four types of anthropological theory : (1) the Jewish-Christian—the creation of man by God and the Fall ; (2) the ancient Greek conception of man as the bearer of reason ; (3) the natural science view of man as the product of the evolution in the animal world ; (4) the decadence theory which regards the birth of consciousness, reason and spirit as biological retrogression, a weakening of life. The latter point of view is expressed most clearly by Klagess, who says " *Was sich in der Extase befreie? Wir antworten, Die Seele. Die Zweite, wovon es sich befreie? Vom Geiste.*"[1] Although Klagess is influenced by Bachofen, M. Scheler is wrong in including Bachofen among the founders of the decadence theory. Bachofen was a Christian and regarded the birth of the spirit, the awakening of personality, the victory of the solar masculine principle over the tellurgic feminine as a tremendous gain and achievement.[2] Nietzsche's

[1] Klagess, *Vom Kosmogonischen Eros.*
[2] See his *Mutterrecht*, a work of genius.

47

conception of man may also be classed in a sense with the decadence theories. Klagess is compelled to regard the very emergence of man as a retrogression. Nietzsche also wants to rise beyond man and return to the ancient demi-God, to the hero-superman.

M. Scheler admirably shows that man's superiority cannot be defended on biological grounds. Biologically man does not differ from animals ; he only differs from them in virtue of the principle which is superior to that of life—the spirit.[1] Man is human only as the bearer of spirit which manifests itself in personality. Man is a being who transcends himself and the world. He is a continual protest against reality. M. Scheler draws a sharp distinction between life and spirit. Spirit moves in a direction that cuts across the temporal flux of life. Spirit brings ideas into life. For M. Scheler, however, spirit is not active but completely passive ; and he does not believe in freedom. Life is active, but spirit is very similar to the ideal values which life has to realize.

The presence of spirit in man greatly complicates the question of man's evolution. From the biological point of view man regresses rather than progresses. He is a divided and weakened being—there can be no doubt of that. Consciousness has weakened in man the power of instinct and made him biologically defenceless. His organs have not been perfected but weakened by the growth of civilization. He has to think with regret of his lost primeval strength. His organs for attack and defence have become social instead of biological ; he relies upon his social environment and its weapons. But this means that his strength has ceased to be biologically hereditary. From the purely biological point of view man does not progress ; his progress consists in an increasing power of consciousness and spirit on the one hand, and in social and technical achievements on the other. But that means that man's wholeness is broken up more and more, and he becomes more and more divided within himself. We shall see how deep that division is when we consider the conflict between civilization and instinct. That conflict is becoming obvious to modern science and philosophy, and utterly disproves the theories of progress and evolution that were predominant in the nineteenth century.

The naturalistic view of man as a product of evolution in the animal world is the feeblest of all anthropological theories. But the ancient Greek conception of man as the bearer of reason is not valid either. The Greek philosophy wanted to discover in man the supreme and eternal principle of reason which rises above the changing world. There is undoubtedly an element of truth in this view, but it has been vulgarized by

[1] M. Scheler, *Die Stellung der Menschen im Kosmos.*

the philosophy of enlightenment. It may be said with equal justice that man is an irrational, paradoxical, essentially tragic being in whom two worlds, two opposite principles, are at war. Dostoevsky, who was a great anthropologist, has shown this with the force of genius. Philosophers and scientists have done very little to elucidate the problem of man. We must learn anthropology from great artists, mystics and a few solitary and unrecognized thinkers. Shakespeare, Dostoevsky, Tolstoy, Stendahl, Proust have done more for the understanding of human nature than academic philosophers and learned psychologists and sociologists. With the great artists may be ranked a few thinkers such as St. Augustine, Jacob Boehme and Pascal in the past, Bachofen, L. Feuerdach and Kierkegaard in the nineteenth century and M. Scheler in our own day. And among men of science the first place belongs to Freud, Adler and Jung.

M. Scheler's classification of anthropological theories is incomplete. The theory most prevalent in modern Europe is that of man as a social being, a product of society and also as an inventor of tools (*homo faber*). At present this theory has more influence than the naturalistic view. We find it in Durkheim and Marx. Social life turns the animal into man. At the present day the social theory shares the field with the rationalistic conception of man.

Anthropology inevitably places man between God and nature, or between civilization and nature, and the types of anthropological theory depend upon the way in which the relation between the two is defined. Anthropologists are bound to draw a qualitative distinction between man and the rest of nature, and they do so by recognizing either that he is a being in whom reason awakens, or that he is a social and civilized being whose instinctive nature is modified by civilization. In any case it is recognized that man masters nature and rises above it. Only the adherents of the decadence theory look back to the lost natural force and call man to return to his primitive state.

The only theory that is eternal and unsurpassed is the Jewish-Christian view of man as a being created by God in His own image and likeness ; but even that theory has not completely revealed the truth about man or shown all the consequences of the Christological doctrine ; it is more in the spirit of the Old Testament than of the New. Christian anthropology should unfold the conception of man as a creator who bears the image and likeness of the Creator of the world. This implies that man is a free and spiritual being capable of rising above nature and of dominating it. But the case is greatly complicated by the dividedness of man, by his fall and sinfulness. Man is both a fallen and sinful creature, split into two and longing for wholeness and salvation, and a creative being called to continue the work of building the world and endowed for the purpose with gifts from above.

Before beginning to discuss ethics as such, it is well to consider certain modern anthropological theories which serve as a basis for ethics. The neo-Kantian idealistic ethics of Hermann Cohen has an anthropology of its own. For Cohen man is a moral idea, and he distinguishes between the anthropological psychology based upon such a conception of man from the naturalistic, zoological psychology for which man does not exist.[1] Cohen is definitely opposed to pantheism which identifies man and nature. Idealistic ethics is not concerned with the destiny of the individual, which it relegates to the sphere of mythology, as it does much else. Cohen regards the very conception of the soul as mythological. A profound difference between the idealistic and the Christian ethics comes to light at this point. Belief in the power of evil, according to Cohen, also has a mythological character and proves to be the source of evil. " Man " really coincides with the moral principle. Cohen's ethics is juridical and social in character. The " I " presupposes another person, the individual presupposes a fellow-man. The whole of Cohen's ethics is inspired by the idea of the future and of activity. All will is will for the future, and ethics is ethics of pure will. Cohen's system of ethics, remarkable in its way, combines Kant with Judaism and exemplifies the formal, legalistic and abstractly moral character of that mode of thought. It does not contain any positive teaching about man and its only interesting feature is the sharp opposition between the natural and the moral. Man is constituted by the ideal or the moral principle ; he belongs to the realm of the " ought " and not of existence.

N. Hartmann's system of ethics is more interesting and more up to date. According to N. Hartmann man's task is to realize through his free activity ideal values which, apart from him, remain unreal. The ideal realm of values lies beyond reality and consciousness. Human will is primarily axiological, it is the bearer of values. In this respect N. Hartmann's theory resembles that of Cohen. But somewhat under the influence of M. Scheler, N. Hartmann works out a different conception of personality—the person is for him the subject of good and evil, the meeting point of value and existence. There can be no doubt of L. Feuerbach's influence on N. Hartmann. Hartmann maintains that ethics generally recognizes, in contradistinction to man, divine attributes and nature conceived as a metaphysical entity ; but such humanization of the

[1] Hermann Cohen, *Ethik des reinen Willens.*

universe means humiliation of man and robs man of what belongs to him. This is Feuerbach's atheistic argument.

According to N. Hartmann man alone is a person, while God is the minimum of personality. N. Hartmann's system of ethics is distinctly personalistic, though personality as conceived by him hangs in the air and has no roots in the world of existence. Only man is a moral being ; the state, the world and God are not moral. Man is not a subordinate part of the whole but has value in and for himself. Purpose exists in man only. To admit a world-purpose is to destroy man's freedom and his moral life. Man is a free mediator between the world of values and the world of existence ; it is he who introduces purpose. Man as a moral being could not exist in a teleologically determined world. Moral freedom may be predicated of personality but not of value. Value does not determine anything and is therefore compatible with human freedom. For religion the supreme reality is God, and for ethics man. The conception of human freedom is incompatible with that of God's will. N. Hartmann postulates atheism for the sake of human dignity, freedom and creativeness ; thus his moral postulate is directly opposed to that of Kant.

N. Hartmann's ethics and anthropology are metaphysically unsound, but there is no denying that he raises questions of profound importance. He formulates the problem of man's freedom and creativeness in all its depth. He rightly protests against systems of ethics based upon a teleological interpretation of the world. He is right in his defence of man's freedom and of his creative vocation. But as I have already said it remains incomprehensible whence come that freedom and creative power. The ideal world of values has no power. And in dealing with the relation between God's will and human freedom N. Hartmann fails to take into account all the complexity of religious and theological thought upon the subject.[1]

Two thinkers of genius, unrecognized in their lifetime but very influential at present—Bachofen and Kierkegaard—are of great importance to anthropology. Kierkegaard, who was a remarkable psychologist, takes fear or terror to be the essential characteristic of man.[2] Fear or terror (*Angst*) is an expression of man's spirituality, of his inability to be content with himself, of his relation to a transcendent God, of his sinfulness and consequently of his fall from a higher state. Awe is unquestionably natural to man and proves that he must be defined by his relation to what is higher than himself. Kierkegaard regards groundless fear, awe before the transcendental mystery of existence, or that which Otto calls

[1] N. Hartmann really reiterates Luther's argument, but reverses the conclusion.
[2] See Kierkegaard's *Der Begriff der Angst*.

Mysterium tremendum[1] as the token of man's spirituality. Bachofen also has an enormous importance for philosophic anthropology. He discovered the deep primeval layer of the human nature, its original connection with the maternal element, the struggle of the masculine solar principle with the feminine tellurgic one, the metaphysics of sex in man. For Bachofen polarity is man's essential characteristic. The cosmic struggle between the sun and the earth, personalism and collectivism takes place in man.[2]

None of the anthropological theories that we know can be said to be exhaustive or satisfactory. The most interesting from the scientific point of view is the definition of man as the maker of tools (*homo faber*). The tool which is a continuation of the hand has singled man out from the rest of the world. Idealism defines man as the bearer of reason and of logical, aesthetic and moral values, but it does not explain the connection between the natural man and reason and ideal values. They constitute a superhuman principle in man. But how does the superhuman descend into man? If man be defined by the presence in him of a superhuman principle, the meaning of humanity as such remains unintelligible. Man is said to be a rational animal, but neither reason nor animality is a specifically human quality. Thus some other problem is substituted for the problem of man.

Naturalism, which regards man as a product of evolution in the animal world, is still less satisfactory. If man is merely a product of cosmic evolution he does not exist as a being *sui generis* which cannot be deduced from or reduced to anything non-human. Man is a transitory natural phenomenon, a perfected animal. The evolutionary conception of man suffers from all the inconsistencies, weaknesses and superficiality of the evolutionary theory as a whole. It is true that human nature is changeable and dynamic, but this has nothing to do with evolution. Man's dynamism springs from freedom and not from necessity. The sociological conception of man is not any better, though man unquestionably is a social animal. Sociology regards man as an animal that has been drilled, disciplined and moulded by society. All that is valuable in man is not inherent in him but received by him from society, which he is bound to revere as something divine.[3] Finally, modern psycho-pathology offers a new conception of man according to which man is first and foremost

[1] See Otto's *Das Heilige.*
[2] See Bachofen's *Das Mutterrecht* and an excellent exposition of the theory in Georg Schmidt's *Bachofen's Geschichtsphilosophie.*
[3] See Durkheim, *Les formes élémentaires de la vie religieuse.*

a sick creature. His fundamental instincts—of sex and of power—have been weakened and repressed by civilization, which creates a painful conflict between man's consciousness and his unconscious mind.

All these theories contain elements of truth : man is a rational being and a bearer of values, he is an evolving being, a social being, a being suffering from the conflict between consciousness and the subconscious. But none of them expresses the essence of human nature as a whole. The biblical and Christian doctrine alone deals with the whole man, with his origin and destination. But biblical anthropology is incomplete and insufficient, it is built upon the Old Testament and does not take into account the fact of the Incarnation. The conclusions that follow from it may with equal justice be used to exalt man or to belittle him. Christian anthropology has been worked out by Roman Catholic thinkers who base it upon a sharp distinction between nature and grace, the act of creation and the act of bestowing grace upon the creature. They conceive of man as a natural and not a spiritual being and therefore do not dwell upon God's image and likeness in him. Protestant anthropology of the school of K. Barth also belittles man.[1] It insists that man is sinful, insignificant and impotent, and that there is nothing divine in him. The merit of this theory, inspired by Kierkegaard, is that it regards man as a tragic and paradoxical creature.

The Christian conception of man is based upon two ideas : (1) man is the image and likeness of God the Creator and, (2) God became man, the Son of God manifested Himself to us as the God-Man. But the conclusions that follow from these two ideas have not been fully worked out. As the image and likeness of the Creator, man is a creator too and is called to creative co-operation in the work of God. Man is not merely a sinful being expiating his sin, is not merely a rational, developing and social being, not merely a being sick with the conflict between his consciousness and the unconscious, but, first and foremost, *he is a creative being*. This is implied in a crude and one-sided way in the definition of man as a maker of tools. But man can only be a creative being if he has freedom. There are two elements in human nature, and it is their combination and interaction that constitute man. There is in him the element of primeval, utterly undetermined potential freedom springing from the abyss of non-being, and the element determined by the fact that man is the image and likeness of God, a Divine idea which his freedom may realize or destroy.

Divine revelation is communicated to the world and acts in it through man. Man passionately longs to hear the voice of God, but he can only

[1] This line of thought is worked out with particular poignancy by E. Brunner. See his books, *Der Mittler* and *Gott und Mensch*.

hear it in and through himself. Man is the mediator between God and himself. God always spoke through man—through Moses, through the prophets, through the great sages, the apostles, the Fathers of the Church, the saints. The only way to God is through man. Man carries within himself the divine principle, the word of God. And as a free being he carries it creatively and actively and not passively and receptively. God expresses Himself in the world through interaction with man, through meeting man, through man's answering His call, through the refraction of the divine principle in human freedom. Hence the extraordinary complexity of the religious life.

There is an element in man which is said to have been created out of nothing and which is in truth uncreated, i.e. freedom. Man has sprung from God and from the dust, from God's creation and non-being, from God's idea and freedom. Therein lies the complexity of human nature and its polarity. The co-existence of opposite principles in man is due not to the Fall, as is often supposed, but to the original duality of human nature and origin. The irrational element in man is not only the result of the Fall but is in the first place the result of freedom, which preceded existence and the creation of the world—of the meonic principle concealed behind all reality. Man is an enigmatic being because he is not the product of natural processes but is God's child and creation, and also because he is the child of freedom and springs from the abyss of non-being. The Fall is merely the return from being to non-being ; it is a free act of resistance to God's creation and God's conception of man. The Fall cannot be expressed in the categories of Creator and creature ; rebellion of the creature against its Maker is impossible. The creature cannot fall away from the Creator, it cannot have the strength to do so, it cannot even think of it. The Fall is only explicable by the third principle—the uncreated freedom, the non-being which is prior to being, the meonic abyss which is neither Creator nor creature and is not a reality co-existent with the reality of God. This is the ultimate mystery behind reality. Endless consequences follow from it. It accounts both for evil and for the creation of what has never existed before. The ethics of creativeness goes back to this primary truth.

2. PERSONALISM. PERSONALITY AND INDIVIDUALITY.
PERSONALITY AND SOCIETY

Our conception of man must be founded upon the conception of personality. True anthropology is bound to be personalistic. Consequently it is essential to understand the relation between personality and individuality. Individuality is a naturalistic and biological category, while personality is a religious and spiritual one. I want to build up a personalistic but certainly not an individualistic system of ethics. An individual is part of the species, it springs from the species although it can isolate itself and come into conflict with it. The individual is produced by the biological generic process ; it is born and it dies. But personality is not generated, it is created by God. It is God's idea, God's conception, which springs up in eternity. From the point of view of the individual, personality is a task to be achieved. Personality is an axiological category. We say of one man that he is a personality, and of another that he is not, although both are individuals. Sometimes a psychologically and biologically remarkable individual may be devoid of personality. Personality is a wholeness and unity possessing absolute and eternal worth. An individual may be lacking in such wholeness and unity, he may be disintegrated, and everything in him may be mortal. Personality is the image and likeness of God in man and this is why it rises above the natural life. Personality is not a part of something, a function of the genus or of society : it is a whole comparable to the whole of the world. It is not a product of the biological process or of social organization ; it cannot be conceived in biological or psychological or sociological terms. Personality is spiritual and presupposes the existence of a spiritual world. The value of personality is the highest hierarchical value in the world, a value of the spiritual order.

It is essential to bear in mind that the value of personality presupposes the existence of superpersonal values and is indeed constituted by them. Personality is the creator and the bearer of superpersonal values and this is the only source of its wholeness, unity and eternal significance. But this must not be taken to mean that personality has no intrinsic value or is merely a means for superpersonal values. It is itself an absolute and exalted value, but it can only exist in virtue of superpersonal values. In other words, the existence of personality presupposes the existence of God ; its value presupposes the supreme value—God. If there is no God as the source of superpersonal values, personality as a value does not exist either ; there is merely the individual entity subordinate to the natural life of the genus. Personality is *the* moral principle, and our relation to all other values is determined by reference to it. Hence the idea of personality lies at the basis of ethics. An impersonal system of ethics is a *contradictio in adjecto*. Ethics is to a great extent the theory of personality. Moral life is centred in the person and not in generalities. Personality is a higher value than the state, the nation, mankind or nature, and indeed it does not form part of that series.

The value and unity of personality does not exist apart from the spiritual principle. The spirit forms personality, enlightens and transfigures the biological individual and makes him independent of the natural order. Personality is certainly not an abstract norm or idea suppressing and enslaving the concrete, individual living being. The idea or ideal value of personality is the concrete fullness of life. The spiritual principle which constitutes personality does not imply a bloodless and abstract spiritualism. Conflict between good and evil or between any values can only exist for a person. Tragedy is always connected with the personality—with its awakening and its struggles. A personality is created by the Divine idea and human freedom. The life of personality is not self-preservation as that of the individual but self-development and self-determination. The very existence of personality presupposes sacrifice, and sacrifice cannot be impersonal. Psychological individualism so characteristic of the nineteenth and twentieth centuries is the very reverse of personalism. Complete disintegration of personality, i.e. of the wholeness and unity of the self, is exemplified in the work of Proust. The self is broken up into elements, sensations and thoughts, the image and likeness of God disappear and everything is enveloped, as it were, in mental cobwebs. The refinement of a soul which ceases to be the bearer of superpersonal values, of the divine principle, leads to dissociation and disintegration. The refined soul needs a stern spirit to give it eternal worth and to hold it together in wholeness and unity.

M. Scheler has worked out an interesting theory of personality. His aim was to build up a purely personalistic system of ethics. Philosophical anthropology which must be the basis of ethics is very little developed, and M. Scheler is one of the few philosophers who have done something towards it. According to M. Scheler, man is a being who transcends himself and the whole of life.[1] We have already seen that Scheler regards man as undefinable biologically. The fundamental opposition is for him not that between man and animal, but between personality and organism, spirit and life. The dualism between spirit and life is essential to Scheler's view. He criticises with great subtlety the conception of autonomy in Kant, Fichte and Hegel and rightly says that it means the autonomy of impersonal spirit and not of personality. German idealism is unfavourable to the idea of personality and is not concerned with it.[2] Scheler tries

[1] Scheler's view of personality is developed in the best of his works, *Der Formalismus in der Ethik und die materiele Werthethik*.

[2] G. Gurvitch in his interesting book, *Fichtes System der konkreten Ethik*, tries to interpret Fichte in the spirit of personalism.

to defend the personalistic view both of man and of God by distinguishing between personality and the self. The self presupposes something outside it, a not-self. But personality is absolute and does not presuppose anything outside itself. Personality is not a part of the world but is correlative to it.

There is no doubt that personality is a whole and not a part ; it is a microcosm. Scheler wants to base his ethics on the value of personality, highest in the hierarchy of values. He means the value not of personality in the abstract but of the concrete individual person, unique and unreplaceable. This is an advance upon the normative legalistic ethics such as Kant's. But Scheler is wrong in saying that personality is self-contained. He maintains this in order to defend the faith in God as a Person, but he is mistaken. Personality from its very nature presupposes another—not the " not-self " which is a negative limit, but another person. Personality is impossible without love and sacrifice, without passing over to the other, to the friend, to the loved one. A self-contained personality becomes disintegrated. Personality is not the absolute, and God as the Absolute is not a Person. God as a Person presupposes His other, another Person, and is love and sacrifice. The Person of the Father presupposes the Persons of the Son and of the Holy Spirit. The Holy Trinity is a Trinity of Persons just because they presuppose one another and imply mutual love and intercommunion.

On another plane the personality of God and of man presuppose each other. Personality exists in the relation of love and sacrifice. It is impossible to conceive of a personal God in an abstract monotheistic way. A person cannot exist as a self-contained and self-sufficient Absolute. Personalistic metaphysics and ethics are based upon the Christian doctrine of the Holy Trinity. The moral life of every individual person must be interpreted after the image of the Divine Tri-unity, reversed and reflected in the world. A person presupposes the existence of other persons and communion between them. Personality is the highest hierarchical value and never is merely a means. But it does not exist as a value apart from its relation to God, to other persons and to human society. Personality must come out of itself, must transcend itself—this is the task set to it by God. Narrow self-centredness ruins personality.

The individual is correlative to the genus, the person is correlative to society. A person presupposes other persons and their intercommunion ; an individual presupposes the existence of the genus. He is nurtured by the genus and is as mortal as the genus. Personality, however, does not share the destiny of the genus but is immortal. The complexity of man lies in the fact that he is both an individual, a part of the genus, and a person, a spiritual being. The individual in his biological self-assertion and self-centredness may sever himself from the life of the genus, but this alone never leads to the affirmation of personality, its growth and expansion. Hence Christian ethics is personalistic, but not individualistic. The narrow isolation of personality in modern individualism is the destruction and not the triumph of personality. Hardened selfhood—the result of original sin—is not personality. It is only when the hardened selfhood melts away and is transcended that personality manifests itself.

The struggle that takes place within the genus is for the self-assertion of the individual and not of personality. The individual's struggle for existence and power within the genus has nothing to do with the vaue of personality. The struggle for personality and its value is spiritual and not biological. In that struggle man inevitably comes into conflict with society, for metaphysically he is a social being. But personality only partly belongs to society ; the rest of it belongs to the spiritual world. Man is bound to determine his relation to society but he cannot be morally determined by society. The ethical problem of the relation between the individual and society is very complex. It is wrongly solved both by individualistic and by universalistic social theories.[1] Two processes are taking place in the world simultaneously : man is becoming both more social and more individual. And there is always a conflict and a struggle between the social and the personal moral consciousness. This leads to the distinction between legal justice and morality. It is remarkable that in the nineteenth and twentieth centuries man allowed himself to be persuaded that society is the sole source of his moral life and values and of the difference between good and evil. He was ready to renounce his birthright and the independence of his spirit and conscience. Auguste Comte, Karl Marx and Durkheim took the moral consciousness of a primitive clan to be the apex of man's moral consciousness. They denied personality and believed that only the individual is correlative to the social group.

Ethics must begin by opposing the final socialization of man which destroys the freedom of spirit and conscience. The socialization of morality means a tyranny of society and of public opinion over the spiritual life of man and his moral valuations. The enemy of personality is the community, but not communalty or *sobornost*. Hegel's philosophy is an instance of false universalism in ethics. Traces of it are to be found also in Wundt's *Ethics* and in the social philosophy of Spann.

[1] See S. Frank's *Duhovniya osnovy obschhestva* (*The Spiritual Foundations of Society*).

Moral life is intertwined with the social, and man's moral experience has social significance. But the first source of moral life is not social. The moral act is first and foremost a spiritual act, and has a spiritual origin. Conscience is not instilled into man by society, although society does affect conscience. Society is an object of moral valuations and cannot be the source of them. Customs and manners have a social origin and are the result of social sanctions, but they are not moral facts.

Philosophical ethics, in contradistinction to sociology, studies not moral ideas, manners and customs but good and evil as such, the original values and valuations. The subject of ethics is the actual good itself and not human sentiments about the good. Westermarck,[1] Durkheim and Lévy-Bruhl make interesting and important investigations, but they are not directly concerned with ethics and leave the essential ethical problem untouched. When Westermarck says that moral emotions arise from resentment he makes an interesting social-psychological suggestion which finds confirmation in modern psycho-pathology, but this has no relation whatever to the problem of good and evil and of the origin of moral distinctions and valuations. He deals with secondary and not with primary facts. All that sociology and social psychology have to say refers to the world after the Fall, in which the distinction between good and evil has already been drawn. Sociology studies human beliefs and judgments, but knows nothing of the underlying reality which provides the ground for them. Personality in its deeper aspects evades sociology, which is concerned with collective units. Thus, for instance, Marx teaches that class-struggle prevents the organized struggle of man with nature, i.e. prevents the development of man's power. Class struggle is transferred in a reflected form to the fictitious ideological sphere of religion, philosophy, morality and art. In saying this Marx himself is making moral judgments and valuations. He regards man's social power and his domination of nature as the highest good. But why should he do so? According to his own theory, this view has been instilled into him by society at a certain stage of its development. Marx naïvely makes use of the categories of good and evil, but he does not ask what good and evil are in themselves as distinct from human opinions about them ; he does not raise the question of the source of our valuations and of values as such. Sociological ethics may be very useful for the study of a particular stage of man's moral development. When sociologists discover that social unity in early society is based upon the totem and not upon the family tie they rightly argue that it depends upon primitive religious beliefs. The conception of the clan becomes

[1] *Origin and Development of Moral Ideas.*

more complicated and includes not only blood relationship but an element of religious faith as well. The totem bond is more important than the blood tie.[1] And yet sociology makes moral consciousness entirely dependent upon the clan or tribe, even if it be understood in a more complex sense.

The early moral consciousness of mankind is wholly dominated by the mystical power of kinship. Man had to wage a heroic struggle to free himself from it. The awakening of personal responsibility is the main feature of man's moral development and it exempts morality from the power of the community and from the competence of sociology. Vengeance, the most ancient and deep-rooted of moral emotions, which man shares with the animal world, has a tribal character. The soul of the victim can have no rest until it is avenged. Blood vengeance is a moral duty. It is with the greatest difficulty man learns to discriminate between personal and collective responsibility. The curse of his kindred hung over the early man ; it was the curse of original sin refracted in the primitive pagan element. The primitive man experienced original sin as the common heritage of the tribe and had as yet no consciousness of personal sin as such.

Primitive, archaic human morality is entirely communal and traces of it have not completely disappeared among the civilized races of to-day. Blood-vengeance has been transferred to the state. Capital punishment is a survival of it. In primitive society blood-vengeance, which was a moral act *par excellence*, was directed not necessarily upon the culprit but upon anyone who happened to be related to him. Vengeance is the chief moral emotion of ancient humanity. Hamlet's tragedy is incomprehensible apart from it. A supreme spiritual effort is required to establish the distinction between the person and his kindred or the social collective unit. This distinction is disappearing once more in modern communism. Modern man lays moral responsibility on families, classes, races, professions, parties and creeds and has difficulty in distinguishing the purely personal responsibility. And indeed the idea of collective responsibility contains a germ of truth—the truth, namely, that everyone is responsible for everyone else, that all are interconnected, that a person is not an isolated entity.

The Greek tragedy is bound up with the idea of hereditary guilt and vengeance, with the idea of punishment for crime committed unwillingly and without any evil motive. Such is in the first place the tragedy of Œdipus. Freud attaches universal significance to the Œdipus complex

[1] See Durkheim, *Les formes élémentaires de la vie religieuse.*

and builds upon it a whole sociological theory. He thinks that the crime of Œdipus lies at the basis of all human societies and primitive religious beliefs.[1] Freud is a true mythologist in this respect. But however much he may exaggerate the importance of the Œdipus complex he does hit upon some ancient truth in his treatment of it. Sociologists are baffled by the instinctive character of the horror of incest, and are not able to account for it. It is a mystical horror and is connected with mystical ideas attaching to the bond of kinship. The commands and prohibitions of the clan are regarded by the primitive man as though they proceeded from the deity. Man is plunged into the great whirlpool of nature, and the power of the cosmic forces over him is, first and foremost, the power of kindred. The clan and not the individual is the bearer of the moral law and moral valuations. The question of personal guilt does not arise, since the individual is not a moral subject, and judgment and valuation are not within his competence.

The myth of Œdipus has a cosmic significance, it reflects the struggle of the ancient cosmic principles in man—of motherhood and fatherhood. It all takes place in the unconscious, and consequently there is no conscious guilt and responsibility. The subject is the genus, and the individual is the innocent victim. Personality as a moral subject was not yet born. Only Christianity finally freed man from the power of cosmic forces and of the blood-tie. In doing so Christianity made the moral life of the individual independent of the tribe or of any collective unit.

If one does not adopt the naturalistic point of view one must recognize the pre-existence of the soul. The soul is not a product of the generic process and is not created at the moment of conception, but is created by God in eternity, in the spiritual world. Only in that case can human personality be metaphysically independent both of its kindred and of society.

3. SEX. THE MASCULINE AND THE FEMININE

The problem of sex is of fundamental importance to anthropology. Man is a sexual being, and sexual polarity is characteristic of human nature. Sex is not a function of the human organism but a quality of it as a whole and of every cell which composes it. Rozanov[2] always maintained this, and Freud has shown it to be true. Man is not only a sexual but a bisexual being, combining the masculine and the feminine principle in

[1] See Freud's marvellous book, *Totem und Tabu*.
[2] See Rozanov's remarkable book, *V mire neyasnago i nereshonnago.* (*The domain of the uncertain and undecided*).

himself in different proportions and often in fierce conflict. A man in whom the feminine principle was completely absent would be an abstract being, completely severed from the cosmic element. A woman in whom the masculine principle was completely absent would not be a personality. The masculine principle is essentially personal and anthropological. The feminine principle is essentially communal and cosmic. It is only the union of these two principles that constitutes a complete human being. Their union is realized in every man and every woman within their bisexual, androgynous nature, and it also takes place through the intercommunion between two natures, the masculine and the feminine. In the fallen world a cosmic struggle is going on between the masculine and the feminine principles : the two not only seek union but also wage a war against each other like deadly enemies. This is due to the polarity of human nature. With the insight of genius Bachofen has shown the presence of this struggle in the world.[1] The sun, according to him, is a masculine principle. The masculine principle is spirit. *Solarismus* is identical with *Paternität*. The moon is masculinely feminine intermediary principle. *Lunarische Tellurismus* is identical with *eheliche Gynaekokratie*. The earth is the feminine principle. It is matter, flesh, in the mystical sense of the term. Matter and maternity are interconnected. *Chthonische Tellurismus* is identical with *hetärische Gynaekokratie*. Bachofen develops a wonderful cosmic symbolism of sex. The solar masculine, the lunar masculinely feminine and the earthly feminine principles meet, interact and come into conflict within the cosmos. World-epochs replace one another according to the predominance of this or that principle. The archaic, primitive epoch is, according to Bachofen, characterized by the predominance of the feminine principle, the mother-earth, the chthonic, subterranean gods. It was Bachofen who discovered the ancient matriarchate. The chief subject of his study is the original archaic religion of humanity, and his marvellous intuition is connected with this. Matriarchate goes together with communism. Bachofen, who belonged to the age of romanticism, was one of the first to discover the significance of chthonic subterranean gods. It is the mystic religion of the Mother-Earth. The maternal principle is the source, the " whence " ; the masculine principle is the goal, the " whither ". The mystical feeling precedes the moral. This proves once more that the bearer of the moral principle is personality. In primitive communism there is as yet no moral life.

[1] *Das Mutterrecht.* Bachofen's view is of the utmost importance for the metaphysics of sex as well as for sociology.

. When people talk of Bachofen they forget that he was a Christian.[1] The awakening of the spirit and of personality, i.e. the solar masculine principle and its victory over the original matriarchy, the primitive cosmic communism and the feminine religion of the earth and subterranean gods was in his view a distinct step in advance. Unlike Klagess he did not consider the victory of the personal spiritual principle a sign of decadence. Bachofen's enormous importance for ethics and anthropology lies in the fact that he discovered the moral significance of the deep underlying layer of the collective subconscious, of instinct and the blood-tie, which most systems of ethics completely overlook. Morality can thus be traced back to cosmic principles.

The Œdipus complex to which Freud and the psycho-analysts attach so universal a meaning may be interpreted symbolically and mystically in the light of the cosmic struggle between the sexes. The masculine and the feminine principles, fatherhood and motherhood, are struggling for predominance. The Œdipus myth is one of the expressions of this cosmic struggle. In the light of day, on the conscious level. Œdipus is an innocent sufferer, but in his subconsciousness he rises against his father, against the conquering masculine principle, and seeks union with his mother, the feminine principle of the earth. It is a profoundly real myth of the ancient struggle going on in man between the solar masculine principle and the feminine principle of the earth. The human being does not easily resign itself to the victory of the sun over the earth, of spirit over matter, of the masculine over the feminine, of personality over the collective unit. Man rebels against the victory of the logos over the maternal element and strives to be absorbed in it once more. He protests against being torn away from the mother-earth, the primary source of life.

The tragedy of Œdipus took place at the time when masculine moral consciousness had conquered and imposed its norm upon society. The revolt against the father was to play an important part in history. It takes the form of struggling against power, against reason, norm, law. Man will always be attracted by the elementary cosmic force, the mainspring of creative energy. This is connected with the struggle between the Dionysian and the Apollonian principles which is going on to this day. Man is struggling for personality, for the possession of the cosmic elements by the logos ; and he rises against the limits imposed by personality, against the complete power of the logos ; he wants to enter into com-

---

[1] It is curious that Bachofen was first recognized by the Marxists because he discovered primitive communism. See Fr. Engels, *Der Ursprung der Familie, des Privateigentums und des Staates.*

munion with the soul of the world, with the depths from which he has sprung. Man rebels against the very fact of birth as a severance from the maternal womb. This is implied in what Rank calls the " trauma of birth ".[1] In this connection Freud speaks of the instinct of death.

Man is both a personality and the cosmos, the logos and the earth, the masculine and the feminine. While man remains a sexual being he cannot live in peace and harmony. Masculine psychology is completely different from the feminine. Mutual understanding is difficult because of the fierce, cruel struggle between man and woman. The great anthropological myth which alone can be the basis of an anthropological metaphysic is the myth about the androgyn. It is told in Plato's *Symposium* and occupies a central place in Jacob Boehme's gnosticism. According to his Idea, to God's conception of him, man is a complete, masculinely feminine being, solar and tellurgic, logoic and cosmic at the same time. Only in so far as he is complete is he chaste,[2] wise and Sophian in his perfect wholeness. As a sexual, halved, divided being he is not chaste, not wise, and is doomed to disharmony, to passionate longing and dissatisfaction. Original sin is connected in the first instance with division into two sexes and the Fall of the androgyn, i.e. of man as a complete being. It involves the loss of human virginity and the formation of the bad masculine and the bad feminine. This leads to incalculable consequences for the fate of the world and for man's moral life.

In the world vitiated by original sin there are accumulations of hidden, unconscious sexual energy which result in explosions and cannot be mastered by man. This energy is characterized by a polarity of attraction and repulsion. Sex driven inwards becomes dangerous and gives rise to crimes and insanity. The great task of man has always been not to destroy but to sublimate sex. Civilization and consciousness try to fetter the sexual energy, the polarity of the human nature. But the force of sex, driven into the subconscious, revolts and produces neuroses. Freud is perfectly right in this, although he does not understand the metaphysical and religious depth of the problem. Rozanov also is right—not in the solution he has to offer but in his statement of the problem. Christian asceticism has made heroic efforts to overcome the horror and the curse of sex. It can claim great achievements, but the problem of sex has never been solved. No power in the world can destroy the horror of sex and its explosive force ; sex cannot be ignored. People tried to conceal it, they

---

[1] See Otto Rank's extremely interesting book, *Le traumatisme de la naissance*.

[2] *Tselomudrie*, the Russian word for chastity, means by derivation " the wisdom of wholeness ". Translator's note.

were ashamed of it, but it went on living subconsciously and out of the hidden depths determined men's lives. Sex is the source of life and the source of death. Eros is bound up with death. Freud understands this. Great poets and artists saw the connection between love and death. The significance of sex is all-embracing because it explains not only life but death as well. Sex which has cleft into two the androgynous image of man dooms man to death, to the bad infinity of lives and deaths. Erotic love always brings death with it. This is brought out with the force of genius in Wagner's *Tristan and Isolde*. Both the religious sanctification of Eros and the attempts to limit it are powerless against this. Man is a sick, wounded, disharmonious creature primarily because he is a sexual, i.e. bi-sected being, and has lost his wholeness and integrity.

The consciousness of our era is engaged in discovering and understanding the mystery of sex. It can be concealed no longer. It is not for nothing that our epoch has produced Rozanov on the one hand and Freud on the other. The problem of sex is fundamental to philosophical anthropology and occupies a central place in the new ethics. Religion has always understood this better than science or philosophy. Asceticism is bound up with sex in the first place. The horror of sex is the horror of life and death in our sinful world, the horror of being unable to escape it. The whole being of man is affected by the horror of sex and the force of sexual polarity—man's thoughts, feelings, creativeness and moral consciousness no less than his physical organism. Man sinks low, overcome by the unregenerate force of sex, and rises high through sublimating it. The concentrated power of sex may be a source of creativeness. To sacrifice one's Eros, diverting its energy in another direction, may increase one's creative power. We see it in Ibsen and in the tragic fate of Kierkegaard, who sacrificed his love and found compensation in his creative genius. The problem of sex involves the problem of birth and creation.

It is highly important, both for cosmology and for anthropology, to draw a distinction between creation and procreation. Its symbolism has a tremendous significance for theology as well. The Son is eternally born of the Father ; the world is created by God. The symbols of birth and creation borrowed from the processes that take place in our world are applied to the mystery of the Divine life. Birth and creation are distinct in principle. Birth is from nature, from the womb, and presupposes that the progenitor hands on some of his matter to the progeny. Creation on the other hand springs from freedom and not from nature, and no matter is handed on by the creator to that which he creates. Creation is out of nothing, i.e. out of freedom, for freedom *is* nothing. Birth is always from something. Through creation there always arises something perfectly new that has never existed before, i.e. the " nothing " becomes " something ". Hegel discovered in his own way the truth that dynamism, becoming, the appearance of the new, presupposes non-being. Birth has none of this creative novelty. Man's creativeness is similar to God's, but God does not need any material for His creation, while man does. A sculptor makes a statue out of marble. Without marble, without material, he cannot create. In the same way, man needs cosmic matter for all his creation. A philospher's creative thought needs the world for its matter and without it would hang in the void.

All this leads people to believe that human creation never is out of nothing. But the creative conception itself, the original creative act, does not depend upon any material. It presupposes freedom and arises out of freedom. It is not marble that gives rise to the sculptor's conception, nor is that conception entirely determined by the statues or human bodies which the sculptor has observed and studied. An original creative work always includes an element of freedom and that is the " nothing " out of which the new, the not yet existent, is created. A philosopher cannot create a philosophical system without reality, without the world. To do so he would have to be God, the Creator of the world. This is what Hegel ventured to do. But the philosopher's creative knowledge is not entirely determined by the world, which is given him as already created by God. He introduces into that knowledge an element that comes from freedom, from nothing, and only in virtue of that his knowledge brings into being something that has never been before, and light comes out of darkness. Creative knowledge always presupposes both the already created world and the darkness of non-being. A creative act is therefore a continuation of world-creation and means participation in the work of God, man's answer to God's call. And this presupposes freedom which is prior to being.

But there is a limit to human creativeness, which shows its fundamental difference from God's. Man cannot create a living being, a person. If man could create living beings they would not be God's creations and would have no Divine image and likeness. If personality could be created by man, it would not be God's conception, i.e. it would not be personality. The thought that personality is a human and not a Divine creation is utterly unendurable to man. The human being, the human personality, is created by God in eternity but is born of man in time. It is born of the mother's womb, which is destined to give birth and not to create. The mother, like the earth, generates but is not creative. And even birth requires fertilization by the masculine principle.

66

Two truths may be affirmed of personality : it is the principle of crea-tiveness and not of generation, and it is the result of creation and not of birth—of creation on the part of God and not of man. The masculine element is essentially creative and the feminine birth-giving. But neither in generation nor in creativeness can the masculine and the feminine principles be isolated ; they interact and complete one another. Woman inspires man to create. Both through creation and procreation man strives to attain the androgynous wholeness of his being, though he can never reach it on the earthly plane.

Eternal motherhood is not only a sexual principle of generation ; it is also the principle of protection, care, preservation, without which the world would perish. The woman-mother not merely gives birth to living beings ; she also radiates beneficent power and warmth, enveloping the helpless, shivering creatures thrown out into a terrible alien world. This is strongly felt in the cult of the Mother of God. There is profound truth in the idea of Our Lady's Intercession. The feminine, maternal principle as the principle of generation remains in force when no birth is taking place. The generating energy is transformed and sublimated.

The primeval furious element of sex rages in human beings ; it is not conquered by civilization but merely banished into the unconscious. But the power of sex may be overcome and sublimated. Instead of being generative it may become creative and be a spiritual power. Creativeness is closely allied to sexuality. Sexlessness makes man sterile. A sexless being can neither precreate not create. The moral task is not to destroy the power of sex but to sublimate it, transforming it into a force that creates values. Erotic love is one of such values. Man generates and creates because he is an incomplete being, divided into two and striving for the completeness and wholeness of the androgyn. Another funda-mental problem of anthropology is that of consciousness and the uncon-scious.

4. THE CONSCIOUS AND THE UNCONSCIOUS

For a long time psychology was one of the dullest and most fruitless of sciences. It investigated abstract mental elements, chiefly cognitive ones, and man as a concrete individual did not exist for it. The English asso-ciational psychology has contributed nothing to the understanding of the human mind. The psychology of Wundt was a little better but equally arid and sterile. It was as though psychologists could not find the lever which was to set their work in motion. The new impetus came not from psychology but from psycho-pathology with its discovery of the unconscious or the subconscious. The unconscious had been spoken of before, but was regarded as the biological, material and physiological basis of mental life.[1] E. Hartmann's theory of the unconscious was a metaphysical system. The true founders of a living, concrete psychology are Janet, Freud, Adler, Jung and Baudouin.[2] Their work is of tremendous importance for philosophical anthropology. They attempt to apply scientific methods to the investigation of the mysteries of mental life. Before their time psychological or anthropological discoveries were made either by great artists or by thinkers of the type of Pascal, La Rochefoucauld, Kierkegaard and Nietzsche. Very few philosophers have done anything for psychology. One may mention the names of Ravaisson,[3] William James, Bergson, Max Scheler.

It is not difficult to see why psycho-pathology has set psychology to work in a new direction. The old psychologists were wrong in assuming that man was a healthy creature, mainly conscious and intellectual, and should be studied from that point of view. Man is a sick being, with a strong unconscious life, and therefore psycho-pathology has more to say about him—though the final word does not belong to it. The discoveries of psycho-pathology are wholly in keeping with the Christian doctrine of original sin. The human soul is divided, an agonizing conflict between opposing elements is going on in it. The modern man has, in addition to his civilized mentality, the mind of the man of antiquity, of the child with its infantile instincts, of the madman and the neurasthenic. The conflict between the civilized mind and the archaic, infantile and pathological elements results in the wonderful complexity of the soul which scarcely lends itself to study by the old psychological methods. Man deceives not only others but himself as well. He frequently does not know what is going on in him and wrongly interprets it both to himself and to others.

The psychologists of the old school altogether missed the sub-conscious, for they accepted unquestioningly the testimony of consciousness. But the distinction between the conscious and the subconscious mind is fundamental for the new psychology. Mental disorders are due to the conflict between the two. Anticipating the discoveries of science, Dostoevsky, with the insight of genius, revealed the part played by the subconscious, and so did Nietzsche in his attempts to understand the origin of

[1] See, for instance, Ribot, *La psychologie des sentiments*.
[2] Valuable contributions to the psychology of nations and civilizations have been made by Keyserling. See his *Das Spektrum Europas*.
[3] See Ravaisson's remarkable book, *L'Habitude*. Very interesting is his distinction between effort and passion.

morality ; but the old psychology was blind and helpless in this respect. Man defends himself against the chaos of his subconscious mind by the " censorship " of consciousness, which is so strict that he has lost the power to study and understand his subconscious. He has lived through a long period of the dictatorship of consciousness. Man is a passionate being who easily loses balance and goes over the brink, and he is bound to use his consciousness as a defence against the abyss of the subconscious. Human nature is rooted in fathomless, pre-existential meonic freedom, and in his struggle for personality, for God's idea in him, man had to fashion consciousness with its limitations, to bring light into darkness, and to subject subconscious instincts and strivings to the censorship of consciousness. There is a demonical element in man, for there is in him the fathomless abyss of freedom, and he may prefer that abyss to God.

It is very difficult to define the unconscious and the subconscious. All definitions of it are inadequate, for it is a limiting notion.[1] Consciousness is an intuitive act of the human ego with regard to itself, in consequence of which experience is remembered, and distinction is drawn between the self and the not-self. Consciousness is the unity of self and its distinction from the not-self. Consciousness is not identical with knowledge, but it always involves a relation to the logical principle which transcends the self-contained mental world. The self can only become conscious of itself through that which is above it. Consciousness is personal and forms personality, but it is also communal, super-personal and social in the metaphysical sense of the term. Consciousness is from its nature opposed to solipsism : the very derivation of the word from *conscire* suggests interaction of several or many minds. If the world contained only one mind there would be no consciousness. Consciousness arises through the meeting and interaction of minds, it springs from the need for distinction and, at the same time, for unity and for mutual understanding—that is, consciousness is social in its very origin. The censorship of consciousness is a social censorship.

Consciousness plays both a positive and a negative part in the formation of human personality. It does a great work with regard to the formless subconscious, but it is inclined to deny the existence of superconsciousness and to close the way to it. Frequently, instead of transfiguring and sublimating the subconscious, consciousness simply represses it and thus gives rise to endless conflicts in the mind. This was discovered by Freud and his

[1] Jung defines the unconscious as " all those psychical contents and processes of which we are not conscious, i.e. which are not perceptibly referred to our self " (*Psychological Types*). This definition is tautological.

followers who explain neuroses and mental disorders by the conflict between the conscious and the unconscious. The subconscious mind of man has wounds and injuries that date back to early childhood ; consciousness conceals rather than heals them. Man ceases to understand what it is that is tormenting him. The social consciousness which triumphs in civilized communities demands that man should altogether suppress his subconscious processes, banish them from his memory and make them conform to the censorship of consciousness.

Turning to the study of the subconscious we find there *libido*, unsatisfied sexual craving inherent in man from his birth ; we find a continually defeated striving for supremacy and power ; we find resentment, wounded pride which suffers mortification throughout life and gives rise to envy and sense of injury. A man may be ill because he cannot endure living not as he would like to live, not in the environment he wants, not with the people who satisfy his subconscious inclinations. A man will often make innocent people suffer for the fact that his life has not been what he wanted it to be and that his subconscious cravings were suppressed and remained unrealized. Subconscious cravings banished from consciousness make a person ill and divided against himself.

Freud ascribes a central and all-embracing place to *libido* and builds up a false pansexualistic metaphysic, but his main conception bears the mark of genius and his method is fruitful. Still greater psychological truth is to be found in Adler's theory of the instinct of power and mastery and in his contention that man is unable to reconcile himself to his humiliating position.[1] Man compensates himself for his defeat and defends himself by means of neuroses. La Rochefoucauld had intuitions for which Alder supplies proofs. The primary subconscious strivings—the sexual impulse and the love of power—can be transformed beyond recognition, be idealized and appear as something lofty. We often find that consciousness misinterprets the life of the subconscious, and it is not easy to detect the falsity. But Freud unquestionably exaggerates the healing power of consciousness.

The new psychology requires intuitive insight and close attention to the study of individual character. It discovers a deep irrational layer in the human soul, hidden from consciousness, and goes beyond the abstractions of the old-fashioned psychology. Following Dostoevsky, Kierkegaard and Nietzsche, modern psychology discovers that man is a being who torments both himself and others and that both masochism and sadism

[1] Adler is the most remarkable psychologist of our time. See his *Le tempérament nerveux*.

are characteristic of him. New psychology alone can establish the existence of different psychological types ; it is only now that characterisation has become possible.[1]

Jung, a psychologist of exceptional talent, whose theory is in many respects more correct than Freud's, distinguishes two main types—the introvert and the extravert.[2] This classification is somewhat artificial. Far more important and true is another classification similar to, but not identical with, Jung's. There is the type of people who are in harmony with their environment, though that harmony is only relative, and the type which is in constant disharmony with it, though the disharmony is not absolute. As a sinful being man is generally disharmonious, but the disharmony may vary in degree and in character. A man may be in comparative harmony with the surrounding world not because he is better and less sinful than it but because he is not sufficiently awake spiritually and is not eager for a different kind of existence, because he is too confined to a narrow circle of interests and is dominated by his surroundings to the point of being completely satisfied with them. Men of disharmonious temperament often have a deeper and more intense inner life, and their melancholy disposition is the result of their longing for a better life and for other worlds. Frequently, however, they are anti-social and incapable of practical activity. Disharmony may be the result of spiritual depth but also of the inferiority complex. Harmony or lack of it depends upon the correlation between man's consciousness and his subconscious.

There always is a conflict between the civilized and socialized consciousness and the subconscious, and it leads to innumerable consequences. If a man is in harmony with the norms and laws of civilized society, even if he himself helps to create and support them, this does not necessarily imply that they have gained possession of his subconscious. He may compensate himself in various ways, and his activity in preserving and supporting the laws and norms may be inspired by love of power and of sexual gratification through cruelty. A champion of legal justice may be a regular sadist. Pillars of society and guardians of the law usually apply different standards to themselves and to others. The main and most disheartening discovery of modern psychology is that man is false and deceitful not merely in relation to others but to himself as well. It shows up the underworld of the human mind, the fathomless sinfulness of man, and destroys all lofty illusions. A man often adopts this or that set of ideas not

[1] See Fr. Seifert, *Charakterologie* in the *Handbuch der Philosophie*, 1929.
[2] Jung, *Psychological Types*.

out of straightforward, pure and disinterested motives but through some kind of resentment, failure in life and a desire " to get even " with himself or others. He may become a vindictive and tyrannical reactionary or a communist because his pride has been wounded and he has failed in something, e.g. his love has been unrequited, or because he has not a spark of talent, or because he has some humiliating physical deformity. Adler is perfectly right in saying that man always tries to compensate himself and, having been through the experience of weakness and humiliation, strives to gain superiority in some other way.[1]

The work of Freud and Adler in psychology and psycho-pathology is in a sense analogous to the work of Marx in sociology and of Nietzsche in ethics. They are all engaged in tearing down the veils and showing up deceits and illusions. Marx did it through his materialistic interpretation of history and bitter criticism of idealistic theories, Nietzsche through his interpretation of the genesis of morality and denunciation of " the good ". It might be said that man is sincerely insincere, deceiving himself and others. The most remarkable thing is that he deceives himself. We constantly observe this in family relations when unconscious jealousy, envy, sense of injury or love of mastery find false and insincere expression in conscious life, fastening on all sorts of fictitious pretexts and appearing in an utterly misleading guise. The human soul is sick, personality is continually disintegrating under the pressure of its subconscious, and man wants to conceal his sickness and his disintegration. Unconscious sexual instincts find expression in consciousness in most unexpected and incongruous ways.

Scientific psychology is as powerless as sociology to defend man's dignity and discover the image of God in him. These sciences are concerned not so much with personality as with its disintegration, with the impersonal (the *Es* of Freud or *das Man* of Heidegger[2]). Psychology and psycho-pathology know the unconscious in its lower forms and they know consciousness ; but they have no knowledge of the superconscious and do not even discriminate between the subconscious and the superconscious.[3] They thus come to interpret the structure of the mind solely as a contraption for self-defence. Our mental structure is the result of external conditions which hinder the satisfaction of our needs and cravings. Man creates fictions in order to have a sense of strength and power and to

[1] See Adler's *Tempérament nerveux.*

[2] See Heidegger's *Sein und Zeit.*

[3] This is noted by Dwelshauvers in his book, *L'inconscient.* See P. Janet, *Lautomatisme psychologique.*

compensate himself for his weakness (Adler). Freud discovers an infinitude of sinful cravings in man, but he does not see the human soul. Psycho-analysis treats man's mental life as though the soul did not exist. It, too, is a psychology without a soul. The image of God in man is completely darkened and concealed it is invisible through the darkness of the unconscious and the falsehoods of consciousness. It is unintelligible where the clear consciousness of the psycho-analysts themselves comes from. Modern psychological knowledge is bitter and pessimistic, and it is a significant fact that Freud has worked out a metaphysic of death. In exactly the same way Karl Marx was blind to the human being as such, to personality. Psychology discovers that man is a sick being but does not recognize that he has been wounded by sin. Christian psychology also sees in man fathomless darkness, sin and evil, but it understands the source of it and therefore does not deny the image and likeness of God in man.

Our attitude to psycho-analysis is bound to be ambiguous. On the one hand we must give it credit for great scientific discoveries and for initiating a new era in psychology and anthropology.[1] It throws light on the source of man's mental and nervous diseases. Freud's school confirms the truth of what Vladimir Solovyov had said : a man may go mad and sacrifice his intellect because he is unable to cope with the moral conflicts of life. The era of intellectualistic psychology of the conscious mind, inaugurated by Descartes, has come to an end. The conflict between consciousness and the unconscious is the greatest discovery of the school of Freud and is true quite apart from Freud's pansexualism. His school studies the symbolism of which our life is full. Life of the unconscious is symbolically reflected in consciousness, and the symbolism must be understood. The psycho-analytical method has great importance for sociology, history of culture and the study of myths. Jung in particular insists upon the existence of the collective as well as of the individual subconscious.[2] The collective subconscious shows the presence of an archaic layer in man. The human soul is sick and tormented by atavistic false moral ideas and by the tyranny of society, which goes back to times immemorial. Myths are rooted in the collective subconscious. This is Jung's main contention, though he does not see all its implications.

Psycho-analysis cannot, however, claim to be a metaphysic of life. The ultimate truths escape it. And in practice it is in many respects mistaken or harmful. As a method of cure it concentrates the patient's attention on

[1] Jung is particularly interesting in this respect.
[2] See his *Wandlungen und Symbolen der Libido*. For the study of the collective unconscious Le Bon's *La Psychologie des Foules* is of value.

sexual life instead of drawing it away from it ; it turns the soul inside out and breaks it up into elements, claiming to be a substitute for confession. But psycho-analysts know nothing of the mystery of the remission of sins and the regeneration of the soul. They moralize and denounce sin without knowing what sin is and what is its source. Freud greatly exaggerates man's ignorance of his own unconscious. Man knows that he is a fallen and sinful being and is especially aware of it when he is conscious of himself as God's creation and God's idea. Freud's chief merit is his discovery of the evil part played by consciousness, especially the moral consciousness.

The optimistic and intellectualistic psychology of Thomism according to which man seeks bliss and loves himself is erroneous. It is a hedonistic view which can no longer be defended. Dostoevsky has shown in a masterly way that man is an irrational being and may long for suffering and not for happiness. This is confirmed by modern psychology. Masochism and sadism are deeply rooted in human nature. Man is a creature that torments himself and others and derives enjoyment from it. He does not strive for happiness at all. Such a striving would be objectless and meaningless. Man strives for concrete values and goods, the possession of which may give him bliss and happiness, but happiness itself cannot be his conscious purpose. When a philosopher or a scientist is engaged in the pursuit of truth, it is the truth he is after and not happiness, though the discover of truth may being happiness with it. When a lover is longing to be united to the woman he loves he is striving not for happiness but for what appears to him as a supreme good and value, the possession, namely, of that particular woman. Joy and happiness may be a consequence of that possession—and so may pain and suffering, as indeed is generally the case. The word "happiness" is the emptiest and most meaningless of human words. There exists no criterion or measure of happiness, and no comparison can be made between the happiness of one man and another.

Nor is it true that man always loves himself above all. Man is an egoistical and egocentric being, but that does not mean that he loves himself. Frequently people do not love themselves at all, and indeed feel an aversion for themselves. And if a man does not love himself, he cannot forgive it to anyone and vents upon other people the bitterness which he feels against himself. The most vindictive people are those who do not love themselves. People who have a liking for themselves are generally kinder and more tolerant of others. This is a moral and psychological paradox. A man may be a hard and heartless egoist but neither love nor like himself ; indeed he may feel a positive aversion for himself. One of the sources of human suffering is disgust with oneself and inability to feel any self-love. There is a self-love which we ought to have in accordance with God's will. We ought to love ourselves as God's creation and love the Divine image and likeness in us. We must love our neighbours as ourselves. This implies that we must love ourselves too and respect the image of God in us. Such a love is opposed to egoism and egocentricity, i.e. to the madness of putting oneself at the centre of the universe. Dislike of oneself, insufficient respect for the Divine image in one, makes a person a divided, morbidly introspective creature and gives rise to all kinds of complexes. The most touchy and proud people are those who do not love themselves.

St. Thomas Aquinas regards man as a healthy being and greatly minimizes the effects of original sin. His philosophy is one of the sources of optimistic naturalism. But in truth man is a sick creature longing to be healed. Man is by nature a divided being, combining such opposites as love and hate, purity and uncleanness, concentration and absent-mindedness, etc. According to Kierkegaard's definition, man is the synthesis of time and eternity, but it is a perpetually shifting synthesis, at one moment inclining towards eternity and at another falling under the sway of time. Consequently neither the psychological doctrine of St. Thomas of Aquinas nor that of Descartes is right. Although man is endowed with reason he is an irrational being, and this is why the psychology of the irrational is so valuable.

Man aspires to the loftiest values and the divine reality. Discovering in human nature fathomless darkness, conflict and pain, psychology ought also to discover that man is a creator of values and the image and likeness of God. The unconscious includes automatism, the lower unconscious or the subconscious in the strict sense.[1] But it also contains the sources of human creativeness, of creative inspiration and ecstasy. Creative inspiration, conception and intuition always have their original basis in the unconscious or the superconscious. The creative process in consciousness is secondary and less intense. The faculty of imagination is the source of all creativeness. God created the world through imagination. In Him imagination is an absolute ontological power. Imagination plays an enormous part in the moral and spiritual life of man. There is such a thing as the magic of imagination. Imagination magically creates realities. Without it there can be no works of art, no scientific or technical discoveries, no plans for ordering the economic or the political life of nations. Imagination springs from the depths of the unconscious, from fathomless

[1] See P. Janet, *L'automatisme psychique*.

freedom. Imagination is not only imitation of timelessly existent patterns, as Platonism in all its forms interprets it, but creation out of the depths of non-being of images that had never existed before.

The unconscious thus plays a double part in human life. It is the source of neuroses and of conflicts with consciousness and at the same time it is the source of creativeness, inspiration, the power of imagination, Two sides or aspects must be distinguished in human creativeness. There is the inner creative conception, the creative image arising out of the darkness, the primary creative intuition, springing from the depths of the unconscious. And then there is the realization of the creative conception, the embodiment of the creative image, the unfolding of the creative intuition in the density of our sinful world. In the inner creative act the spirit is aflame ; the outer creative act, subject to norms and laws, implies a certain cooling down. When a philosophical or a scientific book or a novel is written, when a statue is chiselled and a symphony assumes its final form, e.g. when a machine is built or an economic or political institution takes shape, or even when the earthly, canonical life of the church is organized, the creative activity loses its intensity, the fire dies down, the creator is dragged down to earth. He cannot fly away to heaven, but must descend to this world to realize his idea. This is the tragedy of creativeness. The results never correspond to the original conception and can never give satisfaction. This is the bitterness of all creative work, and it, too, is one of the conflicts between consciousness and the unconscious. Consciousness does violence to the unconscious creativeness and distorts its results. This is particularly obvious with regard to our moral life.

Modern psycho-pathology sees the source of nervous and mental diseases in the insoluble moral conflicts produced by thwarting the unconscious. Moral consciousness through which society dictates its will to the individual comes up against the deep-seated primeval instincts hidden in the subconscious. Man falls a victim to his inability to deal with moral conflicts. It must be recognized as an axiom that moral law is powerless to change human nature and cannot solve any individual moral problem. The chief difficulty of moral conflicts is not the choice between obvious good and obvious evil, but the absence of any single, morally binding solution laid down once for all and the necessity for making each time an individual creative act. There always appear to be several good solutions and one has to choose between them. Both in the life of communities and of individuals the Dionysian forces of life rise up periodically against the laws of civilization and society. Such rebellion cannot always be regarded as an evil. Without it life would become petrified.

We are not aware that we live in madness which is but superficially concealed. Human consciousness lies between two abysses, the upper and the lower, the superconscious and the subconscious. This is why man is inwardly divided, as Dostoevsky has shown in so masterly a way. Proust depicts this splitting up of personality apart from the conflict between good and evil.[1] Moral consciousness which formulates laws and norms comes up both against the instinctive, subconscious, primeval nature and against grace, superconsciousness and the divine. This is what makes the moral problem so complex. It is quite a mistake to imagine that human passions and instincts, suppressed by moral consciousness, are always selfish, self-regarding and pleasure-seeking. To do so is to introduce the rationally teleological point of view into the elemental subconscious life. Man disinterestedly desires power, violence, domination, cruelty, sensuality, and destroys himself. Pleasure, satisfaction, wellbeing as an aim are suggested by consciousness ; such an aim does not exist in the subconscious. Immorality in the sense of desire for sexual pleasure springs from consciousness, from bringing a conscious element into the unconscious life of sex. It is the merit of Freud to have dared to unveil the carefully hidden life of sex. But he wants to make it conscious ; he wants not merely to know about sexual life, which is perfectly legitimate, but also to bring consciousness into the sexual life itself, which is inadmissible. This is the evil of psycho-analysis as a practical method. Sexual life must remain in the sphere of the unconscious. Introspective analysis of the sexual act is as impossible as an aesthetic contemplation of it. *Libido* is not only a striving for sexual union but also a source of creativeness which is always based on polarization. The sublimation of the sexual instinct in creativeness is not achieved by making consciousness predominant. Rationalism does not know the mystery of sublimation. The Freudian school means the end both of naïve idealism and naïve materialism. Naïve materialism was based upon ignorance of the mystery of the unconscious and introduced the rational teleological point of view for the interpretation of the instinctive life of the soul. Naïve idealism is equally ignorant of the mystery of the subconscious.

I have already said that man is sick because he does not do what he wants to do, does not live in the way he wants to live, and has his unconscious strivings repressed by social consciousness. But the remarkable thing is that the conscious and the unconscious pass into each other. That which was conscious in the life of primitive communities—their laws, norms,

[1] This distinction between Proust and Dostoevsky is pointed out by J. Rivière in his articles on Proust.

prohibitions—afterwards becomes subconscious and exists as an atavistic instinct. This shows the limits of consciousness. The ancient taboos were fixed by the social consciousness, which was also moral and religious. But at a later stage of social development those taboos passed into the life of the subconscious and came into conflict with the new forms of consciousness. The dividing line between the conscious and the unconscious is therefore relative. True spiritual victories are won in the domain of superconsciousness, i.e. in the spirit, and not in consciousness. Obsession by some fixed idea—the most usual form of nervous and mental disorder—is a wrong state of consciousness, its narrowing and exclusive fixation upon one object. The disease is really due to the wrong work of consciousness upon the unconscious. Recovery can only take place through the intervention of the superconscious, spiritual principle.

Man's moral recovery cannot be attained through moral consciousness, which is just what causes the disease. It can only be effected through superconsciousness, which belongs to the spiritual world. This presupposes a new ethics, based not upon the norms and laws of consciousness but upon gracious spiritual power. The Christian doctrine of grace has always meant recovery of spiritual health which law cannot bring about ; but it has not been utilized as a basis for ethics. Man desires not only health and victory over sin but also creative activity ; and that activity is a means of healing as well.

There exist three types of ethics—the ethics of law, of redemption and of creativeness. Ethics in the profound sense of the term must teach of the awakening of the human spirit and not of consciousness, of creative spiritual power and not of laws and norms. The ethics of law, the ethics of consciousness which represses subconsciousness and knows nothing of superconsciousness, is the result of the primitive emotion of fear, and we, Christians, see in it the result of original sin. Fear warns man of danger, and therein lies its ontological significance.

The awakening of spirit in man is very painful. At the early stages the spirit divides and fetters man's vital energy, and only later does it manifest itself as creative energy. The spiritual superconscious principle separates man out of nature, and, as it were, dementalizes nature, depriving it of its daemonic power. In man too there is a struggle between spirit and nature. Consciousness becomes the arena of that struggle. The awakening of the spirit may be inspired by the idea of redemption or by creativeness. The idea of redemption subjects the soul to new dangers. The thought of perdition and salvation may become a morbid obsession. In that case salvation of the soul from being possessed by the idea of salvation comes from creative spiritual energy, from the shock of creative inspiration. Redemption is only completed through creativeness. This is the fundamental conception of the new ethics.

The soul is afraid of emptiness, and if it has no positive creative content it becomes filled with falsehoods, illusions and fictions. The ethics of redemption corresponds to the awakening of the spiritual man and his struggle against "nature". Paradoxically enough it develops man's scientific, intellectual and technical mastery over nature. But this mastery transfers the struggle to man's external social environment and produces weapons which are not biologically hereditary ; hence, as has already been said, it leads to man's anthropological regress and dulls the keenness of his senses and instincts. This is a very disturbing problem and one of great importance to anthropology and ethics. It cannot be solved during the dualistic period, when the ethics of redemption co-exists with secularized scientific technique which severs man from nature, and, while giving him mastery over it, weakens him and leads to his degeneration. Consciousness and civilization based upon it are responsible for endless diseases of man and make him weak and divided against himself. The paradoxical part of it is that consciousness is connected with the awakening of the spirit, i.e. of the superconscious principle and with the ethics of redemption which corresponds to it. Man's weakness and morbid dividedness are overcome through superconsciousness and the ethics of creative energy which continues and completes the spiritual work of redemption. In superconsciousness man is no longer alone, but is united to God. We must trace the three stages of moral consciousness—the ethics of the law, the ethics of redemption and the ethics of creativeness. Their interrelation cannot be interpreted chronologically, for they co-exist. But first, it is necessary to consider the question of free will, essential both to ethics and to anthropology.

5. FREEDOM OF WILL AND ETHICS

The religious, metaphysical and moral problem of freedom is by no means identical with the traditional scholastic problem of free will. The doctrine of free will rests upon false presuppositions and psychological doctrines that are no longer tenable. The old conception of will, as an element of the mental life by means of which man chooses between good and evil and becomes responsible for evil, is mistaken. I have already pointed out that such a conception was suggested by utilitarian pedagogical considerations. Free will as *liberum arbitrium indifferentiæ* does not exist. Freedom of will in the sense of freedom of indifference is slavery rather than freedom, and man ought to feel relieved and free when the choice is made and he need no longer remain in a state of indecision. According to the traditional interpretation, freedom of will is in no sense creative, and instead of liberating man keeps him in perpetual fear. It humiliates man rather than exalts him ; he cannot create anything through that freedom, but can only accept or reject what is given him from without. Indeed, one may state the following paradox which has played a considerable part in the history of religious ideas : freedom of will, confronted for ever with the terrifying necessity of choosing between alternatives externally imposed upon it from above, represses and enslaves man ; true liberation comes through grace and not through free will : man is free when he need not choose. In this sense there is a certain amount of truth in Luther's view, though he expressed it wrongly.

N. Hartmann is right in saying that the teleological point of view in ethics involves a denial of human freedom and introduces a notion of necessity ; but his own treatment of ideal values is not altogether free from teleology. The teleological point of view, combined with the doctrine of free will, may be formulated as follows : man must subordinate his life to the supreme end placed before him and make all his lower aims subservient to the highest good. Such a conception, though greatly prevalent, is out of keeping both with modern psychology and with the Christian revelation and results in a slavish morality. The teleological point of view, dating back to Aristotle, must be abandoned altogether. Man's moral dignity and freedom are determined not by the purpose to which he subordinates his life but by the source from which his moral life and activity spring. It may actually be said that in a sense " the means " which a man uses are far more important than " the ends " which he pursues, for they express more truly what his spirit is. If a man strives for freedom by means of tyranny, for love by means of hatred, for brotherhood by means of dissension, for truth by means of falsity, his lofty aim is not likely to make our judgment of him more lenient. I actually believe that a man who worked for the cause of tyranny, hatred, falsity and dissension by means of freedom, love, truthfulness and brotherhood, would be the better man of the two. The most important thing for ethics is man's real nature, the spirit in which he acts, the presence or absence in him of inner light, of beneficent creative energy. Ethics must be based upon the conception of energy and not of the final end. It must therefore interpret freedom as the original source of action and inner creative energy and not as the power of fulfilling the law and realizing a set purpose. The moral good is not a goal but an inner force which lights up man's life from within. The important thing is the source from which activity springs and not the end towards which it is directed.

The doctrine of free will and teleology belong entirely to the ethics of law, the normative ethics. Kant's theory of autonomy has no bearing on human freedom. It is the moral law that is autonomous and not man. Freedom is needed solely for carrying out the moral law. Kant's autonomous ethics really ignores man : all that exists for it is the moral and intellectual nature which suppresses man as a concrete individual. Ethics must be based upon the conception of creative freedom as the source of life, and of spirit as the light which illumines life. Man acts not in order to realize certain ends but in virtue of the creative freedom and energy inherent in him and of the gracious light that irradiates his life from within. The question fundamental to ethics is that of freedom and grace and not of freedom and necessity.

Another question of great importance both to ethics and anthropology is that of the interrelation between freedom and the hierarchical principle. Christians often misconceive it. When the hierarchical principle is considered in relation not to the highest quality, as opposed to quantity or mass, but to the sinful human nature which must be fettered, repressed and guided, the result is a distorted view of man. The object of reverence in that case is not man, not human gifts and qualities, but the bearer of authority, of the impersonal hierarchical principle. Life is organized so as to ensure everywhere the rule and domination of rank. Bishop and priest, monarch and policeman, father and head of family, factory owner and office chief—all these are hierarchical ranks, the qualities of which do not depend upon the individual man's nature but are automatically conferred on the bearer. This implies a peculiar kind of anthropology and ethics. Man's influence and significance in life is taken to depend upon the presence in him of an impersonal, non-human, hierarchical principle. This kind of hierarchism is not human at all. It has nothing in common with Carlyle's worship of heroes and great men.

Impersonal non-human hierarchism is opposed to the hierarchism of human gifts and qualities. Saint and genius, hero and great man, prophet and apostle, artist and man of intelligence, inventor and craftsman—these are the ranks of the human hierarchy ; it implies quite a different kind of subordination than the impersonal, non-human hierarchy. Our sinful world presupposes the existence of both kinds of hierarchy, but the human is the higher of the two. The church cannot exist without bishops and priests, whatever their human qualities may be, but inwardly it lives and breathes through saints, apostles and prophets, religious geniuses, artists, heroes and ascetics. A state cannot exist without the head of the state, ministers, officials, policemen, generals, soldiers, but states progress and carry out their historical missions through great men, heroes, leaders, reformers, men of talent and exceptional energy. Science cannot exist without professors and teachers, however mediocre they may be, without academies and universities organized on the hierarchical principle, but it lives and develops through men of genius and talent, discoverers of new paths, inventors and revolutionaries. A family cannot exist without a hierarchical structure, but it lives and breathes through love and self-sacrifice. Salvation from degeneracy, stagnation and death comes not from the impersonal but from the human hierarchism, from human gifts and qualities. The impersonal, non-human, angelic hierarchy (in the church) is symbolic and representative, while the human and personal hierarchy is real, based on actual qualities and achievements. A priest is symbolic, a saint is real. A monarch is symbolic, a great man is real. It is the business of ethics to give predominance to the real, human hierarchy over the symbolic and non-human. This presupposes a different conception of man. From the ethical point of view the essential human striving is not the striving for happiness any more than for submission and obedience, but the striving for quality, self-development and self-realization, even if it brings suffering and not happiness and be achieved through revolt and rebellion. Man is a free being called to creativeness and therefore he must think not of happiness and satisfaction or of obedience and submission. Man does not exist apart from the divine element in him, not symbolically but really divine.

Man and humanity, the idea and the image of man, have two eternal sources in the world of antiquity—the biblical and the Hellenic. It was there that man was formed and differentiated out of the primeval chaos. But though his first sources are Hebrew-Hellenic, it was only in Christianity, through Christ and the Christian revelation, that man found himself, reached spiritual maturity and became free from the power of the lower natural elements. In the person of Christ the God-Man man has fully come to exist. The fundamental Christian conception of man is real and not symbolic. It implies the transfiguration and illumination of the created nature of man, i.e. the actual attainment of the highest qualities and not a symbolic representation of non-human values in the human world. The central anthropological idea of Christianity is the idea of Divine humanity, of real divinely human kingdom. Christianity leads to the deification of the human and not of the angelic or the animal nature, because Christ was the God-man and not God-angel. Symbolic hierarchism is divinely angelic and not divinely human. Ethics cannot be based upon a separation between God and man, the divine and the human. It is possible to distinguish three types of ethics : theological, humanitarian and theo-andric ethics. It is to the third type, to the divinely human ethics, that the present book is devoted.

PART II

MORALITY ON THIS SIDE OF GOOD AND EVIL

CHAPTER ONE

The Ethics of Law

I. THE DUALISM OF GOOD AND EVIL

MORALITY in our world implies the dualism of good and evil. Dualism is the presupposition of morality. Monistic theories always prove unfavourable to it and weaken man's moral earnestness. Ethical dualism means that the primeval beauty of creation has been disturbed and damaged. It indicates that man is a wounded creature. The very distinction between good and evil is painful and brings no joy with it. Philosophical theories may be classified according to the poignancy with which the problem of good and evil makes itself felt in them. But the poignancy is connected with the experience of evil, for the experience of the good as such is free from it. Plato, the Stoics, the Gnostics, Luther, Jacob Boehme, Pascal, Fichte, Nietzsche, Kierkegaard, Dostoevsky were thinkers whose main interest was ethical ; they were tormented by the problem of evil. Aristotle, Thomas Aquinas, Descartes, Spinoza, Leibniz, Hegel were not mainly concerned with moral issues. To say that a philosopher's main interest is ethical does not mean that he is a moralist ; rather, the reverse is the case. It implies awareness of the tragedy involved in the experience of good and evil which is not solved by moral laws and norms. The source of tragedy is that the good and the moral law are absolutely powerless to overcome evil and conquer the source of evil. This has been expressed once and for all by St. Paul.

Moral consciousness presupposes dualism and opposition between the moral personality and the evil world both around it and within it. And this means that moral acts and valuations have their source in the Fall, in the loss of the original paradisaical wholeness and the impossibility to feed from the tree of life directly, without discrimination and reflection. Discrimination and valuation presuppose dividedness and loss of wholeness. Herein lies the fundamental paradox of ethics : the moral good has a bad origin and its bad origin pursues it like a curse. This paradox is brought to light by Christianity, which shows that the good understood as a law is powerless. For Christian consciousness law is paradoxical.

This is the main theme of St. Paul.[1] St. Paul wages a passionate struggle against the power of the law and reveals the religion of grace. Law comes from sin and makes sin manifest. Law denounces sin, limits it, but cannot conquer it. Man cannot attain righteousness through the works of the law. " By the deeds of the law there shall no flesh be justified in his sight : for by the law is the knowledge of sin." " Man is justified by faith without the deeds of the law." " If they which are of the law be heirs, faith is made void and the promise made of none effect." Law is connected with sin because " sin is not imputed when there is no law ". St. Paul lays particular stress on deliverance from the power of the law. " Ye are not under the law, but under grace." " Now we are delivered from the law, that being dead wherein we were held ; that we should serve in newness of spirit, and not in the oldness of the letter." " Christ is become of no effect unto you, whosoever of you are justified by the law ; ye are fallen from grace." " If ye be led of the Spirit ye are not under the law." The fiery words of St. Paul may lead one to think that he completely rejects the law, and indeed they have been used for preaching lawlessness. But so to interpret St. Paul would be to deny the main antinomy of ethics—to deny the paradox of normative ethics. Christianity reveals the kingdom of grace which is higher than and beyond the law. But Christ came to fulfil the law and not to destroy it. And those who pretend to stand above the law may easily sink below it. Law has a bad origin in that it comes from sin. It denounces sin, it judges and discriminates, but is powerless to overcome sin and evil, and even in denouncing sin it easily becomes evil. But at the same time law has a positive mission in the world, and for that reason the ethics of law cannot be simply rejected.

The ethics of law is the pre-Christian morality ; it is to be found not only in the Old Testament but in paganism, in primitve communities, in Aristotle and the Stoics, and within Christianity in Pelagius and to a considerable extent in St. Thomas Aquinas.[2] At the same time the ethics of law contains an eternal principle which must be recognized by the Christian world as well, for sin and evil are not conquered in it. The ethics of law cannot be interpreted chronologically only, for it co-exists with the ethics of redemption and of creativeness. Its history in the Christian world is extremely complicated. Christianity is the revelation of grace, and

[1] See B. Vysheslavtsev's excellent article in *Put*, *The Ethics of Sublimation as Victory over Moralism* (in Russian).
[2] See *Les moralistes chrétiens (Textes et Commentaires)*, *Saint Thomas d'Aquin* by Etienne Gilson. It is remarkable how Aristotelian St. Thomas's ethics is.

Christian ethics is the ethics of redemption and not of law. But Christianity was weighed down by extraneous elements and underwent changes in the course of time. It has often been interpreted in a legalistic sense. Thus, the official Roman Catholic theology is to a considerable extent legalistic. The Gospel itself has been constantly distorted by legalistic interpretations. Legalism, rationalism and formalism have actually introduced an element of law into the truth of the Christian revelation. Even grace received a legalistic interpretation. Theologians were alarmed by St. Paul's doctrine and did their best to limit and modify it. An element of rationalistic, almost Pelagian legalism penetrated into the very consciousness of the church. Luther protested ardently against the law in Christianity, against legalistic ethics, and attempted to take his stand beyond good and evil.[1] But Luther's own followers were alarmed by him ; they tried to render harmless his passionate protests and modify and rationalize his irrationalism. Only the school of K. Barth, following Kierkegaard, has returned to Luther's paradoxality.[2] Throughout the history of Christianity there has always been a struggle between the principles of grace and spiritual regeneration and the formal, juridical and rationalistic principles.

Legalistic morality is deeply rooted in human society and goes back to the primitive clans with their totems and taboos. The ethics of law is essentially social as distinct from the personal ethics of redemption and creativeness. The Fall subordinated human conscience to society. Society became the bearer and the guardian of the moral law. Sociologists who maintain that morality has a social origin have unquestionably got hold of a certain truth. But they do not see the origin of this truth or the depth of its meaning. The ethics of law means, first and foremost, that the subject of moral valuation is society and not the individual, that society lays down moral prohibitions, taboos, laws and norms to which the individual must submit under penalty of moral excommunication and retribution. The ethics of law can never be personal and individual, it never penetrates into the intimate depths of personal moral life, experience and struggle. It exaggerates evil in personal life, punishing and prohibiting it, but does not attach sufficient importance to evil in the life of the world and society. It takes an optimistic view of the power of the moral law, of the freedom of will and of the punishment of the wicked, which is supposed to prove that the world is ruled by justice. The ethics of law is both very human and well adapted to human needs and standards, and

[1] L. Schestov finds a similarity between the work of Luther and of Nietzsche.
[2] See especially Karl Barth, *Der Römerbrief.*

extremely inhuman and pitiless towards the human personality, its individual destiny and intimate life.

2. THE PRIMITIVE MORAL CONSCIOUSNESS

Anthropologists and sociologists have devoted a great deal of attention to the primitive man, but their methods and principles of investigation were determined by the evolutionary theory of the second half of the nineteenth century. They studied modern savages and from them drew conclusions about the primitive man. Scientific investigation in the strict sense was from the nature of the case impossible, but as a result of philosophic assumptions it was believed that, to begin with, man was at a savage, half-animal stage and then, up to the nineteenth century, he gradually progressed. Man's distant past was inferred from his present, from savages and animals. The scientists' imagination was so poor that in man's distant past they could conceive of nothing different from what they found in modern times at the lower stages of life. But ancient man and his life were infinitely more significant and mysterious than anthropologists and sociologists suppose. In this respect theosophists and occultists are nearer the truth. There is something to be said for the Akasha Records, the Chronicle of the world, though the idea is easily vulgarized. At the dawn of humanity the world was at a different stage than it is now. It was more plastic, and the limits which divide this world from other worlds were less sharply marked. We are told this, in a covert form, in the book of Genesis.

The evolutionary theory of the nineteenth century has been disproved both by science and philosophy, and cannot be used as the basis of the methods and principles of inquiry. It is inadmissible to transfer to the ancient, primitive humanity our habits of thought and feeling and our view of the world. Everything then was different, not at all similar either to the savages or to the animal world of our own day. Lévy Bruhl, criticizing Taylor and Fraser, tries to discover the nature of primitive thought, quite different from civilized people's thought,[1] but his modern positivist and rationalistic mentality prevents him from understanding it. What he calls *la loi de participation* shows that primitive thought was of a higher type than that of the nineteenth-century man, for it expressed the mystical nearness of the knower to his object. Man loses as well as gains through the growth of civilization. He not only progresses but degenerates, falls, grows weaker and poorer. There is no doubt that some ancient know-

[1] See Lévy Bruhl, *Les fonctions mentales dans les sociétés inférieures.*

ledge connected with the proximity to the source of being was lost by man in the course of time, and only a memory of it is left to him.[1] There is no doubt that there existed great civilizations in the past, such as those of Babylon or Egypt, and that their fall meant a period of regress and a loss of tremendous achievements. There are considerable reasons to believe in the truth of the myth about Atlantis, where a very high civilization became morally degenerate and perished. It is far more likely that the savages as we know them are a product of degeneration and retrogression, and do not represent the primary stage of human development. In speaking of the primitive moral consciousness as we know it, we must not draw conclusions with regard to the first origins of mankind. The facts that lend themselves to study and observation are chronologically secondary and not primary. Psycho-pathology has shed more light on the ancient man than sociology.

Westermarck is to a great extent right in saying that moral emotions were born out of resentment. This is why vengeance plays such a tremendous part in primitive moral consciousness. In the primitive mind the ethics of law finds expression first of all in vengeance, and this throws light on the genesis of good and evil. Moral life was to a considerable extent determined by the primitive emotions of terror and awe. Vengeance is connected with that terror. The shade of the victim would haunt his kinsmen until they avenged his death. In ancient times men were keenly conscious of the power of the dead over the living, and their dread of the nether world showed a far deeper insight into truth than the modern man's careless indifference. It is curious that in antiquity the imperative need for vengeance was by no means due to cruelty or ferocity, malice or hatred : it was pre-eminently a moral feeling and a religious duty. This can be seen from the Greek tragedy. Take the instance of Orestes, obsessed by the moral duty of avenging his father's death. Hamlet's case is similar. The ancient morality of vengeance forms a very deep layer of man's moral feelings and makes itself felt in the modern Christian world as well. Moral discrimination, valuation, judgment and condemnation contain an element of primitive vengeance in a sublimated form. Without being aware of it " the good " really want to wreak vengeance on " the wicked ", though it is not a blood vengeance. The moral consciousness of antiquity dreaded the thought of leaving a crime unpunished. Punishment was at the same time vengeance, and the idea of punishment was born out of vengeance. The punisher was the avenger.

[1] This is maintained not only by the occultists. See, e.g., *La Science mystérieuse des Pharaons* by Abbé Moreaux.

This idealization and sublimation of vengeance as a religious and moral duty finds its final metaphysical expression in the doctrine of hell.

The primitive moral consciousness is communal and social. Its moral subject is the group united by kinship and not the individual. Vengeance as a moral act is also communal : it is carried out by one group of kinsmen against another, and not by one individual against another. Blood vengeance is the most characteristic moral phenomenon of antiquity and persists in the Christian world in so far as human nature in it is not transfigured and enlightened. The instinct of vengeance and the mentality it involves, so radically opposed to Christianity, give rise to a curious conception of honour : a man must defend his honour and the honour of his family by the force of arms, by shedding blood. Insult to one's honour must be washed away by blood. The bond of kinship inspires reverential fear. This is connected with the fear of incest, which has haunted man from times immemorial. In Œdipus's union with his own mother incest reached the climax of horror : it meant that man returned, as it were, to where he had come from, i.e. denied the very fact of birth and rebelled against the law of generic life.

In antiquity vengeance was not at all connected with personal guilt. Vengeance and punishment were not primarily directed against the person who was personally guilty and responsible. The conception of personal guilt and responsibility was formed much later. Blood vengeance was impersonal. When the state took upon itself the duty of avenging and punishing crime, the idea of personal guilt and responsibility began to develop. The law, which always has a social character, demands that the primeval chaos of instincts should be suppressed ; but it merely drives that chaos inwards and does not conquer it or regenerate it. Chaotic primeval instincts have been preserved in the civilized man of the twentieth century. The world-war and the communistic revolution have shown this.

After the Christian revelation vengeance, which was at first a moral and religious duty, became an immoral unruly instinct that man had to overcome through the new law. The ancient awe-inspiring tyranny of the clan and kin with its endless taboos and prohibitions ceased to be a moral law as it was in antiquity, and became a part of atavistic instincts against which a higher moral consciousness must struggle. This is one of the important truths of social ethics. To begin with, society subdues and disciplines man's instincts, but afterwards, at the higher stages of moral development, ideas and emotions which had been instilled into man for the sake of disciplining him become, in their turn, unruly instincts. This happened in the first instance with vengeance. Society deprived the individual of freedom because he was possessed by sinful passions ; but social restraint of freedom became an instinct of tyranny and love of power. Superstitions, tyranny and caste privileges had once served the purpose of bringing order into chaos and establishing a social cosmos ; but they degenerated into instincts which stand in the way of a free social organization. Law plays a double part in the moral life of humanity : it restrains unruly instincts and creates order, but it also calls forth instincts which prevent the creation of a new order. This shows the impotence of the law.

Primitive life is communistic as well as social,[1] and this primitive communism is the source of tyrannical instincts in human society. Primary moral emotions were born when the individual was wholly dominated by the clan ; and to this day man cannot free himself from the instincts of clannish morality. Moral conceptions began to be formed while personality was still dormant and merely potential. And our moral consciousness is still torn between ideas that date back to the time when the clan was the subject of moral life, and those that were formed when personality had come into its own and become the subject of moral life. Taboo was the main category of the legalistic ethics of the clan period, and it was preserved when personal conscience had become the source of moral judgments. Primitive morality was formed under the influence of terror inspired by the souls of the departed and was determined by the relations not only between human beings, but between men and gods, demi-gods, demons and spirits. The king was a god or a totem. This is the source of reverential feelings for the monarch which persist to our own day. It is the basis of monarchist morality.

Cruelty in primitive society was not merely an unruly animal instinct, but was connected with moral emotions and had a moral sanction. Indeed, throughout history man has been cruel in virtue of moral emotions and from a sense of duty. When he loses the instinct of cruelty he often loses at the same time moral emotions and the sense of duty that had been formed in earlier epochs. There is nothing more distressing than atavistic moral instincts connected with moral emotions of a by-gone age. They spoil life more than anything else does. The ethics of law is capable of creating such instincts. Rulers of states, hierarchs of churches, owners of business concerns, heads of families are not infrequently cruel not from bloodthirstiness or a love of tyrannizing, but from atavistic moral emotions and a sense of duty which is a torture to themselves. Morality of the law, developed at a time when the community completely suppressed

[1] Bachofen connects communism with matriarchate.

the individual, goes on tormenting him even after the personal conscience has awakened and the centre of moral gravity has been transferred to it.

The element of magic plays a very important part in primitive moral consciousness. It was by means of magic that man waged war on hostile forces ; it was the first expression of his scientific and technical activity. At the same time magic was a highly social force. Power originally meant magical power,[1] and the relations between the ruler and the ruled were based on magic. Magic is from its very nature imperative. The ᴧwer of the moral law with its prohibitions was in the first instance magical. These magical attributes of power remained in force throughout history, and man is not free from them to this day in spite of Christianity, the conception of moral responsibility, and so on. The distinction between the pure and the impure has a magical character. Men believe in the moral magic of words. They are superstitiously afraid of infringing a moral taboo. They are tormented by remorse for things that have no relation whatever to their personal conscience or their personal guilt. They are haunted by the magic of curses and condemnations. And they think that their moral actions and words have power over God and over destiny. At the beginning a moral act was, so to speak, a form of operative magic. Men believed in a merely magical fulfilment of moral commandments. Modern people have inherited this belief from primitive times. Philosophers and moralists, Socrates and the Stoics, Kant and Tolstoy tried to purify the moral law from magic elements. But for many minds something of the nature of primitive magic attaches to the " good works " of the ethics of law.[2]

3. THE SOCIAL CHARACTER OF THE LAW

The ethics of law is the expression of herd morality. It organizes the life of the average man, of the human herd, and leaves altogether out of account the creative human personality which rises above the common level. It deals with personality in the abstract ; the concrete person does not exist for it. The morality of the law is universally binding. The herd life for which Heidegger has invented a special category of *das Man* is social in character. It means the domination of society with its general norms and laws over the inner, intimately personal and unique life of the individual. Herd life means the cooling down of the creative fire ; moral

[1] Frazer especially insists on this in his work on the magical origin of kingly power.

[2] See Frazer, *The Golden Bough* ; Huber et Maus, *Mélanges d'histoire des religions* ; Maxwell, *Magic*.

consciousness in it is determined not by what the person himself thinks or feels, but by other people's ideas and conscience (" *on dit* ", " *man sagt* ", " they say "). Legalistic morality is always social and not personal. The person, the personal conscience, the individual mind cannot be the bearer of the law ; the law is inherent in society, in social conscience and social thought. True, in Kant's autonomous but legalistic ethics, the bearer of the moral law is the person and not the community. But the moral law which the person is freely to manifest in himself is determined by society · it is universally binding, and universality always has a social character The moral law, as well as the logical law, is absolutely binding upon every living being, whatever its unique and individual nature may be. The law does not recognize individuality and uniqueness. The moral law is not in the least concerned with the individual's moral experience and spiritual conflicts. We find in Kant complete indifference to moral experience and struggle. The only thing that matters to the law is whether the individual is going to fulfil it or not. Cohen, who works out a system of legalistic ethics, is perfectly consistent in connecting it with jurisprudence. The ethics of law brings order into the life of the herd. It is concerned only with the universally binding.

The fatal consequence of the legalistic discrimination between good and evil is tyranny of the law which means tyranny of society over the person and of the universally binding idea over the personal, the particular, unique and individual. The hard-set crystallized forms of herd life in which the creative fire is almost extinct oppress like a nightmare the creative life of personality. The law thwarts life and does violence to it. And the real tragedy of ethics lies in the fact that the law has its own positive mission in the world. It cannot be simply rejected and denied. If this were possible there would be no conflict of principles. The ethics of law must be transcended, the creative life of personality must be vindicated. But the law has a positive value of its own. It warps the individual life, but it also preserves it. It is a paradox, but the exclusive predominance of the ethics of grace in a sinful world would endanger the freedom and, indeed, the very existence of personality. A person's fate cannot be made to rest solely upon other people's spiritual condition. This is where the significance of law comes in. No one can be made to depend upon his neighbours' moral qualities and inward perfection. In our sinful world personality is doomed to share to some extent the herd life which both thwarts it and preserves it by means of law and justice. Justice is righteousness refracted in the common life of every day. The realm of the herd-

[1] Zimmel has many interesting remarks on the subject. See his *Soziologie*.

man, *das Man*, is the result of the Fall ; indeed, it *is* the fallen world. The life of personality is inevitably warped in it, and even Christian revelation becomes distorted. The primary evil is not in the law as such which makes sin manifest, but in the sin which gives rise to the law. But the law which denounces sin and puts a limit to the manifestations of it has a way of degenerating into evil.

This is why the history of the ethics of law is so complicated. As early as Socrates Greek thought tried to emancipate itself from the power of law and society and to penetrate to the personal conscience. The moral consciousness of Socrates comes into conflict with the Athenian democracy. He falls a victim to the law of the herd, of *das Man*, of " they say so " of society. Socrates proclaimed the principle that God ought to be obeyed more than men. But this means that God, conscience, truth, the inner man ought to be obeyed more than society and the formal law. Socrates did not rise from the ethics of law to the ethics of grace, any more than the Stoics have done. But he made a tremendous advance towards the moral liberation of personality and the discovery of individual conscience as distinct from the social. When Plato in *Gorgias* says that it is better to suffer injustice than to inflict it on others, he transfers the centre of gravity in moral life to the depths of personality. This is all the more remarkable because Plato arrives at communism, which denies personality. The Greek consciousness never completely liberated personality from the power of the city-state. This liberation was only achieved by Christianity, which means transition to the ethics of grace and redemption.

The violence which legalistic good does to the life of the world and the individual finds expression in the formula *fiat justitia, pereat mundus*. The ethics of law is concerned with goodness and justice, but not with life, not with man or the world. This is its limitation. Legalistic ethics with its universally binding rules leads to the slavery of man to the state and society, to a slavish relation to the monarch, to the chief, to the rich and powerful, as well as to the mass, to the crowd, to the majority. Moral judgments of legalistic ethics are made not by the individual, but by the clan, the tribe, the caste, the state, the nation, the family. The divine principle of truth is invoked to sanction these products of the herd mind. Respect for rank—for the ruler of the state, the hierarch of the church, the chief, the head of the family—is placed above respect for individual gifts and qualities of the genius, the artist, the good man, the scientist or the poet. We touch here upon the main problem of the ethics of law. The ethics of law does not know the inner man ; it regulates the life of the outer man in relation to society ; it rests on what I call the external, as opposed to the inward hierarchism. It may be either conservative or revolutionary, but in either case it is social and based upon imperatives. Social ethics renders primary and virginal moral acts and valuations impossible ; they become overlaid with the social layers of beliefs and preconceived ideas of the group, the family, the class, the party, and so on, so that the pure and free moral judgment is not to be discovered. The greatest task of moral life lies precisely in detecting the primary, virginal moral act, not vitiated by social suggestions. A tremendous influence on our moral judgments is exercised by the state. But state is not only from God, it is also from the devil.

There is something paradoxical in the Pagan and Judaic attitude to the world-reason and to fate. The Greeks and the Romans resigned themselves to fate (as shown by the Greek tragedies and Stoicism), for there was no one to appeal to against it. The ancient Jews rebelled and struggled against God Himself (the book of Job, the prophets, the Psalms). The absolute power of the law which rules the world called forth either dispassionate submission or rebellion and struggle against God. But it was only Job and the prophets on the one hand and tragedians and sages on the other who rose to this ; the main line of life was in accord with the power of the law. In ancient books, in the laws of Manu, in the Bible, in the Talmud, in the Koran, life is regulated throughout and subject to law ; everywhere there is the fear of impurity, of prohibitions and taboos; everywhere there are barriers and dividing lines. Uncleanness and purification, prohibitions and the violation of prohibitions—these are the fundamental categories of the primitive man's moral life. The fear to violate a prohibition and to become unclean is the mainspring of morality. This is the ethics of law at the early stages. In the course of time it is transformed into legalism within Christianity, into the ethics of Kant and idealistic normative morality. The ethics of law is based upon religious fear, an almost animal fear, which later on is sublimated. The fear of the unclean and the forbidden haunts man at the highest stages of culture, merely assuming a more refined form. But the primitive emotion of fear is always at the bottom.

From its very nature law inevitably inspires fear. It does not regenerate human nature, does not destroy sin, but by means of fear, both external and inward, holds sin within certain bounds. Moral order in the world is maintained in the first place through religious fear, which later on assumes the form of the moral law. Such are the direct consequences of the Fall. In the life of the state and the community we find at this stage cruel punishments and executions to which moral significance is attached. The characteristic feature of the ethics of law is that it is concerned with the abstract norm of the good but does not care about man, the unique and individual human personality and its intimate inner life. This is its limitation. It is interested not in man as a living being with his joys and sufferings, but in the abstract norm of the good which is set for man. This is the case even when it becomes philosophic and idealistic and proclaims the principle of the intrinsic value of human personality. Thus in Kant the conception of personality is purely abstract and normative, and has no relation to the concrete and irreplaceable human individuality in which Kant never took any interest.

Kantian ethics is opposed to hedonism, which regards happiness as the end of life ; but hedonism, too, understands happiness as an abstract norm of the good, and is not in the least concerned with the happiness of the concrete living individual. The ethics of law seems to be confined to a closed range of ideas, and can never get hold of the concrete and the individual. Whatever form it takes, it is bound to admit that the abstract good is higher than the concrete individual man, even if the abstract good stands for the principle of personality or of happiness. Moralism, which is always full of condemnation, is born of the law ; but such moralism is immoral from the point of view of a higher, not legalistic, ethics.

The law neither cares about the individual's life nor gives him strength to fulfil the good which it requires of him. This is the essential contradiction of the ethics of law, which inevitably leads to the ethics of grace or redemption. Dried up formal virtue deprived of beneficent, gracious and life-giving energy is frequently met with in Christian asceticism, which may prove to be an instance of legalistic morality within Christianity. A monastically ascetic attitude to life, a kind of resentment towards it, is the expression of the ethics of law within the religion of grace and redemption ; it is powerless to raise life to a higher level. Only when asceticism is combined with mysticism it acquires a different character. The moral law, the law of the state, of the church, of the family, of civilization, of technics and economics, organizes life, preserves it and passes judgment upon it ; sometimes it warps life but never sustains it with a gracious power, never illuminates or transfigures it. The law is necessary for the sinful world and cannot be simply cancelled. But it must be overcome by a higher force ; the world and man must be freed from the impersonal power of the law.

The terrible thing about moralism is that it strives to make man into an automaton of virtue. The intolerable dullness of virtue that gives rise to immorality, often of an extremely thoughtless kind, is a specific consequence of the ethics of law which knows of no higher power. In truth, the ethics of law is built up without any reference to God's help, as though God did not exist. It is inevitable that men should at times rebel against the dull legalistic virtue, and then return to it. Such rebellion is a moral phenomenon and demands careful consideration. The domination of legalistic ethics in all spheres of life is the expression of the objective law intended for the majority, i.e. of the necessary organization of order in the life of the human masses, as well as of the mass of matter in the life of nature. Therein lies the cosmic meaning of law. Freedom which resists the absolute power of law in all spheres of life is, on the contrary, the expression of the law of the minority and is of value, in the first place, for the spiritual aristocracy which is a minority. Freedom is aristocratic and not democratic. Freedom of the minority generally involves repression of the majority by means of the law. This is the paradox of freedom in history. Creative freedom of thought is aristocratic. But not only the spiritual " aristocracy " rebels against the power of the law over life and thought—the " democratic ", Dionysian forces of life rebel against it too. This is the sole reason why revolutions take place in the world and acquire an ethical significance. The aristocracy as such would never make a revolution. The power of custom, of tradition, of public opinion, is " democratic " and always has the majority on its side. But the rising of the masses against custom, tradition and public opinion in order immediately to form a new custom and tradition is also democratic.[1] The ethics of law is based upon contradictions which come to light in its own domain. The ethics of grace alone rises above the opposition between the " aristocratic " freedom and the " democratic " law.

4. NORMATIVE ETHICS. PHARISAISM

The ethics of law is not only religious and social ; it is also philosophical and claims to be based upon freedom and autonomy. But even then its Old Testament character makes itself manifest. Philosophical ethics of law is normative and idealistic ; it is not based upon any external authority but is autonomous. This is pre-eminently true of the Kantian system, which is the most remarkable attempt of constructing a philosophical ethics of law. Though Kant's ethics is autonomous, it is based on the conception of law, as the very term autonomy indicates. It is legalistic because it is concerned with the universally binding moral law, with man's moral and rational nature which is the same in all ; it is not in the least interested in the concrete living man as such, in his destiny, in his

[1] Le Bon writes very well on the conservatism of the revolutionary masses. See his *Psychologie des Foules*.

moral experience and spiritual conflicts. The moral law, which man must freely discover for himself, automatically gives directions to all, and is the same for all men and in all cases of life. Kant's moral maxim that every man must be regarded not only as a means but also as an end in himself is undermined by the legalisic character of his ethics, because every man proves to be a means and an instrument for the realization of an abstract, impersonal, universally binding law. Morality is free in so far as it is autonomous ; man, however, is not free or autonomous at all, but is entirely subject to law. Consequently Kant completely denied the emotional side of the moral life, provoking Schiller's famous epigram. Human personality has really no value for Kant and is merely a formal and universally binding principle. Individuality does not exist for Kantian ethics, any more than do unique and individual moral problems which demand unique and individual, i.e. creative, moral solutions. The formalism of Kantian ethics has been severely criticized by M. Scheler, who insists on the value of personality.[1] Unfortunately in Scheler's own theory the conception of freedom is almost altogether absent.

The moral philosophy of Tolstoy is as legalistic as that of Kant. It is not based on any external authority. Tolstoy regards the Gospel as an expression of the moral law and norm, and the realization of the Kingdom of God is for him on a par with abstention from tobacco and alcohol. Christ's teaching consists for him of a number of moral precepts which man can easily carry out, once he recognizes their rationality. Tolstoy was a severe critic of Christian falsity and hypocrisy, but he wanted to subordinate life to the tyrannical power of legalistic morality. There is something almost daemonic in Tolstoy's moralism which would destroy all the richness and fullness of life. Both Kant and Tolstoy had grown up against a Christian background, but in spite of their love of freedom their teaching is a legalistic distortion of Christianity. They preach righteousness achieved through fulfilling the law, i.e. they return to a philosophically refined form of pharisaism and Pelagianism, which also upheld moralism and had no need of grace.

It was against Pelagian moralism and rationalism, i.e. against legalism in the Catholic church, that Luther rebelled ; but in its further development Lutheranism, too, became legalistic. The legalistic element was strong in Christianity at all times, and even the doctrine of grace was interpreted in that sense. Pharisaism was by no means overcome. Moralism in all its forms was essentially pharisaical. Asceticism assumed a legalistic character. A moralist as a type is a stickler for the law who does not want to know

[1] See his *Der Formalismus in der Ethik und die materielle Werthethik.*

anything about the concrete, living individual. Amoralism is a legitimate reaction against this. The imperatives of legalistic ethics are applicable only to very crude, elementary instances—one must not indulge in vice, steal, commit murder, tell lies—but they are of no help in the more subtle and complex cases which demand an individual, creative solution. The law has been made for the Old Adam, vindictive, tyrannical, greedy, lustful and envious. But the real problem of ethics lies deeper ; it is bound up with the individual complexity of life, which is due to conflicts between the higher values and to the presence of the tragic element in life. And yet it is generally supposed that the business of ethics is to teach that one ought not to be a pick-pocket!

The religious form of legalistic ethics is to be found in pharisaism. It is a mistake to imagine, as many Christians do, that Pharisees were morally and religiously on a low level and to use the word almost as a term of abuse. On the contrary, pharisaism was the highest point reached by the Jews in their moral and religious life. And, indeed, starting from the hard-set ground of the Old Testament religion of the law it was impossible to rise higher. But it was this pure and lofty form of Judaism that Christ denounced. The thing that impresses one most in reading the Gospel is the rebellion against pharisaism, the denunciation of its falsity as compared with the New Testament truth. That means the denunciation of legalistic morality, of the idea of justification by the law, and of complacent self-righteousness. The Gospel puts sinners and publicans above the Pharisees, the unclean above the clean, those who have not fulfilled the law above those who have fulfilled it, the last above the first, the perishing above the saved, " the wicked " above " the good ". This is the paradox of Christian morality which the Christians have found it hard to understand and accept. Christians imagine that the Gospel denunciations refer to Pharisees who lived in the distant past, and themselves join in rhetorically denouncing them as villains. But in truth those denunciations refer to ourselves, to us who are living to-day, to the self-righteous, to the morally " first " and " saved " of all times. The Gospel morality as such will be discussed later. But what does this paradox mean? Why shall the first in the moral sense be last and *vice versa*? Why is it better to be a sinner conscious of his sin than to be a Pharisee conscious of his righteousness? The usual explanation is that the sinner is humble while the Pharisee is proud, like the Stoic, and Christianity is first and foremost a religion of humility. It seems to me that this explanation does not go to the root of the disquieting problem. The Pharisees stood on the confines of two worlds, at the dividing line between the ethics of law and the ethics of grace and redemption. The impotence of the ethics of law to save from sin and evil had to be made manifest in them. The difficulty of the problem lies in the fact that the precepts of legalistic ethics are fully practicable. One can fulfil the law down to the smallest detail and become pure according to the law. This was precisely what the Pharisees did. And then it appeared that the perfect fulfilment of the law and perfect purity do not save, do not lead to the Kingdom of God. The law sprang up as a result of sin, but it is powerless to free man from the world in which he found himself after plucking the fruit of the tree of knowledge. It is powerless to conquer sin and cannot save. Pharisaism, i.e. the ethics of law, is mercilessly condemned in the Gospel because its adherents do not need the Saviour and salvation as sinners and publicans need it, because if the final religious and moral truth were on the side of the Pharisees redemption would be unnecessary. Pharisaism means rejection of the Redeemer and redemption and the belief that salvation is to be found by fulfilling the moral law. But in truth salvation means rising above the distinction between good and evil which is the result of the Fall, i.e. rising above the law engendered by that distinction. It means entering the Kingdom of Heaven, which is certainly not the Kingdom of the law or of the good as it exists on this side of the distinction.

Pharisaism is so deep and stable an element of human nature in its attitude to the law that it misinterprets Christianity in its own particular way. The Christian who thinks that he is saved, justified, pure and superior to the sinners because he often goes to church, makes genuflexions, puts up candles, repeats the regulation prayers, follows all canonical rules and does good works, is, of course, a Pharisee within Christianity, and the Gospel denunciations are meant for him too. The ethics of law is practicable, but it does not help in the struggle against evil thoughts and is powerless to change one's inner spiritual condition. According to the ethics of law a man becomes good because he does good works. But in truth a man does good works because he is good. Luther understood this admirably, though he derived one-sided conclusions from it.

The complexity and paradoxality of the Christian attitude to the law is due to the fact that although Christ denounced pharisaism, He said that He came to fulfil the law and not to destroy it. The Gospel transcends and cancels the ethics of law, replacing it by a different and higher ethics of love and freedom. But at the same time it does not allow us simply to reject the law. Christianity opens the way to the Kingdom of God where there is no more law, but meanwhile the law denounces sin and must be fulfilled by the world which remains in sin. Sinners need salvation, and salvation comes not from the law but from the Saviour ; salvation is attained through redemption and not through law. But the lower sphere of the law exists all the time, and law remains in force in its own domain. The social life of Christendom is still under the power of the law almost to the same extent as the life of the primitive clans and totems. The law is improved and perfected while remaining the same in principle. There is an eternal element in it.

The valuations that are demanded from a Christian are extremely difficult and achieved at the cost of much suffering. Valuations according to the law are comparatively simple and easy, but this ease and simplicity are not for the Christian. He has to pass valuations of the law itself, and these cannot rest on the law. Christian valuations must always rise above pharisaism, but they must not be merely negative with regard to the law. The greatest difficulty lies in harmonizing the claims of the individual and of society. The ethics of law is pre-eminently social. The Christian ethics is more individual than social ; for it the human soul is worth more than all the kingdoms of the world. This attitude creates great difficulties for the ethics of law, which prizes the kingdom of this world above all. To men of the law Christianity must appear as anarchism. This is affirmed, for instance, by C. Maurras, who regards the Gospel as a destructive and anarchical book.[1] According to him the great merit of the Roman Catholic Church is to have transformed the destructive force of Christianity into a constructive one. It is the argument of the Grand Inquisitor in Dostoevsky's *The Brothers Karamazov*. Maurras has a pre-Christian mentality ; he might be one of the Romans who were afraid of the destructive power of Christianity. But the Roman element entered into the Catholic Church and this saved the situation.

All this proves the profoundly paradoxical attitude of Christianity to law and to all social order. The law without which no social life is possible is of pre-Christian origin. The principles of justice have been formulated by the Pagan Roman world, and Christendom accepted Roman law. Hence the Christian world lives a double life—it lives both by law and by grace. And it must be said that individual freedom, the freedom of human personality, is not always protected through grace, but frequently has to be protected by the law. Therein lies the positive mission of the law. Mediaeval theocracy, both Eastern and Western, imperial and papal, claimed to be based upon grace and not upon law, but it was at the cost of interpreting grace in a legalistic sense. The theocratic community based upon grace symbolizes the Kingdom of God in the natural and historical order which is subject to law. It makes man's freedom dependent upon

[1] See his book, *Romantisme et revolution*.

the gracious regeneration of other men, of the rulers and the community as a whole. And when this gracious regeneration does not take place, freedom is absent, a person is subjected to tyranny, and denied every right. This is where the importance of the law for the social life comes in. Human life and freedom cannot be made to depend entirely upon the spiritual condition of other men, society and its rulers. The rights of the individual must be safeguarded in case that spiritual condition proves to be a low one or not sufficiently enlightened by grace. A society that chose to be based solely upon grace and declined to have any law would be a despotic society. Thus the Communistic society may be said, in a sense, to be based upon grace and not upon law, though, of course, it is not grace in the Christian sense of the term. The result is a tyranny, a theocracy reversed.

We are thus faced with the following paradox : the law does not know the concrete, unique, living personality or penetrate into its inner life, but it preserves that personality from interference and violence on the part of others, whatever their spiritual condition may be. Therein lies the great and eternal value of law and justice. Christianity is bound to recognize it. It is impossible to wait for a gracious regeneration of society to make human life tolerable. Such is the correlation of law and grace. I must love my neighbour in Christ, this is the way to the Kingdom of Heaven. But if I have no love for my neighbour I must in any case fulfil the law in relation to him and treat him justly and honourably. It is impossible to cancel the law and wait for the realization of love. That, too, would be sheer hypocrisy. Even if I have no love I must not steal, must not commit murder, must not be a bully. That which comes from grace is never lower but always higher than that which comes from law. The higher does not cancel the lower, but includes it in a sublimated form. A legalistic misinterpretation of love and grace is an evil and leads to violence, denial of freedom and complete rejection of the law. This then is the relation between the ethics of law and the ethics of redemption. The latter cannot take the place of the former : if it does, it becomes despotic and denies freedom. The two orders co-exist, and the order of grace stands for regeneration and enlightenment, and not for tyranny. The highest achievement of the ethics of law is justice.

The conflict between law and grace, between the ethics of law and of redemption, makes itself felt in every concrete moral problem, as we shall see later. It is particularly marked with regard to human freedom and the dignity of human personality. Sometimes the ethics of law and sometimes the ethics of grace proves to be hostile to freedom and personality. Grace itself cannot, of course, be hostile to either, for it regenerates personality and gives it strength and freedom. But the way in which grace is reflected and distorted in the human world may be hostile both to freedom and personality. A double process takes place : in the realm of grace legalism penetrates into the spiritual community, the church, and in the realm of law the principle of grace, distorted by legalism, penetrates into the secular community, the state. In both cases freedom is repressed and personality suffers. The concrete living personality is repressed both by the law and by compulsory grace. In the case of complex moral situations we can see how law warps life instead of leaving it to the free play of the powers of grace, and how compulsory grace also warps life, instead of letting the law protect its rights. This can be seen in the life of the family, the life of the state, in economic relations and in different departments of culture. The problem is further complicated by the fact that in addition to the ethics of law and ethics of grace there exists also the ethics of creativeness connected with man's gift and his vocation.

These conflicts cannot be finally solved within the limits of our sinful earthly life, but it is possible to establish values for which we must strive in solving them. Happiness is not the supreme value. Tragic moral conflicts show the falsity of psychological and ethical theories which take happiness to be the aim of life. The idea that happiness is the supreme good and the final end has been instilled into man in order to keep him in slavery. Human freedom and dignity forbid us to regard happiness and satisfaction in this light. There is an irreconcilable conflict between freedom and happiness. This is the theme of Dostoevsky's Legend of the Grand Inquisitor. I agree to suffer and to be unhappy for the sake of remaining a free being. The ethics of law promises happiness as the result of fulfilling the law. " Do what I tell you and you shall be happy." But the ethics of grace—of grace legalistically misinterpreted—also promises happiness. Roman Catholic theology is particularly inclined to hedonism. The Thomists still hold psychological theories according to which man always strives for bliss and happiness. But modern psychology, following the work of Dostoevsky, Nietzsche and Kierkegaard, has completely disproved that rationalistic doctrine. Man is a free, spiritual and creative being, and he prefers the free creation of spiritual values to happiness. At the same time man is a sick being, divided in himself and influenced by a dark subconscious. Consequently he does not necessarily strive for happiness and satisfaction. No law can make him into a creature that prefers happiness to freedom, rest and satisfaction to creativeness. For this reason alone human life cannot be entirely subject to law. As to grace, it gives us only moments of joy and bliss.

CHAPTER TWO

The Ethics of Redemption

1. THE GOOD UNDER GRACE

To every sensitive mind it is clear that it is impossible to be content with the law and that legalistic good does not solve the problem of life. Once the distinction between good and evil has arisen, it is beyond the power of man to annul it, i.e. to conquer evil. And man thirsts for redemption, for deliverance not only from evil but from the legalistic distinction between good and evil. The longing for redemption was present in the pre-Christian world. We find it in the ancient mysteries of the suffering gods. In an embryonic form it is present in totemism and the totemic eucharist.[1] The thirst for redemption means an earnest hope that God and the gods will take part in solving the painful problem of good and evil and in human suffering. God will come down to earth like fire, and sin and evil will be burnt up, the distinction between good and evil will disappear, and so will the impotent legalistic good which does nothing but torture man. The thirst for redemption is the longing to be reconciled to God, and it is the only way to conquer atheism inspired by the presence of pain and evil in the world. Redemption is the meeting with the suffering and sacrificial God, with a God, i.e., Who shares the bitter destiny of the world and of man. Man is a free being and there is in him an element of primeval, uncreated, pre-cosmic freedom. But he is powerless to master his own irrational freedom and its abysmal darkness. This is his perennial tragedy. It is necessary that God Himself should descend into the depths of that freedom and take upon Himself the consequences of pain and evil to which it gives rise. Redemption is certainly not the reconciliation between God and man, as it wrongly appears to the limited human consciousness (the juridical theory of redemption[2]). Redemption is first and foremost the reconciliation of man to God the Creator, i.e. a victory over atheism or the natural denial of God because of the pain and misery of the world. Atheism as the cry of the indignant human heart can only be conquered by a suffering God Who shares the

---

[1] See Frazer and Durkheim.
[2] See *Le dogme de la Redemption*, by l'Abbé J. Rivière. At present the Roman Catholic theology too is getting over the old juridical theory of redemption.

fate of the world. The conception of such a God leads also to the final victory over idolatry which is always present in abstract monotheism. In the depths of paganism when men knew only the natural gods and not the God Who is above nature, they sought help and healing from the totem, the wise men and magicians, the divine kings or demi-gods. Man could not bear to be alone, left to his own powers and wholly dependent upon the impersonal and inhuman law. The world was full of gods, but the gods were shut in within the immanent circle of the natural life. The gods themselves were subject to fate. There was no one to complain to against slavery. Man was living down the consequence of some unknown guilt for which he was not to blame. This is expressed in the Greek tragedy. The world was full of gods, but the God Who is above the world and nature did not come down into the world, did not share its fate and free men from it. The mysteries of redemption took place within the immanent circle of the natural created life, and they expressed man's longing that God should help him in his agonizing struggle.

If God exists, it is difficult to believe that He could have completely forsaken the ancient pagan world which produced so much that is great and beautiful. God acted in that world, too, but in a different way, through nature and not through history as in the case of the Jews. Man is never left completely alone, abandoned to his own resources. But he is not aware that God is taking part in his life and destiny. This is the result of the ethics of law. God gives the law, but does not take part in carrying it out. When the good is under the law it is, in a sense, a godless good. Law means precisely that God has withdrawn from man. Hence the impotence of the law to change human nature. In law the good is severed from existence and cannot change it. Redemption unites the good and existence, bridging the gulf made by the law as a consequence of sin. It means the entrance of the existent good into the very depths of being. Redemption destroys the roots of sin and evil, and thereby frees man from the absolute power of the law. Redemption means, first and foremost, liberation. The Redeemer is the Liberator. The law does not free from slavery. Redemption means a revolutionary change in moral valuations, a revaluation of all values. It cancels innumerable taboos, it conquers the fear of outer uncleanness, it transfers everything into the depth of the human heart and overturns all the established hierarchies. The ethics of redemption, the morality of the Gospel, is divinely human. The moral act is performed by man together with God, there is between them no break or opposition insisted upon by the law. And that which was impossible for man, becomes possible for God.

Everyone knows that the Gospel morality is totally different from the morality of the law. But the Christian world has managed to live and to formulate its doctrine as though there had never been any conflict between them. No one can deny that there is an opposition between the Christian and the legalistic ethics. The Gospel morality is based upon the power of grace, unknown to the law, so that it is no longer morality in the old sense. Christianity means the acquisition of power in and through Christ, of power that truly regenerates man and does not fear life or death, darkness or pain. The real opposition is between power and law, between something ontologically real and something purely ideal and normative. This is why abstract moralism, so natural to all legalistic and normative theories, is not at all typical of Christianity. We touch here upon the central point of Christian ethics and of ethics in general. The fundamental question of ethics may be formulated as follows : can the idea of the good be the aim of human life and the source of all practical valuations? Moralists are only too ready to base their systems upon the idea of the supreme good and think it, indeed, indispensable to ethics. But as soon as the idea of the supreme good is put at the basis of ethics, ethics becomes normative and legalistic.

Christianity in its original and virginal form not merely questioned the supremacy of the idea of the good, but sharply opposed its own morality based upon it. Christianity is founded not upon the abstract and impotent idea of the good which, in relation to man, inevitably appears as a norm and a law, but upon a living Being, a Personality, and man's personal relation to God and to his neighbours. Christianity has placed man above the idea of the good and thereby made the greatest revolution in history —a revolution which the Christians had not the strength to accept in its fullness. The idea of the good, like every other idea, must yield and make way for man. It is not the abstract idea of the good, but man who is God's creation and God's child. Man inherits eternity, while nothing shall be left of the law. This is how the Gospel passes from the morality of our fallen world, based upon the distinction between good and evil, to the morality beyond, opposed to the law of this world—the morality of paradise and of the Kingdom of God. Man is redeemed from the power of the law.

The ethics of the Gospel is based upon existence and not upon norm, it prefers life to law. A concrete existent, a living being, is higher than any abstract idea, even if it be the idea of the good. The good of the Gospel consists in regarding not the good but man as the supreme principle of life. The Gospel shows that men, out of love for the good, may be vile and hypocritical, that out of love for the good they may torture their fellows or forget about them. The Sabbath is for man and not man for the Sabbath—this is the essence of the great moral revolution made by Christianity, in which man for the first time recovered from the fatal consequences of distinguishing between good and evil and from the power of the law. " The Sabbath " stands for the abstract good, for the idea, the norm, the law, the fear of defilement. But " the Son of man is the lord of the Sabbath ". Christianity knows no abstract moral norms, binding upon all men and at all times. Therefore for a Christian every moral problem demands its own individual solution, and is not to be solved mechanically by applying a norm set once for all. It must be so, if man is higher than " the Sabbath," the abstract idea of the good. Every moral act must be based upon the greatest possible consideration for the man from whom it proceeds and for the man upon whom it is directed. The Gospel morality of grace and redemption is the direct opposite of Kant's formula : you must not act so that the principle of your action could become a universal law ; you must always act individually, and everyone must act differently. The universal law is that every moral action should be unique and individual, i.e. that it should have in view a concrete living person and not the abstract good.

Such is the ethics of love. Love can only be directed upon a person, a living being and not upon the abstract good.[1] To be guided in one's moral actions by the love for the good and not for men means to be a Scribe and a Pharisee and to practise the reverse of the Christian moral teaching. The only thing higher than the love for man is the love for God, Who is also a concrete Being, a Person and not an abstract idea. The love of God and the love of man sum up the Gospel morality ; all the rest is not characteristically Christian and merely confirms the law. Christianity preaches love for one's neighbour and not for " those far off ". This is a very important distinction. Love for " the far off ", for man and humanity in general, is love for an abstract idea, for the abstract good, and not love for man. And for the sake of this abstract love men are ready to sacrifice concrete, living beings. We find this love for " the far off " in humanistic revolutionary morality. But there is a great difference between humanistic and Christian love. Christian love is concrete and personal, while humanistic love is abstract and impersonal ; Christian love cares above all for the individual, and humanistic for " the idea ", even though it be the idea of humanity and its happiness. There is, of course, a

[1] There are very subtle remarks to that effect in M. Scheler's *Wesen und Formen der Sympathie.*

strong Christian element in humanism, for humanism is of Christian origin. Christianity affirmed the supreme value of man through the words of Christ that man is higher than Sabbath and His commandment of love for one's neighbour. But just as in Christianity the Scribes and Pharisees began to gain the upper hand, and " the Sabbath ", the abstract idea of the good, was set above man, so in humanism its Scribes and Pharisees put the idea of human welfare or progress above man as a concrete living being.

A false interpretation of " good works " leads to a complete perversion of Christianity. " Good works " are regarded not as an expression of love for God and man, not as a manifestation of the gracious force which gives life to others, but as a means of salvation and justification for oneself, as a way of realizing the abstract idea of the good and receiving a reward in the future life. This is a betrayal of the Gospel revelation of love. " Good works " done not for the love of others but for the salvation of one's soul are not good at all. Where there is no love there is no goodness. Love does not require or expect any reward, it is a reward in itself, it is a ray of paradise illumining and transfiguring reality. " Good works " as works of the law have nothing to do with the Gospel and the Christian revelation ; they belong to the pre-Christian world. One must help others and do good works not for saving one's soul but for love, for the union of men, for bringing their souls together in the Kingdom of God. Love for man is a value in itself, the quality of goodness is immanent in it.

There are two ways of feeling towards one's neighbour. There is pity. Pity means sharing the desolateness of the creature, its sense of being forsaken by God. And there is love. Love means sharing the life in God and His gracious help. Pity is not the last and the highest state, love is higher —love for others in God. But pity is one of the loftiest human feelings, a true miracle in the moral life of man, as Schopenhauer rightly pointed out, though he gave a wrong explanation of it. The burning, poignant sense of desolation and the readiness to share it embraces the whole of the animal world and all created things. Pity inevitably forms part of love, but love is greater than pity, for love knows others in God. Love means seeing the other in God and affirming him in eternal life ; it is the radiation of energy needed for that eternal life. The Christian ethics of the Gospel is founded upon the recognition of the significance of each human soul which is worth more than all the kingdoms of this world. Personality has unconditional value as the image and likeness of God. No abstract idea of the good can be put above personality.

2. THE MORALITY OF THE GOSPEL AND THE MORALITY OF THE SCRIBES AND PHARISEES

We have already seen that the Gospel morality is opposed to the legalistic morality of salvation by one's own efforts through carrying out the moral law. Since it is based not upon the abstract good but upon the relation to man as a concrete living person, it is highly dynamic in character. Christianity does not recognize the fixed types of " the wicked " and of " the righteous ". An evil-doer may turn into a righteous man, and *vice versa*. St. John of the Ladder says : " You will be careful not to condemn sinners if you remember that Judas was one of the Apostles and the thief was one of a band of murderers ; but in one moment the miracle of regeneration took place in him." This is why Christ teaches us " judge not, that ye be not judged ". Up to the hour of death no one knows what may happen to a man and what a complete change he may undergo, nor does anyone know what happens to him at the hour of death, on a plane inaccessible to us. This is why Christianity regards " the wicked " differently than this world does ; it does not allow a sharp division of mankind into two halves, " the good " and " the wicked "—a division by which moral theories set much store.

Christianity alone teaches that the past can be wiped out ; it knows the mystery of forgetting and cancelling the past. This is the mystery of redemption and it leads to a morality different from the morality of the law. Redemption frees us from Karma, from the Karmic living down of the past in an infinite future. The endless threads stretching from the past into the future are cut. Therein lies the mystery of penitence and of the remission of sins. Man cannot forgive himself his sin and vileness, he is unable to forget his evil past. But Christ has taken upon Himself the sins of the world, and He can take away our sin and forgive it. It is only in and through Christ that the past can be forgiven and forgotten. Man cannot give absolution to himself for sin and evil, and live down its consequences ; he is absolved through Christ. But he must in the name of Christ forgive his neighbour's sin and evil and help him to free himself from their power. If a man is condemned as hopelessly " wicked ", this does not help to liberate or save or improve him. On the contrary, the condemnation ruins him. The evil of the past, regarded as unconquerable and irretrievable, gives rise to fresh evil. A man begins to feel that he is lost anyhow, that there is no turning back, that he is damned. It is against this that the religion and ethics of redemption protests. Christ came not for the righteous but for sinners. And there is no sin which cannot be wiped out and forgiven. The sin against the Son of Man, against Christ Himself, shall be forgiven. Only the sin against the Holy Ghost shall not be forgiven, but here we touch upon the mystery of the final rejection of God which cannot be identified with atheism. Atheism may be forgiven and it may mean a perverted love of truth. We do not know the inmost depths of the human heart ; it is revealed only to love. But those who condemn have generally little love, and therefore the mystery of the heart which they judge is closed to them. This is the limitation of every judgment which divides men into " the good " and " the wicked ", the pious and the rebellious, the faithful and the unbelievers. " The wicked ", " the rebellious ", " the unbelievers " may sometimes prove to be more acceptable to God than " the good ", " the pious " and " the faithful ". This is a stumbling block to the ethics of law, but is intelligible from the point of view of the ethics of redemption.

The Gospel makes a complete change in our moral valuations, but we are not conscious of its full significance because we have grown used to it and adapted it too well to our everyday needs. " I am come to send fire on the earth." In this fire are burnt up all the old, habitual moral valuations, and new ones are formed. The first shall be last, and the last first. This means a revolution more radical than any other. Christianity was born in this revolution, it has sprung from it. But Christian humanity was unable to introduce it into life, for that would have meant rising " beyond good and evil " by which the world lives. When the mysterious words of the Gospel were made into a norm, " the last " became the new " first ". It was just as it is in social revolutions when the oppressed class comes into power and begins to oppress others. This is the fate of all the Gospel words in so far as they are turned into a norm. The paradox is that the oppressed never can be masters, for as soon as they obtain mastery they become the oppressors. The poor never can be masters, for as soon as they obtain mastery they become rich. Therefore no external revolutions can correspond to the radical change proclaimed in the Gospel. The Gospel does not preach laws and norms, and cannot be interpreted in that sense.

The gospel is the good news of the coming of the Kingdom of God. Christ's call to us is the call to His Kingdom and can only be interpreted in that sense. The morality of the Kingdom of God proves to be unlike the morality of the fallen world, which is on this side of good and evil. The Gospel morality lies beyond the familiar distinction between good and evil according to which the first are first and the last are lost. The ethics of redemption is in every way opposed to the ideas of this world.

Most of what Christ says takes the form of " it hath been said, but I say unto you ". Tareyev[1] is right when he insists that the Gospel is absolute in character and incommensurable with the relative naturally historical life. " But I say unto you that ye resist not evil." The ordinary moral life is based upon resisting evil. " Love your enemies, bless them that curse you, do good to them that hate you, and pray for them which despitefully use you, and persecute you." If this call of the Gospel be understood as a law, it is impracticable ; it is senseless from the point of view of the ethics of law, it presupposes a different and a gracious order of being. " Seek ye first the Kingdom of God and His righteousness, and all these things shall be added unto you." Herein lies the essence of the Gospel and of Christianity. But the whole life of the world is based upon seeking first " all these things " which are to be " added ", and not the Kingdom of God. And the morality of our world seeks not the Kingdom of God, but justification by the law. " Not that which goeth into the mouth defileth a man ; but that which cometh out of the mouth, this defileth a man." But the conception of honour in our world is based on the very opposite of this. A man's honour is supposed to be defiled and injured by the fact that he has been insulted or received a blow and not by the fact that he insulted or struck somebody else. " The princes of the Gentiles exercise dominion over them, and they that are great exercise authority upon them. But it shall not be so among you : but whosoever will be chief among you, let him be your servant." Here is another revolutionary change directed against the princes and the great of this world. The greatest is only a servant. The hierarchy of the church which had to act in the world and was marred by human passions and sins found this particularly difficult to follow. Symbolically the church has remained true to the words of Christ but really it has betrayed them. It too was ruled by princes and the great ; in it too the chiefs were not servants. Symbolically the Pope considered himself a servant, but in reality he exercised dominion over princes and the great ones. " The Son of Man came not to be ministered unto, but to minister, and to give his life a ransom for many." Christ lived among sinners and publicans, ate and drank with them. The Pharisees who upheld the ethics of the law, the morality of this world, protested against it in the name of purity. But Christ recognizes no impurity except the impurity of the human heart. " They that be whole need not a physician, but they that are sick. I am not come to call the righteous but the sinners to repentance." The pharisaic ethics

[1] M. Tareyev, " Evangelie " in v. II of *Osnovi Christianstva*. It is one of the most remarkable interpretations of the Gospel.

of law does not like the sick and the sinful ; its representatives live in the company of the pure and righteous and take care of their white garments. But the Son of God says to the Pharisees : " Why call ye Me, Lord, Lord, and do not the things which I say? " " In this place is one greater than the temple." " Ye Pharisees make clean the outside of the cup and the platter, but your inward part is full of ravening and wickedness." These words too are a protest against the ethics of law, the ethics of purity. " Woe unto you, lawyers! for ye have taken away the key of knowledge : ye entered not in yourselves, and them that were entering in ye hindered," Entering the Kingdom of God does not depend upon the lawyers' key of understanding ; they only hinder others. And here again are words that mean a complete overturning of values : " That which is highly esteemed among men is abomination in the sight of God." " Beware of the scribes which desire to walk in long robes, and love greetings in the markets, and the highest seats in the synagogues, and the chief rooms at feasts ; which devour widows' houses, and for a show make long prayers : the same shall receive greater damnation." The Christian world is full of these scribes who find the ethics of law easier and more practicable than the ethics of grace. Here are the words fundamental to the religion and ethics of grace : " Ye know not what manner of spirit ye are of. For the Son of Man is not come to destroy men's lives but to save them." These words were spoken to the Apostles who did not as yet understand their Master. The ethics of law does not save but destroys men's souls. " I am come that they might have life, and that they might have it more abundantly." Christ, the Redeemer and Saviour, is first and foremost the source of life. The ethics of redemption brings us back to the source of life.

The teaching of the Gospel is absolute and uncompromising, but there is nothing harsh about it. Uncompromising moralism is false because it is uncompromising towards other people and insists on their carrying out the law. It is pitiless and condemns everyone. There is nothing like it in the gracious absolutism of the Gospel. It merely reveals to us the Kingdom of God and opens the way to it, but it gives no rules and norms. One must be uncompromising with oneself and not with others. To be strict to oneself and kind to others—this is the truly Christian attitude. There are two kinds of moral enthusiasm : one demands in the first place a high moral standard of oneself and the other begins by denouncing others. The second kind is not Christian. Abstract normative idealism, though it may be found among Christians, is always cruel and fanatical and wants to destroy the wicked. True Christians cannot feel like that, since they care, first and foremost, for concrete living individuals.

Even so inspired and remarkable a thinker as Kierkegaard has an element of un-Christian extremism, devoid of grace and opposed to love. Ibsen with profound insight has shown this type of mind in *Brand*. A man must not think that he is in the right and others in the wrong, he must not feel self-righteous. This brings us to the tremendous change which Christianity has made in our attitude to the sinful and the wicked.

3. THE CHRISTIAN ATTITUDE TO THE SINFUL AND THE WICKED

" He maketh his sun to rise on the evil and on the good, and sendeth rain on the just and on the unjust." Until those words were spoken the ethics of law, which knows not grace or redemption, assumed that the sun rises over the just only and the rain falls on them alone. But the Gospel equalizes in the sight of God the righteous and the unrighteous, the good and the evil. The good and the righteous can no longer pride themselves on their goodness and righteousness. The old legalistic valuations of good and evil apply no more. " The publicans and the harlots go into the Kingdom of God before you." They go before the Pharisees, before those who consider themselves good and righteous. No system of ethics had ever sided with harlots and publicans, with the sinful and the unrighteous. This is how the human conception of the good changes, though it seems absolute and unalterable. In the course of history the Church tried to render harmless the moral change wrought by the Gospel, but it was impossible to conceal altogether that Christian morality is different from the morality of this world. " He that is without sin among you let him first cast a stone at her." But the moralists of this world, the champions of the pharisaic ethics of law, regard it their duty to throw a stone at the sinner. And people who do so and who condemn their neighbours as sinners consider themselves righteous in doing so and think they are fulfilling the moral law.

It is perfectly obvious that true Christianity does not allow of dividing mankind into two camps—" the good " and " the wicked ", " the righteous " and " the sinners ". The wicked and sinful may become good and righteous. The Gospel does not recognize a race of the good who are going to heaven and a race of the wicked who are going to hell. And the righteous, the Pharisees, are certainly not going to heaven. It is all infinitely more complicated, In the early centuries of its existence the Church condemned the practice of sharply singling out the saints, the righteous, the saved (see Hermas's *Shepherd*, controversies in connection with Hippolytus, Calixtus and Montanus). For the ethics of grace and redemption the two camps do not exist. It is an error to seek for a guarantee of salvation (Luther, Calvin, the Baptists). It is wrong to be conscious of oneself as abiding in the camp of the saved and the elect. The idea of hell, of which more will be said later, is connected precisely with this division of the world into the two camps—of the good and the wicked. Pharisaic, legalistic morality easily triumphs over the Gospel, for it is not so hard to live up to it and by doing so to feel oneself justified. That morality triumphs also in Christian asceticism, which so often leads to a coldness of heart. But the gracious morality of the Gospel is revealed in the crises of life, in important and significant circumstances to which the law is not applicable.

In Tolstoy's *Anna Karenin*, Anna's husband is a typical Scribe and Pharisee. His condemnation of Anna is typically pharisaical. He certainly was more sinful than she. His heart was completely cold. But at a moment of great crisis, when Anna was at death's door, Karenin's heart suddenly melted and he ceased judging according to law. It was a moment of grace. And Karenin's attitude to Vronsky ceased to be legalistic and became human. This is how it always is. The law which judges the wicked and the sinners is applicable only in ordinary, everyday cases, while people's hearts are cold and hard. But it is utterly inapplicable and its judgment is of no value in the extraordinary, catastrophic situations when alone the depths of life are revealed. Consequently our judgment about crimes is usually lacking in moral depth. True life is to be found " on the other side " of the law.

Christianity discovers the image of God in every man, even in the wicked and criminal. In the pre-Christian era the image of God was revealed in heroes and kings. Christianity brought with it an entirely new conception of man. It is a paradoxical conception. The paradox is contained in its very attitude to sin. All have sinned, all are affected by original sin ; and therefore one must not judge, must not condemn one's neighbours. Christianity, and it alone, demands mercy for sinners. Consequently, it is Christianity that gives rise to the longing for universal salvation, i.e. for real victory over evil, as opposed to the longing for confining the wicked to hell, first in time and then in eternity. This aspect of Christianity—absence of condemnation, mercy for the sinners— has not been sufficiently realized by the Christians. In the course of history the worst possible condemnations have been deduced from the Christian teaching, This is the tragic fate of Christianity. In the first place Christianity has greatly heightened the consciousness of the infinite value of every human soul, of every human life and personality—and, consequently, of the infinite value of the soul, life and personality of the sinners and " the wicked ". They cannot be treated as merely a means for the realization of goodness and the triumph of the good. Good values " the wicked " no less than " the good ". Indeed, those very terms are false and meaningless. The so-called good are often " wicked " and the apparently " wicked " are often " good ". People managed to deduce from Christianity the most disgusting morality that has ever been known —the morality of transcendental, heavenly egoism. " The good " are so anxious to get to the Kingdom of Heaven that in the crush at the entrance to it they are ready to trample on a great number of their neighbours and push them down to hell, to eternal damnation. And since the gate into the Kingdom is narrow, there is a struggle and a selection. " The good " and the righteous fight their way into Paradise over the corpses of their neighbours, less good and righteous than themselves.

This is the worst defeat that Christianity has suffered in human hearts, a most terrible distortion and perversion of it. The idea of transcendental egoism, of the exclusive concern for the salvation of one's own soul, which some people deduce from ascetic literature, is a satanic idea, a satanic caricature of Christianity. In truth only he saves his soul who is ready to lose it for the sake of his fellow men, in the name of Christ's love. We must not think about our own salvation ; this is a wrong state of mind, and is heavenly utilitarianism. We must think of the highest values and of the Kingdom of God for all creatures—not for men only, but for the whole world. In other words we must think of God and not of ourselves. And no one should dare to regard himself as righteous and others as sinners. This is expressed by the doctrine of humility which Christians have also contrived to interpret formalistically. The influence of Christianity upon human mind has been twofold and paradoxical. On the one hand, man owes to Christianity his loftiest moral consciousness and emotions. But on the other hand it may be said that Christianity has made man morally worse by creating an intolerable conflict between consciousness and the unconscious. The man of the Pagan world was more whole, more serene and harmonious, less overwhelmed by the loftiness of his creed.

4. THE CHRISTIAN MORALITY AS THE MORALITY OF STRENGTH

Nietzsche did not know or understand true Christianity. He had before him the degenerate Christian society which had lost the heroic spirit. And he rose with passionate indignation against this decadent, bourgeois

Christianity. Nietzsche draws a fundamental distinction between the morality of masters and the morality of slaves. He regards Judaism as the moral rebellion of the slaves, i.e. of the weak. Christianity too is for him an expression of the salve morality, based upon the resentment of the weak against the strong, the noble, the aristocratic, upon envy, sense of injury and a desire to receive compensation in the moral sphere. The Romans are for Nietzsche the strong, the aristocratic, the noble. The victory of the Christians over Rome was the victory of the sick over the healthy, of the slaves over the noble. But the chief danger is the sick and not the wicked. Christianity has spoiled the nobility of the race and substituted for the categories of the noble and the base, i.e. the aristocrats and the slaves, the categories of the good and the wicked. Out of a feeling of resentment the slave decided to be first in the eternal life. Christian asceticism is based upon resentment against manly courage and strength.

What Nietzsche has to say of the origin of morality generally and of the Christian morality in particular is very interesting, but absolutely the reverse of truth. The weakness and insignificance of the Christians prevented him from seeing the strength and greatness of Christianity. Christian morality is aristocratic in the spiritual sense and not slavish, it is the morality of the strong in spirit and not of the weak. Christianity calls us to follow the line of the greatest resistance to the world and demands heroic efforts. Christianity rose against the slavish sense of injury and opposed to it the noble sense of guilt. The experience of guilt is a noble, aristocratic experience, while the sense of injury is plebeian and humiliating. Christianity wants to eradicate resentment from the human soul and heal man from envy and wounded self-love. Christianity alone knows the remedy against it. Nietzsche's idea of strength and weakness was much too superficial. He was fascinated by the external beauty of the Roman strength. But a Roman was the type of man entirely subjugated by the world to which he had surrendered himself, i.e. the type of man who had suffered the worst possible spiritual defeat. Christianity is the greatest power of resistance to the power of the world. Christian morality, interpreted not legalistically but in the inner, spiritual sense, means acquisition of spiritual power in all things. Christian virtue is not compliance to norm and duty but strength and power. Nietzsche interpreted Christian morality too much in the spirit of Kant's categorical imperatives. But in truth it is the very opposite of the Kantian conception. Normative idealism is impotent ; it does not know whence to draw the power for realizing the good law. The law and the norm are powerless because they are without grace. But Christianity traces back all good to the source of power, that is, to God. It does not recognize any binding laws and norms ; all that matters is that we should receive spiritual force from God. Sometimes this is called, as St. Seraphim called it, " acquiring the grace of the Holy Spirit ". Christianity teaches us how to be strong in the face of life and of death. Only a decadent Christianity leads man to think of himself as a trembling, weak and timorous creature, having neither strength nor capacity to do anything. Sinful man is powerless without Christ, but he is strong in Christ, for Christ has overcome the world.

In the first place, a false and decadent interpretation has been given to Christian humility. Humility must be understood in an ontological sense. It is a manifestation of spiritual power in the conquest of self hood. Self-centredness is the main consequences of original sin. Man is shut up within himself and sees everything from his own point of view and in relation to himself. He is obsessed by the idea of his own self. We are all guilty of self-centredness. Looked at objectively, nothing could be more comical. Self-centredness distorts all the perspectives of life ; everything is seen in a false light, nothing has its proper place assigned to it. In order to see the world in a true light and everything in its proper shape, in order to contemplate the wide horizon, we must climb out of the pit of self-centredness and rise to a height. We must see the centre of being not in ourselves but in God, where it truly is, and then everything will fall into its right place. Humility in its ontological meaning is the heroic conquest of self hood and ascent to the heights of theocentrism. Humility means escape from one's hardened self hood and the asphyxiating atmosphere of one's own limited self into the pure air of cosmic life. So far from being opposed to freedom, humility is an expression of freedom. No one and nothing in the world can force humility upon me ; I can only arrive at it myself, through a free act. Humility always means acquisition of greater freedom. It is part of our inner, hidden life. One of the most awful perversions of Christianity was the slavish and external interpretation of humility. It is only through the spiritual act of humility that we can overcome resentment and wounded vanity. Man's heart, sick with wounded self-love, is bleeding from the arrows which pierce it all life-long and from which it has no defence. Only spiritual humility can defend us against the agonizing pain. Humility is directed in the first place against self-love and is the power which heals wounded pride.

Christianity alone teaches how to be completely free from the external world which thwarts and injures us. Even the words " obey your masters " may be interpreted as the acquisition of inner spiritual freedom and independence. Be free in spirit, do not be a slave in spirit. Slavish rebellion is a manifestation of the slavish spirit, of the absence of spiritual freedom. Man must be inwardly free even if he happens to be a slave. The acceptance of circumstances which have fallen to one's lot must be interpreted as mastery over the external world, as the victory of the spirit. This does not mean, of course, that a man must not strive to improve his circumstances and struggle for changes and social reforms. But he must remain spiritually free even if those changes do not take place and are not likely to occur soon. He must remain spiritually free even if he is in prison. Holiness is the highest spiritual force and a victory over the world. Love is a force, a radiation of beneficent, life-giving energy. Victory over passions is power. It is to that power that Christianity calls us. The whole of our moral life consists in acquiring spiritual power and conquering the weakness and the darkness of the natural life. Christianity bids us to overcome the world and not to submit to it. Humility is not submission, on the contrary, it is a refusal to submit, and movement along the line of the greatest resistance. And yet the power of Christian morality and spirituality is extremely simple. Simplicity, indeed, is the secret of it, for complexity means division and weakness. Christian morality, unendurable for the world, is possible only because it is divinely human and is the interaction between man and God.

5. SUFFERING. ASCETICISM. LOVE

The relation of Christianity to suffering is twofold and paradoxical. Suffering is a consequence of sin and evil. But suffering is also redemption and has a positive value. Christianity alone accepts suffering and takes up a manly attitude to it throughout. It teaches us not to fear suffering, for God Himself, the Son of God, has suffered. All other doctrines are afraid of suffering and try to escape it. Buddhism and Stoicism—lofty examples of non-Christian moral theories—are afraid of suffering and teach how to avoid it, how to become insensible to it and dispassionate. Buddhism recognizes compassion but denies love, for compassion may be a way of escaping from the pain of existence while love affirms existence and, consequently, the pain of it. Love increases sorrow and suffering. Strictly speaking, Buddhism is concerned with physical and not with moral evil. It is bound to be so if freedom be denied. Evil is pain and suffering. All existence is pain and suffering. Christianity has the courage to accept the pain and the suffering, Buddhism has not and therefore it renounces existence and seeks refuge in non-being. Buddhism does not know how life can be endurable if suffering be accepted ; it does not know the mystery of the Cross. In its own way Buddhism is a great doctrine or salvation without a Saviour. It is salvation from pain and suffering through knowledge of the truth that all existence is pain—i.e. it is salvation for the few, since only a few have knowledge.

Confucius, Buddha, the Stoics and all the sages of the world sought peace and freedom from pain and suffering. The problem of suffering and of escape from it has always been central for religious and philosophical ethics. In the Western pre-Christian world the Stoics are particularly interesting in this respect. Stoicism is the doctrine of self-salvation and of the attainment of peace or " apathy ". Stoic morality testifies to a very high level reached by man's moral consciousness, but in the last resort it is a decadent and pessimistic morality of despair, which sees no meaning in life ; it is inspired by the fear of suffering. One must lose sensitiveness to suffering and become indifferent—that is the only way out. On the surface the Stoics profess to be optimistic, they believe in a World-Reason and want man to be in harmony with It so as to escape suffering ; they seem to recognize that the order of nature is good. But behind all this is concealed much sadness and weakness, and a fear both of the World-Reason and of the order of nature. In this connection the book of Marcus Aurelius is particularly striking—one of the most stirring human documents showing the inner nature of Stoicism. The optimism of the Stoics is artificial.

Both Buddhism and Stoicism are interesting because they recognize that existence is pain ; Buddhism does it directly, Stoicism indirectly. The problem of the meaning of suffering is essential to ethics. It is the main theme of Christianity. Suffering is the inmost essence of being, the fundamental law of life. All that lives endures pain and suffering. In this respect pessimism is metaphysically right. All optimistic metaphysical systems are flat and superficial. But our attitude to life is not determined by the fact that life is pain and suffering. Pessimism is a false doctrine after all, because it is afraid of suffering, renounces existence, flees from the battlefield and betrays life. I may know that life is pain and at the same time accept life, accept its suffering and understand the meaning of it. This is what Christianity does, and it alone.

There are two kinds of suffering—the light and redeeming suffering which leads to life, and the dark and evil suffering which leads to death. A man may go through suffering serenely and graciously and be born into a new life as a result of it. All the sufferings sent to man—the death of his nearest and dearest, illness, poverty, humiliations and disappointments—may serve to purify, raise and regenerate him. But suffering may finally crush man, embitter him, destroy his vitality and make him feel that life has no meaning whatever. Nietzsche says that it is not so much the suffering as the senselessness of it that is unendurable. Man can go through the most terrible sufferings if he sees a meaning in them ; human powers of endurance are enormous. Christianity gives meaning to suffering and makes it endurable. It gives meaning to it through the mystery of the Cross. Man's suffering is twofold. He suffers from the trials that are sent him, from the blows which fate deals him, from death, illness, privations, treachery, solitude, disillusionment and so on, and so on. And he suffers too from rebelling against suffering, from refusing to bear it and from cursing it. And this is another and a bitterer kind of suffering. When man accepts suffering and recognizes that it has a meaning, the pain grows less, becomes more endurable, and a light begins to shine through it. Unenlightened suffering, the most terrible of all, is that which man does not accept, against which he rebels and feels vindictive. But when he accepts suffering as having a higher meaning, it regenerates him. This is the meaning of the Cross. " Take up thy cross and follow me." That means, " accept suffering, understand its meaning and bear it graciously. And if you are given your cross, do not compare it with, and measure it against, other people's crosses ". To try to avoid suffering and run away from it is self-deception and one of the greatest illusions of life. Suffering tracks our steps, even the happiest of us. There is only one way open to man, the way of light and regeneration—to accept suffering as the cross which every one must bear following the Crucified. This is the deepest mystery of Christianity and of Christian ethics. Suffering is bound up with sin and evil, just as death is—the last of man's trials. But it is also the way of redemption, of light and regeneration. Such is the Christian paradox with regard to suffering and it must be accepted and lived through. For a Christian to suffer means voluntarily to take up and bear his cross. Compulsory suffering must be accepted freely. Suffering is closely connected with freedom. To seek a life in which there will be no more suffering is to seek a life in which there will be no more freedom. Hence all hedonistic morality is opposed to freedom.

From what has been said it follows that Christian attitude to compassion is not the same as the Buddhist. In Buddhism compassion means a desire that the sufferer should attain non-being and is a refusal to bear suffering on behalf of others as well as of oneself. In Christianity compassion means a desire for a new and better life for the sufferer and a willingness to share his pain. Compassion may be a renunciation of life or its affirmation. All life in this world means bearing the cross. And I must bear not only my own cross, but my neighbour's. I must desire not that others should suffer but that they should bear their cross, for bearing the cross means bringing light into the pain and misery of life. Humanistic compassion is inspired by the illusion that it is possible to free men from suffering altogether and give them happiness ; it does not accept suffering and struggles against it. But to reject compassion out of love for God, and because suffering is a means of redemption, is a hideous travesty of the Christian teaching. We come here upon the main paradox of the Christian ethics of redemption.

Pity is the most certain and indisputable of man's feelings and it offers most resistance to the power of this world. And if pity finds but little room in the ethics of law and norm, so much the worse for the latter. Blessed are the merciful, those who have pity. The poignant unendurable pity that the eyes of a suffering animal arouse in us is a divine state. But pity may become a source of rebellion against God. Man may renounce the Creator out of pity and compassion for the creature. Atheism may have a very lofty source. I have already said that pity means sharing the creature's sense of being forsaken by the Creator. It is a very real experience, for even Jesus Christ felt that God had forsaken Him ; and it may lead to a rejection of God. Out of pity for the groaning and travailing creation I may rise against the Creator and deny Him. This is Ivan Karamazov's problem which so tortured Dostoevsky. The experience of pity is one of the most overwhelming and transcendental of human experiences. It may possess a man's whole being, it may lead to death, it may lead to a rejection of God, of the world and of man. At the same time pity is the strongest proof of man's belonging to a higher world.

Compassion may have bad results if it fails to respect a person's dignity and freedom. My pity for another man may lead me to deny him freedom and human dignity. Hence, pity, the most beautiful of human feelings, may, like everything else, turn into the worst possible state, into the rejection, namely, both of God and man. Here lies the main paradox of Christian ethics. Love for one's neighbour, which inevitably involves pity and compassion, requires that one should alleviate his sufferings or even completely free him from them. But at the same time suffering is necessary as a means to redemption, light and salvation. One must feel for one's neighbour, share his sufferings, try to alleviate them, and at the same time remember that they are the consequence of sin. As the result of this paradox which, as usual, people are inclined to solve in a purely formal way, Christians constantly prove to be the least compassionate of men, always ready to condemn their neighbours and, after the manner of Job's comforters, to denounce the sin for which the sufferings are the punishment.

This hardening of heart and drying up of the moral sources of life frequently go with the monastically ascetic attitude to men and their sufferings. Asceticism is a dangerous thing and cuts both ways. It may destroy the so-called natural, human pity for men and fail to give rise to gracious Christian love. In that case the dried up soul is left devoid of either love or pity and has nothing but condemnation for sinners. Sinners ought to suffer, they deserve it, it is good for them to suffer. The Scribes and Pharisees of Christianity find excuses for themselves through this moral sophistry. The sophism is this : as a Christian I ought to wish that every man should bear his cross. I want a cross for my neighbour. But does this mean that I want to increase his pain and to make him suffer as much as possible? Certainly not, on the contrary. To want my neighbour to bear his cross means to want that a light should dawn for him through his suffering and that he should find it easier to bear ; and it also means a desire on my part to do all I can to alleviate it. Life is in any case full of suffering and trials. But I must not be a source of suffering and trials of my neighbour.

Christians who want to increase their neighbours' sufferings and are ready to crucify them for their salvation may be compared to those who crucified Christ. The Inquisition was founded upon this wrong conception of the redeeming power of suffering. I must help my neighbour to bear his cross but not to crucify him. The wish that a man should bear his cross is not a desire to lay a heavy cross upon him and to nail him to it for his salvation. Acceptance of the cross can only be a free act and must make the burden easier and not heavier to bear, it must bring light and not be torture in the dark. A false, legalistic asceticism may inspire a disgust for virtue. It loads men with burdens grievous to be borne. The pseudo-Christian attitude to suffering is projected into eternity and takes the form of the doctrine of eternal damnation. Those loving Christians are not satisfied with temporal earthly torments, but would like to have also eternal torments in hell. Ordinary, natural human feeling is incomparably better than such Christianity. I diminish and lighten my own pain by voluntarily accepting it as the cross of life, and I diminish and lighten my neighbour's pain by sharing it, by being compassionate, by taking it upon myself. Our attitude to all men would be Christian if we regarded them as though they were dying, and determine our relation to them in the light of death, both of their death and our own. A person who is dying calls forth a special kind of feeling . Our attitude to him is at once softened and lifted on to a higher plane. We then can feel compassion for people whom we did not love. But every man is dying, I too am dying and must never forget about death.

The whole meaning of love for one's enemies is that it alone overcomes the bad infinity of evil, cuts the chain of evil and transfers men to another plane. Men are in the power of bad and sinful passions and seek defence in the power of the good. But the good is powerless. Christ alone can free us from evil—from sinful passions, from the bad infinity that enchains us. Christ's gracious love is the only way out of the vicious circle. Luther was right in saying that a Christian is not dominated by his works but dominates them. Luther was also right in maintaining that the doctrine of salvation and justification by faith does away with religious utilitarianism. Kierkegaard was right in perpetually insisting that Christ is in the present and not in the past. Being in the present Christ liberates us and makes possible things which for the law are impossible. Christ's own suffering was due to His taking upon Himself the sin and evil of the whole world. It was infinitely greater and more salutary than our sufferings. Christ, like us, passed through the experience of being forsaken by God. But His experience of it was incomparably more bitter and terrible than ours. Through it the freedom of man and of all creation was established once and for all. Man and his suffering are the central conception in the religion of the God-Man. This is the fundamental *motif* of Russian religious thought which is more humane than any other. It is very remote from the religion of personal salvation and self-improvement. The narrow ascetic interpretation of Christianity is connected precisely with this religion of personal salvation and consequently of self-regarding fear and terror of perdition. Emotional states of that kind banish love. The Gospel and the Epistles contain no grounds for such an interpretation of Christianity ; it arose at a later period. False asceticism—asceticism as an end and not as a means—warps life and creates a revolt in the subconscious and contradictions in the conscious mind. Finally such asceticism becomes pharisaic and purely formal. Ascetic metaphysics declares love to be impossible and even dangerous, i.e. it comes into conflict with the main principles of Christianity. But if Christianity is not a religion of personal salvation, for the sake of which people torture themselves and their neighbours, what is its essential message?

6. THE GOSPEL MESSAGE OF THE KINGDOM OF GOD

It is impossible to understand the Gospel as a norm or law. If it is understood in that sense it becomes hostile to life and incompatible with it.

The absolute character of the Gospel teaching about life then becomes unintelligible and impracticable. The chief argument that the world has always brought against the gospel is that it is impracticable and opposed to the very laws of life. And indeed the morality of the Gospel is paradoxical and contrary to the morality of our world even at its highest. The Gospel is opposed not only to evil but to what men consider good. Usually people have tried to make the Gospel fit the requirements of this world and so make it acceptable. But this has always meant a distortion of Christianity. How then are we to understand the absolute, transcendental and uncompromising character of the truth proclaimed in the Gospel? The Gospel is the good news of the coming of the Kingdom of God. This is the essence both of the Gospel and of Christianity as a whole. " Seek ye first the Kingdom of God and all these things will be added unto you." The Gospel reveals the absolute life of the Kingdom, and everything in it proves to be unlike the relative life of the world. The Gospel morality is not a norm or a law because it is the morality of paradise and is beyond our good and evil, beyond our legalistic distinctions between good and evil. It is difficult, almost impossible, to apply the absolute truths of the Gospel to human life and society in which everything is relative and in time.[1] It is only too obvious that the Gospel cannot serve as a basis for the state, the family, the economic life and civilization and that it is impossible to justify by the Gospel the use of force inevitable in the historical development of society. And so the Christians invented all kinds of other norms and rules for their guidance.

Christ came to bring down fire on earth, and everything that men regard as valuable, all the kingdoms built up by them, are consumed in that fire. Be perfect as your Father in heaven is perfect. Is that a norm and a rule of life? Of course not. The perfection of the Heavenly Father cannot be the norm for a sinful world ; it is absolute, while a law or rule is always relative to sin. It is a revelation of an absolute, divine life, different from the sinful life of the world. Thou shalt do no murder, thou shalt not steal, thou shalt not commit adultery—all this can be a norm or a rule for the sinful life of the world and is relative to it. But the perfection of the Heavenly Father and the Kingdom of God are not relative to anything and cannot be made into a rule. The Gospel appeals to the inner, spiritual man and not to the outer man, a member of society. It calls not for external works in the social world but for the awakening and regeneration of the spiritual life, for a new birth that is to bring us into the Kingdom of

[1] Many interesting reflections on this subject are to be found in the work of M. Tareyev, and from a different point of view in K. Barth.

God. The Gospel is addressed to the eternal principle in the human soul independent of historical epochs and social changes, and in a certain sense it is not social. Everything in the Gospel is connected with the person of Christ and is incomprehensible apart from that connection. The injunctions of the Gospel are utterly unrealizable and impossible as rules of action. But what is impossible for man, is possible for God. Only in and through Christ is the perfection similar to the perfection of the Heavenly Father realized, and the Kingdom of God actually comes. The Gospel is based not upon law, even if it be a new law, but upon Christ Himself, upon His personality. Such is the new ethics of grace and redemption. But we live on two planes, under the law and under grace, in the order of nature and in the spiritual order—and therein lies the immeasurable difficulty and complexity of a Christian's life in the world. Human society lives and builds up its kingdoms and civilizations under the power of the law ; the Gospel revelation of the Kingdom of God is for it a catastrophe and the Last Judgment.

We have already seen how great was the change made by the Gospel in moral valuations. It meant the most radical revaluation of values in the whole of the world's history. Everything becomes strange and different from that which the world values and by which it lives. The world has to renounce not only its evil but its good also. Do not resist evil by force. But the world thinks it a good thing to resist evil by force. The sun rises equally over the just and the unjust. But the world thinks it good that the sun should rise over the just only. Love your enemies, bless them that curse you. But the world thinks it good to love one's friends only and not one's enemies. This is why Christianity alone breaks through the vicious circle of vengeance. Publicans and harlots go before the others into the Kingdom of God. But the world thinks that the good, the righteous, the pure, those who have fulfilled the law and norm, lead the way. One must come through the narrow gate. The world goes through the wide gate. That which comes out of the mouth, i.e. the bad state of the human heart, defiles man. But the world thinks that that which comes into the mouth, i.e. other people's attitude, defiles one. The Gospel tells us to be as carefree as the birds of the air and the lilies of the fields and take no thought for the morrow. But the whole life of the world is based upon care and upon taking endless thought for the morrow. A man ought to leave his father, mother, wife, and even to hate them if they hinder him from seeking the Kingdom of God. But the world requires first of all love for one's nearest—for one's father, mother, wife. It is difficult for the rich to enter the Kingdom of Heaven. But the world esteems the rich above all, honours them and regards them as first. The blessed are not those whom the world considers blessed—blessed are those who weep, the meek, the merciful, the pure in heart, those who hunger and thirst after righteousness, and so on, and so on. But for the world the blessed are the rich, the well born, the powerful, the strong, the famous, the gay, and so on. He who takes up the sword shall perish by the sword. But the world defends its existence by the sword. The Gospel breathes the spirit of liberty which frightens the world and appears to it destructive.

The Gospel and the world are utterly opposed and incompatible. The Kingdom of Christ is not of this world. How then can it be brought into the world? Men have been trying to establish it in the world for nearly 2000 years. Christ came not to judge, but to save. But the world loves judgment above all and needs it, and has but a vague idea of salvation, though it needs it more than anything. The absolute revelation of the Gospel about the Kingdom of God cannot be expressed by any social and historical forms, which are always temporal and relative. The truth of the spiritual life cannot be made to fit into the natural life. There never has been and there can be no Christian state, Christian economics, Christian family, Christian learning, Christian social life. For in the Kingdom of God and in the perfect divine life there is neither state, nor economics, nor family, nor learning, nor any social life determined by law. The church in its historic existence was infected by the state, acquiesced in its use of force and fell under the spell of the law. And yet the Gospel revelation of the Kingdom of God brought about a change secretly, inwardly and imperceptibly, in all the departments of life and altered the very structure of the human soul, bringing forth new emotions. The Kingdom of God cometh not with observation. When it came too perceptibly, it was a snare and a delusion. The gracious power of the Gospel revelation liberates men from the torments of fear, of pride, of love of power, and the insatiable lust for life. The solution of many vital and fundamental questions, however, is not made obvious in the Gospel but is, as it were, veiled. It is left to man himself in his freedom to find a creative solution of the problems that continually confront him. The Gospel is concerned not so much with teaching us how to solve them as with healing and regenerating the texture of the human soul.

CHAPTER THREE

The Ethics of Creativeness

I. THE NATURE OF CREATIVENESS

THE Gospel constantly speaks of the fruit which the seed must bring forth if it falls on good soil and of talents given to man which must be returned with profit. Under cover of parable Christ refers in these words to man's creative activity, to his creative vocation. Burying one's talents in the ground, i.e. absence of creativeness, is condemned by Christ. The whole of St. Paul's teaching about various gifts is concerned with man's creative vocation. The gifts are from God and they indicate that man is intended to do creative work. These gifts are various, and everyone is called to creative service in accordance with the special gift bestowed upon him. It is therefore a mistake to assert, as people often do, that the Holy Writ contains no reference to creativeness. It does—but we must be able to read it, we must guess what it is God wants and expects of man.

Creativeness is always a growth, an addition, the making of something new that had not existed in the world before. The problem of creativeness is the problem as to whether something completely new is really possible.[1] Creativeness from its very meaning is bringing forth out of nothing. Nothing becomes something, non-being becomes being. Creativeness presupposes non-being, just as Hegel's " becoming " does. Like Plato's Eros, creativeness is the child of poverty and plenty, of want and abundance of power. Creativeness is connected with sin and at the same time it is sacrificial. True creativeness always involves catharsis, purification, liberation of the spirit from psycho-physical elements and victory over them. Creation is different in principle from generation and emanation. In emanation particles of matter radiate from a centre and are separated off. Nor is creation a redistribution of force and energy, as evolution is. So far from being identical with evolution, creation is the very opposite of it. In evolution nothing new is made, but the old is redistributed. Evolution is necessity, creation is freedom. Creation is the greatest mystery of life, the mystery of the appearance of something new that had never existed

[1] See my books *Smysl Tvorchestba* (*The Meaning of Creativeness*) and *Freedom and the Spirit*.

before and is not deduced from, or generated by, anything. Creativeness presupposes non-being, μή ὄν (and not οὐκ ὄν) which is the source of the primeval, pre-cosmic, pre-existent freedom in man. The mystery of creativeness is the mystery of freedom. Creativeness can only spring from fathomless freedom, for such freedom alone can give rise to the new, to what had never existed before. Out of being, out of something that exists, it is impossible to create that which is completely new ; there can only be emanation, generation, redistribution. But creativeness means breaking through from non-being, from freedom, to the world of being. The mystery of creativeness is revealed in the biblical myth of the creation. God created the world out of nothing, i.e. freely and out of freedom. The world was not an emanation from God, it was not evolved or born from Him, but created, i.e. it was absolutely new, it was something that had never been before. Creativeness is only possible because the world is created, because there is a Creator. Man, made by God in His own image and likeness, is also a creator and is called to creative work.

Creativeness is a complex fact. It presupposes, first, man's primary, meonic, uncreated freedom ; secondly, the gifts bestowed upon man the creator by God the Creator, and, thirdly, the world as the field for his activity. Thus three elements are involved in human creativeness : the element of freedom, owing to which alone creation of new and hitherto non-existent realities is possible, gifts and vocations connected with them, and the already created world from which man can borrow his materials. Man is not the source of his gifts and his genius. He has received them from God and therefore feels that he is in God's hands and is an instrument of God's work in the world. Nothing can be more pitiful and absurd than to pride oneself on one's genius. There would be more excuse for being proud of one's holiness. The genius feels that he acts not of himself, but is possessed by God and is the means by which God works His own ends and designs. The " demon " of Socrates was not his self but a being that dwelt in him. A creator constantly feels himself possessed by a demon or a genius. His work is a manifestation through freedom of gifts bestowed upon him from above.

Man cannot produce the material for creation out of himself, out of nothing, out of the depths of his own being. The creative act is of the nature of marriage, it always implies a meeting between different elements. The material for human creativeness is borrowed from the world created by God. We find this in all art and in all inventions and discoveries. We find this in the creativeness of knowledge and in philosophy which pre-supposes the existence of the world created by God—objective realities without which thought would be left in a void.   God has granted man the creative gift, the talent, the genius and also the world in and through which the creative activity is to be carried out.   God calls man to perform the creative act and realize his vocation, and He is expecting an answer to His call.   Man's answer to God's call cannot entirely consist of elements that are given by and proceed from God.   Something must come from man also, and that something is the very essence of creativeness, which brings forth new realities.   It is, indeed, not " something " but " nothing " —in other words it is freedom, without which there can be no creative activity.   Freedom not determined by anything answers God's call to creative work, but in doing so it makes use of the gift or genius received from God and of materials present in the created world.   When man is said to create out of nothing it means that he creates out of freedom.   In every creative conception there is an element of primeval freedom, fathomless, undetermined by anything, not proceeding from God but ascending towards God.   God's call is addressed to that abyss of freedom, and the answer must come from it.   Fathomless freedom is present in all creativeness, but the creative process is so complex that it is not easy to detect this primary element in it.   It is a process of interaction between grace and freedom, between forces going from God to man and from man to God.   In describing it, emphasis may be laid either on the element of freedom or on the element of grace, of gracious possession and inspiration. But there can be no inspiration without freedom.   Platonic philosophy is unfavourable to the interpretation of creativeness as the making of new realities.

Creativeness has two different aspects and we describe it differently according to whether we dwell upon one or the other.   It has an inner and an outer aspect.   There is the primary creative act in which man stands as it were face to face with God, and there is the secondary creative act in which he faces other men and the world.   There is the creative conception, the primary creative intuition, in which a man hears the symphony, per- ceives the pictorial or poetic image, or is aware of a discovery or invention as yet unexpressed ; there is such a thing as an inner creative act of love for a person, unexpressed in any way as yet.   In that primary act man stands before God and is not concerned with realization.   If knowledge is given me, that knowledge in the first instance is not a book written by me or a scientific discovery formulated for other people's benefit and forming part of human culture.   In the first instance it is my own inner knowledge, as yet unexpressed, unknown to the world and hidden from it.   This alone is real first-hand knowledge, my real philosophy in which I am face to face with the mystery of existence. Then comes the secondary creative act connected with man's social nature—the realization, namely, of the creative intuition. A book comes to be written. At this stage there arises the question of art and technique. The primary creative fire is not art at all. Art is secondary and in it the creative fire cools down. Art is subject to law and is not an interaction of freedom and grace, as the primary creative act is. In realizing his creative intuition man is limited by the world, by his material, by other people ; all this weighs on him and damps the fire of inspiration. There is always a tragic discrepancy between the burning heat of the creative fire in which the artistic image is conceived, and the cold of its formal realization. Every book, picture, statue, good work, social institution is an instance of this cooling down of the original flame. Probably some creators never find expression ; they have the inner fire and inspiration but fail to give it form. And yet people generally think that creativeness consists in producing concrete, definite things. Classic art requires the greatest possible adherence to the cold formal laws of technique.

The aim of creative inspiration is to bring forth new forms of life, but the results are the cold products of civilization, cultural values, books, pictures, institutions, good works. Good works mean the cooling down of the creative fire of love in the human heart just as a philosophical book means the cooling down of the creative fire of knowledge in the human spirit. This is the tragedy of human creativeness and its limitation. Its results are a terrible condemnation of it. The inner creative act in its fiery impetus ought to leave the heaviness of the world behind and " overcome the world ". But in its external realization the creative act is subject to the power of " the world " and is fettered by it. Creativeness which is a fiery stream flowing out of fathomless freedom has not only to ascend but also to descend. It has to interpret to the world its creative vision and, in doing so, submit to the laws of art and technique.

Creativeness by its very nature implies genius. In his creative aspect man is endowed with genius ; it is the image of God the Creator in him. This does not mean that every man has an outstanding talent for painting pictures, writing poems, novels or philosophical books, ruling the state, or making inventions and discoveries. The presence of genius in man has to do with his inner creativeness and not with the external realization of it. It is a characteristic of human personality as a whole and not a specific gift, and it indicates that man is capable of breaking through to the primary source of life and that his spiritual activity is truly original and not determined by social influences. A man's genius may, however, be out of keeping with his powers of realization. The presence of genius and originality together with a great talent for realizing the products of creative activity makes a man a genius in the usual sense of the term. But there may be something of genius in a man's love for a woman, in a mother's love for her child, in a person's concern for other people's welfare, in inner intuitions which find no outer expression, in the pursuit of righteousness and the suffering of trying to discover the meaning of life. A saint may be a genius in his work of making himself into a perfect and transfigured creature, though he may have nothing to show for it. It is wrong to draw comparisons between the extent of men's genius and talent, for it means ignoring their individuality. Creativeness brings with it much sorrow and bitterness. It is a great failure even in its finest achievements, for they always fall short of the creative conception.

There is a tragic conflict between creativeness and personal perfection. The greatness of creative genius is not correlative to moral perfection. A great artist may be an idle pleasure-seeker, " of the world's worthless children the most worthless he may be ". This problem has been stated in all its poignancy by Pushkin, who said the most remarkable things that have ever been said about artistic creation. Creative genius is bestowed on man for nothing and is not connected with his moral or religious efforts to attain perfection and become a new creature. It stands as it were outside the ethics of law and the ethics of redemption and presupposes a different kind of morality. The creator is justified by his creative achievement. We come here upon a curious moral paradox. Creative genius is not concerned with salvation or perdition. In his creative work the artist forgets about himself, about his own personality, and renounces himself. Creative work is intensely personal and at the same time it means forgetfulness of self. Creative activity always involves sacrifice. It means self-transcendence, overstepping the confines of one's own limited personal being. A creator forgets about salvation ; he is concerned with values that are above man. There is nothing selfish about creativeness. In so far as a man is self-centred he cannot create anything, he cannot abandon himself to inspiration or imagine a better world.

It is paradoxical that ascetic experience absorbs a man in himself, makes him concentrate upon his own improvement and salvation, while creative experience makes him forget himself and brings him into a higher world. Creativeness involves renunciation and asceticism of its own, but it is of a different kind. The Christians who suggest that one should first go in for asceticism and attain perfection and then take up creative work have no idea of what creativeness means. Asceticism required by creativeness is different from that which is concerned with personal perfection and salvation. No amount of ascetic practice will give one talent or ability, to say nothing of genius. Genius cannot be earned, it is given from above, like grace. What is required of the artist is intensity of creative effort and not ascetic struggle for self-improvement. If Pushkin went in for asceticism and sought the salvation of his soul, he would probably have ceased to be a great poet. Creativeness is bound up with imperfection, and perfection may be unfavourable to it. This is the moral paradox with regard to creativeness.

When a man begins to seek moral perfection—whether he follows the Catholic, the Orthodox, the Tolstoyan, the theosophical, the Yoga or any other path—he may be lost to creative work. Creativeness requires that a man should forget about his own moral progress and sacrifice his personality. It is a path that demands heroism, but it is different from the path of personal improvement and salvation. Creativeness is necessary for the Kingdom of God—for God's work in the world—but it is not at all necessary for saving one's soul. Or, if it is, it is only necessary in so far as a creator is justified by his creative achievement. If a man feels nothing but humility and a perpetual sense of sin, he can do no creative work. Creativeness means that one's mind passes on to another plane of being. The soul may live simultaneously on different planes, in the heights and in the lowest depths, it may boldly create and be humbly penitent. But creativeness in all its aspects, including the moral—for there is such a thing as moral creativeness—testifies to the presence in man of a certain principle which may be the source of a different system of morality than the ethics of law and the ethics of redemption. Creativeness more than anything else is reminiscent of man's vocation before the Fall and is in a sense " beyond good and evil ". But since human nature is sinful, creativeness is distorted and perverted by sin, and may be evil.

Man's creative activity alone bears witness to his vocation and shows what he has been destined for in the world. The law says nothing about vocation, nor does the ethics of redemption as such. The Gospel and St. Paul's Epistles speak of man's gifts and vocation only because they go beyond the mystery of redemption. True creativeness is always in the Holy Spirit, for only in the Spirit can there be that union of grace and freedom which we find in creativeness. Its meaning for ethics is twofold. To begin with, ethics must inquire into the moral significance of all creative work, even if it has no direct relation to the moral life. Art and knowledge have a moral significance, like all activities which create higher values. Secondly, ethics must inquire into the creative significance of moral activity. Moral life itself, moral actions and valuations have a creative character. The ethics of law and norm does not as yet recognize this, and it is therefore inevitable that we should pass to the ethics of creativeness, which deals with man's true vocation and destiny.

Creativeness and a creative attitude to life as a whole is not man's right, it is his duty. It is a moral imperative that applies in every department of life. Creative effort in artistic and cognitive activity has a moral value. Realization of truth and goodness is a moral good. There may, however, be a conflict between the creation of perfect cultural values and the creation of a perfect human personality. The path of creativeness is also a path to moral and religious perfection, a way of realizing the fullness o f life. The frequently quoted words of Goethe, " All theory is grey but the tree of life is eternally green," may be turned the other way round : " All life is grey but the tree of theory is eternally green." " Theory '' will then mean creativeness, the thought of a Plato or a Hegel, while " life " will stand for a mere struggle for existence, dull and commonplace, family dissensions, disappointments and so on. In that sense " theory " means rising to a higher moral level.

2. THE CREATIVELY INDIVIDUAL CHARACTER OF MORAL ACTS

The ethics of creativeness differs from the ethics of law first of all because every moral task is for it absolutely individual and creative.[1] The moral problems of life cannot be solved by an automatic application of universally binding rules. It is impossible to say that in the same circumstances one ought always and everywhere to act in the same way. It is impossible if only because circumstances never are quite the same. Indeed, the very opposite rule might be formulated. One ought always to act individually and solve every moral problem for oneself, showing creativeness in one's moral activity, and not for a single moment become a moral automaton. A man ought to make moral inventions with regard to the problems that life sets him. Hence, for the ethics of creativeness freedom means something very different from what it does for the ethics of law. For the latter the so-called freedom of will has no creative character and means merely acceptance or rejection of the law of the good and responsibility for doing one or the other. For the ethics of creativeness freedom means not the acceptance of the law but individual creation of values.

[1] See M. Scheler, *Der Formalismus in der Ethik und die materiele Werthethik.* In my book *Smysl Tvorchestva (The Meaning of Creativeness)* I said long ago that moral acts are creative and individual in character.

Freedom is creative energy, the possibility of building up new realities. The ethics of law knows nothing of that freedom. It does not know that the good is being created, that in every individual and unrepeatable moral act new good that had never existed before is brought into being by the moral agent whose invention it is. There exists no fixed, static moral order subordinated to a single universally binding moral law. Man is not a passive executor of the laws of that world-order. Man is a creator and an inventor. His moral conscience must at every moment of his life be creative and inventive. The ethics of creativeness is one of dynamics and energy. Life is based upon energy and not upon law. It may be said, indeed, that energy is the source of law. The ethics of creativeness takes a very different view of the struggle against evil than does the ethics of law. According to it, that struggle consists in the creative realization of the good and the transformation of evil into good, rather than in the mere destruction of evil. The ethics of law is concerned with the finite : the world is for it a self-contained system and there is no way out of it. The ethics of creativeness is concerned with the infinite : the world is for it open and plastic, with boundless horizons and possibilities of breaking through to other worlds. It overcomes the nightmare of the finite from which there is no escape.

The ethics of creativeness is different from the ethics of redemption : it is concerned in the first place with values and not with salvation. The moral end of life is for it not the salvation of one's soul or the redemption of guilt but creative realization of righteousness and of values which need not belong to the moral order. The ethics of creativeness springs from personality but is concerned with the world, while the ethics of law springs from the world and society but is concerned with the personality. The ethics of creativeness alone overcomes the negative fixation of the spirit upon struggle with sin and evil and replaces it by the positive, i.e. by the creation of the valuable contents of life. It overcomes not only the earthly but the heavenly, transcendental selfishness with which even the ethics of redemption is infected. Fear of punishment and of eternal torments in hell can play no part in the ethics of creativeness. It opens a way to a pure, disinterested morality, since every kind of fear distorts moral experience and activity. It may indeed be said that nothing which is done out of fear, whether it be of temporal or of eternal torments, has any moral value. The truly moral motive is not fear of punishment and of hell, but selfless and disinterested love of God and of the divine in life, of truth and perfection and all positive values. This is the basis of the ethics of creativeness.

The ethics of creativeness affirms the value of the unique and the individual.[1] This is a new phenomenon in the moral world. It is with the greatest difficulty and only as late as the nineteenth century that ethics has recognized the value of the individual. An enormous part was played in this by such men as Dostoevsky, Nietzsche, Ibsen, Kierkegaard. The Christian ethics was for a long time blind to the significance of individuality and conceived of moral life as subordinated to a universally binding law. The unique and the individual has a twofold significance for ethics. In the first place moral valuations and actions must proceed from the concrete personality and be unique and individual in character. Each individual man must act as himself and not as another would have acted in his place, and his moral activity must spring from the depths of his own conscience. Secondly, the individual and the individuality must be recognized as a moral value of the highest hierarchical order. The unique, concrete personality is the highest value and not a means for the triumph of the universal, even if that universal be a generally binding moral law. To be a personality to the end and not to betray it, to be individual in all one's actions, is an absolute moral imperative, paradoxical as it sounds. It means " be thyself, to thine own self be true ". Sacrifice of self is a way of being true to one's self. Ibsen's Peer Gynt wanted to be original, he affirmed individualism. But individualism always destroys personality and individuality. Peer Gynt never was himself, he lost his personality and went into the melting-pot. The figure of the button-moulder is one of the most striking images in the world's literature.

The ethics of creativeness is by no means identical with individualism. The difference between personalism and individualism has already been explained. To be oneself means to realize God's idea of one's self. That is the essence of personality as the highest value. Personality is realized spiritually and not biologically. Ethics is based upon personality and cannot exist apart from it. Human personality as God's idea and God's image is the centre of moral consciousness, a supreme value. It is a value not because it is the bearer of a universally binding moral law, as with Kant, but just because it is God's image and idea, the bearer of the divine principle in life. It is therefore impossible to use the moral good in order to humiliate and destroy man. A person's moral activity has not only a personal but a social and even a cosmic significance. A personality emits, so to speak, moral rays which are diffused throughout the world. Human personality always remains a fiery centre of the world. In the moral life of society the fire is cooled down : it is the life of customs, manners,

[1] See G. Gurvitch, *Fichtes System der konkreten Ethik.*

public opinion. Personality is the only truly creative and prophetic element in moral life ; it coins new values. But it suffers for doing so. Creative personality defends the first-hand, pure, virginal character of moral thought and conscience against the constant resistance of the hard-set collective thought and conscience, the spirit of the times, public opinion and so on. In doing so the creative personality may feel itself a part of a spiritual whole and be neither solitary nor self-assertive ; this, however, is another question. A person is connected with a communal spiritual whole through his own free conscience and not through social compulsion and authority. The ethics of creativeness is always prophetic, directed towards the future ; it originates from the individual and not from a collective unit, but it is social in import.[1]

Within the Christian world there are two conflicting moral tendencies : humility and creativeness, the morality of personal salvation and fear of perdition and the creative morality of values, of devoting oneself to the transformation and transfiguration of the world. Both humility and creativeness are based upon sacrifice, but the nature of sacrifice is different in the two cases. Humility may require that a man should give up personal creativeness but go on perpetually thinking of his own personality and of the way to make it perfect ; creativeness may require that, while preserving personal creative inspiration, a man should forget about himself and think only of values and perfect works for the world. The sacrifice is connected with two different kinds of perfection. But the religious ideal of humility, which has, as we have seen, a profound ontological meaning, easily becomes distorted. In the name of the abstract idea of personal perfection and obedience to God man may be required to renounce every kind of creative inspiration, even if it be the inspiration of love for his fellow creatures. Like everything else humility is paradoxical and may lead to the denial of perfection. There is a lack of humility in being too perfect, good and loving. This kind of attitude is inspired by a false conception of God as a Being who requires of man first and foremost sacrifice and suffering, submission and obedience. Humility may become hostile not only to creativeness but to moral life as a whole. It may become a superstition. Our religious life is still full of idolatry, and to get rid of it is a great moral task. Creativeness is by its very nature opposed to idolatry and therein lies its great significance. The ethics of creativeness is concerned with revealing human values and the value of human personality as such, and in doing so it frees man from the unendurable fear for himself and his future—the fear which gives rise to idolatry and superstition. A

[1] See my book, *Freedom and the Spirit*.

man whose spirit is occupied with the creation of objective values ceases to be " a trembling creature ". Creative inspiration is a way to victory over fear which, owing to original sin, is the ruling emotion of life. At moments of creative elation an artist or a man of science becomes free from fear ; afterwards, when he descends to everyday life, he feels it again. He may indeed feel fear in connection with his creative work if he longs for fame and success, if he is complacent and worships his own work. But these feelings have nothing to do with pure creativeness.

The ethics of creativeness strives for the victory of eternity over time. Creative work takes place in time, but the creative act is directed upon the eternal—eternal values, truth, beauty, righteousness, God and divine heights. All the products of man's genius may be temporal and corruptible, but the creative fire itself is eternal, and everything temporal ought to be consumed in it. It is the tragedy of creativeness that it wants eternity and the eternal, but produces the temporal and builds up culture which is in time and a part of history. The creative act is an escape from the power of time and ascent to the divine. An inventor in his creative inspiration is transported beyond the earth and time, but he creates a machine which may prove to be a weapon in the struggle against eternity. It is another instance of the contradictory character of creativeness in our sinful world. Creativeness is the struggle against the consequences of sin, the expression of man's true vocation, but creativeness is distorted and debased by sin. Hence the ethics of creativeness deals with the agonizing struggle of the human spirit. Creativeness needs purification, needs the purifying fire. In the civilized world creativeness becomes so degenerate that it calls forth a moral reaction against it and a desire for ascetic renunciation and escape from the world. We find such degeneration in many tendencies of modern art and literature, in which the spirit of eternity is finally surrendered to the polluted spirit of the time. We find it in the unendurable complacency of scientists and in the new religion of science. We find it in social and political life where the struggle for gain and power destroys the creative desire for social justice. In every sphere the lust of life damps the creative burning of the spirit. It is the direct opposite of creativeness. Creativeness is victory over the lust of life. That lust is overcome through humility and through creativeness.

The soul is afraid of emptiness. When there is no positive, valuable, divine content in it, it is filled with the negative, false, diabolical content. When the soul feels empty it experiences boredom, which is a truly terrible and diabolical state. Evil lust and evil passions are to a great extent generated by boredom and emptiness. It is difficult to struggle against that boredom by means of abstract goodness and virtue. The dreadful thing is that virtue at times seems deadly dull, and then there is no salvation in it. The cold, hard-set virtue devoid of creative fire is always dull and never saves. The heart must be set aglow if the dullness is to be dispelled. Dull virtue is a poor remedy against the boredom of emptiness. Dullness is the absence of creativeness. All that is not creative is dull. Goodness is deadly dull if it is not creative. No rule or norm can save us from dullness and from evil lust engendered by it. Lust is a means of escape from boredom when goodness provides no such escape. This is why it is very difficult, almost impossible, to conquer evil passions negatively, through negative asceticism and prohibitions. They can only be conquered positively, through awakening the positive and creative spiritual force opposed to them. Creative fire, divine Eros, overcomes lust and evil passions. It burns up evil, boredom and the false strivings engendered by it. The will to evil is at bottom objectless and can only be overcome by a will directed towards an object, towards the valuable and divine contents of life. Purely negative asceticism, preoccupied with evil and sinful desires and strivings, so far from enlightening the soul, intensifies its darkness. We must preach, therefore, not the morality based upon the annihilation of will but upon its enlightenment, not upon the humiliation of man and his external submission to God but upon the creative realization by man of the divine in life—of the values of truth, goodness and beauty. The ethics of creativeness can alone save the human soul from being warped by arid abstract virtue and abstract ideals transformed into rules and norms. The ideas of truth, goodness and beauty must cease to be norms and rules and become vital forces, an inner creative fire.

Christian teachers of spiritual life constantly speak of sinful passions and the struggle against them. They are right, of course, in saying that sinful passions torture man and distort his life. But at the same time passions are the material which may be transformed into a higher qualitative content of life. Without passions, without the unconscious element in life and without creativeness, human virtue is dry and deadly dull. The Fathers of the Church themselves say sometimes that passions may become virtues. This shows that in the struggle with passions it is wrong to adopt the exclusively negative point of view and practise solely the negative asceticism. It is necessary to attain positive qualitative states into which passions will enter in an enlightened, transfigured, sublimated form instead of being uprooted and destroyed. This applies in the first instance to the most fatal of the fallen man's passions—that of sex. It is impossible simply to destroy it, and it is useless and even dangerous to concentrate upon a negative struggle with it. Modern psychology and psycho-pathology talk about its sublimation. And it appears that there are many ways in which man can struggle with the sinful sexual passion. Every form of creative inspiration and deep spiritual feeling overcomes and transfigures it. The experience of intense erotic love may weaken passion and make a man forget the physiological sexual craving. This is a well-known paradox verified by experience. An intense feeling of pity and compassion may also paralyse sexual passion and make a man forget about it. The energy of sex transfigured and sublimated may become a source of creativeness and inspiration. Creativeness is unquestionably connected with the energy of sex, the first source of creative energy, which may assume other forms just as motion may pass into heat. Creativeness is bound up with the ultimate basis of life and indicates a certain spiritual direction assumed by the primary vital energy. The whole problem is to give that energy a spiritual direction instead of an unspiritual and thus save spiritual forces from being wasted upon sexual passion. No purely negative asceti-cism, no effort of will aimed at suppressing the sexual or any sinful passion, instead of replacing it by something positive, can be successful ; it is defeated by what modern psychology calls *la loi de l'effort converti*.[1] The only thing that can help is the change of spiritual direction, the sublimation of passion and its transformation into a source of creative energy. Love may overcome the sexual passion that tortures man ; but the sacrifice of love, the suppression of it in oneself for the sake of creative work, may be a source of creative energy. I have already referred to this in the case of Ibsen and of Kierkegaard, who renounced the woman he loved and in-tended to marry.[2] Sexlessness is as bad for creative activity as the waste of vital energy in sexual passion.

Most of the so-called sinful passions can be sublimated and transformed into a source of positive creativeness. The ethics of law with its formal virtues refuses to recognize this, but not the ethics of creativeness with its creative and dynamic virtues. The Greeks succeeded in converting even hatred, one of the most evil and sinful of human passions, into noble rivalry. Anger and ambition and jealousy and love of gambling may undergo a similar transformation. Love is, as it were, the universal vital energy capable of converting evil passions into creative forces. Thus the thirst for knowledge is love directed in a certain way, and the same is true of philosophy, which means love of truth ; and there may be love of beauty and love of justice. Evil passions become creative through Eros.

[1] See Baudouin, *Suggestion et Autosuggestion*.
[2] See an interesting book by Przymara, *Das Geheimnis Kierkegaards*.

Hence the ethics of creativeness, in contradistinction to the ethics of law, is erotic.

But love can only transform evil passions into creative ones if it is regarded as a value in itself and not as a means of salvation. Love in the sense of good works useful for the salvation of the soul cannot give rise to a creative attitude to life and be a source of a life-giving energy. Love is not merely a fount of creativeness but is itself creativeness, radiation of creative energy. Love is like radiun in the spiritual world. The ethics of creativeness calls for actual, concrete realization of truth, goodness, spirituality, for a real transfiguration of life and not for a symbolic and conventional realization of the good through ascetic practices, good works and so on. It demands that we should love every man in his creative aspect, which is the image and likeness of God in him, i.e. that we should love that which is good, true, superhuman and divine in him. We do not know why we love a person ; we love for no reason. One cannot love a man for his merits ; and in this respect love is like grace which is given freely, not for merits, for nothing. Love is a gracious radiating energy. To interpret love for one's neighbour as a means to save one's soul is a complete misinterpretation of love and an utter failure to understand its nature. It is a legalistic perversion of Christianity. Love is taken to be a law, for the fulfilment of which man is rewarded.

Equally false is the position of the idealist who knows love for an idea but does not know personal love and is always ready to turn man into a means for carrying out the idea. This attitude gives rise to religious formalism and pharisaism, which is always a denial of love. The religion of law condemns the man who disobeys the will of God. Ethical idealism condemns the man who disobeys the moral law. The religion of redemption and the ethics of creativeness have no such condemnation. The Christian religion has placed man above the Sabbath, and the ethics of creativeness accepts this truth absolutely. Man is for it a value in himself, independently of the idea of which he is the bearer ; our task in life is to radiate creative energy that brings with it light and strength and transfiguration. Hence the ethics of creativeness does not pass judgment but gives life, receives life, heightens the quality and the value of life's contents. Its tragedy is connected with the conflict of values which are recognized as equally deserving of creative effort. Hence the ethics of creativeness inevitably presupposes sacrifice.

There are two different types of enjoyment—one reminds us of original sin and always contains poison ; the other reminds us of paradise. When a man is enjoying the gratification of sexual passion or the pleasure of eating he ought to feel the presence of poison and be reminded of original sin. That is the nature of every enjoyment connected with lust. It always testifies to the poverty and not to the richness of our nature. But when we experience the delight of breathing the sea or mountain air or the fragrance of woods and fields, we recall paradise, there is no lust in this. We are comparing here pleasures that have a physiological character. But the same comparison may be drawn in the spiritual realm. When a man is enjoying the satisfaction of his greed or vanity he ought to feel the poison and be reminded of the original sin. But when he is enjoying a creative act which reveals truth or creates beauty or radiates love upon a fellow creature he recalls paradise. Every delight connected with lust is poisoned and reminiscent of original sin. Every delight free from lust and connected with love of objective values is a remembrance or a foretaste of paradise and frees us from the bonds of sin. The sublimation or trans-figuration of passions means that a passion is purified from lust and that a free creative element enters into it. This is a point of fundamental importance for ethics. Man must strive first and foremost to free himself from slavery. Every state incompatible with spiritual freedom and hostile to it is evil. But every lust (*concupiscentia*) is hostile to the freedom of the spirit and enslaves man. Lust is both insatiable and bound to pall. It cannot be satisfied, for it is the bad infinity of craving. There exists a different kind of craving which also extends into infinity, e.g. the hunger for absolute righteousness ; those who hunger and thrist after righteousness are blessed because they are concerned with eternity and not with bad infinity. The divine reality which fills our life is the contrary of the bore-dom and emptiness born of the evil lust of life. Lust from its very nature is uncreative and opposed to creativeness. Creativeness is generous and sacrificial, it means giving one's powers, while lust wants everything for itself, is greedy, insatiable and vampirish. True love gives strength to the loved one, while love-lust vampirically absorbs another person's strength. Hence there is opposition both between lust and freedom, and between lust and creativeness. Lust is a perverted and inwardly weakened passion. Power is a creative force, but there is such a thing as the lust of power ; love is a sacrificial force, but there is also the lust of love.

The moral life of our sinful world is made up of paradoxes and contra-dictions. A man is tormented by pride and ambition when he is lower than others ; inaccessible heights lure him on and rouse a lustful desire in him. But when he is higher than the others, when he has attained the longed for pre-eminence, he is tormented by a sense of emptiness and futility. The same thing happens in sexual erotic life. A man suffers because he cannot possess the object of his sexual love, but when he gains possession he tires of it and life becomes dull and empty. All this indicates an uncreative and lustful direction of the will, not giving but taking, absorbing energy instead of radiating it. The greatest mystery of life is that satisfaction is felt not by those who take and make demands but by those who give and make sacrifices. In them alone the energy of life does not fail, and this is precisely what is meant by creativeness. Therefore the positive mystery of life is to be found in love, in sacrificial, giving, creative love. As has been said already, all creativeness is love and all love is creative. If you want to receive, give, if you want to obtain satisfaction, do not seek it, never think of it and forget the very word ; if you want to acquire strength, manifest it, give it to others. The presence of strength and energy does not by any means presuppose a belief in freedom of will. It is paradoxical that movements characterized by remarkable strength and energy, such for instance as Calvinism or Marxism, altogether reject the doctrine of free will. It is a rationalistic doctrine, concerned with judgment and reckoning. It is a product of reflection and dividedness. But true freedom is gracious energy.

The ethics of creativeness is the highest and most mature form of moral consciousness, and at the same time it is the morality of eternal youth. Creativeness is the youth of the soul and its power is bound up with the soul's virginity. The relation between spiritual youth and old age must not be interpreted chronologically. The morality of law is the morality of old age—and yet it is the earliest human morality. The ever-youthful nature of creative activity raises the question as to the relation between creativeness and development. Is creativeness a developed, an unfolded state? It may be said, paradoxical as it seems at first sight, that development and unfolding is the deadly enemy of creativeness and leads to its cooling down and drying up at the source. The highest point reached by creativeness is not the unfolding of results but the first flight of inspiration, its birth and virginal youth and not its final achievement. Development, unfolding, improvement, completion mean deterioration of creativeness, the cooling down of the creative fire, decay and old age. This can be seen in the fate of men of genius and of creative spiritual movements in history, in the fate of prophecy and holiness in the world, and of all inspirations, intuitions and original ideas. Early Christianity cannot be compared with the developed Christianity so far as the creative flame of the spirit is concerned. It is impossible to compare the prophets with those who were guided by prophecies, to compare the Franciscan order with the fire of love in St. Francis, the developed Protestantism of the seventeenth, eighteenth and nineteenth centuries, that has been influenced by Melancthon, with the fiery spirit of Luther. It is impossible to compare the cooled-down results of all the revolutions in the world with the burning enthusiasm in which they began. It is impossible to compare Marxists with Marx or Tolstoyans with Tolstoy, or any established system of thought with the fiery prophetic genius of its founders. It is impossible to compare the tepid love of middle-age with the ecstasy of its early beginning.

The essence of development and evolution is that it conceals first-hand intuitions and first origins of human feelings and ideas. It envelops and stifles them with secondary emotions and social constructions, making access to them almost impossible. This has happened to Christianity also, and herein lies its historical tragedy. This happens to every human feeling and idea. Development destroys creative youth, virginity and originality. That which was born in the free creative act is unrecognizable in its developed form. True life is creativeness and not development, freedom and not necessity, creative fire and not the gradual cooling down and fixation involved in the process of unfolding and perfecting. This truth has particular importance for moral life. Moral life must be eternal creativeness, free and fiery, i.e. perpetual youth and virginity of spirit. It must rest on primary intuitions free from the suggestions of man's social environment which paralyse the freedom of his moral judgments. But in actual life it is difficult to break through to this youth of the spirit. Most of our moral actions and judgments do not come from that primary source. The ethics of creativeness is not the ethics of development but of the youth and virginity of the human spirit, and it springs from the fiery first source of life—freedom. Therefore true morality is not the social morality of the herd.

3. THE PART OF IMAGINATION IN THE MORAL LIFE.
THE ETHICS OF ENERGY

The ethics of creativeness presupposes that the task which confronts man is infinite and the world is not completed. But the tragedy is that the realization of every infinite task is finite. Creative imagination is of fundamental importance to the ethics of creativeness. Without imagination there can be no creative activity. Creativeness means in the first instance imagining something different, better and higher. Imagination calls up before us something better than the reality around us. Creativeness always rises above reality. Imagination plays this part not only in art and in myth making, but also in scientific discoveries, technical inventions and moral life, creating a better type of relations between human beings.

The Ethics of Creativeness

There is such a thing as moral imagination which creates the image of a better life ; it is absent only from legalistic ethics.[1] No imagination is needed for automatically carrying out a law or norm. In moral life the power of creative imagination plays the part of talent. By the side of the self-contained moral world of laws and rules to which nothing can be added, man builds up in imagination a higher, free and beautiful world lying beyond ordinary good and evil. And this is what gives beauty to life. As a matter of fact life can never be determined solely by law ; men always imagine for themselves a different and better life, freer and more beautiful, and they realize those images. The Kingdom of God is the image of a full, perfect, beautiful, free and divine life. Only law has nothing to do with imagination, or, rather, it is limited to imagining compliance with, or violation of, its behests. But the most perfect fulfil-ment of the law is not the same as the perfect life.

Imagination may also be a source of evil ; there may be bad imagination and phantasms. Evil thoughts are an instance of bad imagination. Crimes are conceived in imagination. But imagination also brings about a better life. A man devoid of imagination is incapable of creative moral activity and of building up a better life. The very conception of a better life towards which we ought to strive is the result of creative imagination. Those who have no imagination think that there is no better life at all and there ought not to be. All that exists for them is the unalterable order of existence in which unalterable law ought to be realized. Jacob Boehme ascribed enormous importance to imagination.[2] The world is created by God through imagination, through images which arise in God in eternity and are both ideal and real. Modern psychologists and alienists also ascribe great importance to imagination, both good and bad. They have discovered that imagination plays an infinitely greater part in people's lives than has been thought hitherto. Diseases and psychoses arise through imagination and can also be cured through it. The ethics of law forbids man to imagine a better world and a better life, it fetters him to the world as given and to the socially organized herd life, laying down taboos and prohibitions everywhere. But the ethics of creativeness breaks with the herd-existence and refuses to recognize legalistic prohibitions. To the " law " of the present life it opposes " the image " of a higher one.

[1] See B. Vysheslavtsev's articles in *Put : Suggestion and Religion* and *The Ethics of Sublimation as the Victory over Moralism* (in Russian).

[2] See his *Mysterium magnum* and *De signatura Rerum*. A. Koyré emphasizes the part played by imagination in Boehme's philosophy. See his book, *La Philosophie de Jacob Boehme.*

The ethics of creativeness is the ethics of energy. Quantitative and qualitative increase in life's intensity and creative energy is one of the criteria of moral valuation. The good is like radium in spiritual life and its essential quality is radio-activity, inexhaustible radiation. The conceptions of energy and that of norm come into conflict in ethics. The morality of law and the morality of creative energy are perpetually at war. If the good is understood as a real force, it cannot be conceived as the purpose of life. A perfect and absolute realization of the good would make it unnecessary and lead us completely to forget moral distinctions and valuations. The nature of the good and of moral life presupposes dualism and struggle, i.e. a painful and difficult path. Complete victory over the dualism and the struggle leads to the disappearance of what, on the way, we had called good and moral. To realize the good is to cancel it. The good is not at all the final end of life and of being. It is only a way, only a struggle on the way. The good must be conceived of in terms of energy and not of purpose. The thing that matters most is the realization of creative energy and not the ideal normative end. Man realizes the good not because he has set himself the purpose of doing so but because he is good or virtuous, i.e. because he has in him the creative energy of goodness. The source is important and not the goal. A man fights for a good cause not because it is his conscious purpose to do so, but because he has combative energy and the energy of goodness. Goodness and moral life are a path in which the starting point and the goal coincide—it is the emanation of creative energy.

But from the ontological and cosmological point of view, the final end of being must be thought of as beauty and not as goodness. Plato defined beauty as the magnificence of the good. Complete, perfect and harmonious being is beauty. Teleological ethics is normative and legalistic. It regards the good as the purpose of life, i.e. as a norm or a law which must be fulfilled. Teleological ethics always implies absence of moral imagination, for it conceives the end as a norm and not as an image, not as a product of the creative energy of life. Moral life must be determined not by a purpose or a norm but by imagery and the exercise of creative activity. Beauty is the image of creative energy radiating over the whole world and transforming it. Teleological ethics based upon the idea of the good as an absolute purpose is hostile to freedom, but creative ethics is based upon freedom. Beauty means a transfigured creation, the good means creation fettered by the law which denounces sin. The paradox is that the law fetters the energy of the good, it does not want the good to be interpreted as a force, for in that case the world would escape from the power of the law. To transcend the morality of law means to put infinite creative energy in the place of commands, prohibitions, and taboos.

Instinct plays a twofold part in man's moral life : it dates back to ancient, primitive times, and ancient terror, slavishness, superstition, animalism and cruelty find expression in it ; but at the same time it is reminiscent of paradise, of primitive freedom and power, of man's ancient bond with the cosmos and the primeval force of life. Hence the attitude of the ethics of creativeness towards instincts is complex : it liberates instincts repressed by the moral law and at the same time struggles with them for the sake of a higher life. Instincts are repressed by the moral law, but since they have their origin in the social life of primitive clans, they themselves tend to become a law and to fetter the creative energy of life. Thus, for instance, the instinct of vengeance is, as has already been said, a heritage of the social life of antiquity and is connected with law. The ethics of creativeness liberates not all instincts but only creative ones, i.e. man's creative energy hampered by the prohibitions of the law. It also struggles against instincts and strives to sublimate them.

Teleological ethics, which is identical with the ethics of law, metaphysically presupposes the power of time in the bad sense of the word. Time is determined either by the idea of purpose which has to be realized in the future or by the idea of creativeness which is to be carried out in the future. In the first case, man is in the power of the purpose and of the time created by it, in the second he is the master of time for he realizes in it his creative energy. The problem of time is bound up with the ethics of creativeness. Time and freedom are the fundamental and the most painful of metaphysical problems. Heidegger, in his *Sein und Zeit*, formulates it in a new way, but he connects time with care and not with creativeness. There can be no doubt, however, that creativeness is connected with time. It is usually said that creativeness needs the perspective of the future and presupposes changes that take place in time. In truth, it would be more correct to say that movement, change, creativeness give rise to time. Thus we see that time has a double nature. It is the source both of hope and of pain and torture. The charm of the future is connected with the fact that the future may be changed and to some extent depends upon ourselves. But to the past we can do nothing, we can only remember it with reverence and gratitude or with remorse and indignation. The future may bring with it the realization of our desires, hopes and dreams. But it also inspires us with terror. We are tortured with anxiety about the unknown future. Thus the part of time which we call the future and regard as dependent upon our own activity may be determined in two ways. It may be determined by duty, by painful anxiety and a command to realize a set purpose, or by our creative energy, by a constructive vital impulse through which new values are coined. In the first case time oppresses us, we are in its power. The loftiest purpose projected into the future enslaves us, becomes external to us and makes us anxious. Anxiety is called forth not only by the lower material needs but also by the higher ideal ends. In the second case, when we are determined by the free creative energy, by our free vital force, we regard the future as immanent in us and are its masters. In time everything appears as already determined and necessary, and in our feeling of the future we anticipate this determinateness ; events to come appear sometimes to us as an impending fate. But a free creative act is not dominated by time, for it is not determined in any way : it springs from the depths of being, which are not subject to time, and belongs to a different order of existence. It is only later that everything comes to appear as determined in time. The task of the ethics of creativeness is to make the perspective of life independent of the fatal march of time, of the future which terrifies and torments us. The creative act is an escape from time, it is performed in the realm of freedom and not of necessity. It is by its very nature opposed to anxiety which makes time so terrible. And if the whole of the human life could be one continuous creative act, there would be no more time ; there would be no future as a part of time ; there would be movement out of time, in non-temporal reality. There would be no determination, no necessity, no binding laws. There would be the life of the spirit. In Heidegger reality subject to time is a fallen reality, though he does not make clear what was its state before the Fall. It is the realm of the " herd man ". It is connected with care for the future and anxiety. But Christ teaches us not to care about the future. " Enough for the day is the evil thereof." This is an escape from the power of time, from the nightmare of the future born of anxiety.

The future may or may not bring with it disappointment, suffering and misfortune. But certainly, and to everyone, it brings death. And fear of the future, natural to everyone, is in the first place fear of impending death. Death is determined for everyone in this world, it is our fate. But man's free and creative spirit rises against this slavery to death and fate. It has another vista of life, springing from freedom and creativeness. In and through Christ the fate of death is cancelled, although empirically every man dies. Our attitude to the future which ends for us in death is false because, being divided in ourselves, we analyse it and think of it as determined. But future is unknowable and cannot be subjected to analysis. Only prophecy is possible with regard to it, and the mystery of prophecy lies precisely in the fact that it has nothing to do with determinations and is not knowledge within the categories of necessity. For a free creative act there exist no fate and no predetermined future. At the moment when a free creative act takes place there is no thought of the future, of the inevitable death, of future suffering ; it is an escape from time and from all determinateness. In creative imagination the future is not determined. The creative image is outside the process of time, it is in eternity. Time is the child of sin, of sinful slavery, of sinful anxiety. It will stop and disappear when the world is transfigured. But transfiguration of the world is taking place already in all true creativeness. We possess a force by means of which we escape from time. That creative force is full of grace and saves us from the power of the law. The greatest moral task is to build up a life free from determinateness and anxiety about the future and out of the perspective of time. The moral freedom to do so is given us, but we make poor use of it.

Freedom requires struggle and resistance. We are therefore confronted with the necessarily determined everyday world in which processes are taking place in time and the future appears as fated. Man is fettered and weighed down. He both longs for freedom and fears it. The paradox of liberation is that in order to preserve freedom and to struggle for it, one must in a sense be already free, have freedom within oneself. Those who are slaves to the very core of their being do not know the name of freedom and cannot struggle for it. Ancient taboos surround man on all sides and fetter his moral life. In order to free himself from their power man must first be conscious of himself as inwardly free and only then can he struggle for freedom outwardly. The inner conquest of slavery is the fundamental task of moral life. Every kind of slavery is meant here—the slavery to the power of the past and of the future, the slavery to the external world and to oneself, to one's lower self. The awakening of creative energy is inner liberation and is accompanied by a sense of freedom.[1] Creativeness is the way of liberation. Liberation cannot result in inner emptiness—it is not merely liberation *from* something but also liberation *for the sake of* something. And this " for the sake of " is creativeness. Creativeness cannot be aimless and objectless. It is an ascent and therefore presupposes heights, and that means that creativeness rises from the world to God. It moves not along a flat surface in endless time but ascends towards eternity. The products of creativeness remain in time, but the creative act itself, the

[1] Maine de Biran justly connects freedom with inner effort.

creative flight, communes with eternity. Every creative act of ours in relation to other people—an act of love, of pity, of help, of peacemaking —not merely has a future but is eternal.

Victory over the categories of master and slave[1] in the moral life is a great achievement. A man must not be the slave of other men, nor must he be their master, for then other people will be slaves. To achieve this is one of the tasks of the ethics of creativeness which knows nothing of mastery and slavery. A creator is neither a slave nor a master, he is one who gives and gives abundantly. All dependence of one man upon another is morally degrading. It is incomprehensible how the slavish doctrine that a free and independent mind is forsaken by the divine grace could ever have arisen. Where the Spirit of God is, there is liberty. Where there is liberty, there is the Spirit of God and grace. Grace acts upon liberty and cannot act upon anything else. A slavish mind cannot receive grace and grace cannot affect it. But slavish theories which distort Christianity build up their conception of it not upon grace and liberty but upon mastery and slavery, upon the tyranny of society, of the family and the state. They generally recognize free will but only for the sake of urging it to obedience. Free will cannot, however, be called in merely to be threatened. The " freedom of will " which has frequently led to man's enslavement must itself be liberated, i.e. imbued with gracious force. Creativeness is the gracious force which makes free will really free, free from fear, from the law, from inner dividedness.

The paradox of good and evil—the fundamental paradox of ethics—is that the good presupposes the existence of evil and requires that it should be tolerated. This is what the Creator does in allowing the existence of evil. Hence absolute perfection, absolute order and rationality may prove to be an evil, a greater evil than the imperfect, unorganized, irrational life which admits of a certain freedom of evil. The absolute good incompatible with the existence of evil is possible only in the Kingdom of God, when there will be a new heaven and a new earth, and God will be all in all. But outside the Divine kingdom of grace, freedom and love, absolute good which does not allow the existence of evil is always a tyranny, the kingdom of the Grand Inquisitor and the antichrist. Ethics must recognize this once and for all. So long as there exists a distinction between good and evil, and consequently our good which is on this side of the distinction, there must inevitably be a struggle, a conflict between opposing principles, and resistance, i.e. exercise of human freedom. The absolute good and perfection outside the Kingdom of God turns man into an

[1] Hegel has some striking things to say about this category.

automaton of virtue, i.e. really abolishes moral life, since moral life is impossible without spiritual freedom.

Hence our attitude to evil must be twofold : we must be tolerant of it as the Creator is tolerant, and we must mercilessly struggle against it. There is no escaping from this paradox, for it is rooted in freedom and in the very fact of distinction between good and evil. Ethics is bound to be paradoxical because it has its source in the Fall. The good must be realized, but it has a bad origin. The only thing that is really fine about it is the recollection of the beauty of Paradise. Is the struggle waged in the name of the good in this world an expression of the true life, " first life "? Is it not bound by earthly surroundings and is it not only a means to life? And how can " first life ", life in itself, be attained? We may say with certainty that *love* is life-in-itself, and so is *creativeness*, and so is the *contemplation* of the spiritual world. But this life-in-itself is absent from a considerable part of our legalistic morality, from physiological processes, from politics and from civilization. " First life " or life-in-itself is to be found only in the first-hand, free moral acts and judgments. It is absent from moral acts which are determined by social environment, heredity, public opinion, party doctrines, etc., i.e. it is absent from a great part of our moral life. True life is only to be found in moral acts in so far as they are creative. Automatic fulfilment of the moral law is not life. Life is always an expansion, a gain. It is present in first-hand aesthetic perceptions and judgments and in a creatively artistic attitude to the world, but not in aesthetic snobbishness.

Nietzsche thought that morality was dangerous because it hindered the realization of the higher type of man. This is true of legalistic morality, which does not allow the human personality to express itself as a whole. In Christianity itself legalistic elements are unfavourable to the creative manifestation of the higher type of man. The morality of chivalry, of knightly honour and loyalty, was creative and could not be subsumed under the ethics of law or the ethics of redemption. And in spite of the relative, transitory and even bad characteristics which chivalry has had as a matter of historical fact, it contained elements of permanent value and was a manifestation of the eternal principles of the human personality. Chivalry would have been impossible without Christianity.

Nietzsche opposes to the distinction between good and evil, which he regards as a sign of decadence, the distinction between the noble and the low. The noble, the fine, is a higher type of life, aristocratic, strong, beautiful, well-bred. The conception of " fineness " is ontological while that of goodness is moralistic. This leads not to a-moralism which is a misleading conception, but to the subordination of moral categories to the ontological. It means that the important thing is not to fulfil the moral law but to perfect one's nature, i.e. to attain transfiguration and enlightenment. From this point of view the saint must be described as "fine" and not as "good", for he has a lofty, beautiful nature penetrated by the divine light through and through. But all Nietzsche knew of Christianity was the moral law, and he rebelled against it. He had quite a mistaken idea about the spirit and spiritual life. He thought that a bad conscience was born of the conflict between the instincts and the behests of the society—just as Freud, Adler, and Jung suppose. The instinct turns inwards and becomes spirit. Spirit is the repressed, inward-driven instinct, and therefore really an epiphenomenon. The true, rich, un-repressed life is for Nietzsche not spirit and indeed is opposed to it. Nietzsche is clearly the victim of reaction against degenerate legalistic Christianity and against the bad spirituality which in truth has always meant suppression of the spirit. Nietzsche mistook it for the true spirituality. He rejected God because he thought God was incompatible with creativeness and creative heroism to which his philosophy was a call. God was for him the symbol not of man's ascent to the heights but of his remaining on a flat surface below. Nietzsche was fighting not against God but against a false conception of God, which certainly ought to be combated. The idea, so widely spread in theology, that the existence of God is incompatible with man's creativeness is a source of atheism. And Nietzsche waged an agonizing struggle against God. He went further and asserted that spirit is incompatible with creativeness. while in truth spirit is the only source of creativeness. In this connection, too, Nietzsche's attitude was inspired by a feeling of protest. Theology systematically demanded that man should bury his talents in the ground. It failed to see that the Gospel required creativeness of man and confined its attention to commands and laws ; it failed to grasp the meaning of parables and of the call to freedom ; it sought to know only the revealed and not the hidden. Theologians have not sufficiently understood that freedom should not be forced, repressed and burdened with commands and prohibitions. Rather it ought to be enlightened, transfigured and strengthened through the power of grace. A curious paradox is exemplified in the teaching of the Jesuits.[1] Jesuitism is in a sense an apotheosis of the human will : a man may increase the power of God. Jesuitism teaches a new form of asceti-

---

[1] See an interesting book by Fülop Müller, *Macht und Geheimnis der Jesuiten*. The author is not a Catholic, but his book is a curious apology for the Jesuits and contains instances of subtle psychological analysis.

cism—asceticism of the will and not of the body. It takes heaven by storm and gains power over the world. And at the same time Jesuitism means slavery of the will and a denial of man's creativeness. The real problem of creativeness, so far from being formulated and solved by Christianity, has not even been faced in all its religious implications. It has only been considered as the problem of justifying culture, i.e. on a secondary plane, and not as the question of the relation between God and man. The result is rebellion and rejection of the dominant theological theories.

Human nature may contract or expand. Or, rather, human nature is rooted in infinity and has access to boundless energy. But man's consciousness may be narrowed down and repressed. Just as the atom contains enormous and terrible force which can only be released by splitting the atom (the secret of it has not yet been discovered), so the human monad contains enormous and terrible force which can be released by melting down consciousness and removing its limits. In so far as human nature is narrowed down by consciousness it becomes shallow and unreceptive. It feels cut off from the sources of creative energy. What makes man interesting and significant is that his mind has so to speak an opening into infinity. But average normal consciousness tries to close this opening, and then man finds it difficult to manifest all his gifts and resources of creative energy. The principles of *laisser faire*, so false in economics, contains a certain amount of truth in regard to moral and spiritual life. Man must be given a chance to manifest his gifts and creative energy, he must not be overwhelmed with external commands and have his life encumbered with an endless number of norms and prohibitions.

It is a mistake to think that a cult of creativeness means a cult of the future and of the new. True creativeness is concerned neither with the old nor with the new but with the eternal. A creative act directed upon the eternal may, however, have as its product and result something new, i.e. something projected in time. Newness in time is merely the projection or symbolization of the creative process which takes place in the depths of eternity.[1] Creativeness may give one bliss and happiness, but that is merely a consequence of it. Bliss and happiness are never the aim of creativeness, which brings with it its own pain and suffering. The human spirit moves in two directions : towards struggle and towards contemplation. Creativeness takes place both in struggle and in contemplation. There is a restless element in it, but contemplation is the moment of rest. It is impossible to separate and to oppose the two elements. Man is called

[1] See my book, *Freedom and the Spirit*.

The Destiny of Man

to struggle and to manifest his creative power, to win a regal place in nature and in cosmos. And he is also called to the mystic contemplation of God and the spiritual worlds. By comparison with active struggle contemplation seems to us passive and inactive. But contemplation of God is creative activity. God cannot be won through active struggle similar to the struggle we wage with cosmic elements. He can only be contemplated through creatively directing our spirit upwards. The contemplation of God Who is love is man's creative answer to God's call. Contemplation can only be interpreted as love, as the ecstasy of love—and love always is creative. This contemplation, this ecstasy of love, is possible not only in relation to God and the higher world but also in relation to nature and to other people. I contemplate in love the human faces I love and the face of nature, its beauty. There is something morally repulsive about modern activistic theories which deny contemplation and recognize nothing but struggle. For them not a single moment has value in itself, but is only a means for what follows. The ethics of creativeness is an ethics of struggle and contemplation, of love both in the struggle and in the contemplation. By reconciling the opposition between love and contemplation it reconciles the opposition between aristocratic and democratic morality. It is an ethics both of ascent and of descent. The human soul rises upwards, ascends to God, wins for itself the gifts of the Holy Spirit and strives for spiritual aristocratism. But it also descends into the sinful world, shares the fate of the world and of other men, strives to help its brothers and gives them the spiritual energy acquired in the upward movement of the soul. One is inseparable from the other. Proudly to forsake the world and men for the lofty heights of the spirit and refuse to share one's spiritual wealth with others is un-Christian, and implies a lack of love, and also a lack of creativeness, for creativeness is generous and ready to give. This was the limitation of pre-Christian spirituality. Plato's Eros is ascent without descent, i.e. an abstraction. The same is true of the Indian mystics. But it is equally un-Christian and uncreative completely to merge one's soul in the world and humanity and to renounce spiritual ascent and acquisition of spiritual force. And when the soul takes up a tyrannical attitude towards nature and mankind, when it wants to dominate and not to be a source of sacrificial help and regeneration, it falls prey to one of the darkest instincts of the subconscious and inevitably undermines its own creative powers, for creativeness presupposes sacrifice. Victory over the subconscious instinct of tyranny is one of the most fundamental moral tasks. People ought to be brought up from childhood in a spirit completely opposed to the instincts of tyranny which exhaust and destroy creative energy. Tyranny finds expression in personal relations, in family life, in social and political organizations and in spiritual and religious life.

Three new factors have appeared in the moral life of man and are acquiring an unprecedented significance. Ethics must take account of three new objects of human striving. Man has come to love *freedom* more than he has ever loved it before, and he demands freedom with extraordinary persistence. He no longer can or wants to accept anything unless he can accept it freely. Man has grown more *compassionate* than before. He cannot endure the cruelty of the old days, he is pitiful in a new way to every creature—not only to the least of men but also to animals and to everything that lives. A moral consciousness opposed to pity and compassion is no longer tolerable. And, finally, man is more eager than ever before *to create*. He wants to find a religious justification and meaning for his creativeness. He can no longer endure having his creative instinct repressed either from without or from within. At the same time other instincts are at work in him, instincts of slavery and cruelty, and he shows a lack of creativeness which leads him to thwart it and deny its very existence. And yet the striving for freedom, compassion and creativeness is both new and eternal. Therefore the new ethics is bound to be an ethics of *freedom*, *compassion* and *creativeness*.

CHAPTER FOUR

Concrete Problems of Ethics

1. THE TRAGIC AND PARADOXICAL CHARACTER
OF THE MORAL LIFE

IN dealing with concrete problems of ethics it must be remembered that the difficulty of solving them is bound up with the tragic and paradoxical character of the moral life. As has already been said, the tragedy lies not in the conflict between good and evil, the divine and the diabolical, but in the conflict between different kinds of good and value—between the love of God and the love of man, the love of one's country and of one's nearest and dearest, the love of science or art and the love and pity for men, and so on. A moral value in the narrow sense of the word comes into conflict with a cognitive or aesthetic value, a personal value with a superpersonal national one, etc. The love of knowledge or of art, or of one's country or of civilization, has a moral value and must be recognized as a good, if the good be understood in the full sense of the term. A man is bound to be cruel because he is confronted with the necessity of sacrificing one value for the sake of another—for instance, of sacrificing his family for the sake of his country or of the struggle for social justice, or of sacrificing patriotic or social activity for the sake of artistic or scientific work. A man may sacrifice his artistic or intellectual calling for the sake of religious values, ascetic discipline and greater personal perfection, or he may sacrifice the pursuit of personal perfection for the sake of being a poet or a philosopher. The life of love is full of such tragic conflicts. The most terrible thing is to have to sacrifice one kind of love for the sake of another. Sometimes a man sacrifices a love which he regards as the greatest good and value for the sake of a value of a different order—for the sake of remaining true to a peculiar conception of freedom, or of family affections, or out of pity for other people who suffer from this love. And on the other hand a man may sacrifice the unquestionable values of his freedom, his work in the world, his family and his compassion for others for the sake of the infinite value of love. The important point is that no law or norm can help to solve a moral conflict of that kind. The greatest liberty is given man in solving the moral conflicts which make life so difficult. Man is left free not only to act worse or better but also to decide for himself what is worse and what is better. The law does not recognize tragedy, it knows only the categories of good and evil. Hence a legalistic solution of tragic conflicts is impossible. If life were limited to the categories of law, there would be no tragedy, for although the struggle between good and evil may be very painful it is not in itself tragic.

The problem is greatly complicated by the fact that the conflict is between values which are called moral and values which are not recognized as moral, e.g. cognitive, aesthetic or erotic. Legalistic ethics settles the question very simply : if there is a conflict between moral duty and love, even if that love has a high moral value, love ought to be sacrificed to duty ; if there is a conflict of a purely moral value with creative vocation in art and science, the creative vocation must be sacrificed for the sake of the purely moral duty. Thus the domain of the "moral" is very much narrowed down and life is fettered by law. The ethics of creativeness which has passed through the ethics of redemption takes a different view of life and its purpose. The tragic conflicts of life are solved for it through man's creative freedom, and the domain of the "moral" is widened, i.e. moral significance is attached to things which are not generally regarded as forming part of moral values. Thus, for instance, the question of man's creative vocation in art or in science acquires a moral significance. At the same time religious values connected with eternal salvation and the attainment of perfection cease to form a realm of their own, from which they dominate as it were the rest of existence, but become extended to life as a whole and are seen to form its deepest foundation. If a man is conscious of himself as a free and creative spirit, he will make the solution of the tragic conflicts of life depend upon his freedom and creativeness and not upon a uniform and universally binding law. He will sacrifice one value for the sake of another. But his solution will not be binding upon others who may do the very opposite. In such cases one person can claim no superiority over another. The moral law is concerned with elementary, straightforward situations—do not kill, do not steal, do not indulge in vice, etc., and its injunctions are the same for all men. The law may say that no one ought to be cruel, but it knows nothing of cases in which a man is bound to be cruel because it is inevitable that he should sacrifice one value for the sake of another. "Do not kill" is an absolute norm, the same for all men ; but sometimes a man has to take upon himself the sin of killing so that there should be less killing in the world and that the highest values might be preserved.

But the pure element of tragedy is so lost in the complexity of life, so mixed up with other elements, that it is not easy to detect it. In the tragedies of life there is a great deal of what is conventional, temporal and transitory, connected with social norms and institutions, with false beliefs and superstitions. The tragedy then lies in the conflict between the social law and the personality struggling for the higher values. Such, e.g., is the tragedy of Antigone—Antigone defends against the law of the community her right to give burial to her brother, which is her religious duty. Yet the tragedy in this case springs not from the eternal source of life but from conflict with social institutions. The tragedy of Hamlet is connected with the ancient belief that blood vengeance is a moral duty and is rooted in the fact that Hamlet has outgrown this belief. The instinct of vengeance was weakened in him by reflection ; thought had too great a power over his life. Christianity has greatly intensified the tragic contradictions of life, for it came into conflict with man's primitive instincts and ancient beliefs that had degenerated into superstitions. Consciousness, which has brought a new faith with it, is in conflict with instinct, which is the old faith plunged into the subconscious. It is difficult to realize Christian righteousness in life because it runs counter both to our deep primeval instincts and to values which we find difficult to renounce.

The pure and eternal element of tragedy can only be revealed when man is completely free from the temporal conditions of social life, from prejudices and superstitious fears. We have pure tragedy when a free personality is confronted with a choice between conflicting values. Moral life is overlaid with social conventions which lead to difficulties that have nothing to do with the nature of the tragic as such. If love comes into conflict with social institutions that fetter man, and the tragedy is due to the impossibility of obtaining a divorce, to fear of public opinion, etc., it is not an instance of the pure and eternal element of tragedy. The only really tragic element in it is the eternal conflict between the individual and society. But there is something tragic in love itself and not in its conflict with the transitory and temporal social environment. The love of Tristan and Isolde or of Romeo and Juliet contains an element of the eternal tragedy of love which lies in the connection between love and death, but it is complicated and concealed by the conflict with the social environment. Love contains an eternal tragic element which has nothing to do with social forms but is mysteriously and indissolubly connected with death. It would be present if there were only two loving hearts in the world. There is tragedy in unrequited love, but perhaps even more in love that is returned. This is seen at the deepest level of love when all social obstacles are removed. Pure tragedy arises when people are completely free and when a conflict of values takes place between the value of love and the value of freedom or of creative vocation, or of the higher value of the love of God and divine perfection, or when one has to defend the eternal god-like image of man which is connected with love, though sometimes love may be a danger to it. Enmity is disclosed in the depths of love. Too often people are afraid to open their hearts out of wrong instincts, false beliefs, false fears of society, and this prevents the possibility of true intercommunion. Man's life is poisoned by atavistic terrors. Liberation from them is a great moral task ; yet it brings with it not only joy but new tragedies.

The purely spiritual and moral problems of life arise only when man is outwardly free. Then the tragedy is no longer in the conflict of personality with its social environment but is transferred to the inner spiritual life. A free man, whose moral judgments are not dictated by the community in which he lives, is faced with an inner conflict of values and with the necessity of making a free and creative choice. And sometimes he feels he would welcome the social compulsion, for then the inner strain would be less intense. Such is the difference between the inner and the outer tragedy. Of course, external tragedy dependent upon social forms and relations has an inner aspect as well, for man is a social being and is bound to live in the community. But this is not the final depth of tragedy. Man's struggle for inward freedom and for liberation from the fetters of the state, the society and social customs may be tragic ; but the real tragedy of the human spirit, soluble only by the gracious power of God, takes place when man is completely free. In true tragedy man appeals not to society but to God, calling to Him *de profundis*. Hence man's liberation from social forms which oppress and enslave him has an enormous moral and religious significance and puts before him the moral and religious problem in its pure form. Man's liberation from social oppression shows that the pain and suffering of life is not due to social causes and cannot be cured by them. Herein lies the paradox of the relations between the individual and society. Life becomes outwardly less tragic as a result of liberation from social fetters and prejudices, but inwardly its eternally tragic nature is deepened and intensified. Man's social liberation shows how false, superficial and illusory are all social dreams and utopias. This does not mean of course that one must not struggle for social liberation. One must struggle for it if only in order to reveal the depths of life and its inner conflicts ; liberation thus acquires a spiritual, religious and moral significance. Thus the object of freeing love from social fetters, prejudices and restrictions is not to enable people to enjoy love and satisfy their desires, but to reveal love's inner tragedy, depth and earnestness. It is the same in everything, It is true of all freedom. For freedom is not satisfaction, delight and ease, but pain, toil and difficulty. A time must come in the life of man when he will take upon himself the burden of freedom, for he will come spiritually of age. In freedom life will be harder, more tragic and fuller of responsibility. The ethics of freedom is stern and demands heroism.

I have already spoken about the fundamental paradox of the struggle between good and evil : struggle with evil perpetually generates new evils—intolerance, fanaticism, violence, cruelty, evil feelings. In their struggle with " the wicked " the virtuous are often wicked too. The love of the good and constant striving for it makes men spiteful, hard and merciless towards their fellows.[1] Love of the good and a merciless attitude to evil leads to pharisaism. Moral hypocrisy springs from the same source. But when men are " shamefully indifferent to good and evil ", when they are too tolerant and broad-minded and renounce moral struggle, the result is demoralization and decadence. There is something truly tragic in the fact that the reaction of righteousness against unrighteousness may result in fresh evil. And yet this is the case. The Gospel alone understands this and points out new ways, unintelligible to the law. It tells us to love our enemies, not to condemn others ; it says that sinners and publicans go before the others into the Kingdom of Heaven, that man is higher than the Sabbath, and so on. We have already seen that the Gospel morality alone breaks through the vicious circle in the struggle between good and evil, the virtuous and the wicked. The tragedy of morality is that moral consciousness cannot conquer cruelty, greed, fear, envy and so on, for all these states have a way of coming to life again under the guise of the good. The virtuous in their virtue may be cruel, greedy, envious, trembling with fear. This brings us up against the problem of the good. We cannot break through to the other side of good and evil, as Nietzsche would have us do, for we are trapped by the same evil as on this side of the distinction, and we cannot remain entirely on this side of the good, for that good easily degenerates into evil. Ethics must recognize to the full that human life is the arena of the tragic conflict between good and good, between conflicting goods and values. Both good and evil can assume contradictory forms. The good may prove to be a hidden form of evil. The evil may prove to be a new and not yet recognized form of the good. The good does a great deal of harm in family life, in the state, in economic relations, in social customs. Those who rebel against it may bring about the realization of new forms of the good.

[1] Max Scheler speaks very well about this.

The problematic nature of the good leads in the first place to the rejection of *a priori* ethics, *a priori* principles of morality, which are utterly incompatible with the ethics of creativeness. Moral valuations and actions are based upon spiritual and moral experience. Ethics is based upon experience, not, of course, as rationalistic empiricism understands the term, but upon experience as the fullness of spiritual life. And that experience teaches us that relations between good and evil are complex and paradoxical, that we must both struggle against evil and treat it with tolerance that we must be merciless to it and yet allow it a certain amount of freedom. We have learnt the bitter lesson that the most merciless to evil and to the wicked, the most fanatical champions of the good and the true, are by no means the most good and righteous. In the name of the highest values, of truth, faith, righteousness and God, men become cruel, hard, heartless, pitiless, incapable of understanding other people or of having sympathy with anyone. We constantly find this among people wholly devoted to their religious ideas.

Only freedom from tyranny and external compulsion puts the moral problem before us in all its purity. But at this point, too, we come up against a fundamental paradox. If for the sake of realizing the pure form of moral life we strive for a perfect social and political order in which perfect freedom is to be realized in a new way, we come into conflict with the very essence of human liberty and may deprive moral life of all meaning. In the utopias of the perfect social order man's moral experience and his free moral efforts prove impossible and unnecessary. The perfect man is automatically created by the perfect social order in which no immoral acts are either admissible or possible. This is the same old paradox of evil in a new form. Evil must be possible if good is to be possible. Such is the world on this side of good and evil, i.e. the world after the Fall. The paradox of evil is the paradox of liberty. And here we come upon another moral tragedy. Man's moral life and activity is a striving for perfect life. The moral act in its purity presupposes complete freedom from external violence and compulsion. But in the perfect social order, in which there will be no violence or compulsion of any kind and it will be impossible to do evil, man's moral activity will be unnecessary and impossible. Such is the paradox of freedom. Man must be free and must struggle for his liberation. But freedom needs resistance and presupposes struggle. In a politically free community a man may be far from free in spirit ; he may be reduced to a dead level, enslaved by society and public opinion ; he may have lost his originality and in his moral life be determined from without and not from within. Complete socialization of man, and regulation of the whole of human culture, involved in the idea of a perfect social order, may lead to a new and complete enslavement of personality. And in the name of personality and its birthright of freedom it will be necessary to struggle against this perfect socialization. It is so already in democratic communities and will be still more so in socialistic communities. It does not follow, of course, that one must not struggle for the realization of social justice. But social justice is unthinkable without spiritual justice, without spiritual change and regeneration. For moral consciousness there always exists an irreducible conflict between the individual and the society, the individual and the family, the individual and the state, and between one individual and another.

There is always a tragic conflict between the personal and the social morality. Religious values come into opposition with political and national values, love for an individual, with the love for creative work, and so on. No set, rationalistic, standardized solution of these conflicts is possible. The good is realized through contradictions, sacrifices and suffering. The good is paradoxical. The moral life is tragic, for the very appearance of the distinction between good and evil was a terrible tragedy. There will always be a fundamental contradiction between social and personal morality, the morality of the genus and of the creative personality. Equally fundamental is the contradiction between ends and means. Means prove to be contrary to ends and absorb the whole of life. A man may strive for freedom as an end and be so engrossed in repression as a means to that end that he forgets about freedom. A man may strive for love and brotherhood as an end but be so engrossed in hatred and dissension as a means to it that he forgets about love and brotherhood. For the sake of truth people have recourse to falsehood, for the sake of salvation they torture heretics and burn them at the stake. The means are morally heterogeneous to the ends. Tolstoy suffered acutely from the tragic contradiction between ends and means ; in that he was on the side of truth, though he never found a solution. The contradiction can only be solved through gracious and creative love for living beings.

2. ON TRUTH AND FALSEHOOD

Ethics has not paid sufficient attention to the monstrously big part played by falsehood in man's moral and spiritual life. What is meant here is not the falsehood which is regarded as an expression of wickedness, but falsehood which is morally sanctioned as good. People do not believe that the good may be preserved and established without the aid of falsehood. The good is the end, the lies are the means. In the nineteenth century Tolstoy, Ibsen, Nietzsche and Kierkegaard passionately protested against the falsity of our moral life. The religious life of mankind, and perhaps of Christendom in particular, is permeated with falsity. Falsity has received an almost dogmatic significance. I am not speaking here of external falsity which is obvious and easily condemned. I mean the inner, hidden falsity, falsity to oneself and to God which eludes detection and comes to be regarded as a virtue. There is a kind of falsity which is considered a moral and religious duty, and those who reject it are said to be rebels. There exist social accumulations of falsity which have become part of the established order of things. This is connected with the essential character of moral perception and judgment—with the absence of what I call first-hand moral acts. Conventional, as it were, socially organized falsity clusters round all social groupings, such as the family, the class, the party, the church, the nation, the state. Such conventional falsity is a means of self-preservation for these institutions ; truth might lead to their break up. The conventional falsity of socially organized groups (I include among them schools of thought and ideological tendencies) deprives man of the freedom of moral perception and moral judgment. The moral judgment is made not by a free personality in the presence of God, but by the family, the class, the nation, the party, the denomination, etc. This does not imply that in order to make truthful, free and first-hand moral judgments a man must be cut off from all social and super-personal unities —from his family, his people, his church, and so on ; it means that he must consider at first hand, in the light of his own conscience, the judgments of the social groups which influence him and separate truth from falsity in them. Our conscience is confused and polluted not only because of the original sin, but because we belong to various social units, which find falsity more useful than truth for purposes of self-preservation. What an amount of conventional falsity accumulates in family life ! And it is regarded as essential for its existence and self-preservation. How many true feelings are concealed, how many false ones expressed, how conventionally false the relations between parents and children, husbands and wives often are ! Hypocrisy acquires the character of a family virtue. What never finds expression in consciousness, or does so in quite a misleading and inintelligible way, is stored up in the subconscious.

Falsity has its own symbolism, and that symbolism is regarded as something good. When a lie acquires the character of a social symbol it is always regarded as good. It is considered evil only so long as it is individual. The social lies have come to be regarded as truths. Such lies are to be found in the socially organized judgments of all denominations—in the judgments of the Catholics about the Orthodox, of the Orthodox about the Catholics, of Christians about non-Christians and *vice versa*. The amount of these lies is truly terrifying. It is almost impossible to get at the truth, at the pure, free, first-hand, original judgments. A Catholic has to speak of Luther in a certain way, although it is against his conscience and his own free judgment ; and he is not even aware of this, for his conscience is socially organized and completely permeated with the conventionally useful lies. Exactly the same must be said about the Protestants, the Orthodox and people of other denominations. An incredible amount of falsity has accumulated in all the denominational histories of Christianity, systematically distorting the historical truth. The whole of the Roman Catholic account of Papacy is based upon conventional lies and falsification which serve to create the myth of Papalism.[1] There is a conventional social falsity in the judgments of the Orthodox about the separation of the Churches, of the Protestants about the Reformation and so on, and so on.

Science tries to free itself from conventional lies and preconceived ideas whether they be religious, philosophical, social or national ; it seeks for pure, unadorned truth, however bitter truth might be. Such is the great task of science. But what an amount of falsity accumulates round science ! A new denomination of Scientism has been created and the greatest values are sacrificed to the new idol. Men of science struggling against faith, against Christianity, against God, imagining that in doing so they serve truth and justice. The freedom of scientific thought degenerates into freethinking, i.e. into a new kind of dogmatism. And this new dogmatism makes use of conventional lies for its own purposes. Academicians, professors, scientists are certainly not the type of men free from preconceived ideas and conventional falsity which is widely used by socially organized science. Scientists stand in superstitious awe of science and frequently prove to be its slaves and not its masters. Their judgments do not spring from a free and clear source. There is a conventional public opinion in the world of science, very tyrannical and destructive of the freedom of judgment. The conventional falsity of judgments passed by people of one nationality upon those of another or by members of one class upon those of a different class is known only too well. That falsity has been accumulating in the national and class consciousness for centuries and has come to

[1] I am far from wishing to minimize the enormous significance of Papalism for the history of Western Christianity.

be regarded as good and true. There is no need to point out that almost the whole of politics and the relations between political parties are based on falsity. The same must be said of judgments inspired by a definite school of thought. Marxists, idealists, positivists, Thomists, Tolstoyans, theosophists, all are influenced by conventional lies of their own in judging about other trends of thought ; they have no pure, free perception and judgment. The same must be said of tendencies in art and literature— classicism and romanticism, realism and symbolism. In aesthetic valuations snobbishness plays a simply incredible part. An aesthete is a creature devoid of all freedom of perception and judgment. A school of art creates conventional falsity of its own. An overwhelming amount of conventional falsity is accumulated in the family, the nation, the state, the church, in history, morality, art and science. They all have a conventional rhetoric which is false and means severance from the original sources of being. People have managed to convert the Christian revelation itself into conventional rhetoric, thus throwing doubt upon its truth. So-called " public opinion " is based upon conventional falsity and uses lies as a means to impose itself on people. Every social fashion is a conventional lie.

Lying is considered useful for organizing and preserving the life of the community and performs a social function. This is the tragedy of the problem of falsity. Falsity is pragmatically justified, while truth is often regarded as dangerous and harmful. The most lofty ideas acquire the character of conventional falsity. There exists a conventionally false rhetoric of love, of justice, of learning ; there is such a thing as a conventionally rhetorical attitude to the idea of God. From the spiritual depths of the human nature a protest is raised in the name of pure truth and reality against conventional falsity, rhetoric and false idealization. There arises a longing for ontological truthfulness, a desire to break through to freedom and purity of judgment—to what I should call *original and virginal conscience*. Sometimes it takes rhe form of a return to nature from the falsity of civilization, but in truth it is a return to God. Only the pure, free and original conscience stands in the presence of God, and its judgments alone are authentic. The will to originality is not the will to be peculiar and unlike anybody else ; it means the desire to derive one's consciousness from its primary source.

A morally justified falsity converted into a virtue is the fruit of utilitarianism, and utilitarianism was concerned with heaven before it came down to earth. The heavenly utilitarianism, so strongly marked in theology, chronologically precedes the earthly, but logically the heavenly utilitarianism is a reflection of the earthly. Utilitarian morality is built on the pattern of the heavenly utilitarianism, which regards good works and love of one's neighbour as a means for the salvation of the soul and the attainment of the bliss of paradise. But a heavenly utilitarianism of this kind was simply the old earthly utilitarianism translated into the terms of infinity. It is a form of hedonism, and not an ethics of values. But the introduction of hedonistic and utilitarian motive into morality always leads to falsity and transforms falsity into a good, since it may be useful for attaining happiness and bliss. There are two types of morality : the transcendentally utilitarian which regards everything as a means to an end external to the actual attainment of the spiritual good, and the immanently spiritual which regards everything from the point of view of spiritual quality. In the first case there is inevitably a hiatus and a lack of resemblance between means and ends. Truth is the end, and falsity is the means. But a hiatus between ends and means in ethics is not permissible of only because morality is the way of life and not the final end. Hence utilitarian ethics, whether earthly or heavenly, wrongly teaches both about the means and the end. Welfare, happiness, bliss, is certainly not the end of life, and a useful lie or useful violence is certainly not the means for realizing that end. Falsity is the child of fear and anxiety. One of the main problems of ethics is to overcome the dualism between means and ends, and make the means more and more conformable to ends. The discrepancy between ends and means comes about in two ways. On the one hand, people may be so engrossed in their purpose, in the attainment of some good—the good of the state, the nation, the family, the earthly church, the civilization—that they are ready to use any means to bring it about. On the other hand, people may be so taken up with the means that they forget their end. Both these things are constantly happening in politics. Politics is the sphere in which the discrepancy between ends and means reaches its maximum ; it therefore admits of the greatest falsity. Thus parliament is a means for bringing about public welfare which is supposed to be the aim of democracy. But parliamentarianism with its rival parties, each of which strives for power, applies false means to achieve its ends at any cost and at the same time forgets those ends and becomes an end in itself. Parliamentary politics are permeated with lies which are essential for securing the majority of votes at elections. Power is a means of realizing the good of the state, of the nation, of civilization, of humanity. But power always tends to become an end in itself and to replace all other ends. The approximation between ends and means takes place in the wrong way, through substituting the bad means for an end. Monarchy and socialism are alike in severing ends from means, in taking means for ends and using lies for the realization of their ends. The original end is public welfare, the secondary end is power which at first had been only a means. The same thing happens with every bureaucracy : it is essentially a means, but tends to become an end in itself. Opportunism and a fanatical pursuit of ends regardless of means results in falsity which comes to be regarded as good and obligatory. The Russian communists have created a whole system of lying which they regard as a moral duty, since the object of it is the realization of world-communism and the preservation of their own power which has become an end in itself. The tragic part of it all is that falsity, lying, cruelty are practised both for the sake of ends which are regarded as supreme and by way of means which are regarded as necessary and, in the process, come to replace the ends. In this way a fictitious environment is created and hypocrisy ceases to be a sin, but becomes a duty. What is horrible is not the lying which is recognized as a sin, but the lying which is taken to be a virtue. The life of the state, of the family, of individual people and of our civilization as a whole, is full of lying and hypocrisy. It is the moving power of monarchy, democracy, aristocracy, bureaucracy, the bourgeoisie and the proletariat. One set of lies replaces another. The same thing is true of parties, political movements and schools of thoughts. The cause of this is to be found not merely in the severance between ends and means, but in the fact that the teleological point of view which regards the end as something external to man's spiritual life is itself false. In the spiritual life there is no distinction and opposition between ends and means. The essential thing is of what spirit a man is, from what source he draws the creative force of life. In other words, the important point is what man himself is like, what his nature is. If he is bad, if he is not of God's spirit, no lofty aims will improve him and he will always apply bad means, substituting them for ends. Men may torture and destroy others, be tyrannical and suppress freedom of the spirit in the name of God, in the name of truth and justice. And those whose aim is to destroy evil in others are frequently themselves full of evil. Lofty Platonism (as an end) and low materialism (as a means) in politics have been equally dangerous and resulted in evil, falsehood and misery.

Only the qualitative attainments of the spiritual life lead to the affirmation of truth and to victory over falsity. This is precisely because in the spiritual realm there are no " ends " for the sake of which one may and ought to lie, and no " means " for the sake of which one might forget about " ends " and turn falsity into a virtue. Love of truth is the fundamental ontological virtue, the first of virtues. Above all, be truthful to

God, to yourself and to other people. This is the beginning of the moral life, i.e. of discrimination between moral realities and of living among realities and not among fictions. The devil is a liar and the father of lies, he is the falsification of reality and his kingdom is the kingdom of falsity, It is therefore essential to build up an ethic of ontological truthfulness, to seek in everything for what is primary, first-hand, original, i.e. to seek for the source of life and power. Evil is evil solely because it is falsehood, untruth, non-being.

The question of truth and falsehood in the moral life is envisaged here on a totally different plane than is done for instance by Kant, who does not allow a most innocent lie for the sake of saving a person's life, and falls into legalistic pedantry. The problem of truth and falsity is ontological and not formal and legalistic, and it cannot be solved by moral pedantry. The source of falsity is the herd-mind (Heidegger's *das Man*). The deliberate falsity and hypocrisy of the herd-morality extend to the most intimate aspects of life, leaving out of account both the human soul and the Divine spirit. The herd-morality, concerned with masses and averages, prevents the upward flight of the soul and adapts everything to its own purposes—love, mystical experience and creativeness. It allows only the universally binding, the average, the conventional. It not only puts up with socially useful falsity, but actually demands it and makes it a norm of communal existence, cutting man off from the first sources of life. The herd-mentality distorts and perverts religious revelation and turns Christianity into a religion of the law. Mystical experience, love and creativeness are not a part of the herd-life, but the church, the family and civilization are. This is a profound tragedy. It is impossible simply to renounce the herd-life. That life is the consequence of man's fall into the sinful world, the world of falsity. And the final victory over it is the victory over sin. However lofty a man's spirit may be, he must bear his share of the world's burden. The moral problem is to share the burden in the name of love and yet to have no share in the world's falsity. The falsity required by the herd-life must not be accepted. We must live that life without taking part in its falsity. This creates a tragic conflict which cannot be solved by human resources alone. The falsity in which the herd-life abounds and which it requires as a good must be opposed not by lofty abstract ideas (which are frequently used to cover up the falsity) but by a lofty spirit, by creative spiritual force. And these must be derived from the gracious primary source of life.

There is a great deal of truth, though only of negative truth, in Tolstoy's teaching. He suffered from the incongruity between lofty aims and low means. Tolstoy thought that we could avoid using evil, violent means if we carried out the law of the Master of life—i.e. the way out was for him still the old, legalistic, normative way. One must not resist evil by force just as one must not smoke or drink wine. This was Tolstoy's limitation. But the only way out is spiritual regeneration, acquisition of gracious spiritual force. Tolstoy justly denounced the unworthy love for the strong, the rich and the powerful, for royal palaces, military leaders, and so on, and he rightly saw terrible falsity in all this. But the falsity cannot be overcome by a law, even though it be a new law. It can only be overcome by the spirit, a new spirit, by a gracious creative force that brings light and regeneration.

3. CONSCIENCE AND FREEDOM. THE CRITIQUE OF PURE CONSCIENCE

Conscience is that aspect of man's inmost nature which comes into contact with God, is receptive to His message and hears His voice. A " critique of pure conscience " ought to be written. Conscience may be repressed, hidden and perverted, but it is connected with the very essence of man, with the divine image and likeness in him. In a hidden form it exists even in the Hottentot who defined good and evil by saying, " It is good if I steal somebody else's wife and bad if my wife is stolen ". In our sinful existence conscience is remembrance of God and of the divine life. When conscience is roused in the most sinful and criminal man, it means that he thinks of God and of living in God's way, even though he may not express it in those words. Conscience is the organ of perception of the religious revelation, of goodness, righteousness and truth in its entirety. It is not a special department or function of human nature, but the wholeness of man's spiritual being, its centre or its heart in the ontological and not in the psychological sense of the term. Conscience is the source of original, first-hand judgments about life and the world. Moreover, conscience judges God or judges about God, for it is the organ for the apprehension of God. It can only judge about God because it is the organ whereby we become aware of God. God acts upon man's conscience and rouses it, i.e. rouses the memory of the higher, celestial world. Conscience is the memory of what man really is, of the world to which he ideally belongs, of his Creator, of the purpose for which he has been created. Conscience is the spiritual, supernatural principle in man and it is not of social origin at all. It is rather the perversion and confusion of conscience that is of social origin. Conscience is human nature at the depth at which it has not completely fallen away from God but has preserved its connection with the Divine world. Repentance and remorse are only possible because man has a conscience that is not irreparably damaged. Conscience is the meeting point of freedom and grace. What theology describes as the action of grace upon the human soul is the awakening of its depths, the recollection of the Divine source of life. Repentance is the experience of pain and horror at the disharmony between my present life and the memories of the true life for which I was created and from which man fell into this world of sin and sorrow. Repentance presupposes the dualism of the two worlds, and assumes that man is the meeting point of two orders of existence. Repentance would be impossible if man were rooted in this world alone and had no recollection of any other. Repentance shows the disharmony between the Idea of man as a part of the intelligible world and his empirical existence on earth.

The very existence of conscience proves that it is free. To deny the freedom of conscience, as is done by the official Roman Catholic theology, is unintelligible from the spiritual point of view and is due to worldly considerations and the love of power. Freedom is logically prior to authority. The power of authority as a spiritual fact and not as a manifestation of material force presupposes that it is freely accepted and recognized as commanding respect and obedience. The naïvely realistic conception of authority is untenable. Authority does not pass from the object to the subject like some material force. A spiritual authority must be accepted by my conscience, and if it is not, it ceases to be an authority for me. The conscience that makes valuations and passes judgment must be free from everything external to it and be subject only to the action of God's grace, obedient only to the memories of the divine celestial world. The question of *sobornost* and of the church is secondary and belongs to a different order. In the phenomenon of what may be called *pure conscience* the soul stands before God and is free from the influences of the world. Pure conscience is precisely what is meant by freedom from the world, which is the true freedom of the human spirit and is prior to freedom *in* the world. A conscience enslaved and seduced by the world is no longer an organ for the perception of truth; it does not judge but is judged by a deeper and purer conscience.

What might be called the communal conscience of the church, which perceives truth and judges untruth collectively and not individually, does not by any means imply that the personal conscience, prior to appearing before God in all its purity, combines with other people's and the world's consciences ; it means that spiritually and immanently a man bears in his own conscience the common fate of his brothers in spirit. Communalty—*sobornost*—is the immanent quality of the personal conscience as it stands in the presence of God. The individual soul appears before God in a free union with other souls and the soul of the world. But its relation to other souls and to the world-soul is determined by its own free conscience. Freedom of conscience does not necessarily imply individualism and isolation. Protestantism interpreted the freedom of conscience in too individualistic a manner. In any case, *sobornost* does not mean any kind of external authority over the personal conscience. In religious spiritual life I cannot accept anything apart from, and contrary to, my conscience. It would not be a spiritual act if I did, for spirit is freedom. Free conscience is the greatest moral good and conditions the very possibility of moral life. No force in the world can destroy the inward freedom of conscience ; it remains when a man is imprisoned or led to execution. But outwardly the freedom of conscience may be violated ; it may receive no social recognition and be denied as the personal right of the individual, and therefore struggle for the freedom of conscience is both possible and inevitable. Inwardly, freedom of conscience is repressed and perverted by sin, and struggle for the purity of free conscience means struggle with sin. But outwardly it is repressed and violated by the " herd-man ", always jealous and despotic. Social violence to the freedom of conscience is done not only by the state and the church, which makes use of machinery of the state, but also by " public opinion "— opinion of the family, the nation, the class, the party, and so on. And it is perhaps the most difficult question of ethics to decide how we are to struggle for the purity and freedom of conscienec against the tyrannical public opinion of definite social groups to which a man belongs? The " free " democratic public opinion is constantly doing violence to personal conscience. A struggle must be waged for the originality, the first-hand character of moral acts.

The church itself may be interpreted in two ways in this connection— on the one hand it is the spiritual community with which I am freely united and stand together before God, and on the other hand it is a socially organized historical institution capable of externally violating my conscience and of depriving my moral acts of purity, freedom and originality, i.e. the church may play the part of " public opinion ". From the point of view of the ethics of creativeness, the principle of correlation between freedom and the social unit may be formulated as follows : your conscience must be determined not by the social group, or public opinion, but by the depths of your spirit, i.e. it must be free and feel that it is in the presence of God ; at the same time you must be a social being, i.e. you must determine your relation to society and to social questions out of the depths of your free spirit. We must proceed from spirituality which is primary to sociality which is secondary, and not *vice versa*. Conscience is distorted by social environment ; and most of all, perhaps, it is distorted by economic dependence.

Fanaticism is one of the most painful distortions of conscience. It almost completely destroys its freedom and the capacity for pure and first-hand moral valuations, though fanatics may be pure, idealistic, disinterested people, and frequently complete ascetics. Fanaticism is a curious instance of the degeneration of personality under the influence of motives which as such are not evil and are connected with disinterested devotion to some belief or idea. A fanatic is always an idealist in the sense that an idea means more to him than concrete human beings and that for the sake of the idea he is ready to oppress, torture, and kill others— whether it be the idea of God and theocracy or of justice and the communist regime. Fanaticism is a species of madness due to incapacity to grasp the whole of truth. Christendom has suffered from such madness. Subconscious instincts of cruelty, violence and tyranny in their crude form were expelled from Christian consciousness, but they asserted themselves under cover of the Christian virtues of love and faith. The Inquisition was established in the name of faith in God, love of men and concern for their salvation. Christians have found it difficult to take in the fullness of the Christian revelation about God-in-Man, love and freedom. A fanatic does not understand the mystery of freedom, of Christian freedom —it is utterly beyond him. Though he is so proud of his faith in God, he is as far as possible from the perfection of the Heavenly Father. God tolerates evil and the wicked, He bases His idea of the world and man upon freedom, and apart from freedom no amount of goodness, virtue, faith and piety has any value for God. God's infinite toleration of evil and the wicked has not been sufficiently dwelt upon, although it is of ontological significance. And if we want to strive for perfection similar to the perfection of the Heavenly Father we must be tolerant and beware of fanaticism. Tolerance is not indifference to good and evil, it is the virtue of humaneness and love of freedom, a considerate attitude to human souls and their path in life which is always complex and painful. A fanatic is a person incapable of entertaining more than one thought at a time. He sees everything in a straight line and does not turn his head to see all the complexity and variety of God's world. A fanatic does not see concrete human beings and is not interested in them, he sees only his idea and is interested in it alone. He is completely devoted to his idea of God, but he has almost lost the faculty of contemplating the living God.

In the dialectics of human feelings and passions it is remarkable that fanaticism, which always implies a dislike of freedom and an incapacity to understand it, may take the form of being possessed by the idea of freedom. There exist fanatics of freedom who perform acts of the worst tyranny in the name of freedom. What they are concerned with is not freedom as a reality but the idea of freedom, which justifies every means for its attainment. The idea of freedom gets such complete possession of them that it excludes all other ideas. Fanaticism invariably means that one idea excludes all the others; it thus sins against the fullness of life. A fanatic of love may commit the greatest crimes and acts of tyranny in the name of the idea of love which leaves no room for freedom, justice, knowledge, and so on. Fanatics of justice do the same. The striving for the fullness of life is a moral imperative which a fanatic never carries out. This is why moral extremism is false—it is generally based not upon the greatest fullness of life but upon being possessed by some one idea. A paradoxical moral imperative might be formulated as follows : in your striving for perfection you must strive for the perfect fullness of life and never allow a moral principle as such to become predominant to the exclusion of everything else. A fanatic may be full of vital energy, but he is an enemy of life, he is blind to it and spoils it. Asceticism has a truth of its own without which moral life would be impossible, but ascetic fanaticism means a hatred of life and hostility to human beings. The same must be said of religious fanaticism. It is possession by one idea which crowds out everything else, and for its sake men spoil their own lives and other people's. Every idea can become the source of fanatical madness—the idea of God, of moral perfection, of justice, freedom, love, knowledge. When this happens, the living God, the living perfection, the actual justice, love, freedom and knowledge disappear, since everything living and concrete can only exist in the full and harmonious correlation of parts in a whole. Every value turns into an idol and becomes a lie and a deception.

In this respect it is very interesting to consider the fate of the idea of " heresy " which became the source of the most sinister fanaticism, cruelty, violence and malice. In the history of Christianity heresy in the strict sense has meant onesidedness, incapacity to grasp the fullness of truth, violation of spiritual and intellectual harmony. Every heresy contained some particle of truth, some correct idea, but it was affirmed at the expense of other aspects of truth and exaggerated to the point of falsity.

Ecclesiastical orthodoxy which fought against the onesidedness of heresies and strove to express the fullness of the divinely revealed truth degenerated into fanaticism in the minds of its devoted champions. A fanatic of orthodoxy does not live in the fullness and harmony of the revealed truth, but is obsessed by the " idea " of it which excludes all the other ideas and makes him blind to the complexity and manifoldness of life. It is an instance of the sinister dialectics of human feelings and passions and their transformation from good ones into bad. A fanatic of orthodoxy who denounces heresies and exterminates heretics has lost the vital fullness and harmony of truth, he is possessed by one emotion only and sees nothing but heresy and heretics everywhere. He becomes hard, forgets about the freedom of the spirit and has but little attention to bestow upon men and the complexity of their individual destinies. Heaven preserve us from being obsessed by the idea of heresy ! That obsession plays an enormous part in the history of Christianity and it is very difficult to get rid of it. A conviction has been bred for centuries that a religious fanatic, who mercilessly denounces heresies and heretics, is more religious than other men, and those who think that their own faith is weak respect him. In truth, however, a religious fanatic is a man who is obsessed by his idea and completely believes in it, but is not in communion with the living God. On the contrary he is cut off from the living God. And for the sake of the fullness of the divine truth, for the sake of freedom and love and communion with God, it is essential to uproot in oneself the evil will to denounce heresies and heretics. A heresy should be opposed by the fullness of truth and not by malice and denunciations. Fanatical denunciations of heresies sometimes assume the guise of love and are supposed to be inspired by love and pity for the heretics. But this is hypocrisy and self-deception. Heresy hunters simply flatter themselves and admire their own orthodoxy.

As a matter of fact, enthusiasm for orthodoxy is a social phenomenon. It is generated by the herd-life, by the obligation to profess the same faith as the whole of a given social group and to impose it on others. This has nothing to do with the actual contemplation of truth and of God. In the spiritual life and spiritual world this insistence on uniformity of faith, inevitably accompanied by a search for heresy, simply does not exist. The spiritual unity of truth and of life is a unity of a totally different kind. It is only when spiritual life is translated into the terms of the herd-mentality that it gives rise to religious fanaticism and denunciation of heresies. Suspiciousness which sees everywhere heresy, evil and perdition indicates a disturbance in the harmony of the spiritual life and is the beginning of a psychosis. It is a moral imperative that we should rise above suspicion and morbid imagination, and never suspect anybody of anything. To suspect evil in others always means being blind to evil in oneself. Not to succumb to suspiciousness and evil imaginings is the first rule of moral and mental hygiene. This is closely connected with heresy-hunting. Its psychology is the same in Communist and Catholic and Orthodox " orthodoxy ", in religious thought and among " freethinkers ". A Russian communist looks out for " heretics " and treats them in the same way as zealous Christians used to in the old days. His attitude also has a social origin ; herd-life, whether it be conservative or revolutionary, religious or atheistic, affects human psychology in the same way and in its own interests makes use of man's subconscious instincts. What is opposed to it is true spiritual life, life based upon grace, love and freedom. But it would be a mistake to think that fanaticism takes the form of external violence only : it finds a still stronger expression in inner violence. Suggestion and will-power may do damage to people's minds and kill the soul and not the body, and this is more terrible. In modern democratic states people's lives and liberty are safeguarded by the law, so that their bodies are comparatively safe from the attacks of fanatics. But men's souls may be damaged and distorted by fanatical will-power, and those who can kill the soul are to be feared more than those who can kill the body. This is true of all fanatics, the pious and religious as well as the godless and revolutionary. No fanaticism of any kind must ever be allowed. We must struggle for spiritual freedom and spiritual liberation in the realm of thought, in the state, in the family, in social life. This is a moral imperative. But freedom must not become a fanatical idea by which man is possessed, for then it degenerates into tyranny. Strive for freedom, but never forget about truth, love, justice—or freedom will become empty, false and meaningless. Strive for the fullness of life. Strive for truth, love and justice, but do not forget about freedom. Strive for goodness and perfection, but heaven forbid that you should forget about freedom and try to realize goodness and perfection by force. Strive for real spiritual unity and brotherhood. But if it cannot be attained, let multiplicity have free play and give a chance to a free search for the still undiscovered single truth. Strive for the liberation of human emotions, but do not allow yourself to be overpowered by feelings or let them become detached from the fullness of life which includes thought and life of the intellect, will and the moral life, relation to God and the religious life. Only the spirit synthesizes the life of the soul ; without it the soul disintegrates into elements of thought, sensations, volitions, emotions, etc.

Strive for spirituality, i.e. for the wholeness of life and for creativeness in every sphere of existence. Fanaticism destroys both that wholeness and creativeness ; it is the very opposite of aesthetic contemplation.

4. FEAR, TERROR AND ANGUISH. THE DULL AND THE COMMONPLACE. PHANTASMS

Fear experienced by the creature is a consequence of original sin and of separation from God. Fear has frequently been a determining factor in religious beliefs, philosophical theories, social customs and institutions. Fear is the basis of our sinful life and penetrates into the loftiest spiritual regions, poisoning the moral and the religious life. It is essential to distinguish between fear and terror or anguish. Roughly speaking this corresponds to the distinction which Kierkegaard draws between *Furcht* and *Angst*[1] and partly to Heidegger's distinction between *Sorge* and *Angst*.[2] Fear is the state of the shuddering, trembling, fallen creature on the low plane of existence, threatened with dangers on all sides. Fear is the expectation of helpless suffering, illness, poverty, blows, privations, attacks of enemies who may take away all that a man has and his very life. The experience of fear has no reference to the heights of being which man longs to attain and in separation from which he suffers. In the state of fear man generally forgets all about the heights and is quite ready to live on the low-lying plain so long as he is safe from dangers, privations and sufferings. Fear is opportunistic, and in a state of acute fear a person will agree to anything. Fear humiliates man instead of exalting him. Primitive humanity was possessed by fear, *terror anticus*—the fear of chaos and of the unknown forces of nature that rendered man helpless, the fear of spirits and demons and gods and magicians and kings who had magic power. Ancient man fought against fear by means of magic and totemic beliefs ; he sought protectors and magic formulae which give power over the gods themselves. Fear is the most ancient of man's affective states ; it accompanies his very birth and is always present in the subconscious layer of human nature. Magic is a means of acquiring power and combating dangers and fears, but at the same time it is itself a source of them. Man is afraid of magic powers and seeks protection from them first in religion and then in science. The first emotion that Adam felt after the Fall must have been fear. Absence of fear is a feature of the life of Paradise. And the coming of the Kingdom of God is the final victory over fear—the fear

[1] Kierkegaard, *Der Begriff der Angst* and *Furcht und Zittern*.
[2] See *Sein und Zeit*.

both of life and of death. Religion means struggle against this *terror anticus* and liberation from it. But fear penetrates into religious beliefs and distorts them. Religion is the relation of sinful humanity to God, and since sinful humanity is dominated by fear, religious beliefs are permeated with the fear of God or of the gods. Man is afraid not only of chaos but of God also. Religion creates innumerable taboos, and man stands in fear and trembling of their possible violation. Superstitions are shadows of beliefs and are a sign of fear. A superstitious man is full of terrors. Religion creates the distinction between the sacred and the profane and calls forth fear of the sacred. Religion creates the distinction between the clean and the unclean and evokes a special kind of fear of one and of the other. A religion of the law creates fear of the law and makes man tremble at the idea of violating the law which determines the whole of his life. Religious beliefs both liberate man from fear and create endless new fears, for they are dominated by a sense of sin. The Gospel alone liberates us from fear, and that is the effect of the grace of Christ.[1] The significance of fear for ethics is enormous.

A different meaning attaches to what I should call anguish and terror. In contradistinction to fear, anguish implies yearning, striving upwards and pain from being down below. Anguish and mystic terror have nothing to do with the dangers that threaten us in this sinful world, but are rooted in the mystery of existence from which man is severed. The experience of mystic terror and anguish is very different from that of trembling at the expectation of danger or pain and may indeed be incompatible with it. Mystic terror is anguish at the highest pitch of intensity. Anguish passes into terror before the mystery of existence. It is not due to the dangers and privations of everyday life and comes about for no reason ; its cause is to be found in another world, on a different plane of being ; the yearning has no object. Kierkegaard understood this but he brought into anguish and mystic terror an element of fear. His *Angst* is a misture of *terror anticus* and the biblical fear of God. Anguish and terror not merely testify, as fear does, that man is a low and fallen creature but prove that he has a lofty, godlike nature and is destined for a higher life. Anguished yearning can only be felt for a higher world than the one we are living in ; terror can only be inspired by the mystery of existence or the dark chaos, and not by the dangers of everyday life. The Care (*Sorge*) from which Heidegger tries to deduce the temporal existence in the fallen world is a weak, incipient form of fear. When anxious care

---

[1] Luther passed through a shattering tragedy in this connection. See a very interesting book by Lucien Fevre, *Un destin. Martin Luther.*

reaches a certain pitch of intensity it becomes fear.   But yearning is not connected with fear, and awe does not involve anxiety.   One may experience fear and anxiety if someone we love is dangerously ill, but when the moment of death comes there is no longer any anxiety or ordinary fear but mystic terror before the mystery of death and a yearning for the world in which death is no more.   To fear God is impossible and wrong ; the expression " fear of God " is inaccurate and must be re-interpreted. What we feel towards God may be mystic terror—terror at the fathomless mystery—and we may feel a yearning for God.   To introduce fear into our attitude to God is to introduce a category of ordinary natural life into a higher realm to which it is not applicable.   There may be fear of wild beasts or of infectious disease, but not of God.   One may be afraid of the powers of this world, of tsars, commissars or gendarmes, but not of God. Our attitude to Him may be one of terror or of yearning, but not of fear. This is an important and far-reaching distinction.

The herd-morality born of sin tries to convert the category of fear into one of the fundamental categories of moral and religious life.   The distinction between good and evil, as that between the sacred and the profane, gives rise to fear.   A man must stand in fear and trembling of the " good " and also of evil, though in a different sense.   Man is permanently intimidated by sin and by morality, he is in a state of panic fear and is ready to do anything to escape that fear.   Intimidation with eternal torments in hell had that effect.   Man's moral and spiritual life was determined by the fear of God and of the good and not by holy terror before the mystery of God, not by yearning for the divine righteousness, not by love for God and for the divine good.   Fear makes man agree to anything, and he can be terrorized by the prospect of torments in this life and in eternity.   He becomes a trembling, fearful, shuddering creature, begging for respite and comparative peace.   Even if fear assumes a moral and religious character it is never an ascent towards God, but bondage to the low plane of everyday existence.   Moral distinctions, valuations and actions which are entirely inspired by fear can have no moral significance or be an expression of man's spirituality.   Torture never leads to the discovery of truth.   Fear perverts all moral valuations and actions.   Fear is opportunistic.   The morality of fear has no spiritual source but is rooted in the herd-life.   Fear paralyzes the freedom of conscience and soils its purity.   In order to make moral valuations and act morally one must be free of fear.   A man who is completely terrorized loses the faculty of performing purely moral actions.   Actions and valuations inspired by the fear of temporal or eternal torments are not purely moral.   And yet the herd-mind, which makes itself felt even in the domain of religion, seeks to rule the individual morally through the emotion of fear, though in a softened and modified form. This results in a tragic conflict. A socially determined ethics is always an ethics of fear, though it may take a very liberal guise. All utilitarian morality is based upon fear ; spiritual ethics is the only one that is not. Do not be determined in your moral judgments and actions by the emotion of fear, rise superior to it in your spirit, be inspired by the pure striving for the lofty, for the divine, for pure love— this is an absolute moral imperative. A hedonistic ethics, whether its hedonism be earthly or heavenly, rests in the last resort upon fear, since man is bound to fear for his happiness and the happiness of others ; happiness is threatened with dangers on all sides and is bought at the cost of opportunism in actions and judgments. If I make happiness my aim, I am doomed to fear all the time.

The attraction of the divine heights alone liberates us from fear, but it gives rise to anguished yearning and sacred terror. The meaning of these emotions for the moral and spiritual life is quite different from that of fear. Yearning is not, of course, man's highest spiritual achievement ; it has to be overcome, it is transitory, it is a sign of man's noble dissatisfaction with the ordinary world and his striving towards a higher realm. That which I call " terror " is disinterested, not utilitarian, not hedonistic ; it does not indicate anxiety or fear of sufferings to come but is a pure experience of the gulf which separates our sinful world from the divine, celestial world and the infinite mystery of being. Hence yearning and terror may have a purely moral and spiritual value. But fear is not an experience of standing before an abyss, before a mystery, before infinity ; on the contrary, it plunges man into the lower, ordinary world on this side of the veil. Eschatological fear connected with the final destiny of man and the world means substituting practical interested motives for the disinterested and transcendental terror. The attainment of the divine heights of perfection and love is not a means of avoiding perdition and gaining bliss but an end in itself, *is* bliss and salvation. Anguish and terror are interconnected, but terror comes nearer to the mystery of existence; it is more spiritual than anguish.

The herd-mind creates an ethics of fear, substituting anxiety for transcendental terror and intimidating man with future retribution. But it also creates a mental attitude of another kind, devoid of fear and below it —commonplace smugness. The daily life of the human herd stands in serious danger of it. Smugness frees man from fear not through rising to higher spheres but through sinking to the lower. It means being thor-

oughly acclimatized on the lower plane, no longer yearning for the celestial world, or feeling a sacred terror before the transcendental mystery, or
even having any fear. The mountains finally recede from the horizon
and there is nothing left but an endless flat surface. Commonplace smugness hides the tragedy and the terror of life, and in it the "herd-man",
begotten by the Fall, forgets his transcendental origin. He becomes
perfectly content and is pleased to live on the dead level of unreality, to
be completely thrown out on to the surface and finally severed from the
depths, from the kernel of being, to which he is afraid to return. The
realm of the commonplace is this world in so far as it has completely
forgotten the existence of any other and is thoroughly satisfied. It means
a loss of all originality ; life is determined wholly from without and sinks
to an incomparably lower level than that of existence weighed down by
toil, fear and anxiety. Fear, difficulties and anxiety are a cure for smugness, which makes everything easy because it gives up the struggle for a
higher reality. Boredom is an anticipation of non-being and means
suffering from the greyness and emptiness of life ; it implies a recognition
of the contrast between being and non-being, fullness and emptiness ;
commonplace smugness is free from that suffering. No dualism, which
is always painful, exists for it ; it is a special low kind of monism. Civilization has a fatal way of engendering smugness and complacency, of
destroying originality and individuality, and severing man from the
primary sources of life. The commonplace is characterized by endless
repetition and monotony. Judgments and valuations which had once
been deep and earnest may become platitudes, and so may moral and
aesthetic judgments that have grown fashionable and are reiterated over
and over again. A tendency to paradoxes may become dull and commonplace. Few things have been more vulgarized than erotic love. The
amount of hackneyed commonplaces that have been said about it is so
overwhelming that soon it will be impossible to speak of love at all.
Emotions and instincts rooted in the inmost depths of reality have lost all
depth, and become so light and superficial as to be utterly unreal. Classes,
professions, nations, churches, ideological tendencies may be complacent
to the point of vulgarity. Communism, which is essentially tragic and
earnest, gives rise to incredible smugness. Nothing can be more complacent than a parrot-like repetition of Marxist formulae. The same kind
of smugness is to be met with in aesthetic movements, in fashionable
ideas which in themselves may not be platitudes at all, in the preaching of
moral virtues that have lost their original force. Christianity itself may
become habitual and commonplace.

Smugness acquires an eschatological character : it may be man's final destiny. And one of the most important moral imperatives is to cut it down at the root. Any amount of fear and difficulty is better than smugness. People were further away from it when they lived in perpetual fear of eternal damnation. Liberation from that fear and from all transcendental terrors gave birth to the kingdom of bourgeois commonplace smugness. This is one of the paradoxes of emancipation. Emancipation is a great blessing, but it brings with it the danger of vulgarizing life, of making it flat, shallow and commonplace. If liberation is taken to mean throwing off the burdens and difficulties of life, attaining satisfaction and getting rid of tragedy and of transcendental terror, it always ends in smugness. Such liberation is opposed to spiritual freedom, which gives rise to tragedy and to an acute awareness of the abyss that divides our world from the divine. The herd-man thinks that the process of liberation leads to his triumph and satisfaction and ends in his being comfortably settled in the world. That means the loss of depth and originality and the transition to the realm of bourgeois smugness. This is one of the paradoxes of the ethics of freedom, which is connected with the ethics of creativeness. But creativeness is by its very nature opposed to commonplace smugness, which consists precisely in the absence of creativeness and incapacity for it. Hence creativeness is a way of combating smugness.

The good itself is becoming unendurably stale and commonplace because it is no longer creative. The flatness and dullness of the " good " calls forth a reaction and leads people to imagine that " evil " is deeper, more poignant or passionate. They turn to " evil " as a remedy against dullness. And we often find that movements which are inspired by malice and hatred and contain dark passions and a " demonic " element are more alive, more active and interesting than movements inspired by the good which has lost its creative fire and grown flat and stale. This may be observed in political life and in the history of ideas. New ideological tendencies, active, sharp, bitter and passionate, often contain malice, hatred, lust for destruction and a " demonic" will to victory ; by comparison, the habitual virtuous phrases seem flat and commonplace. We are conscious of this in incipient revolutionary movements, in the early clash between romanticism and classicism, in new tendencies in art, in liberal moral ideas, in new schools of thought, in the struggle for spiritual reformation. Luther, who was a religious genius, had something " demonic " in his character. The greatest moral problem is to make the " good " fiery, creative, capable of active spiritual struggle and prevent it from becoming dull, flat, and commonplace. The most sinister manifestation of smugness is complacent virtue ; complacent vice is morally less terrible. The ethics of creativeness alone can solve the problem, for it is based upon creative originality and insists that moral judgments and actions should spring from the depths of the spirit and be first-hand.

A question that has real metaphysical importance is that of phantasms which play a truly overwhelming part in human life. Phantasms must be distinguished from fantasy and imagination. The difference is this. Creative fantasy is constructive ; it raises the soul, and instead of destroying and perverting realities, transfigures them and adds new ones to them, i.e. it is a way of enriching existence. Phantasms are destructive in their results, they destroy and pervert realities and lead from being to non-being. St. Athanasius the Great says that evil consists of phantasms. In so far as man creatively participates in God's work and realizes His plan in continuing the work of creation, he strives towards the fullness of being. But phantasms replace God's plan by another which means breaking up reality and refusing to participate in God's work and to continue the creation of the world. Phantasms spring from self-centredness, i.e. they are the result of original sin. A man who generates phantasms and is possessed by them does not see the world in its true perspective. In a phantasmagoric world realities are misplaced and wrongly correlated and everything is made to refer to an egocentric being obsessed by his passions. Phantasms spring from passions. And the horror and sinfulness of passions lies not in their original elementary force, in their ontological kernel—on the contrary, that is valuable in them—but in their egocentric tendency and the creation of phantasms in which being passes into non-being. Passions are sinful in so far as they disturb inner wholeness and harmony, destroy the Divine image and likeness in man and deprive him of spiritual power which synthesizes the life of the soul and the body. All sinful passions create phantasmagorical worlds of their own, destroy man's sense of reality and make him an idealist in the bad sense of the term. The struggle against destructive passions is the struggle for the image and likeness of God in man, for harmonious wholeness, or, in other words, for spirituality. Imagination is a creative force and a source of creativeness. But if imagination distorts the direct perception of reality, man loses sight of being and is left with phantasms of non-being. Every passion, every vice has its own bad imagination which stands in the way of direct perception and falsifies reality. When a man allows himself to be possessed by morbid pride, ambition, envy, jealousy, sensuality, morbid eroticism, greed, miserliness, hatred or cruelty, he finds himself in the world of phantasms and no longer apprehends things as they really are. Everything appears to be correlated to the passion by which he is obsessed and which deprives him of spiritual freedom.

Self-love—the worst wound dealt man by original sin—prevents a true perception of realities because at every encounter with life it wants either to defend itself from pain by means of a phantasm or to obtain satisfaction, inevitably a transitory one, through some other phantasm. Out of self-love a man will exalt some people and run down others and not be aware of any of them as they really are. Self-love always seeks compensation and in doing so falsifies reality.[1] A man regards as real a world which gives him most compensation and in which his self-love feels least wounded. A man may construct for himself a pessimistic metaphysic because such a conception of the world is less wounding to him. A man may adopt revolutionary views because they compensate his wounded self-love and make him less vulnerable. A man may join this or that party, school of thought or political group because they are the least wounding to his self-love and give him the most satisfaction. A man will make friends with some people and be hostile to others, ascribing reality and importance to them according to whether they gratify his self-love or wound it. This goes so far that sometimes a man loses faith or becomes a believer for the sake of defending or compensating his self-love. Self-love creates a phantasmagorical world of its own in which all realities are misplaced. And since everyone has a certain amount of self-love—it is the wound of original sin—everyone lives, more or less, in a world of phantasms. Victory over the sin of self-centredness, acquisition of spirituality and the unfolding in oneself of the Divine image and likeness is a return to the real world of being. All the defences and compensations which self-love seeks to find in phantasms are powerless to cure the pain ; the wound goes on bleeding and arrows pierce the sick heart on all sides. The only way really to heal it is by spiritually conquering self-centredness and replacing it by theocentrism, that is, by a spiritually enlightened view of the world. In religious practice this way is exoterically described as humility. In the deep sense of the word humility is nothing other than liberation from phantasms created by self-centredness and opening the mind to realities. Resentment creates endless phantasms both in the individual and the social life. Nietzsche used this fact to explain the genesis of religious and moral consciousness, and indeed he made too much of it. Freud's school and Adler in particular have thrown a great deal of light on the subject.

All mental states derived from the original sin of pride and self-

[1] Adler shows this admirably.

centredness—the various forms of resentment, ambition, love of power, envy, jealousy, sense of injury—create phantasmagorical worlds of their own and destroy one's sense of reality. It is very difficult to bring back to realities a person who has succumbed to envy, jealousy, lust of fame or power. A man who longs for power looks at everything from the point of view of acquiring power, and a man who longs for fame looks at everything from the point of view of acquiring fame. Men obsessed by envy and jealousy are sick men, they can no longer see the realities of God's world but are surrounded by phantasms which feed their feelings of envy and jealousy. Masochism and sadism—torturing oneself and torturing others—are always characteristic of people obsessed by envy or jealousy and indeed by any form of resentment. The desire to tyrannize others becomes an imperative need. A tyrant is always a sadist and a masochist, he both seeks compensation and increases his own pain. Resentment and envy may reach such a point that a man will not be able to endure another man being richer, handsomer, more famous, more powerful, more successful than himself, or even his being purer, nobler and better : the light of holiness is more than he can bear. He can no longer discriminate realities or judge them correctly. The chief characteristic of an aristocrat of the spirit is that he does not suffer from resentment.

A person who lives in a world of phantasms is always partially insane. This may come about through obsession by some phantasmagorical idea which upsets the balance, harmony and wholeness of the mental life. There is such a thing as rationalistic madness, *folie raisonnante*, which means obsession by the idea of regulating the life of the world by reason. It is characteristic of those who create utopias. Lenin suffered from rationalistic madness. A phantasmagorical world may become real. Utopias are realizable ; it is a mistake to imagine that they are not. The madness of rationalism makes use of real forces for its realization, but it has a devastating effect upon the mental life. A man who strives to realize some utopian idea at all costs may be entirely disinterested and guided by moral motives, since he strives for the perfect life, but he is self-centred and may become a moral idiot, losing the power of distinguishing between good and evil.

The lust of greed and the lust of sensuality have a destructive influence on mental life and create phantasms and illusory worlds of their own which replace for man the real world of God. The lust of greed and love of money for its own sake creates one of the most fantastic worlds, furthest removed from the real world of being—the world of capitalism, of banks, stock-exchanges, paper money, cheques, IOU's, advertisement, competition and pursuit of easy gain. The financial world is a terrible phantasmagoria, utterly remote from the world created by God and adding nothing to its richness, fullness or perfection. Léon Bloy was right in saying that finance is a peculiar kind of mystery-play.[1] And this fantastic world obeying its own laws and disregarding the law of God is the creation of lust and egocentric passions in which man loses his freedom and the divine likeness. Phantasms always enslave the spirit. In exactly the same way sexual lust creates an illusory world of its own which severs man from reality and enslaves him. It does not spring from the ontological centre of sex as an elemental passion. It is the product of evil imagination and is illusory, phantasmagorical, opposed to the reality of God's world. The lust of sensuality is joyless and is not really a passion ; it belongs to a realm in which the primary passion, ontological in its significance, has cooled down and been replaced by fictitious passions which condemn man to the bad infinity of insatiable longing. From its very nature lust is insatiable and incapable of satisfaction ; this is true of all lust—the lust of sexuality, of greed and acquisitiveness, of fame and power or of the baser lust of gluttony. This is why it brings man into an illusory world and is the way to non-being. The whole of world-literature bears witness to the illusory world created by sexual lust. The phantasms of sex destroy love, which belongs to the world of real being. The power of woman with her love for wealth and luxury in modern bourgeois society rests upon that lust. N. Fyodorov rightly says that capitalism and its phantasms are to a considerable extent built up by sexual lust.[2] Through lust for the other sex man comes to love money and to commit crimes, entering a world of phantasms. Luxury largely depends upon the lust of sexuality and belongs to an illusory world, different from God's real world of beauty. Sexual lust is a violation of the ontologically normal relation between consciousness and the unconscious ; in it the bad unconscious poisons consciousness, and consciousness, divided against itself and suffering from morbid fancies, perverts and distorts the healthy unconscious. What is usually called debauchery is a product of consciousness ; the unconscious as such is innocent.[3] Phantasms are not produced by the unconscious as such ; they are always a product of consciousness severed from the primary sources of being.

Every phantasm created by lust leads to death—not voluntary but inevitable death. Such is the structure of being. Morbid dreaminess

[1] See L. Bloy's remarkable book, *Le salut par les Juifs.*
[2] *Filosofia Obschago Dela.*
[3] See S. Troitsky's articles in *Put* (in Russian).

which often appears innocent is an evil and builds up an illusory world. It is not creative but tends to exhaust the mind. Whereas love is directed upon personality, upon the image of God in man, and strives to affirm it for all eternity, lust is concerned with itself only, is egocentric and perceives no realities in the world. This is why it is a phantasm. By a phantasm I mean all that fails to take man out of himself to his " other ", to overcome self-centredness and is self-seeking, regardless of reality and not rooted in it. Lust and phantasms do not bring man into contact with the world, other men and God. This is the curse of lust ; this is why it is essentially uncreative. Production of phantasms is not creativeness, which always implies transcendence of self. Auto-suggestion plays an enormous part in moral life. It may be either good or evil. Auto-suggestion may consist in fertilizing the unconscious by a creative idea or in poisoning it with a destructive lust and phantasms which mean mistaking evil for good.

Fear creates quite a special kind of phantasms. Fear prevents the discrimination and perception of realities. A man obsessed by fear sees everything in a wrong perspective. " Fear has large eyes," says the proverb. And since fear in some respect or other is to some extent natural to every man, it may be said that in this sinful world man as a rule wrongly perceives reality and that all his life-perspectives are distorted by phantasms. Cowardice which always seeks pretexts for fear invariably creates illusions. The paradoxical thing is that a coward who wants to protect himself does not seem at all eager to discover the real dangers. He greatly exaggerates the existing dangers, he invents non-existing ones, but often fails to notice what really threatens him. A coward is a phantasm-monger and has a world of his own, like the sensualist or the man obsessed with love of power, or fame, or money. Fear, and especially fear carried to the point of cowardice, is a poor guide to the knowledge of things as they are in themselves. The highest form of fear—the religious fear of eternal damnation—is very unfavourable to knowledge, to pure objective contemplation and discovery of the relations between realities. And in so far as theology is founded upon the fear of eternal torments it cannot be a pure, disinterested form of knowledge and contemplation. Freethinkers in their attacks upon religion like to trace its origin to fear. This assertion, like almost every other, contains a certain amount of truth, but this truth is perverted, mixed with falsity and understood in a purely superficial sense. Fear had its part in the genesis of religious beliefs. Hence freethinkers say that religion creates an illusory world generated by fear and is at the same time intended to save men from fear. In truth, the whole thing is much deeper and more complex. The terror that haunted the primitive man, his helplessness and desolation, his longing for help and protection is a mixture of the holy, transcendental terror before the fathomless mystery of being and of animal fear that reigns in the fallen world—fear in the narrow sense of the term. In the history of religious consciousness, including Christian times, the spiritual fear or holy terror has always been mixed with animal and morbid fear, which vitiated the purity of religious faith. By its very meaning religious faith leads sinful man, tortured by the world, to the discovery of reality and liberates him from phantasms produced by fear. But it has phantasms of its own, also born of fear. Superstition is such a phantasm. Under the influence of fear, faith may easily turn into superstition. We find this in the faith of the people, in popular Christianity which cultured Christians often strive to imitate—at any rate in appearance. Least of all, of course, the word "phantasms" is applicable to myth-making, for a profoundly real element enters into the creation of myths, testifying to the spiritual health of the people. A phantasm is always morbid and pathological.

Fear of disease gives rise to a world of phantasms. It itself becomes a disease, so that a man sees everywhere dangers of infection, microbes ready to attack him on all sides, and loses the normal, healthy attitude to his body. He sees the whole of reality as a source of infection and lives in a world of phantasms just as a man obsessed by envy, jealousy or sensuality. Out of fear of death he loses touch with life and cannot see it in its true light. He finds everywhere a lurking menace of death which he fears so greatly. The transcendental terror at the mystery of death does not confine man to an illusory world of his own; on the contrary, it shows that he does not remain on the surface but penetrates to the depths of reality. But a pathological, animal fear of death is a sinful perversion of that terror, which, indeed, it banishes altogether. A man obsessed by the fear of death is wholly on this side of life, in this world, and is incapable of feeling the transcendental terror : he is too much absorbed in his own bodily states, too much attached to the earthly life and dreads to lose it. And here again we come upon a psychological paradox. Phantasms created by fear bring no deliverance from fear. Phantasms created by envy, jealousy, inordinate ambition, sexual lust, greed, etc., do not free man from his sufferings but increase them. The production of phantasms is not a teleological process determined by the purpose of attaining satisfaction, happiness, liberation, and so on ; it merely increases the dissatisfaction, the suffering and the slavery. This shows how mistaken the hedonistic point of view is. Creation of phantasms is not a solution.

Pain, suffering and death grow all the more fearful. A man's fear of pain, suffering and death depends upon his spiritual condition ; it reaches its maximum if he dwells among phantasms. But life on a high spiritual level, creative work and service of truth or righteousness lessen the fear and free one from it. The chief characteristics of evil phantasms is that they enslave the mind and centre it on itself, i.e. they are essentially unspiritual and uncreative. They also tend to destroy truthfulness, in the first place truthfulness to oneself. This can be clearly seen in hysterical women who live in a world of illusions and lie both to themselves and to others. The vice which we call hypocrisy or, in its weaker form, insincerity is also the result of phantasms and of dwelling in an illusory world. A fully crystallized hypocrite lives in a world of his own invention. He is untruthful and insincere not only with others but with God and with himself, i.e. he has lost touch with the real world of being. Hypocrisy is not necessarily based upon interested motives. A thorough hypocrite is a person who acts the part of somebody different from himself because he has lost his own personality. Phantasms produced by sinful fears always mean isolation and egocentric self-assertion, as well as obsession and madness, and make it impossible to attain satisfaction, true joy and spiritual liberation.

What, then, is the source of phantasms? Evil phantasms that constitute a world unlike the world created by God do not form part of God's plan of creation or of God's idea of man. They spring from some other source. Health is from God, but disease is not. Evil phantasms spring from primeval non-being and return to it. " Non-being " is always present in man. Evil phantasms come from primeval pre-existential meonic freedom which affirms the spirit of non-being within reality. They mean a return to non-being, a refusal to take part in God's creative activity. Primeval freedom is lost through them and turns into slavery. An evil, illusory world is the creation of the empty, non-existential, nether world of insatiable craving. Thus a return to non-being takes place, but it is to evil non-being. The primary, pre-cosmic non-being was not evil. It becomes evil when freedom has been put on trial and failed to respond to God's call to participate in His creative work.

It would be false, godless and inhuman to divide mankind, before God's last judgment, into two camps—of those who live in God's world of being and are in contact with realities and of those who live in an illusory world of non-being and have lost the faculty of perceiving reality. This division takes place in everyone of us, for we all share in non-being and create phantasms of one sort or another. Christian consciousness does not

186

allow us to regard ourselves as abiding in truth and others in untruth. No one perceives the fullness of truth and lives in it ; no one has passed into the realm of pure being.   The evil world of phantasms springs from a sense of injury and from making false claims upon God and His world. This false sense of injury gives rise to envy, pride, ambition, love of power, sensuality, etc.   But the sense of guilt liberates us from phantasms and brings us back to real being.

5. LOVE AND COMPASSION

Now we pass from the world of phantasms and non-being to the world of love, i.e. to the world of reality.   Real love is always for the concrete and the individual.   It is impossible to love the abstract and the general. Love always sees the loved one in God and in eternity through radiating its own gracious power.   Love is creative life and an inexhaustible source of light, warmth and energy.   The true purpose and meaning of love is not to help our neighbours, do good works, cultivate virtues which elevate the soul, or attain perfection, but to reach the union of souls, fellowship and brotherhood.   Love is a two-term relation and presupposes the meeting of two, their communion and unity, and the formation of a third—fellowship and brotherhood.   A man who does good works may think that he deserves salvation and is on the way to perfection although he is isolated and does not care for other men or even feel the need for friends and brothers.   That means that he has no love which truly unites us to others and brings us to the Kingdom of Heaven.

Love cannot be neutral and directed equally upon everyone without distinction.   A different word is needed for that—*caritas,* charity, mercy. One must be merciful to all, but it is impossible to love all alike.   Rozanov described such impersonal equalitarian love as "love made of glass", and in patristic literature it is sometimes called spiritual love, abstracted from the emotions and from all concreteness and individuality.   Love implies by its very nature discrimination and choice ; it is individual and goes from one personality to another.   Love is personalistic.   Indian consciousness does not know love because it does not know personality and believes in a metaphysic of identity.   For the lover the loved one is not identical with him, is not *tat twam asi*.   And it is only because of this that it is possible to pass from one to the other, to have intercourse, communion and brotherhood.   Ascetic Christian literature lowers the significance of love and interprets it in an anti-personalistic sense.   In the last resort the only love that proves to be possible is the love for God, which is man's only purpose. Love for men, for neighbours, friends and brothers in spirit, is either denied or interpreted as an ascetic or philanthropic exercise useful for the salvation of one's soul. Personal love for man and for any creature is regarded as positively dangerous for salvation and as leading one away from the love of God. One must harden one's heart against the creature and love God alone.[1] This is why Christians have often been so hard, so cold hearted and unfeeling in the name of virtues useful for their salvation. Love in Christianity became rhetorical, conventional and hypocritical. There was no human warmth in it. And, to make matters worse, this " glassy ", fossilized love was regarded as pre-eminently spiritual and was favourable contrasted with the warm personal love, springing from man's emotional nature. A contrast was also drawn between the natural and the supernatural love. And it appeared that the spiritual and perfect love, i.e. the very highest, did not resemble love at all but was impersonal, abstract and inhuman. Ordinary sympathy and com-passion is more gracious and more like love than this theological virtue. This is one of the most painful problems of Christian ethics. It shows that Christians have not been able to receive the fullness of the divinely human truth and that it is difficult for man to unite the love for God with the love for man, love for the Creator with love for the creature. Love for the creature in general, for animals, plants, minerals, for the earth and the stars, has not at all developed in Christian ethics. It is a problem for cosmic ethics and has yet to be formulated. Christianity gained strength and was victorious through its ascetic attitude to the cosmic life, through renouncing all that is natural and created, including the natural man. It has not worked out an ethics of love for the world, for all created things and all living beings. Even love for one's neighbour, for man who bears the image and likeness of God, was understood solely as a means of salvation, as an ascetic exercise in virtue. The Gospel commandment not to love " the world nor that which is in the world " was interpreted as a call not to love God's creation, cosmos and man, while in truth " the world " meant only sinful passions. In this respect a creative completion of Christian ethics is particularly necessary. Love cannot be merely a means to salvation and redemption. Love is the creation of a new life.

Love cannot be abstractly spiritual, blind to the concrete personality as a whole ; it must embrace both the spirit and the soul and be based upon

---

[1] See the works of St. Isaac the Syrian, St. John of the Ladder, St. Maxim the Confessor and Bishop Feofan the Hermit. Roman Catholics were more ready to admit the personally human element in love—as, for instance, St. Francis of Assisi, St. Francis de Sales, etc.

the union of those two principles. The spiritual principle abstracted and isolated from the soul and the body cannot give rise to love for a living being. Love means descent of the spirit into soul and body. The spiritual principle from its very nature must bring light and wholeness into the life of the soul. It plays the same part in love. It gives meaning and connection to everything. Without the spiritual principle the life of the soul breaks up into disconnected and meaningless experiences. The spiritual principle alone constitutes personality and gives it a permanent centre. Personality is created by the logos—the cosmos can only produce the individual. Without the logos, without the spiritual principle, personality disintegrates. The synthesizing spiritual principle embraces both the soul and the body. Love is born of the union of the spirit and the soul. The spirit in abstraction from the soul cannot give rise to love. Love is directed upon the concrete personality and seeks union with its kindred. Abstract, bloodless and impersonal spiritual love, that takes no cognizance of the soul, is not love and may be cruelly fanatical and inhuman. It is the love for an idea and not for a living being. They say it is love for God, which is higher than love for men. But God is then conceived as an abstract idea in the name of which men are sacrificed. The living personal God does not demand human sacrifice, He demands that love for Him should at the same time be love for man and mercy for all creatures. This is revealed to us in the Gospel, but it is badly understood and badly applied in Christian practice. Christianity does, of course, reveal to us gracious spiritual love as distinct from the natural love, but that has quite a different meaning. It means that natural human love is fragmentary and disjointed, mixed with lower cravings and passions which distort it and prevent us from seeing another's personality as a whole and directing our feeling upon it. So-called natural love is often impotent because it is unenlightened and partial, spoiled by selfishness and bound up with strivings that are contrary to the meaning of love. It is distorted by jealousy and leads to tyranny and idolatry. The so-called spiritual love is not meant to destroy the natural love but to transfigure, enlighten and strengthen it with spiritual power which gives it wholeness and meaning. Natural love must be spiritualized and acquire meaning which is always to be found in the realm of the spirit ; it must not be an irrational craving. Such cravings have a way of disintegrating and even destroying the personality both of the loved one and of the lover. The revelation of the spiritual principle in love can alone save from the destructive power of natural cravings. When it is unspiritual, blind and unenlightened, the love of parents for children or of friends for each other may be destructive of life and personality and sow the seeds of death. I am not speaking for the moment of love between man and woman, which easily assumes a demonic form. Natural love which leads to the adoration of the creature is idolatry and always bears evil fruit, stifling the one who is adored. We must love God above all. That means that we must not adore or worship anyone and anything in the world, neither men—whether they be our relatives or rulers—nor ideas, neither humanity nor nature. The meaning of life for man always lies in God and not in the world, in the spiritual and not in the natural. And from God man receives power to love other men and all creation with a creative and enlightened love so as to realize righteousness in the world. The primary source of life is in God and not in man. Love is determined not by the relation of the natural to the supernatural but by the relation of person to person—of the human personality to the Divine, or of one human personality to another. But is there such a thing as love of ideas, of values, of truth, of justice, of beauty, of science, of art, and so on? This is the most difficult question in the whole doctrine of love.

My life is determined not only by the love for living beings but also by the love for values—truth, beauty, righteousness—and these two kinds of love may come into conflict. The conflict is so real and poignant that it is equally revolting when personal love is sacrificed to the love of truth and righteousness and when truth and righteousness are sacrificed to personal love. The whole of the Platonic doctrine of Eros is abstract in character : through a series of abstractions from the sensuous world of living beings the mind gradually ascends to the world of ideas, where there can only be love of truth, beauty, the highest good, and so on. Plato calls us to sacrifice the love for living beings, for persons, to the love of ideas. His Eros is not personal, it does not know the mystery of personality and of personal love, it is idealistic. This was the limit of Greek thought. Christianity alone transcended that limit and revealed the mystery of personality and of personal love. From the point of view of abstract idealism there can be no solution of the conflict between love for a living being and love for an idea, between love for a person and love for the ideal values of truth, goodness and beauty. Christianity solves it in principle through the revelation of the God-man and of love for God and love for men ; but in practice the tragic conflict remains and can only be solved through experience and creative effort.

Love of ideas and values, of truth, goodness and beauty, is merely the unconscious and imperfect expression of the love for God and the divine. One ought to love God more than man, and the love for God ought to give us strength to love man. We may have to sacrifice love of our neighbours to the love of God, and in one of life's tragic conflicts this may take the form of putting the love of truth and righteousness above love for a fellow creature. But we must not sacrifice the love for our neighbours, for living beings, for God's creation for the sake of purely abstract ideas of justice, beauty, truth, humanity and so on. The living Truth, Goodness and Beauty may be put above love of one's neighbours—but the abstract idea of truth, goodness and beauty may not. Only the divine is above man—but never the abstract. The abstract idea of God is also worth nothing. It is therefore wrong to sacrifice love for living beings, for persons, for the sake of love for man in general or humanity as an abstract idea. The so-called humanistic love includes many elements and among them a false abstract love for humanity which is an idea and not a being, i.e. love for the "far off". In so far as humanistic love is only for the "far off" and not for the "neighbour" it is a lie and a deception. We must not sacrifice "the neighbours" to those "far off", i.e. must not sacrifice love for concrete living persons to the love for impersonal abstract humanity or its future welfare. The only "far off" Being Who is also the nearest is Christ, the living God, and He demands love for one's neighbour and unites in His divinely human life love for God and love for man. Love of values—of truth, justice, beauty—must be understood as an expression in this world of the love for God and the divine. It is godless and inhuman to love such "far off" entities as Nietzsche's superman, Marx's ideal communistic state, the moral law and abstract justice of legalistic morality, the state, the revolutionary utopias of perfect social order, the scientific truth of "scientism", the "beauty" of the aesthetes, or the abstract orthodoxy of religious fanatics. Love of Truth must at the same time be love of man and *vice versa*. Abstract love for man must not be opposed to the love for concrete, living men whom one meets in life.

Tragic conflicts between these two kinds of love bring much pain and difficulty in actual life. No smooth and rational solution of them is possible, and no general rules can be prescribed. Their solution is left to man's creative freedom. But the principle upon which it must be based is the principle of the divinely human love which is always concrete and personal and not abstract and general. In our sinful world human feelings may undergo such terrible transformations that the highest of them may become false and evil. Even the idea of love may prove to be false and evil and lead to great miseries. Much evil is perpetrated in the name of love—love of God, love of men, and especially love of ideas and goodness. When love of goodness and of ideas becomes abstract and fanatical, all is lost and nothing but evil comes of it. Love for God must be infinite, but when it turns into love for the abstract idea of God it leads to devastating results. Love for man must be boundless, but when it turns into love for the abstract idea of humanity and becomes idolatry, it is evil and destructive. Hunger and thirst for righteousness are blessed, but when righteousness becomes an abstract idea hostile to everything living, personal and concrete, the consequences are evil and destructive. We must not love only the divine in man, only the truth, goodness and beauty in him, i.e. only the valuable content of personality : we must love the human as well, be merciful to this actual living being, love him for nothing. And yet human personality exists only because it has a valuable content, because there is something divine in it, because it is the image of God in man. Love is always for that divine image which is to be found in every man, however low and sinful, but it embraces both the divine and the human in a person. We ought to love not only God in man but also man in God.

Compassion or pity differs from love in so far as it presupposes suffering. This is not necessarily so in the case of love. Compassion means union in suffering, while love may be union in joy and bliss. I have already defined compassion as union with the suffering creature in its God-forsakenness, whereas love is union with the creature in God the Creator. At one time it was the fashion to reject compassion and oppose it to love. This can probably be traced to Nietzsche. Compassion was entirely relegated to Buddhism and banished from Christianity. But this is a terrible moral blunder. Although in Christianity love is not limited to compassion and has higher forms, compassion cannot be excluded from love. Moreover, morality is impossible apart from it. In a sinful and fallen world compassion more than anything else testifies to the existence of another world and to our memory of it. The new ethics must make compassion one of its corner-stones, together with freedom and creativeness. The faculty for compassion has grown in the world together with new forms of cruelty and pitilessness. The capitalistic system is the most pitiless of all. There is no progressive increase of good in the world, there is an increase in it both of new good and new evil. It is the same with cruelty and compassion. A new feeling of pity for every creature has come into being. The cosmic feeling of pity was more characteristic of the East, of India, than of Christian Europe. But there it was not connected with individuality and was impersonal. The cosmic principle in ethics has generally been connected with impersonalism, but this is a mistake, for personality is found not only in the human world. All existence is personal, in however elementary a form. Pain is bound up with personality. Christian consciousness has not yet developed a moral relation to animals and to nature in general. Its attitude to nature has been too much that of spiritual aloofness. And yet the look in the eyes of a helpless animal in pain gives us a moral and metaphysical experience of wonderful depth. It bears witness to the fallen state of the world and the desolateness of the creature, including every one of us. At moments of pain and suffering a look of depth comes into the eyes of the most commonplace and shallow people, testifying to the hidden depths of life. Suffering is a proof not only of the God-forsakenness of creation but of the depths of being. If there were no suffering in a fallen and sinful world, it would be finally severed from being ; the depth of being shows itself in it as suffering. The mystery of existence is revealed in suffering. Hence the twofold attitude of Christianity to suffering ; I have alluded to it already. Suffering is a consequence of sin, a sign of sin, and at the same time redemption from sin and liberation from it. This is the meaning of Christ's suffering on the cross. This is implied in all ideas of a suffering God. Consequently, our attitude to suffering is complex. To have compassion, pity and mercy on those who suffer is an absolute moral duty. To help the suffering, the poor, the sick, the prisoners, is an absolute moral imperative. But suffering is a sign of sin and may bring deliverance. It would be monstrous to conclude from this that we ought not to pity and help the suffering, and that it would be a good thing to increase the amount of pain in the world. This kind of argument is sheer hypocrisy on the part of those who do not want to help and pity their neighbours and have no sympathy for anyone or anything in the world. God preserve us from resembling Job's conforters who, instead of helping and pitying Job, denounced his sins as the probable source of his sufferings ! They were condemned by God, and Job who struggled against God was justified.

Suffering may be of two kinds—unto life and unto death ; it may raise and purify man or crush and humiliate him. Compassion must make us strive to free our fellow creatures from the crushing and humiliating kind of suffering and to help them to feel the regenerating and purifying effect of it. Only bigots and hypocrites want to increase their fellows' sufferings as a means to moral regeneration. It is godless and inhuman. The human thing to do is to pity and help the sufferer, however sinful and wicked he might be. For after all, every one of us is sinful and wicked. The dreadful thing is that the sufferer often takes advantage of his suffering in order to torture and exploit other people. We ought to help our fellow men to bear the cross of suffering and to understand the meaning of it, but not to lay upon their shoulders a heavy cross ostensibly for their spiritual salvation. The conception of punishment as a moral duty to impose suffering in order to reform and regenerate the criminal is false and always has a touch of bigotry and hypocrisy about it. The principle of cruelty in punishment belongs to the past and in our day remains either as a belated survival or finds expression in terrorism. Sin has inevitable consequences, evil must be thrown into the flames, crime brings its own retribution with it—such is the structure of being. But those who bring to light the inevitable consequences of sin, who cast evil into flames and impose penalties for crime, are by no means bearers of the highest good and frequently are just as sinful, evil and criminal as the wrongdoers whom they punish. Bearers of the highest good are those who help, pity, visit the prisoners, save the guilty from execution and work miracles. The work of forcible destruction of evil is generally carried out by evil men—evil devours evil. This is the fate of the fallen world. We can observe it in the succession of political reactions and revolutions, of revolutions and counter-revolutions.

There is being born in the world a new morality of compassion for human beings, for animals, for all creatures, for everyone who feels pain. This is a tremendous spiritual achievement. But like everything else, this fact has a double significance. Modern civilized man cannot endure cruelty, pain and suffering and is more merciful than men of the past, but this is not only because he is morally and spiritually higher than they. He fears pain and suffering more than they did ; he is more effeminate, less firm, patient and courageous than they ; in other words, he is spiritually less strong. This is the reverse side of the growth of pity and compassion, and of decrease in cruelty. Russian literature and thought have revealed wonderful depths of pity and compassion, and have had an enormous significance for the development of the moral consciousness of humanity. It was the mission of Russian creative genius to display exceptional mercy, pity and compassion. The Russian mind at its highest could not rest happy while others were miserable. Complacency and self-sufficiency, individual, national, family, or class, is foreign to the Russian moral consciousness, and this throws light on its ethical mission. Russian moral consciousness puts love and pity for man higher than love for the state and the nation, or for science, civilization, abstract morality, and so on. But pity and compassion have their limits, beyond which they may result in evil. Man always has to choose, and choice always involves cruelty. Sometimes one has to suppress compassion, act pitilessly and cause suffering in order to save the world from greater suffering. Pity and compassion must not be a sign of effeminacy and cowardice. Only manly compassion has a moral significance. Hatred is a principle opposed to love, but anger may be a dark and passionate manifestation of love. But anger is deceptive because it often gives people an illusory sensation of strength and power.

6. THE STATE, REVOLUTION AND WAR

It is not my purpose in the present book to consider the state as such. I am only interested in the state as a moral institution and in the attitude that ought to be adopted towards it. This involves the question of the relation of the state to freedom and to the individual. In its origin, essence and purpose, the state is not inspired by enthusiasm for freedom, justice, or human personality, although it has to do with all these. In the first place, the state brings system into chaos ; it strives for order, strength, power, expansion, the formation of big historical units. Forcibly maintaining a minimum of justice and righteousness, the state does it not out of kindness or love of justice—those feelings are foreign to it—but because without such a minimum original chaos would re-assert itself and the state, instead of being strong and stable, would disintegrate. First and foremost, the state is an embodiment of power and it loves power more than legality, justice or righteousness. Striving for power is the doom of states and the demonic principle in them. It lures them on to conquests and expansion, and may bring prosperity, but may also bring destruction. In any conflict between might and right the state always is on the side of might. It is an expression of the balance of forces.[1]

There can be no ideal form of state ; all political utopias are radically false. There can only be relative improvements, generally connected with limiting the power of the state. In its demonic will to power the state always strives to exceed its limits and to become an absolute monarchy, an absolute democracy, an absolute communism. The ancient Greco-Roman world did not recognize any limits to the state : the city-state was for it absolute. Limits were fixed by Christianity, which liberates man from the power of the world. The human soul is more precious than the kingdoms of this world, than the state. Christianity introduced a dualism which is in principle insoluble, though in modern times attempts have been made to make the state absolute once more. The state belongs to the world of sin and does not in any way resemble

---

[1] There is a great deal of truth in Lassal's speech, " About Constitutional Monarchy ".

the Kingdom of God. The state has a double character : it both struggles against the consequences of sin by externally limiting the expressions of evil will, and is itself contaminated with sin, reflecting it in all it does. The greatest mistake in the history of the church and of Christianity was the attempt to ascribe a sacred, theocratical character to the kingdom of the Caesar. It dates back to Constantine the Great, and that epoch is now over. Holy Christian monarchies, both papal and imperial, were a monstrous mixture of the kingdom of the Caesar and the Kingdom of God, predominance always being given to the Caesar. The sacred state, the holy power of the monarch, was supposed to guide human souls and to look after their salvation, i.e. the kingdom of the Caesar was charged with a task that belongs solely to the church.

The relations between the church and the state are paradoxical, for it may equally well be said that the state forms part of the church and that the church forms part of the state. The spiritual, mystical church is the Christianized cosmos, the soul of the world endowed with Christian grace, and the state, like everything else, is a part of it, though a part the least gracious and Christianized, the most subject to the power of sin and therefore of law. But on the empirical plane, historically and socially, the church forms part of the state, is subject to its laws, is protected or oppressed by it. This is the tragedy of the historical life of the church. The church as a social institution is connected with the state and dependent upon it. The state is the realm of the " herd-man " inspired by the demonic will to power. The democratic state is just as much a kingdom of the Caesar as a monarchy is. To ascribe an absolute and sacred significance to democracy is as wrong as to ascribe it to monarchy. The state has a good mission in the world. Those in authority do not bear the sword in vain, i.e. authority is needed in the sinful, fallen world. Even the worst kind of state carries out that good mission ; but every state perverts it through its will to power and an inclination to overstep its borders. The state in all its forms is subject to passions—to the passion for power, for expansion, for tyranny. Tyranny and disregard for human personality and freedom may exist in a democratic state as much as in an absolute monarchy, and are at their worst in a communistic state. The state cannot be sacred and absolute, it cannot be in the least like the Kingdom of God, because it is always based upon compulsion. But compulsory power has its origin in sin and does not belong to the Kingdom of God. The relation of the ruler and the ruled is foreign to the kingdom which knows only the relations of love. The state is under the sign of law and not of grace. True, it is an expression of human creativeness and not only of law, but that creativeness is without grace and does not open the way into the Kingdom of God. There can be no perfect, ideal state, for every state means the rule of one set of men over others. The ideal, perfect life puts an end to such rule and indeed to all compulsory power, even to that of God ; for it is only to a sinful world that God can appear as a source of compulsion.

There is a certain amount of truth in anarchism. Anarchism is not applicable to our sinful world which is under the law, and anarchic utopias are a snare and a delusion. But the perfect life, the Kingdom of God, can only be conceived in terms of anarchism, which is the apaphatic and the only true way of thinking about it, for it avoids any similarity with the kingdom of the Caesar and severs all connection with the categories of this world. The unholy and unrighteous nature of the state power shows itself in the fact that power is always demoralizing ; it unbridles passions and lets loose subconscious instincts. From the moral point of view power ought to be regarded as a duty and a burden and not as a right and a privilege. The lust of power is as sinful as every other lust. The trouble is that exercise of power kindles the lust, so that only people of exceptional spirituality avoid succumbing to it. Power is generally exercised by that type of the " herd-man " which seldom reaches a high moral or spiritual level. Manifestations of power cannot be regarded as a theophany ; and tyranny is a thing that ought not to be endured.

There are two truly moral principles : love and gracious regeneration of life on the one hand, and freedom and justice on the other. The state is not the gracious kingdom of love and is but partly connected with freedom and justice, since it always tends to violate them. The fundamental moral problem with regard to the state is the relation between the state and the individual. At this point we see most clearly that the state is devoid of grace and holiness and has a non-Christian nature and origin. The state does not recognize concrete and unique personalities ; the inner world of the individual and his destiny are closed to it. It is limited to the abstract and the general ; the mystery of the individual does not exist for it. Personality is for it merely a general term. This is characteristic of herd-morality. The state may reluctantly admit in the abstract the personal rights of a man and a citizen, but it will never recognize the particular and qualitatively unique rights of individual human beings, each of which has a destiny of his own. Indeed it is impossible to demand this from the state. The state is not interested in personal destinies and can take no notice of them. There is a perennial struggle, a tragic conflict between the individual and the state and from the ethical point of view their interrelation is hopelessly paradoxical. The individual cannot live without the state ; he recognizes the state as a certain value and is prepared to work in it and make sacrifices for its sake. But at the same time the individual rebels against " the cold monster " which oppresses all personal existence. The spheres of personal life and of the life of the state never coincide but only partially intersect. The value of personality is hierarchically higher than that of the state—personality belongs to eternity and the state to time, personality bears the image and likeness of God and the state does not, personality is going towards the Kingdom of God and may enter it, while the state never can. In the herd-life of our sinful world the state with its glory and power may appear as a superpersonal value inspiring individuals to heroic deeds. But from the point of view of Christian personalism it is the individual who has to pass moral judgment on the state. All forms of state organization and power are temporal and transitory ; not one of them may be treated as absolute or regarded as sacred. The only political principle which is connected with absolute truth is the principle of the subjective rights of the human personality, of the freedom of spirit, of conscience, of thought and speech. The state in all its forms has a tendency to violate that principle. The monistic state, whether it be an absolute monarchy or a form of socialism, is particularly dangerous and hostile to personal freedom ; the mixed and pluralistic forms of state organization are not so apt to be tyrannical and are a lesser evil. The individual, the free social organizations and the state must freely interact and limit one another.

Sociologically the individual and society are correlative ; the individual cannot be conceived apart from society, and society presupposes the existence of individuals. Society is a certain reality and not merely the sum total of its members.[1] Society has an ontological kernel, which the state has not ; the Kingdom of God is a society, an ontologically real communion between persons. In the hierarchy of spiritual values the first place belongs to personality, the second to society and the third to the state. But in the sinful world of the herd-man the lower value acquires the highest significance, and the highest has the least importance. The state has most power, then comes society, and personality, which has the greatest value, has the least. Spiritual freedom is the highest value, but in the realm of the herd-man it has not the greatest importance. This tragic conflict between values is insoluble in the sinful world where power and value do not coincide, and quantity has precedence over quality.

[1] Many valuable ideas are to be found in Zimmel's *Sociologie*. But Zimmell's sociology has no ontological basis.

Morally one must strive for a social organization in which the principles of personality, society and the state interact and mutually limit one another, giving the individual the greatest possible freedom of creative spiritual life. There is something incommensurable between the state which cannot penetrate into the infinity of the spirit and the infinite spiritual life going on in the depths of personality. But that life cannot be understood individualistically : it is also life in society, in communion with others, i.e. it is metaphysically social and rooted in the Kingdom of God. Personality lives in the spiritual society, i.e. in the church. From the ethical point of view the principle of the absolute supremacy of the state is wrong and immoral, and so is Communism, which finally socializes man and suppresses personality.

The moral problem of the state grows particularly acute during war. The state gives rise to wars, is based on military power and does not recognize the higher moral tribunal which prevents wars. It regards as permissible all that serves its preservation, expansion and power. It is utterly impossible to apply to the state the same moral standards as to an individual. Actions considered evil, immoral and deserving of condemnation in an individual are regarded in the case of the state not merely as permissible but as fine and noble. It is apparently impossible to require that the state should obey the ten commandments : they are only applicable to individuals. Individuals are forbidden to kill, and murder is considered a great sin. But the same individuals acting on behalf of the state as its organs and instruments not only may kill but must kill and, so far from being regarded as a sin, it is considered their duty. A very complex and painful conflict is thus created for the human conscience. A man performs moral acts in a different capacity—as a private person and as an instrument of the state, i.e. as a judge, a soldier, etc. A person belongs to superpersonal social wholes, such as the family, a corporation, a class, a nation and, first and foremost, the state. His life is bound up with a very complex hierarchy of values. A man cannot perform pure moral acts as though he stood alone before the absolute good. He acts in the world, in a dark, sinful environment, and all his moral actions and valuations are complicated by the multiplicity and relativity of the world-life and present difficulties for conscience. Absolutely uncompromising moral actions and valuations are mistaken if only because they ignore the existence of the world in which men live and recognize nothing but the moral law and norm. To condemn war from the point of view of absolute morality is easy enough, but this does not solve the painful problem. War is a great evil. This is indisputable from the moral and especially from the

Christian point of view. It is desirable and indeed imperative to reach a condition in which wars would be impossible. But this does not solve the concrete and painful question of our attitude to war. From the absolute, normative point of view it may be a lesser evil and even a good, because absolute moral norms have to be applied to a dark and sinful world. The fundamental ethical paradox is that the distinction between good and evil, i.e. the very origin of our good, is bound up with the Fall, and in a fallen and sinful world the good is never found in its pure form. The pure and absolute good can only be manifested in a world which will be beyond good and evil. But then the kingdom of the good will be the Kingdom of God which is above good. Hence uncompromising moral absolutism is out of place both in the sinful world and in the Kingdom of God. This is apparent in relation to war. War is the result of sin and is possible only in a sinful world. But in the darkness of that world it may prove to contain an element of light and be a source of heroism and nobility. In the history of mankind war has been an expression of chaos but it has also been a victorious struggle against chaos and has served to create great historical bodies with their splendid civilizations. It brutalized man and unbridled his lower instincts, but was also a source of the lofty virtues of courage, honour, loyalty, chivalry and nobility. War is therefore a highly complex moral phenomenon. For the individual conscience it is always a tragedy and means taking upon oneself the burden of sin and guilt ; but the state of the world may be such that the acceptance of sin and guilt raise man to a morally higher level than an easy rejection of them. Personal conscience is always confronted with a conflict between various kinds of values and the decision always involves a sacrifice of one of them. The conflict is particularly acute in the case of war. The defence of one's country, the defence of the cultural and spiritual values of one's nation, may make war itself a value for the sake of which other values must be sacrificed. A will guided by moral conscience cannot perform absolutely moral acts because it is opposed by the evil will of the world. A moral act could be pure and absolute only if there were no evil will in the world and if it were confronted with other acts as pure and absolute. But the sinful world is the arena for the struggle of conflicting and inter-acting wills, and thus in a sense the world is at war.[1]

Two entirely different questions must be distinguished with regard to war. There is the question of the prevention of war, of the struggle for the spiritual and social order of life in which it would be impossible, and there is the question of the personal attitude to war once it has begun and

[1] Proudhon has written a famous justification of war.

become a part of the nation's destiny. The problem is further complicated by the fact that it is differently formulated at different historical epochs. There were epochs when war still had meaning and justification. Ethics cannot therefore give a straightforward answer to the painful questionings of the moral conscience with regard to war. In the past war had meaning and justification, although wars were often senseless and unjust. But after the horror of the world-war we are entering an epoch when war loses meaning and can be no longer justified, and when struggle against the possibility of new wars becomes a moral obligation. Ethics must give a double answer to the question of war ; we must do our utmost to prevent war, to develop a moral attitude which condemns it and makes it unlikely, to create social conditions which make wars unnecessary ; but once a war has begun and can no longer be stopped, the individual must not throw off its burden or give up his share of the common responsibility ; he must take upon himself the guilt of the war for the sake of higher ends, but h must feel the tragedy and the inevitable horror of it. War is a part of man's destiny and this is why it repels the Christian conscience which resists destiny. War is retribution. And it must be accepted in an enlightened spirit, as all other trials of life. In the same way we ought to accept with Christian enlightenment and spiritual humility the death of the people we love, though we ought to do everything in our power to prevent their death. But the meaning of war, as of all great historical events, is generally quite different from what it is taken to be by those who take an active part in it. The last world-war has a meaning of its own but, of course, it is not what the belligerent countries took it to be. It means the end of a whole historical epoch and the beginning of a new one.

Wars are due to a complex interaction of causes, and economic forces play a considerable part in this connection. But emotionally wars are bound up first and foremost with national passions. Wars are declared and carried on by states which do not ask the peoples' permission to wage war. But behind the state is the nation, national interests and conflicts, national love and hate. The nation is undoubtedly a higher value than the state, which has a purely functional significance. The state serves merely to form the nation, to defend it and further its development. But, like every other value, nationality may become perverted and claim to have a supreme and absolute significance. Self-centred nationalism, hostile to every nation except its own, puts itself above all other values. All countries suffer from the disease of nationalism and this is the emotional source of wars. Ethics must recognize the value of nationality and at the same time condemn nationalism, which is as false as moralism or aestheticism or the worship of the state, or of science. All these are forms of idolatry. The logical opposite of nationalism is internationalism, which is equally false. Nationality as a positive value enters hierarchically into the concrete unity of mankind, which embraces the whole multiplicity of nations. The horror and evil of war cannot be conquered by the anaemic gospel of pacifism, which is generally connected with abstract cosmo-politanism. Pacifism is the opposite of militarism, but there is no final moral truth in either. Pacifism is optimistic and ignores the tragic nature of history. There is a certain amount of truth in it—the will, namely, that wars should cease. But pacifism does not recognize the spiritual condi-tions needed to end wars ; it remains on the surface, in the domain of unreal politics and legal formulae, unconscious of the irrational forces at work in the world. Pacifism is a form of rationalism. The preaching of peace and of the brotherhood of nations is a Christian work, and Christian ethics must take it over from rationalistic pacifism. For Christian con-sciousness the problem is complicated by the understanding of the evil and irrational forces of history.

War has a fatal dialectic of its own which will bring it to an end sooner than the preaching of peace. War is connected with the development of technical sciences. Recent discoveries of new means of attack and de-struction are so monstrous that they must lead to the self-negation of war and make it impossible. War is going to be waged not by armies and not even by peoples but by chemical laboratories and involve horrible de-struction of nations, towns and civilizations, i.e. it will threaten mankind with annihilation. The chivalrous aspects of war connected with courage, manliness, honour and loyalty are disappearing and losing their signifi-cance. They played hardly any part in the last war. War is becoming quite a different kind of thing and requires another name. War will be destroyed by the technique of war. The question of the spiritual and moral communion of nations thus becomes the question of the further existence of mankind, which is threatened with destruction through the new and more perfect means of warfare. States and civilizations breed forces which impel them to their doom.

Ideas bred by war had far greater significance for the moral education of mankind than war itself. The type of the warrior, the knight, the man who defends by force of arms his honour, the honour of the weak, the honour of his family, the honour of his country, was the predominant moral ideal and had enormous influence upon social morality. The aristocrat, the nobleman, was first and foremost a warrior ready to fight for his honour. The ancient cruel and warlike instincts of man took the form of inborn nobility, a manly courage in life and in death, and readiness always to put honour and loyalty higher than life. A military code of morals always developed strength of character, prevented the masculine type from becoming soft and effeminate and succeeded in imparting to cruel instincts a character of nobility. It cannot be denied that although historic chivalry connected with the military caste is dead, some of the features developed by it became permanent characteristics of the higher, non-bourgeois type of man. The bourgeoisie which put into the foreground enterprise and economic interests has not succeeded, like chivalry, in developing high moral characteristics ; the virtue of industry is not a specific characteristic of the bourgeois. Aristocratic nobility still remains the highest type outside of religious ethics. A warrior is a man with a strong sense of honour and a special conception of it. And here we come upon a tragic conflict between lofty human conceptions and the lofty ideas revealed by God and contained in the Gospel. The military code of honour, which became binding on the upper class in general, presupposes that it is better to injure than to be injured, better to insult than to be insulted ; it is based on the principle that every stain upon honour must be washed away in blood and always implies that man is humiliated not by what he does but by what is done to him. A warrior, a man belonging to the nobility, a man of good birth, is one who is always afraid that his honour may be assaulted and his nobility called in question. He believes that his honour and nobility depend not upon his personal virtues and qualities but upon his belonging to a certain class or caste. He is not primarily conscious of personal honour but of the honour of the family, the class, the regiment, the army, and is ready to forget himself and sacrifice his life for the sake of that honour. At that stage, personal moral consciousness is not as yet awakened ; all moral valuations have an impersonal, generic, regimental, class character, and their worth depends precisely on their being impersonal. Even the insults that must be washed away by blood are not insults to the person as such, unique and irreplaceable, but to the person as representative of the family, the class, the army, the regiment and so on. Blood is always connected with kinship and implies the awakening of the ancient unconscious instincts of the clan which have not yet been mastered by the personal consciousness. The consciousness of personal honour, nobility and dignity is only revealed in the Gospel, which finally overcomes all generic, impersonal morality.

There exists a sharp conflict and opposition between the morality of the Gospel and the aristocratic moral code created by warriors at a time when armed struggle was regarded as a man's noblest occupation. If the mind and conscience of the Christian world were more sensitive and less influenced by hereditary instincts, that conflict would cause us much pain and bitterness. The Christian morality of the Gospel knows nothing about the honour of the family, the class or the regiment ; it is only concerned with personal honour. And personal honour is determined by man's spiritual quality and his being unable to inflict, rather than to endure, injuries. Turning the other cheek is an expression of spiritual heroism which presupposes inner humility and victory over the old hereditary instincts, but it seems revolting to a man who is ruled by those instincts and has a warrior's code of morals. A man who turns the other cheek may always be suspected of cowardice. This is what makes the problem so difficult. Turning the other cheek must be an act of grace, a deed of light and of spiritual heroism, a manifestation of a greater force than the physical violence displayed in attacking the offender, fighting a duel, etc. But mere passivity and indifference to insult or, worse still, cowardice are morally revolting and far beneath the military conception of honour.

It is remarkable that the military ethics of chivalry, so contrary to the Gospel morality, has developed chiefly within Christendom. Chivalry ennobled the dark barbarian world and brought light into it ; it spiritualized the blind and savage instincts. Chivalry emphasized the idea of service, of devotion to faith, of respect for woman, of defending the weak and the humble—and all these ideas have a permanent moral value. But chivalry also gave rise to the institution of duelling, which is based upon an un-Christian, clannish conception of defending honour by blood and is a paradox in a Christian world. A military man cannot refuse to fight a duel if he has been insulted or been challenged by the injured party. If he puts up with the insult he is disgraced, considered a coward and driven out of his regiment. But at the same time duelling may be forbidden by law and punished as a crime. Duelling was not only an expression of an unconscious instinct but a conscious moral duty as well. It is of course radically opposed to Christianity and to the morality of the Gospel. It is inspired by the archaic instinct of blood vengeance, though in a transformed and civilized form. Duelling is connected with the affective states of injury and vengeance. A man who challenges another to a duel considers himself injured and longs for blood vengeance. In special cases a duel is provoked by the fact that two men feel there is not room enough for both of them in the world because they both love the same woman. In such cases the sense of injury and desire for vengeance may be absent, or in any case very much refined and transformed. But there certainly is jealousy, which is morally no better, there is the evil will to own a human being and there is the wrong conception of honour. A man's honour is made to depend not on what proceeds from him but on what proceeds from another, i.e. to depend not on his own but upon another person's feelings. This is spiritual slavery. A man who challenges another to a duel is always in a state of spiritual slavery though he may display courage and fortitude. Not infrequently duels are due to moral cowardice, to the fear of public opinion or of the corporation to which one belongs. A duel is not murder, for in a serious duel both parties are prepared to face death. But it involves murder and bloodshed, often for trifling reasons and for the sake of a false conception of honour. In a sense duel is a form of suicide and must be judged in the same way. Although a duel seems a very personal, intimate affair and is a conflict between two persons, it is in truth an impersonal act inspired by unconscious herd instincts. It could only be fought between gentlemen, which alone shows how strong the impersonal, class element was in it. Duelling is connected with military ethics and psychology. It is an un-Christian and an anti-Christian but a comparatively noble manifestation of the military spirit. War and the military spirit give rise, however, to another fact which is absolutely low and ignoble, has no justification whatever and has nothing to do with nobility, fortitude, or sense of honour. I am referring to capital punishment.

The condition of people's moral consciousness may be gauged in a sense by their attitude to capital punishment. It is an ominous moral sign that the peoples of Western Europe and America approve of capital punishment and actually go to look at executions. Capital punishment is rooted in the ancient instinct of blood vengeance and human sacrifice, though it has assumed a civilized and legal form. War and duel are not murder because those who take part in them are ready not only to kill but also to die, and always risk their lives ; but capital punishment is murder pure and simple. It may be said that it does not involve a moral subject who commits the murder. Death is inflicted not by an individual but by the " cold monster ", the state. Hence there is no one who acts from motives of hatred and vengeance. In defence of capital punishment it is said that it has nothing to do with human desires, emotions and passions but is merely an expression of the social instinct of self-preservation. The only thing that is true in this contention is that capital punishment is absolutely inhuman. The " cold monster ", the state, which performs the executions dispassionately and without malice, consists, after all, of living men and women with their instincts, thoughts and feelings. A whole people's instincts of vengeance and fear are active in capital punishment and approve of it. The existence of capital punishment is a reflection on the moral consciousness of a nation and its rulers. It is a mistake to think that capital punishment is the work of abstract law, wholly non-human and dispassionate ; and in any case the " dispassionateness " of capital punishment is the most horrible thing about it, the chief argument against it. Those who inflict capital punishment sacrifice nothing and run no risk of death ; this is what makes it so vile. And who inflicts it? Not the executioner with his axe, who is himself a victim, for he is required to renounce his divine image and likeness. It is the whole people who inflict it, in so far as they demand capital punishment and approve of it. It is the most striking instance of the state overstepping its legitimate boundaries, for human life belongs to God and not to man. The final settlement of human destiny, the final judgment over personality, is outside the province of the state. The state cannot and ought not to know the hour of a man's death, for this is the supreme mystery which must be treated with reverence. Capital punishment is violence done by the state to God, to the Divine Providence. It is violence like every other murder. In war and in a duel a man takes his chance and, in spite of all, relies on a higher power. In capital punishment there is no element of chance ; the result is certain and known beforehand and the whole thing is absolutely rationalized. This is the baseness of it.

The conflict of Christian morality with the state is particularly acute in the case of capital punishment. The state takes upon itself to regularize the concentrated instincts of blood vengeance and to make them thoroughly rational and subservient to utilitarian ends. But ferocious instincts are a thousand times worse in a rationalized than in an irrational form. Capital punishment is a rational and utilitarian institution, but it springs from unconscious instincts. It is not my purpose to consider how far capital punishment is useful in preventing and abolishing crime and securing order and safety. That is not a purely ethical problem. I believe that capital punishment is socially pernicious and demoralizing. People who thought that the death penalty has a redeeming significance took a higher view of it, though they did not understand the Christian meaning of redemption and interpreted it in a pagan and superstitious sense.[1] But their attitude was higher because they did not rationalize the idea of capital punishment ; it is the rationalization of it which makes it particularly revolting. To kill a man out of vengeance is morally better than to

[1] J. de Maistre's ideas are particularly interesting in this connection. See his *Sur les délais de la justice divine dans la punition des coupables.*

inflict capital punishment. From the point of view of religion capital punishment has been abolished by the fact that the Son of God, the Redeemer and Saviour of the world, was put to a shameful death, and the instrument of His execution became the means of salvation for us. In the pre-Christian pagan world capital punishment was discredited by the fact that it was inflicted on Socrates. The law which sentenced to death Socrates and afterwards Jesus Christ can no longer be regarded as competent to decide on matters of life and death ; it must moderate its claims. Capital punishment is the most sinister product of the ethics of law and of herd-morality.

It is the fate of sinful communities on this side of good and evil to form states. Human society is destined to live both under the moral law and under the law of the state, both under the law that takes the form of duty and the law that must be obeyed under compulsion. The state not only curtails manifestations of evil will but enables men to realize their possibilities and consequently it strives to embrace the whole fullness of life, including spiritual culture and religion. Men have come to love the state and are fascinated by its growth and power, by the task of defending or perfecting it. They devote their creative instincts to the state. They give it both their good and their bad ; but the bad proves to outweigh the good. The state has a double nature ; it has a good and providential mission which it vitiates by its sinful lust for power and by every sort of wrong. At certain epochs not only the state as such is regarded as sacred but definite forms of state, e.g. monarchy or, later on, democracy. But all forms of state and authority are sacred only so long as people believe in them. When faith in the sacredness of this or that form of authority disappears and the ruling power has to rely on force alone, it ceases to be sacred and passes away. The political organization of the state rests both on force and on faith. When faith is gone, force proves to be powerless. The phenomenon of the state in our sinful world has its corrective in that of the revolution. Revolution too is providential and has a mission of its own. It is essential to take up a moral attitude towards revolutions and this is not easy, for they have a double and ambiguous character in which good and evil are completely mixed. Revolutions are the destiny, the inevitable doom of nations, and it is impossible to take a superficial view of them, explaining them by external political and economic causes, as both the revolutionaries and the counter-revolutionaries generally do. A revolution is a spiritual phenomenon, though it may and usually does deny the reality of spirit. It is only as a spiritual event that it interests me at present. Revolutions bring out much evil and vindictiveness. But it would be a mistake to think that the evil is caused by revolutions ; to suppose this would be as superficial as to imagine that revolutions are manifestations of justice and righteousness and establish a perfect social order. The cause of evil is the failure to realize the good. The existence of evil is the fault of the good. This is one of the paradoxes of ethics. The Good has formulated its lofty principles but failed to realize them in life. Thus Christianity has proclaimed the highest principles of life— love, brotherhood, spiritual freedom. But the Christians have succeeded in turning them into mere rhetoric and an edifying convention. Their social and political life has been based not upon love, brotherhood and spiritual freedom, but upon indifference, hostility, injustice, violence and lack of respect for human personality. The structure of reality, however, is such that falsity is bound sooner or later to come to light, and the order of existence based upon falsity is bound to perish. If the Good does not bring about its own realization and establish justice and righteousness, evil takes this task upon itself. Such are the dialectics of good and evil. A revolution takes place. A revolution always means that there had been no creative spiritual forces working to improve and regenerate life. A revolution is a punishment sent men for having failed to manifest their creative spiritual powers and build up a better life. Morally one cannot desire a revolution any more than one can desire death ; one ought only to desire a better life, spiritually social regeneration and the realization of the greatest possible measure of justice. But once a revolution has been decided upon in Heaven and taken place, we must accept it in an enlightened spirit, inwardly and not externally ; we must not stoop to vindictive opposition or succumb to despair at the horror of it. Revolutions are sent by Providence and only appear to be caused by political and economic causes and by the activity of revolutionary leaders and revolutionary masses.[1]

An enormous, an overwhelming amount of evil and malice is released in revolution, but the evil and malice are not created by it. They had been accumulating for ages, and the revolution merely releases them. Everything that was rotten in the old regime crumbles away in a revolution. There is general demoralization because objects of piety and beliefs in them had disintegrated in the old pre-revolutionary days, acquired a purely rhetorical and legalistic character and been used as means of restraint and repression. Revolutions happen because creative activity

[1] J. de Maistre in his *Considérations sur la France* and Carlyle in his *French Revolution*, the best book written on the subject, speak about revolution with the insight of genius.

becomes impossible. This does not mean that revolutions are favourable to creativeness ; on the contrary, they are unfavourable to it. A revolution cannot be regarded as a new and better life, it is an illness, a catastrophe, a passage through death. A revolution always brings with it an avenger who performs the greatest cruelties and acts of violence. The revolutionary element, i.e. the released collective subconscious, is saturated with vengeance. But those on whom the revolution wreaks its vengeance and whose old wrongs have caused its abuses and cruelties cannot claim to be the champions of righteousness as against its unrighteousness, for the revolution itself embodies a measure of right as compared with their wrong. There always is a certain relative justice in a revolution though it may be wrapped up in falsity, malice and violence. Those who had behaved unjustly in the past and failed to create a new and better life before the revolution cannot claim to have justice on their side, for it is they who are responsible for the injustice of the revolution. Vengeance is hideòus, but it is not for those whose wrongs have provoked it to denounce its hideousness. Spiritually speaking they are the very people who ought to see a certain measure of justice in that vengeance.

The disease of the revolution can never be cured by counter-revolutionaries and reactionaries. Both they and the revolutionaries live in a world of falsity and self-deception. What is realized in and through revolutions is very different from the dreams of the revolutionaries, and what takes place after revolutions is very different from the dreams of the reactionaries. Revolutions have a purifying and regenerating effect quite apart from the malicious and vindictive acts performed by their leaders and the masses. They have enormous spiritual consequences for national life and often bring about a religious regeneration. They do not as such create a social order based on freedom and justice, but they get rid of many old wrongs, of much injustice and falsity. They reshift the social layers and call to creative work men who had been repressed in the past and had no chance of occupying the foremost places. A revolution not merely destroys the old political order of the state but enables the state to put an end to the tyranny of some social classes over others.

From the moral point of view our attitude to revolutions is bound to be very complex. Christian morality is opposed to the revolutionary ethics which is based on vengeance, envy, malice and violence. A revolution unites and organizes the most vindictive, envious and embittered elements of a nation. This is what gives it victory. It is the law of every revolution. Revolution is by its very nature devoid of grace and is a symptom of man being forsaken by God. Divine Providence acts in it, but its ways are so mysterious and unfathomable that they may lead through a complete separation from God. From the moral point of view revolutions must be condemned because they create the type of man possessed by vengeance, malice and thirst for violence. They are condemned by the very expression in the eyes of their renowned leaders and by their terrible lack of spirituality. From the religious point of view revolutions must be condemned because they are not only graceless, and as it were abandoned by God, but for the most part godless and hostile to religion. But we cannot rest content with these judgments. Moreover, we cannot lightly pronounce this religious and moral condemnation. Religiously and morally we must take upon ourselves the blame for revolutions and regard them as part of our own destiny. No one can regard himself as innocent and others as guilty. A revolution, like every other great and significant event in the destinies of mankind, involves me and every one of us. It is not something which is wholly external to me, even though I might be free from the ideas and illusions of the revolutionaries. This is why poets have a foreboding of a coming revolution (in Russia this was the case with Alexander Blok). In this case as in every other it is morally wrong to think of two camps—the camp of revolutionary injustice and the camp of those who condemn it, or *vice versa*. Justice and injustice, right and wrong, are to be found in both camps and are present in every one of us. Vengeance of the counter-revolutions is even more hideous than that of the revolutions.

The right to revolt is morally justifiable when the wrongs of the old regime have grown outrageous and its spiritual foundations have crumbled away. But a revolution does not trouble about rights ; it is elemental and resembles a geological cataclysm. It releases the subconscious instincts of the masses which were repressed by the old forms of life so long as those forms corresponded to their beliefs and were regarded by them as sacred. The question as to the right to revolt is asked by the reflective moral consciousness before or after a revolution has taken place but never at the time. A revolution is the manifestation of the subconscious and not of the conscious mind—of the collective and not of the individual subconscious—and it obeys its laws. But the paradox of revolutions is that they are generally inspired by rationalistic theories and are directed towards rationalistic ends. Thus the Russian revolution in which passionate forces of subconscious mass instincts are at work is ideally dominated by the rationalistic Marxian theory requiring absolute order and regularization of life. Hegelian rationalism has been forced upon the unconscious elemental instincts of the Russian people. Something analogous happened in the French revolution which on the conscious level was connected with the eighteenth century rationalistic philosophy of enlightenment. Revolutions always combine the collective unconscious of the masses with utilitarian and rationalistic theories which leave no room for the irrational. The rational logical consciousness thus itself becomes a part of the irrational subconscious. Russian Marxism, for instance, is precisely such an irrational unconsciously elemental fact.

A revolution means the rejection of the unjust and wicked old world and to that extent is elemental and irrational ; but in so far as it also means a belief in the good and just world which it is supposed to create, it is rationalistic, idealistic and utopian. Hence a revolution generally proves to be a rationalistic madness, a rationalized irrationality. The irrational submits to the tyranny of the rational, and the rational, in imposing the tyranny, becomes irrational. Revolutions are inspired by the desire to struggle against tyranny, by ideals of liberty and instinctive love of it, but when they take place freedom is forgotten and a new and worse tyranny is created. The forces of revolution are opposed to the value of personality, of freedom, of creativeness and, indeed, to all spiritual values. The most terrible thing is that revolutions suppress and destroy personality, the source of moral judgments and actions, and therefore free and original moral judgments become impossible. Revolutions are catastrophic, exceptional events, and yet they always bring about the triumph of a conventionality of their own which inevitably comes into conflict with personalistic ethics. It is impossible to expect personal, free, original and first-hand moral judgments from Jacobins or Communists. Their personal conscience is paralysed and replaced by the collective mass-conscience of the new herd-man. Hence a triumphant revolution generally comes into conflict with personal creativeness and the free spirit. It is a different kind of conflict from that with the counter-revolutionary forces. The latter also belong to the realm of the herd-man and are guided not by the personal and original conscience but by the impersonal mass-conscience. The evil aspects of the old regime and of the revolution correlative to it, as well as the element of fate in both of them, are equally hostile to the freedom of the spirit, equally opposed to the infinite value of personality. The conflict between them is a tragedy that can find no solution in our sinful work. Utopias of the perfect state are even more opposed to the value of freedom and of personality than the present imperfect political and social order. This is true of all utopias, theocratic and communistic alike. We find it already in Plato, who created the prototype of utopias. His aristocratic idealistic communism is a thorough-going tyranny, a denial of all freedom and of the value of personality. Christian ethics is utterly opposed to this. Even anarchist utopias lead to a denial of freedom and of personality.

7. THE SOCIAL QUESTION, LABOUR AND TECHNICAL PROGRESS

It was only in the nineteenth century that the social question was clearly formulated, for it was only then that social contrasts and contradictions came fully to light ; but the source of it is in the Bible. " In the sweat of thy face shalt thou eat bread." Man cannot live in the fallen world as in the garden of Eden. His economic life is based upon care and constant fear for the next day ; the amount of material goods is limited and is out of proportion to the population and their needs. The biblical curse pursued man throughout the history of his economic struggle. "Bread" is the the symbol of material goods needed for the preservation and development of life. Yet lust inherent in sinful nature strives not for the daily "bread" but for the bad infinity of material goods which satisfy not real but imaginary needs. The most real economic basis of life gives rise to a world of phantasms, the furthest removed from reality. The " bread " is earned in the sweat of the face, that is, it is earned by labour. Hence the universal significance of labour for life and at the same time its twofold character. Labour is a curse in so far as it is painful, accompanied by suffering and destined to build up a sinful and not a paradisaical material life. It is only at the cost of labour and effort that the fallen man can attain anything, whether it be material goods necessary for the preservation of life or the Kingdom of God. But at the same time labour suggests man's creative calling ; according to God's conception of him man is called to labour and creatively to transform by his spirit the elements of nature. Creative work gives man a regal position in nature, but the tragedy is that work is not always creative. The great mass of humanity is doomed to uncreative labour, painful, at times terrible and always servile, though the slavery may take a concealed form as in the capitalistic state. Labour is both a curse and a blessing ; like bread it is sacred and bound up with the deepest foundations of life and is the most certain of realities. Men may be forced to devote their labour to making fictitious, fantastic things, objects of useless luxury, but labour as such, the strain and effort of it, is holy. Labour has a redeeming significance for men, as child-bearing has for women. The heaviest and most uncreative labour is sacred, and slave labour is sacred too, though it is a curse for those who enslave and own their fellow creatures. The most meaningless labour has an ascetic value.

Economic and social theories are not as a rule concerned with the religious and moral significance of labour. The problem of labour in the deep sense does not as yet exist either for capitalism or for socialism.[1] The champions of capitalism want to justify and to preserve the form of economic slavery hypocritically called "free labour". The champions of socialism strive for freedom from labour, understanding by it freedom from heavy work and long hours, or for compulsory organization of labour as a means of increasing to the utmost the power of the collective social unit. The bourgeois and the socialist ideology make it impossible even to formulate the spiritual problem of labour, for they do not recognize personality as a supreme value. The value of personality, of its inner life and destiny, is overlaid and concealed for them by the values of material wealth, of the economic power of society or the just distribution of economic goods in it. Both capitalism and socialism adopt the economic point of view, i.e. distort the hierarchy of values, putting the lower and subordinate values above the higher. The so-called individualism, characteristic of the bourgeois capitalistic society and connected with economic freedom and unlimited right of private property, has nothing to do with personality and is hostile to it. The individualism of the bourgeois capitalistic civilization destroys personality. Marx did not invent economism which distorts the hierarchy of values, he found it in the life of the nineteenth century society. The "credit" of denying the value of human personality does not belong to Marx and his communism. This had been done before him by capitalist and bourgeois ideologies. Capitalism and communism taken as symbols—for in their pure form they do not exist in real life—equally deny the inherent value of personality. Personality is for them merely a part of the social and economic process, and personal characteristics are only a means for obtaining the maximum of economic goods and power. From the point of view of social individualism a personality endowed with economic freedom and an unlimited right of property is as much a tool of society and a means to social welfare as it is from the point of view of communism, which at any rate has the advantage of sincerely denying the value of personality in the name of the collective whole. In its struggle for the liberation of the workers socialism, no less than capitalism, is prepared to regard personality as a function of society. Consequently, Christian ethics is opposed to the ethics both of capitalism and of socialism, though it must recognize the

[1] De Man is trying to formulate it at the present time.

partial truth of socialism, at any rate the negative truth of its struggle with capitalism. The morally objectionable aspects of socialism have been inherited by it from capitalism.[1]

The conception of *homo oeconomicus* who is always actuated by self-interest is utterly false. It is a fiction of the bourgeois political economy and is in keeping with capitalistic morality ; the " economic man " has never existed in reality. But he is regarded as a permanent type and used as an argument against the new social organization of labour.

The inward and ethical problem of labour is in the first place a personal and not a social problem. It is only secondarily that it becomes social. Labour as a curse, as the struggle for the daily bread, is precisely what gives rise to the realm of the herd-man, repressive of personality and of free and original moral judgments. The overwhelming power of the herd is crystallized in the capitalist system based upon " free " labour, and it may be crystallized in a socialistic system based upon " organized " labour. The herd-mind can never reach to the sources of life or understand the meaning of labour. Although labour creates the realm of the herd-man in the conditions of the sinful world, its meaning lies beyond it, for it is connected with the mainsprings of life. In its origin and meaning labour is sacred and has a religious foundation. Everything religious is connected with spiritual freedom. Labour is hard and compulsory, it is under the power of the law and shares in its righteousness. But we can carry it out freely and regard it as redemption, and then it will appear in a different light. The compulsory law of labour will then be changed into spiritual freedom. The possibility of this spiritual freedom is always open to us and no social environment can deprive us of it.

Society requires of man different forms of work, ranging from compulsory slave labour to compulsory socially organized labour. But personality as a free spirit accepts labour as its own personal destiny, freely taking it upon itself as a part of the burden of the sinful world. The spiritual attitude to labour, determined from within and not by external circumstances, includes, however, more than this. A person may feel that his work is his vocation and transmute it into creativeness, thus bringing out the true ontological kernel of labour, independent of the herd-life which turns creativeness into drudgery. Labour is transfigured and enlightened when it is experienced in spiritual freedom as redemption or as creativeness. But the chances of experiencing it as one or the other are

[1] The psychology and ethics of socialism is discussed in a remarkable book by Henri de Man, *Au delà du Marxisme*, and the psychology and ethics of capitalism in W. Sombard's *Der Bourgeois*.

not the same. Every kind of work may be regarded as redemption, but not every kind of work is creative. Creative work is the privilege of a smaller portion of mankind and presupposes special gifts.

This raises the problem of the qualitative hierarchy of workers which socialism does not recognize, for it is based entirely upon a quantitative conception of labour. Most forms of socialism insist upon equality and ignore the quality of work and the special gifts connected with that quality. But culture implies a hierarchy of qualities, distinction between the quality of work, and personal gifts. Spiritual, intellectual and creative work is different in quality from physical labour which creates material goods, and it has a different place in the scale of values. Every human being, however insignificant, is called to creativeness, but those whose life is taken up with elementary forms of labour cannot manifest their creativeness directly in their work. If a man is not endowed with special gifts which qualify him for creative work of a higher kind, he cannot rise any higher through envy of those whose work is creative—on the contrary, envy can only enslave and humiliate him still further. A social movement based upon envy must be spiritually and morally condemned. Envy of another person's gifts which may be as bitter as envy of another person's wealth cannot be remedied by any social reforms and changes. It is born of sin and must be struggled against as a sin. But pride and conceit on the part of a gifted man engaged in work of a higher kind are equally wrong and sinful. For every gift which raises one to a relatively higher position implies service and responsibility, and presupposes spiritual struggle and suffering unknown to those who have not that gift. All true creators know this.

The ancient Greco-Roman world despised work, did not consider it sacred and thought it only fit for slaves. That world was based upon the domination of aristocracy—democracy itself was aristocratic ; and consequently the greatest philosophers of Greece, Plato and Aristotle, failed to see the evil and injustice of slavery. When the Stoics began to recognize it and to gain insight into the truth of human brotherhood and equality, it was a symptom of the decline and fall of the aristocratic culture of antiquity. Christianity introduced a totally different attitude to labour. Respect for work and for workers is of Christian origin. It was Christianity that made contempt for work morally untenable. Jesus Christ Himself was a carpenter. The Christian attitude to work has its sources in the Old Testament. The Greco-Roman world left us a true conception of the qualitative value of aristocratically creative work, and it must be reconciled with the biblical and Christian idea of the holy and ascetic nature of labour and of the equality of all men before God.

The following moral principles may be deduced from all this with regard to labour. The individual ought to transmute all labour into a work of redemption and at the same time strive to render it creative, to however humble an extent. Society on the other hand must strive to free its members from labour and to make the conditions of it less hard and painful ; it must recognize the right to work—i.e. the right to bread, i.e. the right to existence. The more individual a person's work is and the less regulated by society, the more freedom and joy there is in it. The individual is made to subserve society in the capitalistic bourgeois system just as in social systems based upon slavery ; and socialism goes still farther in that direction. Work is, of course, social and takes place in a community. But from the ethical point of view we ought to make it more individual. Partial de-socialization does not in the least imply that man becomes anti-social, since social life and activity is the vocation of personality. It implies that he realizes the freedom of his spirit and is determined in his actions and judgments at first hand, i.e. in accordance with his inmost nature and not under social pressure. It is in society that the individual must manifest his originality, i.e. his conscience at first-hand.

The struggle against capitalism for the liberation of the workers need not by any means be a struggle for the socialization of the individual and of the whole of life, since this would be tantamount to the suppression of personality and of spiritual freedom. The struggle against the injustice of capitalism is first of all the struggle for the economic rights of the individual, for the concrete rights of the producer and not for the abstract rights of the citizen. Liberation of labour is the liberation of personality from the oppressive phantasms of the bourgeois capitalist world, from the oppressive power of herd-life. This moral purpose is, however, only partly realizable, for the tragic conflict between the individual and society cannot be finally solved within the confines of our sinful world. The conflict must not be taken to imply any hostility towards society on the part of the individual. Personality is essentially social, and its partial de-socialization, attained through liberating it from the tyranny of the herd, enables it to realize its social and cosmic vocation in spiritual freedom. A society should consist of workers, and the various kinds of work, including the highest spiritual creativeness, should form a hierarchical whole. Only such a society can be religiously and morally justified.

From the moral point of view the social problem is closely allied to that of private property. Like everything else in ethics it is beset with paradoxes and antinomies. Socialism has called into question, and no doubt rightly, the institution of private property. An unlimited and absolute right of property has bred the evils and iniquities of feudalism and capitalism and resulted in unendurable social inequality, proletarianization of the masses and the loss by the workers of the means of production. It gives rise to a revolutionary mentality accompanied by so much envy, malice and vindictiveness that the oppressed lose all human semblance. But at the same time there is something essentially right in private property ; it is connected with the principle of personality, as can be seen from the attempts to establish a materialistic communism. If a man is deprived of all personal power over the material world of things, of all personal freedom in his economic life, he becomes a slave of society and the state which will deprive him as well of the freedom of thought, conscience and speech, of the right to move about and even of the right to live. If the community or the state is the sole owner of material goods of every description it can do what it likes to the individual. The individual is then helpless against the tyranny of the state and becomes completely socialized. Economic dependence deprives man of freedom, whether it be dependence upon capitalists or upon the community and the state. The inner freedom of conscience and spirit remains inviolable, it cannot be destroyed by any power in the world, but it can only manifest itself in martyrdom.

From the Christian point of view the principle of absolute unlimited ownership of material things and economic goods is altogether wrong and inadmissible. Property is the result of sin. No one can be an absolute unlimited owner—not the individual, not the community, not the state. The Roman conception of property as the right to use and to abuse material objects and values, which is not at all Christian, lies at the basis of European individualism.[1] No one can claim an absolute and unlimited right of property or absolute and unlimited power, neither the individual, nor the community, nor the state. If an individual is given an absolute right of property he becomes a tyrant and inevitably tyrannizes over other people ; and the same thing happens in the case of the community or the state. Both the individual and the state abuse their absolute right of property and the power which it gives them, and become tyrants and exploiters. Liberation from the tyranny of individuals who have abused their right of property and acquired enormous wealth—from feudal lords or from capitalists owning banks and factories—does not consist in depriving them of the absolute right of property and vesting it in the community or the state. This would merely change the subject of the tyranny

[1] See Declareuil, *Rome et l'organisation de droit.*

and exploitation and might result in still greater restrictions of freedom. The liberation consists in denying spiritually and morally the very principle of an absolute right of property, by whomsoever it might be exercised. This is quite analogous to the principle of power. To transfer the right of unlimited power from the monarch to the people means merely to create a new tyranny. True liberation consists in denying the very principle of unlimited power. It is godless and anti-Christian to believe that any man or any group of men can have absolute ownership of the material world.

The absolute right of property belongs to God alone, the Creator of the world and of man, but certainly not to the creature. God as the subject of the right of property does not exploit creation but gives it liberty, while man cannot be an owner without being a tyrant. I have no absolute right of property even over the pen with which I am writing this book ; I may not do anything I like with it and break it to pieces for no reason at all. This pen has been given me for writing and its significance is simply that of a certain good function. The same thing is true of every object that I possess. Property is given man for use and must be used to a good purpose, otherwise he loses his moral right to it. The right of private property must be morally recognized as a limited right, as the right to use but not to abuse. The right of property is justified by its creative result. The same limited right of property must be accorded to society, to free co-operations and to the state. The right of owning material things and economic goods must be divided and apportioned between the individual, the society and the state, and in all cases must be limited and functional. Property enables man to realize freedom in the world and is also a means of tyranny and exploitation. The maximum of freedom and the minimum of tyranny is achieved when God is recognized as the absolute owner, and man merely as a steward and a user. A man is responsible for his property both to God and to other men. He is responsible for the material objects which he owns, for the land which he tills, for the machines he uses, for his garden and the house in which he lives, for the furniture in it, for his pen and paper, for the money he happens to have and certainly for his dog, horse and cow. He has no absolute right to do what he likes with it all and cannot use it for exploiting and oppressing his neighbours. Property must not be infinitely expanded and increased. The desire to do so is a sinful lust bred by economic phantasms. The longing for infinite expansion lies at the basis of the capitalist world with its deceptions and contradictions. Property requires self-control and self-limitation, otherwise it becomes an evil. Property has a dialectic of its own which destroys it.

Capitalism shows this clearly. An absolute right of property inspired by lust of greed tends to defeat itself. Property ceases to be a relation to the real world and becomes fictitious. This is what happens in the capitalistic world with its trusts, banks, stock-exchanges, and so on. It is no longer possible to distinguish who is the owner and what he is supposed to own. Everything passes into a world of phantasms, an abstract realm of papers and figures. It is not socialism but capitalism that destroys the reality of property. In struggling against capitalism we must reinstate that reality, and re-establish the spiritually personal attitude to the world of things and material goods, the intimate bond between personality and the world in which it is called upon to act. The moral task is to make property on the one hand more personal, and on the other to limit private property by the state and the community, to attain the greatest possible freedom and the least possible compulsion. A wrong use has often been made of freedom in social life. The principle of freedom may prove to be false, as it is in economic liberalism. In a sinful world freedom must have limits. The spirit is free in its very essence and indeed *is* freedom. But matter diminishes the activity of the spirit so that in the spatial physical world freedom varies in degree. Absence of freedom means repression of spirit by matter. In spiritual life there must be a maximum of freedom. This implies the subjective rights of human personality—freedom of conscience, of thought, of creative activity, and the dignity of every human being as a free spirit and the image and likeness of God. Freedom in political life is less complete ; it is restricted by the material world. In the economic life freedom must be reduced to its minimum, for in this realm it leads to the greatest abuses and can deprive men of their daily bread, making it impossible for the free spirit to exist in the physical world. Socialists are right in this respect. The state must protect one social class from the tyranny of another which has concentrated in its hands the ownership of material goods or, what it comes to, the state must protect the individual.[1] The ideal is to get rid of social classes altogether and to replace them by professions.

This is what morality demands in the external world of social life. In the inner world of spiritual life it demands freedom of the human spirit from the power of property, an ascetic attitude towards material possessions, victory over the sinful lust for material goods, a refusal to be enslaved by the world. Property may be a source of initiative and of freedom of action but it has also been the source of man's enslavement. Man

[1] Lorenz Stein is still very interesting on this point. See his *Geschichte der sozialen Bewegung in Frankreich*.

became the slave of his possessions and the idea of the absolute right of property has distorted his moral consciousness and made him unjust. The ideas of property and of wealth have distorted the very conception of honesty. The Gospel brings this to light. The moral value set upon a man is determined not by what he is but by what he has. The inner man is replaced by the outer man, possessing material goods which give him power. Honesty is made to depend upon a man's attitude to property and not to poverty. It is a bourgeois, an anti-Christian conception of honesty to regard as honest the man who respects property and wealth and not the one who respects poverty and is kind to the destitute. This is one of the distortions of moral consciousness brought about by the idea of property.

Finally, the conception of private property has been transferred to human beings. Slavery was founded upon it. Although slavery in its crude forms was condemned and abolished long ago, it goes on existing in a more refined and less noticeable form. It exists in family relations, where the principle of absolute property still holds good. It penetrates into the most intimate aspect of love between man and woman. The lover still consider himself as the absolute master and owner of the loved one. The right of property is connected with the emotion of jealousy, which is the affective aspect of the instinct of ownership at a level so deep and intimate that no control of it is possible. But the claim to the absolute ownership of another person insisted upon in jealousy is as wrong and illusory as the claim to any other form of absolute ownership.

The falsity of communism and its tyrannical character is due to the fact that it does not rise superior to the conception of the absolute right of property but merely wants to transfer this right to the community or to the state. The collective social unit is the absolute owner, feudal lord, capitalist and banker. It is the most merciless of owners, recognizing no tribunal, no authority, no higher power of any kind. The individual is completely enslaved by the herd and deprived of spiritual freedom, of the freedom of conscience and thought. Property in the sense of man's attitude to the material world of things is always bound up with herd-life and may become a means of enslaving personality. Man may be enslaved both by his own property and by the property of others. But property is also the source of man's free activity in the social world and, as it were, its continuation in the cosmos. Such is the paradoxical and contradictory nature of property.

Struggle against the enslaving principle of property is in the first place struggle against the sinful lust which is the source of enslavement. In social life freedom is, apparently, best attained through a complex pluralistic system combining private ownership with ownership by the state and limiting both, so that property is least likely to become a means of tyranny and exploitation of one man by another. Man's power over the world and nature must not include power over other men. Socialism is absolutely right in this respect, but its truth must be spiritualized and given a deeper religious meaning. Growth of economic production, increase of material wealth and of man's power over the elemental forces of nature, are good in themselves and a means to a fuller life. But these economic values must be subordinated to values of a higher order and, first of all, to the value of human personality and its freedom. Economic life cannot be perfectly autonomous, it must be subordinated to moral principles. An isolated personality is powerless to struggle against exploitation and tyranny in order to improve its standard of living ; it can only wage that struggle together with other people—and that is the justification of the labour movement. This brings us up against a fundamental problem of Christian ethics. Ought the individual to engage only in spiritual struggle against sin, accepting every social system as inevitable and a dispensation of Providence—or ought he to struggle for social justice?

Conservative Christianity is prepared to defend and justify the most iniquitous social system on the ground that original sin has made human nature essentially bad, and that social justice is therefore unattainable. Such an argument against social reform is both hypocritical and sociologically false. In the first place, Christianity teaches not only about original sin but also about seeking the Kingdom of God and striving for perfection similar to the perfection of the Heavenly Father. It does not follow that because human nature is sinful we must talk of nothing else and give up all attempts to realize social justice. The bourgeois capitalistic system certainly is the result of original sin and its projection on the social plane, but this is not a reason for justifying it and declaring it to be unchangeable.

The sinfulness of human nature does not mean that social reforms and improvements are impossible. It only means that there can be no perfect and absolute social order, i.e. there can be no Kingdom of God on this earth and in this aeon of time, before the transfiguration of the world. But the will to realize the greatest possible social justice does not imply any belief in earthly paradise or in the final triumph of justice as an inevitable result of social progress. The will to bring about social justice is based upon freedom, without which no moral life is possible, and is therefore essentially moral in character. If I am a Christian I must do my best to realize Christian truth in the social as well as in the personal life.

Whether it will be realized, and how great are the forces of evil opposed to it, is another question, and it must never disturb the purity of my moral will.

The paradox connected with the sinfulness of human nature has been formulated with great force by K. Leontyev.[1] From the fact that Christian prophecies are pessimistic and do not foretell the triumph of love and justice on earth, he drew the conclusion that it is best not to strive to realize them in social life, but to uphold injustice. The real reason why Leontyev argued in this way was that aesthetically he preferred the unjust social order based upon sin. He was afraid that a social system which embodied more justice would be the reign of petty bourgeois complacency and unendurable hypocrisy of the smug believers in progress. K. Leontyev's attitude was determined by disinterested aesthetic motives, but in case of other people the same kind of attitude is due to distinctly interested motives and a desire to preserve their own privileged position. Those who oppose social reforms on the ground of original sin enjoy a privileged position themselves, though probably they are no less sinful than the men who are suffering from oppression and iniquity of the social system in question. It is impossible to defend injustice and wrong on the ground that original sin makes them inevitable. And there is no reason whatever for concluding that a world afflicted by original sin is bound to have absolute monarchy, absence of political freedom and a capitalist economic system based upon the exploitation and oppression of the workers.

Those who misuse the argument about original sin still have in mind Rousseau's theory of man's natural goodness and virtue and imagine that all attempts to realize social justice on a large scale are inspired by Rousseau. But this view is completely out of date. Socialism takes a pessimistic rather than an optimistic view of human nature. Optimism was characteristic of the philosophy on which capitalism was based, with its belief in the natural harmony of human interests and the coincidence between might and right in the realm of economics. But socialism wants to organize and regulate society because it believes that human nature is evil and consequently social life ought not be left to the free play of interests. Marx was, of course, the last person to believe in the natural goodness of man. If Christianity refuses to realize social justice on the assumption that the sinfulness of human nature makes it impossible, the task will be undertaken by that sinful nature without its help. and the idea of justice will be distorted and spoiled. We find this in revolutionary

[1] See my book, *Konstantin Leontyev.*

socialistic movements, which certainly do not take a rosy view of man, and in its extreme form in communism which *is* organized sin. The good does not want to realize itself on the excuse that sin is too strong, and then evil tries to realize by its own means the task which the good has shirked. Socialism and communism are possible just because human nature is sinful and not at all on the ground of Rousseau's theory.

It is equally wrong to argue against democracy on the ground that human nature is sinful. Memories of Rousseau prove confusing in this connection also. Whatever one's attitude to democracy may be, it must be admitted that it is certainly not an ideal social system and least of all presupposes victory over original sin. Democracy suits the fallen man perhaps better than any other form of social order and enables him to express himself most. The ideal of an autocratic monarchy on the other hand is a utopia pre-supposing victory over sin and a spiritual unity which man's sinfulness makes impossible. It is perfectly absurd to uphold the principle of authority in every department of life and to admit no freedom in anything because of original sin. It is as though the representatives of hierarchical power and authority were exempt from original sin or less sinful than other people. But as a matter of fact they are particularly subject to sin and introduce an element of sinful lust into their power and authority.

Sin cannot be destroyed by force, for the force that destroys it is itself sinful in so far as it is destructive. This is an insoluble contradiction. Sin can be conquered, though only partially, by the spirit being directed towards truth and righteousness. The doubt which prevents us from realizing righteousness and suggests that it is impossible because our nature is sinful, is an evil and sinful doubt. Christianity takes up a realistic attitude towards human nature and allows no fantastic utopias or false social dreams ; but it demands that our will should be bent upon the realization of justice and righteousness at every moment of our lives. The Christian conception of social justice is, however, different from that of materialistic socialism. Christian ethics in general and the ethics of creativeness in particular does not accept the materialistic view of the world, based upon quantity versus quality and upon reducing everything down to the lowest level ; it does not recognize the metaphysics of equality which denies personality with its spiritual life and devastates reality. The idea of communism has a religious origin and is connected with that of community and intercommunion, but materialistic communism distorts it in a hideous way, organizing by mechanical and violent methods a society in which there is no spiritual communion whatever.

There may be a tragic conflict between social justice and cultural and spiritual values. Materialistic socialism does not recognize at all the tragic nature of this problem : it knows only one value—social justice and social prosperity and welfare. The same kind of conflict exists between the highest values of the spirit and the imperialistic will to expansion and political power. It also creates painful contradictions for the moral conscience. From the ethical point of view it must be recognized that the values of spiritual life are higher than the values of social life. The social problem itself can only be solved if there is a spiritual regeneration. Such solutions of it as lead to the oppression and enslavement of the spirit are illusory and lead to social disintegration. The social question is inevitably a question of the spiritual enlightenment of the masses, without which no justice can be achieved. There is also a tragic conflict between the value of freedom and that of equality. It is connected with the fundamental paradox of evil.

Evil that finds expression in social injustice and hatred cannot be abolished by external and mechanical means. A certain amount of evil in social life must be left free, and the complete disappearance of evil can only be thought of as spiritual transfiguration. The final victory over evil is the business of the church rather than of society or the state. But it would be wrong and impossible to abandon society to the free play of evil forces and passively to await a miraculous transfiguration of the world, a new heaven and a new earth. It would be sheer hypocrisy to do so. Society must struggle against evil, but in doing so it must preserve the value of personality and spiritual freedom. The amount of freedom allowed to evil in bourgeois capitalistic society is morally intolerable ; in a similar way, at a certain level of development, moral consciousness found intolerable the freedom of evil that existed in societies based upon slavery, upon turning man, made in the image and semblance of God, into an article for sale. The awakening of a slumbering conscience and of a higher moral consciousness is bound to lead to a struggle against crystallized social evil.

Moral problems created by the wrongs of the capitalistic society and the new forms of slavery engendered by it are particularly complex and acute. Capitalistic society with its new forms of slavery claims to be based upon liberty, and its champions denounce every attempt to limit the evil in it as an attack upon liberty. Socialists rightly condemn the hypocrisy of these appeals to freedom which is a cloak for slavery. But the trouble is that for the most part socialists themselves do not recognize the value of freedom, of personality and of the spirit. Consequently, in the conflict between the capitalistic and the socialistic world neither side can be said to be completely right, although there is more to be said for socialism than for capitalism. The slavery created by capitalism, based upon economic freedom—slavery in the realm of money—is even more inhuman than the old slavery which was softened by patriarchal customs and the Christian religion. It is an absolutely cold world in which one cannot even see the face of the master and enslaver : it is slavery to abstract phantasms of the capitalistic world. All spiritual bonds between men are finally severed, society is completely atomized, and the " free " individual is utterly forsaken and left to himself, helpless in a terrible and alien world. In the bourgeois capitalistic world a man is terribly lonely. It is therefore inevitable that individuals should form mechanical, materialistic combines to struggle for improving their life. But from the moral and spiritual point of view socialism is as bourgeois as capitalism. It does not rise above the bourgeois conception of life, the higher values are closed to it ; it is plunged into the kingdom of this world and believes in visible things alone. Thus the social problem necessarily assumes a moral and spiritual form and demands the birth of a new, spiritual man and of new spiritual relations between men. In so far as the social problem is connected with human relationships it inevitably leads up to the relation between man and God. The other aspect of the social problem is connected with man's relation to nature and with the growth of his power over it. It is, first and foremost, the problem of technical inventions, which is acquiring a tremendous significance in our time and must be considered from the moral point of view.

Our moral attitude to technical inventions is bound to be ambiguous and contradictory. Those inventions are a manifestation of man's power, of his kingly place in the world ; they bear witness to his creativeness and must be recognized as good and valuable. Man is the inventor of tools which he puts between himself and the natural elements ; the invention of the simplest tool is the beginning of civilization. The justification of technical progress in the wide sense of the term is the justification of human culture and a negative attitude to it means a desire to return from civilized to primitive life. The romantic rejection of technical progress does not stand criticism. Ruskin could not reconcile himself to railways and drove in a carriage beside the railway track ; he could afford to do it because he was rich. Romantic people who denounce technical inventions make use of them at every step and cannot dispense with them. But the romantic dislike of technical progress does indicate that there is some evil connected with it. Technical progress testifies not only to man's strength and power over nature ; it not only liberates man but also weakens and enslaves him ; it mechanizes human life and gives man the image and semblance of a machine.

The overwhelming technical achievements of the nineteenth and twentieth centuries produced the greatest revolution in human history, far more important than all political revolutions. They brought about a radical change in the whole rhythm of human life, a break with the natural, cosmic rhythm and the appearance of a new, mechanically determined rhythm. Machinery destroys the old wholeness and unity of human life, it tears away, as it were, the human spirit from organic flesh and mechanizes the material life of man. Machinery alters man's relation to time. Time is quickened, human life becomes less stable. An established order of things is less likely to continue for long. Machinery makes human existence dynamic. The latest achievements of practical science have an even deeper significance—not merely social but cosmic as well. The remarkable developments in physics and scientific discoveries based upon it have brought to light the existence of new and hitherto undiscovered realities. Forces which man had not known before and which were hidden in the mysterious depths of nature have now been made manifest. The reality which is being built up through technical inventions is different from the reality which had surrounded man before and which he strove to know. The discovery of radium has a cosmic importance. If man succeeds in breaking up the atom and releasing the monstrous energy contained in it, the result will be a cosmic and not merely a social change. A terrible destructive and constructive power is being given to man. It will depend upon his spiritual condition whether he employs this power to destroy or to construct.

Scientific discoveries which transcend the limits of space and time give man a new and somewhat alarming feeling of the earth being merely a part of the solar system. This means that at a certain stage of its development scientific progress severs man from the maternal bosom of the earth and transfers him into interstellar space. Man's conception of the world and his feeling of life have been very intimately connected with earth. A special tellurgic mysticism has been natural to man. Man came from the earth and to the earth he must return. This is an ancient and deeply rooted belief. But now scientific discoveries confront man with quite a different kind of cosmic reality, no longer connected with the earth. They transfer man to interplanetary space, they surround him with new and hitherto unknown energies the effect of which has not yet been investigated. This means that technical science and machinery have a cosmic significance. Human spirit is eternal and independent of any discoveries, but the flesh is dependent upon them, and the intimate bond between the spirit and the flesh, which had seemed eternal, may be weakened and changed.

Technical progress has a twofold influence on man's moral and social life. On the one hand it lessens spirituality and makes life more material and mechanical. On the other hand it stands for dematerialization and disincarnation, opening up possibilities of greater freedom for the spirit. This is what renders the ethical attitude to the problem so complex. The sensuous beauty of form characteristic of preceding historical epochs, which had not known the achievements of practical science and the power of machinery over life, is disappearing. Technical progress is the death of beauty which had seemed eternal. Great architecture is no longer possible in our age. Machinery acquires a universal significance and puts its seal upon everything, making all into its own semblance. It is an expression of man's strength, but it weakens his physique, lowers the type and decreases his natural resourcefulness. Man no longer relies on his bodily strength but trusts to mechanical means, and his organism grows weaker. Life is no longer bound up with the earth, animals and plants and becomes connected with machinery, with a new reality which seems to us not to have been created by God. And the human spirit must find the inner strength to endure this change and not to be enslaved by this new reality ; man must use the power given him by science for construction and not for destruction.

One of the consequences of scientific progress is that everything which had appeared as neutral acquires a spiritual and religious significance. Technical achievements are morally neutral up to a point. When they reach a certain level they lose this neutral character and may turn into black magic if the human spirit does not subordinate them to a higher purpose. Scientific and technical progress may eventually lead to the destruction of the greater portion of mankind and even to a cosmic catastrophe. The moral and spiritual condition of man, who has acquired an unheard of power over nature, becomes of paramount importance. Nature was at first full of gods, then it was regarded as a dark power and finally, in modern times, it has been completely neutralized. But the progress of practical science confronts man with a new nature which can no longer be considered neutral. Man's power over natural elements may serve either the work of God or of the devil, but it cannot be merely neutral. Hence it is essential to develop a moral attitude towards technical achievements. This is particularly imperative with regard to the question of war. Scientific discoveries may be a great power in dealing with poverty, famine and disease. It is for science to solve that aspect of the social problem which is connected with man's relation to nature. Karl Marx did not see this, for he had no imagination to foresee the technical and scientific achievements of the twentieth century. He was too much occupied with the narrow vista of life as it was lived in the middle of the nineteenth century. For him the social problem was solved in the first instance by the class struggle, the conflict between class interests and increase in class hatred. Accordingly, he minimized and almost denied the morally and technically creative aspect of the social question. The development of practical science was for him merely a subordinate function of social processes.

Our moral attitude towards technical achievements presents an important problem, worked out but little as yet. It has a significance for the world as a whole. The ethics of creativeness must admit that the progress of practical science has positive value and is a manifestation of man's free spirit and of his creative vocation in the world. But at the same time it must clearly recognize that such progress brings with it the greatest danger of new slavery and degradation for the human spirit. We must be keenly sensitive to this and rise above a neutral attitude to scientific progress. It is wrong and unspiritual to oppose to the new world discovered by science the old primeval " earth " and " nature " to which man ought to remain subordinated. The " earth " is a religious symbol but it may be understood materialistically. And it must be recognized that science, destroying as it does many illusions born of weakness and dependence, may help us to overcome religious materialism and attain greater spirituality, though, on the other hand, it threatens to materialize life through and through. The achievements of practical science put the human spirit to the test and bring out its essential qualities. The right attitude towards scientific progress inevitably presupposes a spiritual asceticism and control of the lust of life to which science is always ready to pander. Practical science has an eschatology of its own, opposed to the Christian, and its goal is to conquer the world and to organize life without God and apart from a spiritual regeneration of mankind.

Another consideration which complicates the social problem, regarded from the spiritual point of view, is this : We ought to do our utmost to improve the position of the masses and to attach greater importance to labour ; but at the same time we must not give preponderance to quantity over quality, allow the masses to dominate personality, and let material values outweigh the spiritual. And this means that however radical the social reforms may be, it is essential to preserve a spiritual aristocracy. The demagogues who play so prominent a part in revolutionary movements dominate the masses by flattering them and sacrificing the higher values to them. They always betray quality for the sake of quantity, distort the hierarchy of values and renounce spiritual nobility out of lust for power. The masses need symbolism whether it be religious, national or revolutionary, and it alone inspires them and helps them to rise above their drab everyday existence. The masses live by emotions and affective states. Ideas, conceptions and theories exist for them merely as myths or symbols. Thus, for instance, in the Russian revolution Marxism became a myth and a symbol. In the French revolution the same thing happened to the philosophical theory of freedom, liberty and equality. Conservative and nationalist ideologies serve as myths and symbols in exactly the same way. There is such a thing as a collective unconscious, and this is what the masses chiefly live by. The primitive instincts at work in the collective unconscious find expression in symbols and symbolic images which focus the social energy. The psychology of the crowd is a reflection of the collective unconscious. The symbols and myths which inspire the crowd are always expressive of unconscious erotic cravings seeking an outlet. Thought plays a very small part in the psychology of the masses, which can only be ruled through the unconscious. A crowd, even if it be possessed by enthusiasm, always lowers and weakens the quality of the individual who becomes subordinated to the herd.

The masses can be ruled with the help of symbols which inspire them. But the symbolism may either be profound and connected with ontological realities or it may be shameless claptrap. Stable religious symbolism based upon tradition can alone claim to have depth and reality. It is only through religion that the life of the masses can be rightly directed and organized. All other symbols used for the purpose prove to be mere catch-words and appeal to low instincts and interests. Religious symbols, however, may also be turned into catch-words and used to incite low instincts. This is what makes the problem of mass psychology so painful and complicated. Individuals can be furiously fanatical only because of the masses ; apart from them personal fanaticism would be impossible. Fury and fanaticism are expressions of the collective unconscious and are inspired by collective symbolism. The individual unconscious as such does not create fanaticism and fury, for those states are nurtured by mass emotions. Socialism creates for the masses a symbolism of its own, similar to the religious or the national, and also capable of generating fanaticism and fury. Socialism strives to rationalize, organize and regulate the social life, but it is based upon the collective unconscious of the masses, upon mass instincts and cravings which need satisfaction. And it is ready to sacrifice the spiritual aristocracy and cultural values to the masses moved by the unconscious instincts of envy, vindictiveness and malice. This is the morally low side of revolutionary socialism. In this respect it is lacking in purity, freedom and originality of moral actions and judgments. Socialism must therefore be spiritually ennobled. Only aristocratic socialism is morally justifiable. Distinction must be made between " workers " and " proletarians ". A worker has a sacred significance and every man ought to be a worker. But the chief characteristic of the proletarian is resentment, and both his psychology and his ideology arise from a mistaken attitude on the part of the worker. The " bourgeois " springs from the working class and is valuable as a man of activity, initiative and energy. But he has betrayed the working people, forsaken them and created a class which oppresses labour. The value of the " aristocrat " depends on the fact that he is free from resentment and sense of injury and that his qualities are a free gift. The type of the " aristocrat " has a more abiding significance than that of the " bourgeois ".

The life of the masses is always merged in the collective unconscious. That unconscious, with its instincts, emotions and affective states, must be ennobled and sublimated. This is precisely what true religious faith does. Spiritual life is a whole in which separate mental elements are synthesized. There may be more truth and wholeness in the unconscious than in consciousness which introduces division and separation. But this may only be the case when the unconscious is hallowed, purified from resentment and ennobled by lofty religious symbolism. From the point of view of Christian and creative ethics the social problem is solved by improving the life of the masses, by engaging them in creative activity, raising them up and increasing the significance of labour, but not by giving them the mastery and letting power rest with the collective whole.

What is eternal in Christian ethics is its attitude to the poor and the rich. It is revealed in the Gospel and does not depend upon changes in social conditions. A Christianity which upholds the rich against the poor betrays and falsifies the teaching of Christ. Christianity certainly does not preach enmity against the rich ; and envy of the rich is utterly alien to it. In a certain sense Christianity admits the privileged position of the poor. The categories of " rich " and " poor " are in this connection not social at all but spiritual and indicate freedom from the material goods of this world, or slavery to them. But although a man whose lot it is to be " rich " easily becomes a slave to his wealth, the " poor " who is deprived of material goods may easily become a slave to the lust of wealth and be possessed by envy. Christianity proclaims the cult of voluntary poverty, carried out to perfection by St. Francis. Christianity affirms the positive value and blessedness of poverty.[1] Such an attitude to poverty and wealth is certainly not to be found in socialism. In its prevailing forms socialism wants wealth and bases itself upon the lust of wealth and the envy of the poor for the rich. When socialism is victorious the poor become rich and vindictively strive to make the rich poor. The conception of asceticism is alien to socialism.

The Gospel theories of wealth and poverty cannot be translated into social categories. The absolute Christian truth about the poor and the rich which reveals the Kingdom of God to us does not warrant the conclusion either that the envious and vindictive poor ought to destroy the rich or, still less, that there is no need to improve the position of the poor or to limit the power of the rich. The question of creating a better social system in which there will be neither inevitable and unendurable poverty nor unendurable wealth is on a different plane than the spiritual question of " poverty " or " wealth ". It would be wrong to conclude that Christianity requires us to be indifferent to social life and humbly and obediently to accept the existing social order. No social system is eternal and absolute ; they are all created and changed by men, are in a state of flux and have only a temporal and relative stability. And there is no ground for thinking that changes and improvements in social life will always be the work of other people, and that I, a Christian, must always bow down before the social structure created by others. It is perfectly obvious that Christians, too, must take a creative part in changing, reforming and improving the social order. The economic system based upon slavery was not eternal, the capitalistic system is not eternal, nor will the socialistic system, if it comes, be eternal either. All these are relative historical formations. Consequently everyone must choose for himself what he is to defend and to create. Everyone is responsible for the social order, and therefore no one has a right to determine his relation to society as obedient acceptance of the existing state of things. Man is called to creativeness and to social life. Christian ethics demands social realism and is hostile to social dreams and utopias. Such dreams are based upon the ancient Messianic idea and the hope of its realization. But the true religious kernel of the hopes for a millennium and the coming of the Kingdom of God is utterly misrepresented in social utopias. A perfect society is only

[1] Ch. Péguy makes a very interesting distinction between poverty (*pauvreté*) and destitution (*misère*). Destitution must not be tolerated in human society.

thinkable in a perfect cosmos and means the transfiguration of the world, a new heaven and a new earth, the new Jerusalem and the coming of the Kingdom of God. It is not a social and political system in the conditions of our earthly life and time. Upon our earth, in our aeon of time, all social achievements are relative; they may mean improvement but not perfection.

8. SEX, MARRIAGE AND LOVE

The problem of sexual and erotic morality is one of the most profound, difficult and metaphysical problems of ethics. Sexual morality is particularly dominated by social conventions. The most intimate aspect of personality, which simply cannot be judged from outside and of which the person is shy of speaking to anyone at all, is the most organized and regulated socially. This is due to the fact that sexual life results in the birth of children, the continuation of the human race. Something intimately personal and absolutely non-social has social consequences. This is why sex life provides the field for particularly tragic conflicts between the individual and society, for a fatal clash between personal and social destinies. In the life of the community what is personal and intimate becomes socially regulated and the individual has to answer to society for feelings and actions which have no reference to it and have a social bearing in their consequences only. The result is that no other sphere of life is so vitiated by hypocrisy and cowardice. In their judgments about sex people are terrorized by society and particularly cowardly and insincere. But judgments and valuations of pure ethics must be free from the power of social conventions, i.e. as a matter of principle ethics must be individual and not social.

The first thing to be recognized is that for the herd-man sexual life exists merely as a physiological and social fact. As a physiological fact it leads either to procreation and a happy continuance of the human species, or to immorality and break up of the race. As a social fact sexual life results in the family which is organized in the interests of society in accordance with the general structure of the community. But the herd-mind is absolutely blind to the fact of erotic love, of love between man and woman. It simply fails to observe it and judges of the relations between the sexes merely from the physiological and the social point of view.

Love as such lies outside the social sphere and has no relation whatever to the community. It is absolutely individual and wholly connected with personality. It is between two persons, and any third is an intruder. The sexual instinct is connected with the life of the genus and therefore comes under the notice of the herd-mind which regulates its social and generic consequences. But love has nothing to do with the species and the community and is usually not mentioned in traditional systems of ethics which deal only with the problem of marriage and the family.

It is remarkable that Christian writers and Fathers of the Church failed to observe the phenomenon of love and said nothing interesting about its meaning. All that has been said about marriage and the family in patristic literature and by Christian theologians generally is on an extraordinarily low level. The treatise of St. Methodius of Pathara, " *The feast of the ten virgins* ", is pitiful in its banality. It is partly a description of physiological processes and partly a praise of virginity. It does not show any depth in dealing with the problem of sex and marriage. The treatise of St. Augustine is so bourgeois and conventional in spirit that it scarcely bears reading.[1] In truth, St. Augustine's and other theologians' treatises on sex and marriage are concerned with regulating the generic life and strongly remind one of treatises on cattle breeding. Personal love, personal destiny are completely ignored by those writers. Not one of them mentions the fact of love, which is utterly different both from the physiological gratification of the sex instinct and from the social organization of the generic life in the family. The fact of love is apparently relegated to the domain of poetry and mysticism and regarded with suspicion. And yet, although sexual life remained for Christian thought a purely social and physiological fact, connected with the genus and not with personality, the Church established the sacrament of marriage. But a sacrament is always connected with the intimate life of personality. Thus there arises a great tragedy in the Christian world. Personality is sacrificed to the family and society.

The very nature of the sacrament of marriage is incomprehensible and out of keeping with other sacraments. It is difficult to grasp what forms the *matter* of the sacrament of marriage. The church binds by this sacrament the destinies of any man and any woman who are outwardly and formally free, and outwardly and formally express their consent to the marriage. The intimate, hidden life of the persons concerned and their real attitude to each other remains as impenetrable for the church as it is for the community. The church will marry a girl of seventeen to an old man of seventy, to whom she is given in marriage by her parents for mercenary reasons against her will; all that the church wants is the girl's formal consent, which may be insincere and due to fear. The church has

[1] St. Augustine's attitude to the woman with whom he lived for sixteen years and by whom he had a child shows how low was his conception of love. See Papini, *Saint Augustin.*

no means of ascertaining whether one of the parties is already inwardly united by the bond of love to someone else. Under such conditions the sacrament of marriage frequently proves to be a merely formal rite deprived of spiritual content but having fatal consequences for people's lives. The only thing that is really profound and mystical in the Orthodox marriage service is the comparison of marriage crowns to martyrs' crowns. For in a true marriage that has meaning husband and wife have to suffer and bear each other's burdens, since life upon earth is always full of pain. And true love means tragedy and suffering.

Marriage constantly turns out to be a trap in which people are caught either by being forced into it, or through mercenary motives, or through thoughtlessness and passing infatuation. To prohibit divorce, as the Roman Catholic Church in particular insists on doing, is one of the most cruel things that can be done to human beings, forcing them to live in an atmosphere of falsity, hypocrisy and tyranny and to profane their most intimate feelings. Marriage as a sacrament, mystical marriage, is by its very meaning eternal and indissoluble. This is an absolute truth. But most marriages have no mystical meaning and have nothing to do with eternity. The Christian consciousness must recognize this. The reference to the Gospel which is supposed to proclaim the indissolubility of marriage is particularly unconvincing. The Gospel always reveals absolute life, there is nothing relative about it, but that absoluteness is a revelation of the Kingdom of God and not an external norm and law. The prohibition of divorce is based upon a legalistic interpretation of Christianity. It is striking how differently Christians interpret the Gospel teachings about sex and marriage and the Gospel teaching about wealth and property. They regard marriage as absolute and indissoluble and make this a law of social life, quoting the Gospel in support of their view. But then they might with equal justice make poverty compulsory and quote Gospel texts in favour of abolishing wealth and private property. The Gospel injunctions are absolute in both cases—it is the absoluteness of the Kingdom of God where a marriage, mystical in its meaning, is eternal and indissoluble and where there is no property, no slavery to material wealth. But the Christians did not venture to interpret the Gospel teaching about property in this uncompromising way and to insist on the abolition of wealth and compulsory poverty. Instead they consolidated the family by connecting it with property. The family as a social institution is bound up with private property, and it is always very much feared that any weakening of the principle of private property may lead to the break up of family ties. It is perfectly clear that the herd-man has adapted the

Gospel truth to suit his own ends. The doctrine of the indissolubility of marriage and the prohibition of divorce are social conventions which have no relation to the inner life of personality, have nothing mystical about them and are thoroughly rationalistic. Marriage is eternal and indissoluble, but only if its essence is eternal and not social, if it brings about the realization of the androgynous image of man and is a union of those who are truly " intended " for each other. In other words the eternity and indissolubility of marriage is an ontological and not a social truth. Marriage is a sacrament, but only if it is based upon love that is ontologically real and not upon a passing infatuation and attraction. The sacrament of marriage is ontological and not social. In that case, however, the fundamental characteristic of true marriage and true love is freedom. All social compulsion and tyranny deprives wedlock of the mystical inner meaning which is found in love alone. But love is not a social fact that can be fixed and determined from outside, it eludes the observation both of the state and of the church as a social organization.

Marriage and family which are not based upon love and freedom must be recognized as legal and economic institutions determined by laws and social conventions. They must be distinguished as a matter of principle from the sacrament of marriage and decisively pronounced to be neither sacred nor mystical in their significance. Only love, real love, one and eternal, that leads to the Kingdom of God, is sacred, mysterious and mystical. It is a fact of completely different order from the physiological life of sex and the social life of the family. And this mystical, sacred meaning of love has not been made manifest in the Church. It is the task of the ethics of creativeness to reveal it. Hitherto sexual life, marriage and family have been under the power of *das Man*. Rozanov, who must be acknowledged as the finest critic of Christian hypocrisy with regard to sex, rightly says that conventional Christianity defends not the marriage, not the family, not the reality, but the form, the law, the marriage-rite. This is pure nominalism, a denial of ontological realities.[1] The life of sex and of family is more dominated by the power of empty legalistic formulae than any other sphere of existence. This nominalism and formalism are responsible for some of the worst miseries of human existence. Personal life is sacrificed to meaningless appearances, to abstract laws and words that have lost all real content. In this domain as in every other a return to realities brings liberation. Morally we ought to welcome the process of liberation in the family and sex life. For the Christian consciousness it

---

[1] Many remarkable ideas are to be found in Rozanov's book, *V mire neyasnago inereshonnago.*

means something quite different from what it does for the non-Christian and by no means implies a vindication of the rights of the flesh. An ascetic attitude towards sex is of paramount significance to Christianity and may be even more exacting than before. But such asceticism is a personal matter and is for the free spirit to adopt ; it implies an increase in spirituality and is not a matter of social compulsion. Human personality ought to be made both outwardly and socially free, but inwardly and spiritually subordinated to the ideal of free asceticism, and to have the meaning of love revealed to it. Spiritual liberation from the slavery to sexual lust, humiliating to human dignity, and the sublimation of unconscious sexual cravings are an essential requirement of ethics. This spiritual liberation, however, is not attained through negative asceticism alone, but presupposes turning sexual energy into creative channels. True love is the most powerful remedy against sexual lust, which is the source of man's slavery and degradation. To attain chastity through love means to attain the wholeness of one's nature and rise above the sinfulness and dividedness of sex.

The hidden life of sex and sexual love is a mystery of two persons. No one and nothing third can judge between them or even perceive its reality. It is the most intimate and individual aspect of human personality, which it does not want to show to others and sometimes conceals even from itself. Sexual life is connected with shame, and this proves that it has its origin in the Fall. The shame and terror that one sex has of the other is overcome either positively through love, i.e. through sublimation of shame, or through depravity, i.e. the loss of shame. The tragedy of sexual love lies first of all in the fact that something secret, sacred and intimate, which only the two lovers can see and understand, is profaned by being made public and brought to the notice of the community. Normally no one except the lovers themselves ought to know anything about it. But sexual love has consequences which bring it within the domain of the herd-life and make it subject to its laws, though in its essence it does not belong to that domain. The personal element in sex eludes the herd-mind, but the social aspect of it does not. And therefore sexual love is tragic for the individual ; it is profaned by being submitted to the judgment of society and is the ruin of personal hopes.

Sexual love is profaned both by society and by the individual himself, his sinful passions, strivings and emotions. Love is a flight upwards towards eternity and a descent into time where it becomes subject to corruption and death. Two elements are present in love—the heavenly and the earthly, the eternal and the temporal, Aphrodite Urania and

Aphrodite Pandemos. And it is the temporal, earthly and vulgar element in love that brings it under the sway of the herd-man. Passing infatuation connected with a transitory attraction is mistaken for love. And in view of the fatal connection of love with procreation, society begins to control the quality of love—which proves to be beyond its power and leads to unexpected results. Only mystical love which is personal to its inmost depths and entirely free from the generic element lies outside the realm of social conventions and is free from the power of society. From the onto-logical point of view God alone, as a higher principle, can come between the lovers. Only the lovers' sinfulness places them in the power of other people and society.

Love as such, in its pure and original essence, is a personal fact. But the family is a social fact. Herein lies the insoluble tragedy of love in this world—for true love comes into this world from another sphere. Sexual love in the realm of the herd-man forms the family. The structure of the family is as changeable as is man's social life, which is not sanctified by the spirit of eternity. Conservative social conventions preserve the temporal, not the eternal. The monogamic family, which appears to us eternal and unchangeable, is, as a matter of fact, temporal and came into existence at a certain period of time. Other forms of family had existed before. Bachofen's work had enormous significance in this respect, for he was one of the first to show the existence of primitive sexual communism, out of which the monogamic family came to be formed only after the awakening of spirit and of personality.[1] Originally it was the maternal principle that was predominant, and mankind passed through the stage of matri-archy. This was only natural since the feminine principle is more in-timately connected with sex than the masculine. The feminine element is essentially generic, while in the masculine the principle of personality is more pronounced. Man's slavery to sex is slavery to the feminine element, going back to the image of Eve.

Only in woman sex is primary, deep and all-pervasive. In man sex is secondary, more superficial and more differentiated into a special function. Hence in sexual love woman displays greater talent and genius than man. It is only in woman that the generic aspect of sex has depth and signifi-cance. Man strives to be free from it on the surface. The depth of the generic element in sex is, in the case of woman, bound up with mother-hood. Motherhood is a deep and eternal metaphysical principle which is not exclusively connected with child-bearing. It is the cosmic principle

[1] See Bachofen, *Das Mutterrecht*, and also Engels, *Der Ursprung der Familie, des Privateigentums und des Staates*.

of care and protection against the dangers that threaten life ; it means bringing up children not only in the literal sense but of the ever helpless children such as most people are. Motherhood alone knows the ways of this care, protection and preservation. The demonic element in the feminine nature is conquered by cosmic motherhood. A woman is potentially a mother, not only in relation to individual being but to nature as a whole, to the whole world, fallen and helpless in its fall. Masculine heroism and conquering energy could not preserve the world from destruction, from final desolation. The element of eternal motherhood enters into all true love. A wife is also a mother. Complete absence of the maternal principle is only characteristic of the type of the courtesan, the haetera, who, like a vampire, takes without giving. Motherhood has become distorted in our fallen world and is itself subject to sinful passions and lusts and therefore needs spiritual enlightenment and transfiguration. From the moral point of view the aim is always to transmute physical bonds into spiritual ones, and physical motherhood, which may be a source of slavery, into spiritual. The image of the eternal transfiguration of motherhood is given in the Mother of God.

The family belongs to the realm of the herd-man and is subject to its laws. Family life frequently cools down love. But it would be a mistake to think that family has no spiritual depth or meaning. That meaning is to be found not only in the fact that in our everyday world love takes the form of family. First and foremost, that meaning lies in the fact that the family is a school of sacrifice and of bearing each other's burdens. The importance of the family is that it is the union of souls in the face of the miseries and horrors of life. Like almost everything in our fallen world it has a twofold character. It both lightens the sufferings and burdens of life and creates innumerable new ones. It liberates man spiritually, but it also enslaves him and comes into tragic conflict with his vocation and spiritual life. And therefore one ought sometimes, in accordance with the Gospel, to leave one's father and mother, husband and wife. Sometimes man has to escape from the warmth and closeness of the family into the wide circle of society, and sometimes to flee from the cold of public life to the family circle.

The eternal tragedy of the family is due to the fact that man and woman represent different worlds, and their ends never coincide. This is the tragic element of love which is crystallized in the family, though it is deeper and more primary than it. In family life everything becomes more solid and heavy, and the very tragedy acquires a commonplace character. Woman's mentality and her feeling of life is different from man's. She expects infinitely more from love and family life than man does. There is something absolute and wholehearted about woman's attitude to sex ; man's partial and relative attitude to it can never correspond to hers. Strictly speaking, most marriages are unhappy. They conceal painful conflicts between consciousness and the unconscious. Consciousness disciplined by social conventions suppresses the unconscious, and the unconscious gives rise to endless conflicts and misery in family life. True love can alone overcome those conflicts and harmonize in its own miraculous way the relation between consciousness and the unconscious. But true love is a rare flower in our world and does not form part of everyday existence.

If love is the ontological basis of the marriage union, the question whether marriage ought to be strictly monogamous is simply irrelevant. This question is only raised when there is no real love, when love has cooled down or died, when the outer is substituted for the inner, and grace is replaced by law. The provision that marriage should be indissoluble is made for the unhappy cases. There is no occasion to talk about it and appeal to the law when a marriage is happy. The contradictions of monogamy spring from the failure of love and fatal disharmony. It must be recognized once for all that monogamous marriage is not the natural law of sexual union. It is not at all characteristic of the " natural " man, rather the contrary. It did not exist always but came into being at a certain stage of civilization. Monogamous marriage is possible through grace but not through nature or law. It belongs to the spiritually mystical rather than to the social and natural order. This is the fundamental paradox. Monogamy is required by the herd-man, to whom it is not in the least natural. This is why monogamic marriage in the world of herd-life exists in name only and not in reality. In the civilized world it finds its correlative and corrective in prostitution, in the broad sense of the term—that is, in one of the most shameful and terrible features of human life legitimized by social conventions. Strictly speaking, in the modern everyday world there is no real monogamous marriage, it is merely a conventional lie and an expression of legalistic nominalism. It is perfectly natural that there should be a revolutionary revolt against the old monogamic family. It is the rebellion of unconscious realism against conscious nominalism, i.e. a demand for being true to realities. Rozanov was profoundly right in his criticism.

And in the world of true realities the question of monogamic marriage is solved in quite a different way. From the spiritually mystical point of view " infidelity " is terrible, for it is the betrayal of the eternal to the

239

temporal, the victory of death over life. It is a religious and ontological question, rooted in the very depths of reality. But from the point of view of social conventions and bourgeois legalism there is no such thing as " infidelity " in a spiritual sense ; all that is required is conformity to social norms and the external forms of marriage and family. " Infidelity " is a perfectly natural and naturally social fact and there is nothing very dreadful about it. It is only for man as a spiritual being, standing face to face with eternity, that the problem is deep and serious. " Infidelity " is bad from the point of view of eternity, but from the point of view of time it is the most ordinary thing in the world. The herd-man is concerned not with the spiritual question, not with personality, but with the organization of the family and society. Hence he has to lay down rules and enforce laws about things to which he is really quite in-different.

The conventional everyday world proclaims by the mouth of many Christian thinkers and theologians a conception of marriage quite striking in its moral falsity and incongruity with Christian personalistic ethics. Child-bearing is declared to be the only moral purpose of the union between man and woman which forms the family. A generic process which is a part of the unenlightened nature and knows nothing of per-sonality is regarded as a supreme religious and moral principle. But a morality based upon the consciousness of the dignity of the spirit and of personality must pronounce immoral a union the sole purpose of which is procreation. This is transferring the principle of cattle-breeding to human relations. The meaning and purpose of the union between man and woman is to be found not in the continuation of the species or in its social import but in personality, in its striving for the completeness and fullness of life and its longing for eternity.[1] From a purely psychological point of view there is nothing to be said in defence of the view that the meaning and purpose of the marriage union is child-bearing and continu-ation of the race. As a matter of fact no one has ever married for that purpose, though he may have hypocritically said so for the sake of public opinion. People marry because of an irresistible desire, because they love and are in love, because they want to be united to the loved one, and sometimes through interest. No one longs for physical sexual union because he wants to beget children. It is an invention of the conscious mind. There is more truth in Schopenhauer's contention that the genius of the race laughs at the individual who is the victim of erotic illusions, and turns

[1] See Solovyov's *The Meaning of Love*—the best book that has ever been written on the subject.

him into its own instrument. Strictly speaking those who see the meaning and value of marriage in procreation ought to maintain that Eros—from the elementary forms of sexual attraction up to the highest forms of love —is merely an illusion and self-deception. They consciously side with the genius of the race and regard it as morally right that personality should be its tool. And there is none of Schopenhauer's bitter irony about their view. All this is due to the fact that the question as to the meaning of love has never been asked. Ethics must not merely ask but answer it, and recognize that the meaning of love is personal and not generic. Curiously enough it was on the basis of Christianity and in Christian times, in the Middle Ages, that the love between man and woman blossomed out and produced its highest flower in chivalry and the cult of " the fair lady ". And yet Christian theology which reflects the herd-mind denies love and ignores it.

We come here to the most difficult question of religious metaphysics. Christianity has put forward the cult of virginity, connecting it with the worship of the Virgin Mary. This is the only thing that was profound in the Christian attitude to sex. The Christian conception of marriage and the family has always been opportunist and adapted to the herd-level. Virginity was connected with personality, but marriage was connected with the race, and family with society. The sole purpose and justification of marriage was declared by Christianity to be procreation, dependent upon physical sexual intercourse, accompanied by loss of virginity. But it regarded this loss as a lower state and metaphysically despised it. The meaning and purpose of marriage proved to be physiological and necessitating the loss of virginity, i.e. of man's highest estate. The continuation of the human race presupposes the loss of virginity or wholeness, and implies the enslavement of personality and the spirit by matter or the unconscious generic element. The fact that sexual union which involves the loss of virginity, particularly catastrophic for women, is the means of continuing the human race shows that there is a profound rift in the sexual life and that it is essentially affected by the Fall. But the meaning of love, its idea and principle, is victory over the fallen life of sex in which personality and the spirit have been made subservient to the genus, and a bad infinity is attained instead of eternity. Love is the reinstatement of the personal element in sex, not natural but spiritual.

Empirically love is a mixture of the higher and the lower : it is drawn downwards and distorted by physical desire. Love has an element of terror in it, and a suspicious attitude to it is justifiable. But in its idea and meaning love is something very different from sexual lust, has no necessary connection with the physiological craving and may actually be a deliverance from it. Therefore the spiritual meaning of the marriage union can only be found in love, in personal love between two beings and in the striving to be united in one androgynous image, i.e. in over-coming loneliness.[1] This higher truth is not a denial of the fact that woman is saved by child-bearing. Such is the ethics of redemption in this sinful world ; motherhood is holy in it. If there were no child-bearing, sexual union would degenerate into debauchery. But the ethics of creativeness reveal a higher ideal of love as the final meaning of the marriage union and as victory over the vicious circle of natural processes. Love must conquer the old matter of sex and reveal the new, in which the union of man and woman will mean not the loss but the realization of virginity, i.e. of wholeness. It is only from this fiery point that the trans-figuration of the world can begin.

9. HUMAN IDEALS. THE DOCTRINE OF GIFTS

In the nineteenth and twentieth centuries the ideal of man has grown dim and almost disappeared. When man was recognized as the product of society, a result of social environment, the ideal of man was replaced by the ideal of society. But perfect society can be achieved apart from man's moral efforts. Thus the ideal image of man, of the complete human personality, is bound to disappear. For the last time this ideal image showed itself for a moment in the Romantic movement as the ideal of a complete personality. This is what the ideal of man has always been in the past and is indeed bound to be : it cannot be one-sided. The Greco-Roman world put forth the ideal of the sage, and that ideal embraced the whole man and indicated that his attitude to life was complete and har-monious. It signified spiritual victory over the horror, evil and suffering of life and the attainment of inward peace. It was an intellectual ideal in which knowledge held a central place, but intellectualism meant the enlighten-ment of human nature, and knowledge had a practical meaning. Socrates Plato and the Stoics were of this type. The ideal of the sage, familiar not only to the Greco-Roman world but to the East as well, to China and India, is the highest conception of man attained in the pre-Christian era. The Christian world created the ideal of the saint, i.e. of man completely

---

[1] Homosexual love is ontologically condemned by the fact that androgynous wholeness is not achieved through it, the separate halves remain each in its element without communing with their opposites, i.e. the law of the polarity of being is violated.

enlightened and transfigured, a new creature that had conquered its old nature. This is the highest point that the new, spiritual man can reach. In the Middle Ages the Christian world created also the ideal of the knight, the image of chivalrous nobility, loyalty and sacrificial devotion to faith and duty. The knightly ideal influenced the formation of the general type of man in the Christian era. Chivalry helped to form personality.

What image of man, comparable with the ideals of the sage, the saint and the knight, has been created by modern history? There is no such image. The ideal image of the citizen cannot be put on the same level as that of the sage, the saint or the knight, for it is too exclusively connected with political and social life. A number of professional types which have their own ideal qualifications have appeared—the type of the scientist, the artist, the politician, the business man, the workman. That of the workman is the only one which people are trying to convert into a complete ideal image—the image of the " comrade " which is to replace the sage, the saint and the knight for our era. But in the " comrade " the ideal of man is finally extinguished, the Divine image and likeness is distorted. It is characteristic of our age that the ideal of man is split up into a number of professional images and ideals, so that the wholeness is lost. The scientist or the artist bears no likeness to the sage, the politician or the business man has certainly no resemblance to the knight. And all of them are blotted out by the image of the " bourgeois " which penetrates into each one of the professional types. The bourgeois is the man in whom the herd element is finally triumphant. The bourgeois is the completely socialized being, subordinate to *das Man*, deprived of originality and of freedom of judgment and action. The bourgeois is a man who has no personality. The ideal of the " comrade " is a bourgeois ideal in which man's spiritual being is socialized down to its very depths, i.e. it is the type of man who has lost his spiritual liberty. A bourgeois workman is no better than a bourgeois proprietor. The bourgeois mentality has its source in the herd-life whether it be capitalistic or communistic in structure. It implies the loss of spiritual freedom and originality, the loss of personality under the pressure of the herd, of the majority.

Ethics must defend the ideal image of man as a personality, as a free and original being, having access to the first sources of being, and oppose all attempts to derive that image from the herd-life. The ideal image man is first and foremost that of an ideal personality. Ideal society is based upon personality. A spiritual society is a reality, but it does not exist apart from persons. The ideal human personality is one in which the image and likeness of God are fully revealed. The ideal image of man is the image of

God in him. And that image embraces the whole nature of man and not certain aspects of it only.

The eternal elements of holiness and chivalry must be supplemented by a new element—that of creativeness—so that all man's potentialities may come to light. The image of man-the-creator carrying out his vocation in the world and realizing his God-given talents in the service of God is an all-embracing human ideal. Man's creative calling may be realized in different spheres, professions and specialities, but the image of man-the-creator is not a professional ideal, it is not the image of a scientist or an artist, a politician or an engineer. The idea of the creative calling and vocation of man is connected with the doctrine of gifts. In Christianity this doctrine was taught by St. Paul, but it has never been fully worked out. Man has no right to bury his talents in the ground, and indeed it is his duty to wage a heroic struggle for the realization of his creative vocation, however much the herd-life of every day—family, economic, political, professional and so on—may drag him down. The struggle to realize one's gifts and vocation gives rise to a number of tragic conflicts due to the clash between different kinds of values. It is a struggle not for one's selfish interests but for the ideal image of man-the-creator.

In speaking of the human image we must not make abstraction from sex. The ideal will always be different for man and for woman. Only the ideal of holiness has always been the same for both. But other ideal types have been chiefly masculine. The ideal images of woman have always been those of the mother, the wife, the virgin, the faithful beloved and, in one way or another, have always been connected with sex as the universal characteristic of human nature. Woman has been the inspirer of man's creative activity rather than herself a creator. Not infrequently she suppressed man's creativeness by establishing a tyranny of love and making a fetish of it. The creative principle in woman found expression chiefly in the domain of love in all its forms. Feminine nature is characterized by the principle of birth rather than that of creation, and this is its specific feature. Birth should be taken to mean not merely child-bearing, but all sacrificial surrender of matter and force ; woman stands for the cosmic principle in contradistinction to the personal. Woman is the soul of the world and the soul of the earth, bringing forth life and protecting it. The feminine principle is not only motherhood but also virginity, i.e. the source of chastity. In this aspect of it the feminine principle calls forth man's reverence and worship. The ideal image of the eternal feminine is that of the Virgin-Mother.

Woman bestows the reward for man's creative achievement. She is more intuitive than man, and her intuition helps man's creativeness. But she also hinders it and enslaves man to sex and the race in her quality of haetera the mistress and of the mother of a family who cares for nothing but her home and children. Creativeness is connected with Eros, and the creative ideal is erotic. But Eros is twofold and contradictory and may enslave and degrade as well as raise up and liberate. Hence the complex part which woman plays in human creativeness. At the primitive, archaic stage woman, apparently, had predominance. Then the masculine principle asserted itself and enslaved the feminine. All the potentialities of woman's nature could not be realized during the period of subjection. But now the era of the liberation of woman is coming. The feminine principle is gaining weight once more. But, like every other process, the emancipation of woman has a double character and may be good or bad. It is bad if it means the distortion of the eternal feminine, an attempt to imitate man and to be a bad copy of him. Such emancipation humiliates woman, deprives her of originality and makes an inferior man of her. The only kind of emancipation which has moral and religious significance is that which brings out the feminine principle in its true depth and original-ity, and enables woman to realize her genuine potentialities, i.e. her feminine genius which is different from the masculine. Man as such is always the bearer of the personal human principle. But this personally human principle in itself, in separation from the feminine element, is helpless, abstract and impotent, and cannot build up the ideal image of man. Without relation to the feminine principle there can be neither a knight nor a creator. Man is called to heroism in every sphere of life. This is the most universal characteristic of the human ideal.

10. SYMBOLISM AND REALISM IN ETHICS

The essential task of morality is to get over nominalism and symbolism and come into contact with spiritual realities. Symbolic morality which is almost universally prevalent must be distinguished from real morality. By symbolic morality I mean morality which seeks not really to transfigure life, but to perform conventionally significant actions. Spiritual life is understood symbolically and therefore does not mean the transfiguration of the psychical and material existence. Thus, for instance, one may proclaim brotherhood as a spiritual symbol, finding expression in definite words and gestures, when as a matter of fact there is no spiritual or religious brotherhood at all, or indeed when there is positive hostility. We constantly find this symbolic brotherhood in the Christian world, among the clergy, for instance, and it inevitably degenerates into conventional hypocrisy. The life of the state, of the family, of smart society, is full of such conventional, symbolic morality. Instead of actually realizing the good, people make conventional signs to show that they have realized it. They regard it as important, significant and praiseworthy to make certain signs—of respect and reverence, of love and compassion, and so on. This might be described as a ritualistic morality. It includes politeness, which is symbolic in character but has an enormous moral importance, not sufficiently recognized as yet. Politeness is a symbolically conventional expression of respect for every human being, and therefore it is the most realistic form of symbolism.

Strictly speaking, ethics of law is always ritualistic and symbolic because it requires of man a certain line of conduct, whatever his nature may be and regardless of whether such conduct indicates any real change of heart. A man is required to act as though he were feeling love and respect, while in truth he is full of hatred and contempt ; he must conform to the standards of good conduct and behave as though he had a clear conscience, though in reality he is a low and unscrupulous man.

Symbolic ethics is derived from sacramentalism, and realistic ethics from prophetism. Symbolic ethics is closely connected with respect and reverence for hierarchical rank which is always a symbol of a certain reality, and generally implies insufficient respect and attention to man as a unique and individual personality. Symbolic ethics is non-human. But realistic ethics is human, for it demands a real transfiguration of life, genuine good qualities and realization of righteousness. The fundamental principle of realistic ethics is not to do symbolic good works but to be good, to radiate the quality of goodness ; not to utter conventional expressions of love but to be loving and to radiate love, not to reverence rank which merely symbolizes greatness but to reverence man's human qualities, actual greatness. Gospel morality is not symbolic but realistic ; it calls us to a perfection similar to the perfection of the Heavenly Father and tells us to seek first the Kingdom of God, real transfiguration and not conventional signs of it. It appeals to the depths of the human heart, i.e. to the source of the perfect, transfigured life.

Realistic morality is much more difficult than the symbolic. Indeed it may be said that the good can be realized symbolically but not actually. This is what people say about the Gospel morality. But everything depends upon the fact whether our spirit, will and consciousness are primarily intent upon a symbolic expression of the good or upon its actual realization in the world and in our own hearts. Realism in ethics means victory of spirituality. In symbolism spirituality is expressed merely in signs and symbols ; it is the ethics of the carnal and not of the spiritual man. Realistic ethics, on the other hand, is the ethics of the spirit ; spirituality is actually realized in it and gains possession of the carnal life. Men cling to all kinds of symbols to escape the hard task of gaining victory for the spirit and of dealing with actual good and evil. Even the expectation of the anti-christ may be a symbol, preventing the realization of Christian righteousness in life. It is easier symbolically to sanctify life than really to transfigure it.

For a realistic ethics struggle with evil is a spiritual struggle. And spiritual struggle, spiritual growth and enlightenment must take precedence over legalistic asceticism and conventional good works. Moral realism and symbolism are connected with the religious. Man fails to realize perfection in life and to attain the Divine likeness, and so he makes up for it by rendering symbolic homage to God. Instead of the actual realization of love, righteousness, perfection and divine likeness there is a conventional, symbolic, rhetorical, doctrinal realization of them. Perfection is transferred from man to signs and symbols, words and doctrines. This is a triumph of nominalism in ethics ; it is a terrible evil and a hindrance to the real transfiguration of life. Moral rhetoric, conventional, symbolic, high-flown sentiments poison the moral life of mankind. There is danger in symbolic promises given in an overwrought emotional state, monastic vows, vows of chastity, of eternal faithfulness, and so on. All this is symbolic and not real morality. Habit plays an enormous part in moral life. It is the crystallization of the conventionally symbolic morality, working automatically. Realistic ethics must struggle against habit. Realism in ethics means love of truth, ontological veracity, absolutely unattainable for legalistic ethics ; and it also means a striving to be truly human.

The real transfiguration and enlightenment of human nature means the attainment of beauty. The good realized actually, and not formally and symbolically, is beauty. The highest end is beauty and not goodness, which always bears a stamp of the law. Beauty will save the world, i.e. beauty *is* the salvation of the world. The transfiguration of the world is the attainment of beauty. The Kingdom of God is beauty. Art gives us merely symbols of beauty. Real beauty is given only in the religious transfiguration of the creature. Beauty is God's idea of the creature, of man and of the world. But that idea is not intended to suppress personality, the concrete living being, or to turn it into a means. At this point we come up against the last paradox of ethics—the paradox of the relation between the personal and the general, the individual and the universal, the life of the personality and the idea. Personality, a living individual being, cannot be a means or an instrument for the realization of a super-personal, universal whole or idea. This is an inviolable principle of per-sonalistic ethics. But in its metaphysical aspect personalistic ethics does not deny the value of the universal and the superpersonal. Personality as the supreme moral value does not exist apart from the superpersonal and the universal, apart from the value of the idea of which it is the bearer. As has already been shown personality ontologically presupposes the superpersonal. This is an imperfect way of expressing the truth that the existence of man presupposes the existence of God. Human personality is the highest value for ethics, but it is only because it is the bearer of the divine principle and is the image and likeness of God. This does not in the least imply that the human is a means for the divine. For God the human personality is an end in itself, a friend from whom He expects responsive love and creative achievement. For man God is the final end, the object of his love, the One for Whose sake he performs creative acts. The paradox of the relation between the personal and the superpersonal (imperfectly described as the universal) is solved by the religion of the God-man, by the idea of the divinely human love—the only idea which does not destroy personality. The realization of beauty is the theosis of the creature, the revelation of the divine in the human personality. At present this is expressed in symbols, but when time is ripe it must be realized as a fact. This brings us to the last, the most anxious and painful problem of all. Ethics must have an eschatological part dealing with the problem of death and immortality, of hell and the Kingdom of God.

CHAPTER ONE

Death and Immortality

ORDINARY systems of philosophical ethics do not deal with the problems of eschatology. If they treat of immortality, they do so without going deep into the question of death but discuss it chiefly in connection with man's moral responsibility, rewards and punishments, or, at best, with the need of satisfying his longing for infinity. The conception of immortality has been defended on the ground of naturalistic metaphysics and the idea of the soul as a substance. It left completely untouched the problem of death, so fundamental for the religious and especially for the Christian consciousness. Death is a problem not only for metaphysics but also for ontological ethics. Thinkers like Kierkegaard and Heidegger recognize this. It also acquires a central significance in Freud. It is the problem of death, inseverably connected with that of time, that has a primary significance ; the problem of immortality is secondary, and as a rule it has been wrongly formulated. The very word " immortality " is inexact and implies a rejection of the mysterious fact of death. The question of the immortality of the soul forms part of a metaphysic that is utterly out of date. Death is the most profound and significant fact of life, raising the least of mortals above the mean commonplaces of life. The fact of death alone gives true depth to the question as to the meaning of life. Life in this world has meaning just because there is death ; if there were no death in our world, life would be meaningless. The meaning is bound up with the end. If there were no end, i.e. if life in our world continued for ever, there would be no meaning in it. Meaning lies beyond the confines of this limited world, and the discovery of meaning presupposes an end here. It is remarkable that although men rightly feel the horror of death and rightly regard it as the supreme evil, they are bound to connect with it the final discovery of meaning. Death—the supreme horror and evil—proves to be the only way out of the " bad time " into eternity ; immortal and eternal life prove to be only attainable through death. Man's last hope is connected with death, which manifests so clearly the power of evil in the world. This is the greatest paradox of death. According to the Christian religion death is the result of sin and is the last enemy, the supreme evil which must be conquered. And at the same time in our sinful world death is a blessing and a value. It inspires us with terror not merely because it is an evil, but because the depth and the greatness of it shatter our everyday world and exceed the powers accumulated by us in this life to meet this world's requirements. Spiritual enlightenment and an extraordinary intensity of spiritual life are needed to give us a right attitude towards death. Plato was right in teaching that philosophy was the practice of death. The only trouble is that philosophy as such does not know how one ought to die and how to conquer death. The philosophic doctrine of immortality does not show the way.

It might be said that ethics at its highest is concerned with death rather than with life, for death manifests the depth of life and reveals the end, which alone gives meaning to life. Life is noble only because it contains death, an end which testifies that man is destined to another and a higher life. Life would be low and meaningless if there were no death and no end.

Meaning is never revealed in an endless time ; it is to be found in eternity. But there is an abyss between life in time and life in eternity, and it can only be bridged by death and the horror of final severance. When this world is apprehended as self-sufficient, completed and closed in, everything in it appears meaningless because everything is transitory and corruptible—i.e. death and mortality in this world is just what makes it meaningless. This is one-half of the truth seen from a narrow and limited point of view. Heidegger is right in saying that the herd-mentality (*das Man*) is insensitive to the anguish of death.[1] It feels merely a low fear of death as of that which makes life meaningless. But there is another half of the truth, concealed from the ordinary point of view. Death not merely makes life senseless and corruptible : it is also a sign, coming from the depths, of there being a higher meaning in life. Not base fear but horror and anguish which death inspires in us prove that we belong not only to the surface but to the depths as well, not only to temporal life but also to eternity. While we are in time, eternity both attracts and horrifies us. We feel horror and anguish not only because all that we hold dear dies and comes to an end, but still more because we are conscious of a yawning abyss between time and eternity. Horror and anguish at having to cross the abyss contain at the same time a hope that the final meaning shall be revealed and realized. Death holds hope as well as horror for man, though he does not always recognize this or call it by an appropriate

[1] See *Sein und Zeit*, chapter *Das mögliche Ganzsein des Daseins und das Sein zum Tode*.

name. The meaning that comes from the other world is like a scorching flame to us and demands that we should pass through death. Death is not only a biological and psychological fact but a spiritual fact as well. *The meaning of death is that there can be no eternity in time and that an endless temporal series would be meaningless.*

But death is a manifestation of life, it is found on this side of life and is life's reaction to its own demand for an end in time. Death cannot be understood merely as the last moment of life followed either by non-being or by existence in the world beyond. Death is an event embracing the whole of life. Our existence is full of death and dying. Life is perpetual dying, experiencing the end in everything, a continual judgment passed by eternity upon time. Life is a constant struggle against death and a partial dying of the human body and the human soul. Death within life is due to the impossibility of embracing the fullness of being, either in time or in space. Time and space are death-dealing, they give rise to disruptions which are a partial experience of death. When, in time, human feelings die and disappear, this is an experience of death. When, in space, we part with a person, a house, a town, a garden, an animal, and have the feeling that we may never see them again, this is an experience of death. The anguish of every parting, of every severance in time and space, is the experience of death. I remember what anguish I felt as a boy at every parting. It was so all-embracing that I lived through mortal anguish at the thought of never seeing again the face of a stranger I met, the town I happened to pass through, the room in which I spent a few days, a tree or a dog I saw. This was, of course, an experience of death within life.

Space and time cannot enfold the wholeness of being but condemn us to severances and separations, and death always triumphs in life ; it testifies that meaning is to be found in eternity and in fullness of being, that in the life in which meaning will triumph there shall be no parting, no dying, no corruption of human thoughts and feelings. We die not only in our own death but in the death of those we love. We have in life the experience of death, though not the final experience of it. And we cannot be reconciled to death—to the death neither of human beings nor of animals, plants, things or houses. The striving for eternity of all that exists is the essence of life. And yet eternity is reached only by passing through death, and death is the destiny of everything that exists in this world. The higher and more complex a being is, the more it is threatened with death. Mountains live longer than men, although their life is less complex and lower in quality ; Mont Blanc appears to be more immortal than a saint or a genius. Things are comparatively more stable than living beings.

Death has a positive significance, but at the same time it is the most terrible and the only evil. Every kind of evil in the last resort means death. Murder, hatred, malice, depravity, envy, vengeance are death and seeds of death. Death is at the bottom of every evil passion. Pride, greed, ambition are deadly in their results. There is no other evil in the world except death and killing. Death is the evil result of sin. A sinless life would be immortal and eternal. Death is a denial of eternity and therein lies its ontological evil, its hostility to existence, its striving to reduce creation to non-being. Death resists God's creation of the world and is a return to the original non-being. Death wants to free the creature by bringing it back to primeval freedom that preceded the creation of the world. There is but one way out for the creature which in its sin resists God's conception of it—death. Death is a negative testimony to God's power and to the Divine meaning manifested in the meaningless world. It might be said that the world would carry out its godless plan of an endless (but not eternal) life if there were no God ; but since God exists, that plan is not realizable and ends in death. The Son of God, the Redeemer and Saviour, absolutely sinless and holy, had to accept death, and thereby He sanctified death. Hence the double attitude of Christianity to death. Christ has destroyed death by His death. His voluntary death, due to the evil of the world, is a blessing and a supreme value. In worshipping the cross we worship death which gives us freedom and victory. In order to rise again we must die. Through the cross death is transfigured and leads us to resurrection and to life. The whole of this world must be made to pass through death and crucifixion, else it cannot attain resurrection and eternity.

If death is accepted as a part of the mystery of life, it is not final and has not the last word. Rebellion against death in our world is rebellion against God. But at the same time we must wage a heroic struggle against death, conquer it as the last evil and pluck out its sting. The work of Christ in the world is in the first instance victory over death and preparation for resurrection and eternity. The good is life, power, fullness and eternity of life. Death proves to be the greatest paradox in the world, which cannot be understood rationally. Death is folly that has become commonplace. The consciousness that death is an ordinary everyday occurrence has dulled our sense of its being irrational and paradoxical. The last achievement of the rationalized herd-mind is to try to forget about death altogether, to conceal it, to bury the dead as unobtrusively as possible. It is the very opposite of the spirit expressed in the Christian prayer "ever to remember death". In this respect modern civilized people are incomparably inferior to the ancient Egyptians.

The paradox of death takes an aesthetic as well as a moral form. Death is hideous, the acme of hideousness, it is dissolution, the loss of all image and form, the triumph of the lower elements of the material world. But at the same time death is beautiful, it ennobles the least of mortals and raises him to the level of the greatest, it overcomes the ugliness of the mean and the commonplace. There is a moment when the face of the dead is more beautiful and harmonious than it had been in life. Ugly, evil feelings pass away and disappear in the presence of death. Death, the greatest of evils, is more noble than life in this world. The beauty and charm of the past depends upon the ennobling influence of death. It is death that purifies the past and puts upon it the seal of eternity. Death brings with it not only dissolution but purification as well. Nothing perishable, spoiled and corruptible can stand the test of death—only the eternal can. Terrible as it is to admit it, the significance of life is bound up with death and is only revealed in the face of death. Man's moral worth is manifested in the test of death, which abounds in life itself.

But at the same time struggle with death in the name of eternal life is man's main task. The fundamental principle of ethics may be formulated as follows : act so as to conquer death and affirm everywhere, in everything and in relation to all, eternal and immortal life. It is base to forget the death of a single living being and to be reconciled to it. The death of the least and most miserable creature is unendurable, and if it is irremediable, the world cannot be accepted and justified. All and everything must be raised to eternal life. This means that the principle of eternal being must be affirmed in relation to human beings, animals, plants and even inanimate things. Man must always and in everything be a giver of life and radiate creative vital energy. Love for all that lives, for every creature, rising above the love for abstract ideas, means struggle against death in the name of eternal life. Christ's love for the world and for man is victory over the powers of death and the gift of abundant life.

Asceticism means struggle with death and with the mortal elements within oneself. Struggle with death in the name of eternal life demands such an attitude to oneself and to other people as though both I and they were on the point of death. Such is the moral significance of death in the world. Conquer the low animal fear of death, but always have a spiritual fear of it, a holy terror before its mystery. It was death that first gave man the idea of the supernatural. Enemies of religion such as Epicurus thought they disproved it by showing that it originated in the fear of death. But they will never succeed in disproving the truth that in the fear of death, in the holy terror of it, man comes into touch with the deepest mystery of being and that death contains a revelation. The moral paradox of life and of death can be expressed by a moral imperative : treat the living as though they were dying and the dead as though they were alive, i.e. always remember death as the mystery of life and always affirm eternal life both in life and in death.

Life, not in its weakness but in its strength, intensity and super-abundance, is closely connected with death. This is felt in the Dionysian cults. This is revealed in love which is always connected with death. Passion, i.e. the expression of the highest intensity of life, always holds the menace of death. He who accepts love in its overwhelming power and tragedy, accepts death. He who attaches too much value to life and avoids death, runs away from love and sacrifices it to other tasks of life. In erotic love the intensity of life reaches its highest pitch and leads to destruction and death. The lover is doomed to death and involves the loved one in his doom. In the second act of *Tristan and Isolde* Wagner gives a musical revelation of this. The herd-mind tries to weaken the connection between love and death, to safeguard love and settle it down in this world. But it is not even capable of noticing love. It organizes the life of the race and knows only one remedy against death—birth. Life seems to conquer death through birth. But the victory of birth over death has nothing to do with personality, with its fate and its hopes ; it is concerned with life of the race only. The victory over death through birth is an illusion. Nature does not know the mystery of conquering death ; the victory can come only from the supernatural world. Throughout their whole history men have tried to struggle against death, and this gave rise to various beliefs and theories. Sometimes the struggle took the form of forgetting about death and sometimes of idealizing it and revelling in the thought of destruction.

The philosophical idea of the natural immortality of the soul deduced from its substantiality leads nowhere. It ignores the fact of death and denies the tragedy of it. From the point of view of such a doctrine there is no need to struggle against death and corruption for the sake of eternal life. It is rationalistic metaphysic without any tragic element in it. Scholastic spiritualism is not a solution of the problem of death and immortality, but is a purely abstract and academic theory. In the same way idealism does not solve the problem or indeed does not even face it. The idealism of the German metaphysics has no place for personality, regards it merely as a function of the world-spirit or idea, and therefore the tragedy of death does not exist for it. Death is a tragedy only when there is an acute awareness of personality. It is only because personality is experienced as eternal and immortal that death is felt to be a tragedy. The death of that which is eternal and immortal in its meaning and destination is alone tragic ; there is nothing tragic about the death of the temporal and the transitory. The death of personality in man is tragic because personality is God's eternal idea of him. It is unendurable that a complete personality containing the unity of all human powers and possibilities should die. Personality is not born of the father and the mother, it is created by God. There is no such thing as immortality of man as a natural being, born in the generic process ; there is no natural immortality of his soul and body. In this world man is a mortal being. But he is conscious of the Divine image and likeness in him and feels that he belongs not only to the natural but to the spiritual world as well. Man regards himself, therefore, as belonging to eternity, and yearns for eternity. What is eternal and immortal in man is not the psychical or the physical element as such but the spiritual element which, acting in the other two, constitutes personality and realizes the image and likeness of God. Man is immortal and eternal as a spiritual being belonging to the incorruptible world, but his spirituality is not a naturally given fact ; man is a spiritual being in so far as he manifests himself as such, in so far as the spirit in him gains possession of the natural elements. Wholeness and unity may result from the work of the spirit in the psychic and bodily elements and constitute personality. But the natural individual as such is not yet a personality, and immortality is not characteristic of him. Natural immortality belongs to the species or to the race but not to the individual. Immortality has to be won by the person and involves struggle for personality.

Idealism affirms the immortality of the impersonal or the superpersonal spirit, of the idea and value, but not of the person. Fichte and Hegel have nothing to say about personal human immortality. Human personality and its eternal destiny are sacrificed to the idea, the value, the world-spirit, world-reason, etc. There is an element of truth in this. It is true that it is not the natural, empirical man who is immortal and eternal but the spiritual, ideal, valuable element in him. The idealists, however, fail to recognize that this spiritual, ideal and valuable element forms an eternal personality and transmutes all man's powers for eternity ; they are wrong in separating it out and abstracting it into an ideal heaven as an impersonal and non-human spirit, abandoning the rest of man to death and corruption. A realized and completed personality is immortal. But in the spiritual world there are no self-contained personalities, they are united with God, with other personalities and with the cosmos.

Materialists, positivists and followers of similar theories accept death, legitimize it, and at the same time try to forget about it, building up life on the graves. Their views show a lack of " memory of death " and are therefore shallow and commonplace. The theory of progress is entirely taken up with the future of the species, of the race, of the coming generations, and has no concern with personality and its destiny. Progress, like evolution, is absolutely impersonal. For the progressing species death is an unpleasant fact, but one that has nothing deep or tragic about it. The species has an immortality of its own. It is only for the person and from the personal point of view that death is tragic and significant.

Theories of a nobler variety take up a sad and resigned attitude towards death. They recognize the tragic nature of it, but as conceived by them the human personality, though conscious of itself, has not the spiritual force to struggle with death and conquer it. The Stoic or the Buddhist attitude to death shows impotence in the face of it, but it is nobler than the naturalistic theories which completely ignore death. The emotional as distinct from the spiritual attitude to death is always melancholy and coloured by the sadness of memory which has no power to raise the dead ; only the spiritual attitude to death is victorious. The pre-Christian view of it implies resignation to fate. Christianity alone knows victory over death.

The ancient Hebrews were not familiar with the idea of personal immortality. We do not find it in the Bible. Personal self-consciousness had not yet awakened. The Jewish people were conscious of the immortality of their race but not of persons. Only in the book of Job there is awareness of personal destiny and its tragedy. It was not until the Hellenistic era, just before the coming of Christ, that the spiritual element in the Jewish religion came to be to some extent disentangled from the naturalistic, or, in other words, that personality was liberated and no longer dissolved in the collective, racial life. But the idea of immortality was truly revealed in the Greek and not in the Jewish thought.[1] The development of that idea in Greece is very instructive. At first man was recognized as mortal. Gods were immortal, but not men. Immortality was an attribute of the divine and not of the human nature. It came to be ascribed to man in so far as the divine, superhuman element was manifested in him. Not ordinary men but demigods, heroes and demons were immortal. The Greeks knew well the heartrending grief caused by death.

[1] See Erwin Rohde, *Psyche, Seelenkult und Unsterblichkeitsglaube der Greichen.*

Greek tragedy and poetry is full of it. Man was resigned to inevitable death ; he was denied immortality which the gods appropriated for themselves alone. The mortal human and the immortal divine principles were dissevered and became united only in heroes and supermen. Man descended into the subterranean realm of shadows and nothing could be sadder than his destiny. The melancholy, characteristic of the Greek and alien in this form to the Hebraic feeling for life, was rooted in the fact that the Greeks were able to reveal the human principle but not to connect it with the divine. It was the humanity of the Greeks that gave rise to the melancholy. And it was from the Greeks we heard the words that it was better for man not to be born. This is not the Indian metaphysical pessimism which denies man and regards the world as an illusion. It is an expression of human sadness for which both man and the world are real. Greeks were realists. But the Greek genius could not endure for ever the hiatus between the divine and the human world that doomed men to death and reserved immortality for the gods. A struggle for human immortality began.

The religious mythological consciousness of Greece recognized that although the divine principle was immortal and the human mortal, man's thought brought him into communion with the divine and enabled him to rise up to it and acquire it. This was the teaching of the Mysteries, of the Orphics and of Plato's philosophy. The human soul contains a divine element, but it must be freed from the power of matter ; only then will man become immortal. Immortality means that the divine element of the soul forsakes the lower, material world and does not transfigure it. Immortality is ideal and spiritual. It belongs only to that which is immortal in its metaphysical nature, but is not won for elements that are mortal and corruptible, i.e. death and corruption are not conquered. According to the Orphic myth the soul descends into the sinful material world, but it must be freed from it and return to its spiritual home. That myth had a great influence upon Plato, as can be seen particularly from *Phaedo,* and is one of the most profound human myths. It is connected with the ancient doctrine of reincarnation—one of the few attempts to understand the destiny of the soul in its past and future. And Orphism does contain a certain eternal truth. Christianity teaches of resurrection, of the victory over death for every life, for all the created world, and in this it is infinitely superior to the Greek conception of immortality which dooms a considerable part of the world to death and corruption. But the Christian view does not make clear the mystery of the genesis of the soul. The presence of the eternal element in the soul means eternity not only in the future but in the past as well. That which has an origin in time cannot inherit eternity. If the human soul bears the image and likeness of God, if it is God's idea, it arises in eternity and not in time, in the spiritual and not in the natural world. But Christian consciousness can interpret this dynamically and not statically as Platonism does. In eternity, in the spiritual world, there goes on a struggle for personality, for the realization of God's idea. Our natural earthly life is but a moment in the process which takes place in the spiritual world. This leads to the recognition of pre-existence in the spiritual world, which does not by any means involve reincarnation on earth.

The fact that man belongs to the eternal spiritual world does not imply a natural immortality of the spirit. Our natural world is the arena of the struggle for eternity and immortality, i.e. of the struggle for personality. In this struggle the spirit must gain possession of the natural elements of the soul and body for their eternal life and resurrection. Christianity teaches not so much of natural immortality which does not presuppose any struggle as of resurrection which presupposes the struggle of spiritual gracious forces with the powers of death. Resurrection means spiritual victory over death, it leaves nothing to death and corruption, as abstract spiritualism does. The doctrine of resurrection recognizes the tragic fact of death and means victory over it—which is not to be found in any doctrines of immortality, whether Orphic or Platonic or theosophical. Christianity alone faces death, recognizes both its tragedy and its meaning, but at the same time refuses to reconcile itself to it and conquers it. Eternal and immortal life is possible for man not because it is natural to the human soul, but because Christ rose from the dead and conquered the deadly powers of the world—because in the cosmic miracle of the Resurrection meaning has triumphed over meaninglessness.

The doctrine of the natural immortality of the human soul severs the destiny of the individual soul from the destiny of the cosmos, of the world-whole. It is metaphysical individualism. But the doctrine of the Resurrection links up the destiny of man with world-destiny. The resurrection of my body is at the same time the resurrection of the body of the world. "Body" in this connection means of course "spiritual body" and not the material frame. A complete personality is connected with the body and the eternal form of it and not merely with the soul. If it had not been for the coming of Christ and for His Resurrection, death would have triumphed in the world and in man. The doctrine of immortality is paradoxical : man is both mortal and immortal, he belongs both to the death-dealing time and to eternity, he is both a spiritual and a natural being

Death is a terrible tragedy, and death is conquered by death through Resurrection. It is conquered not by natural but by supernatural forces.

Two Russian religious thinkers have said remarkable things about life and death, from two entirely opposed points of view—V. Rozanov and N. Feodorov. For Rozanov all religions fall into two categories according as to whether they are based on the fact of birth or of death. Birth and death are the most important and significant events in life, and in the experience of them we catch a glimpse of the divine. Judaism and almost all pagan religions are for Rozanov religions of birth, while Christianity is the religion of death. Religions of birth are religions of life, since life springs from birth, i.e. from sex. But Christianity has not blessed birth, has not blessed sex, but enchanted the world with the beauty of death. Rozanov struggles against death in the name of life. In his view death is conquered by birth. Life is for ever triumphant through birth. But then death is conquered by life only for the newly born and not for the dead. To regard birth as victory over death is only possible if one is utterly insensitive to the human personality and its eternal destiny. For Rozanov the primary reality and the bearer of life is the genus and not the individual. In birth the genus triumphs over the personality : the genus lives for ever, the person dies. But the tragic problem of death is the problem of personality and not of the genus, and it is experienced in all its poignancy when personality is conscious of itself as a true reality and the bearer of life. However flourishing the life of the new generations may be, it does not remedy the unendurable tragedy of the death of a single living being. Rozanov knows nothing about eternal life, he knows only the endless life through child-bearing. It is a kind of sexual pantheism. Rozanov forgets that it was not with Christ that death came into the world and that the last word of Christianity is not death, not Calvary, but Resurrection and eternal life. Rozanov seeks escape from the horror of death in the vital intensity of sex. But sex in its fallen state is the very source of death in the world, and it is not for it to conquer death.

For N. Feodorov the problem is quite different. No one in the whole of human history has felt such pain at the thought of death as did Feodorov, nor such a burning desire to restore to life all who died. While Rozanov thinks of the children that are being born and finds comfort in the thoughts of life in the future, Feodorov thinks of the dead ancestors, and finds a source of sorrow in the thought of death in the past. For Feodorov death is the worst and only evil. We must not passively resign ourselves to it ; it is the source of all evils. Final victory over death consists, in his view, not in the birth of a new life but in raising up the old, in bestowing resurrection upon the dead ancestors. This feeling for the dead shows how lofty was Feodorov's moral consciousness. Man ought to be a giver of life and affirm life for all eternity. This is the supreme moral truth, whatever we may think of Feodorov's " plan " of raising the dead.

There was a great deal of truth, but also a great deal of error, in Feodorov's attitude to death. He wrongly understood the mystery of it. Feodorov was a believing Christian, but he apparently failed to grasp the mystery of the Cross and to accept the redeeming meaning of death. Death was not for him an inner moment of life, through which every sinful life must inevitably pass. While Rozanov was blind to the Resurrection, Feodorov failed to see the Cross and its redeeming significance. Both wanted to struggle with death in the name of life and to conquer death—one through birth and the other through raising the dead to life. There is more truth in Feodorov's view, but it is a one-sided truth. Death cannot be conquered by denying all meaning to it, i.e. by denying its metaphysical depth. Heidegger rightly says that the source of death is " anxiety ", but that is a source visible from our everyday world. Death is also a manifestation of eternity, and in our sinful world eternity means terror and anguish. The paradoxical fact that a man may be afraid of dying in an accident or from a contagious disease, but is not afraid of dying on the battlefield or as a martyr for his faith, shows that eternity is less terrifying when we rise above the level of commonplace everyday existence.

Both individual death and the death of the world inspire horror. There is a personal and a cosmic Apocalypse. Apocalyptic mood is one in which the thought of death reaches its highest intensity, but death is experienced as the way to a new life. The Apocalypse is the revelation about the death of the cosmos, though death is not the last word of it. Not only the individual man is mortal, but also races, civilizations, mankind as a whole, all the world and all created things. It is remarkable that the anguish of this thought is even greater than that of the anticipation of personal death. The fate of the individual and of the world are closely interconnected and intertwined by thousands of bonds. Man suffers anguish not only because he is doomed to death but because all the world is doomed to it. During historical epochs which were not marked by apocalyptic moods a man's death was softened by the thought of the race continuing for ever and preserving the results of his life and activity. But Apocalypse is the end of all perspectives of racial or cosmic immortality ; in it every creature and all the world is directly faced with the judgment of eternity. There can be no comfort in the thought that we shall be immortal in our children and that our work will last for ever, for the end is coming to all consolations that are in time. Apocalypse is a paradox of time and eternity that cannot be expressed in rational terms. The end of our world will come in time, in time as we know it. But it is also the end of time as we know it and therefore lies beyond its limits. This is an antinomy similar to Kant's antinomies of pure reason.[1] When the end comes there shall be no more time. And therefore we must paradoxically think of the end of the world both as in time and in eternity. The end of the world, like the end of each individual man, is an event both immanent and transcendent. Horror and anguish are caused by this incomprehensible combination of the transcendent and the immanent, the temporal and the eternal. For every one of us and for the world as a whole there comes a catastrophe, a jump across the abyss, a mysterious escape from time which takes place in time. The death of an individual is also a deliverance from time taking place in time. If our sinful temporal world as we know it were endless, this would be an evil nightmare, just like the endless continuation of an individual life. It would be a triumph of the meaningless. And the presentiment of the coming end calls forth, together with horror and anguish, hope and expectancy of the final revelation and triumph of meaning. Judgment and valuation of all that has happened in the world is the final revelation of meaning. The Last Judgment of individuals and of the world, interpreted in an inner sense, is nothing other than the discovery of meaning and the affirmation of qualities and values.

The paradox of time and eternity exists for the destiny both of the world and of the individual. Eternal and immortal life may be objectified and naturalized, and then it is spoken of as life in the world beyond. It appears as a natural realm of being though different from ours. Man enters it after death. But eternal and immortal life regarded from within and not objectified is essentially different in quality from the natural and even the supernatural existence. It is a spiritual life, in which eternity is attained while still in time. If man's existence were wholly taken up into the spirit and transmuted into spiritual life so that the spiritual principle gained final possession of the natural elements of the body and the soul, death as a natural fact would not take place at all. The transition to eternity would be accomplished, without the event which externally appears to us as death. Eternal life is revealed in time, it may unfold itself in every instant as an eternal present. Eternal life is not a future life but life

[1] Kant's genius is seen at its best in his treatment of the antinomies of pure reason. See *Kritik der reinen Vernunft, Die Antinomie der reinen Vernunft.*

in the present, life in the depths of an instant of time. In those depths time is torn asunder. It is therefore a mistake to expect eternity in the future, in an existence beyond the grave and to look forward to death in time in order to enter in to the divine eternal life. Strictly speaking, eternity will never come in the future—in the future there can only be a bad infinity. Only hell can be thought of in this way. Eternity and eternal life come not in the future but in a moment, i.e. they are a deliverance from time, and mean ceasing to project life into time. In Heidegger's terminology it means the cessation of " anxiety " which gives temporal form to existence.

Death exists externally as a certain natural fact which takes place in the future, and it signifies that existence assumes a temporal form, and life is projected into the future. Inwardly, from the point of view of eternity unfolded in the depths of the moment and not projected into time, death does not exist ; it is only an element in the eternal life. Death exists only " on this side of things ", in temporal being, in the order of nature. The unfolding of spirituality, the affirmation of the eternal in life and participation in a different order of being mean transcendence of death and victory over it. To transcend death and conquer it is not to forget it or be insensitive to it, but to accept it within one's spirit, so that it ceases to be a natural, temporal fact and becomes a manifestation of meaning which proceeds from eternity.

The personal and the cosmic Apocalypse bring to light our failure to fulfil eternal righteousness in life and are a triumph of righteousness in the dark world of sin. The death of the world and of individuals, of nations, civilizations, customs, historical forms of state and society, is a catastrophic reminder on the part of truth and righteousness of the fact that they have been distorted and not fulfilled. This is the meaning, too, of all great revolutions which indicate an Apocalypse within history, and the meaning of catastrophic events in the individual life. The Revelation about the coming of the antichrist and his kingdom shows that the Christian truth has not been fulfilled and that men are incapable and unwilling to realize it. Such is the law of spiritual life. If men do not freely realize the Kingdom of Christ, the kingdom of the antichrist will be brought about with necessity. Death comes to all life which does not fulfil the divine meaning and the divine truth. The triumph of irrationality is the revelation of meaning in the darkness of sin. Hence death, both cosmic and individual, is not merely a triumph of meaningless dark forces and a result of sin but also a triumph of meaning. It reminds man of the divine truth and does not allow unrighteousness to be eternal.

Theoretically, N. Feodorov was right in saying that the world and man could pass into eternal life without the catastrophe of the end and the Last Judgment, if humanity were fraternally united for the sake of the common task of realizing Christian righteousness and raising the dead.[1] But the world and mankind have gone too far in the path of evil, and judgment has come upon them already. Irrational, meonic freedom prevents the realization of Feodorov's " plan ". He was too optimistic and undervalued the forces of evil. But the affirmation of eternity, of eternal life for every being and for all creation, is a moral imperative. Act so that eternal life might be revealed to you and that the energy of eternal life should radiate from you to all creation.

Ethics must be eschatological. The question of death an immortality is fundamental to a personalistic ethics and confronts us in every act and every expression of life. Insensitiveness to death and forgetfulness of it, so characteristic of the nineteenth and twentieth century ethics, mean insensitiveness to personality and to its eternal destiny, as well as insensitiveness to the destiny of the world as a whole. Strictly speaking, a system of ethics which does not make death its central problem has no value and is lacking in depth and earnestness. Although it deals with judgments and valuations, it forgets about the final judgment and valuation, i.e. about the Last Judgment. Ethics must be framed not with a prospect to happiness in an unending life here, but in view of an inevitable death and victory over death, of resurrection and eternal life. Creative ethics calls us not to the creation of temporary, transitory and corruptible goods and values which help us to forget death, the end, and the Last Judgment, but to the creation of eternal, permanent, immortal goods and values which further the victory of eternity and prepare man for the end.

Eschatological ethics does not by any means imply a passive renunciation of creative activity. Passive apocalyptic moods are a thing of the past, they are a sign of decadence and an escape from life. On the contrary, eschatological ethics based upon apocalyptic experience demands an unprecedented intensity of human creativeness and activity. We must not passively await in horror and anguish the impending end and the death of human personality and the world. Man is called actively to struggle with the deadly forces of evil and creatively to prepare for the coming of the Kingdom of God. Christ's second coming presupposes intense creative activity on our part, preparing both mankind and the world for the end. The end itself depends upon man's creative activity and is determined by the positive results of the cosmic process. We must not passively wait for

[1] See *Filosofia obshtchago dela.*

the Kingdom of Christ, any more than for that of antichrist, but must actively and creatively struggle against the latter and prepare for the Kingdom of God which is taken by force.

To regard apocalyptic prophecies with passive resignation means to interpret them in a naturalistic sense, to rationalize them and deny the mysterious combination of Divine Providence and human freedom. It is equally wrong to take up a passive and fatalistic attitude to one's own death, to the death of personality, and regard it as a predetermined natural fact. We must accept death freely and with an enlightened mind, and not rebel against it ; but this free and enlightened acceptance of death is a creative activity of the spirit. There is a false activity which rebels against death and refuses to accept it. It leads to unendurable suffering. But there is also the true activity which is the victory of eternity over death. An active spirit does not really fear death—only a passive spirit does. An active spirit experiences an infinitely greater fear and terror than that of death—the fear of hell and eternal torments. It lives through its own eternity ; death exists for it not inwardly but merely as an external fact. It experiences terror at the thought of its eternal destiny and of the judgment which is in eternity.

We come here upon a psychological paradox which to many people is unknown and incomprehensible. An active spirit which has a direct inward experience of being eternal and indestructible may, so far from fearing death, actually desire it and envy those who do not believe in immortality and are convinced that death is the end. It is a mistake to imagine that the so-called faith in immortality is always comforting and that those who have it are in a privileged and enviable position. Faith in immortality is a comfort and makes life less hard, but it is also a source of terror and of an overwhelming responsibility. Those who are convinced that there is no immortality know nothing of this responsibility. It would be more correct to say that the unbelievers rather than the believers make life easy for themselves. Unbelief in immortality is suspicious just because it is so easy and comforting ; the unbelievers comfort themselves with the thought that in eternity there will be no judgment of meaning over their meaningless lives. The extreme, unendurable terror is not the terror of death but of judgment and of hell. It does not exist for the unbelievers, only the believers know it. A passive spirit seldom experiences it, but an active one experiences it with particular intensity, because it is apt to connect its destiny, and consequently judgment and the possibility of hell, with its own creative efforts. The problem of death inevitably leads to that of hell. Victory over death is not the last and final victory. Victory over death is too much concerned with time. The last, final and ultimate victory is victory over hell. It is wholly concerned with eternity. Still more fundamental than the task of raising the dead, preached by Feodorov, is the task of conquering hell and freeing from it all who are suffering " eternal " torments. The final task, which ethics is bound to set us in the end, is creative liberation of all beings from the temporal and " eternal " torments of hell. If this task is not realized, the Kingdom of God cannot be realized either.

CHAPTER TWO

Hell

PHILOSOPHICAL ethics has left untouched the problem of hell, which existed for religious ethics only. And yet hell is not only the final but the fundamental problem of ethics and no thoroughgoing system of ethics can dispense with it. It is remarkable how little people think about hell or trouble about it. This is the most striking evidence of human frivolity. Man is capable of living entirely on the surface, and then the image of hell does not haunt him. Having lost the sense of immortal and eternal life man has freed himself from the painful problem of hell and thrown off the burden of responsibility. We come here upon a moral antinomy which, apparently, cannot be solved rationally. The soul conducts an inner dialogue with itself about hell, and neither side has the final say. This is what makes the problem so painful. Modern rejection of hell makes life too easy, superficial and irresponsible. But a belief in hell makes moral and spiritual life meaningless, for then the whole of it is lived under torture. The idea of hell is torture, and torture may force man to do anything. But things done under torture have no value or significance and are not a moral and spiritual achievement. Sufficient attention has not been paid to this aspect of the belief in hell. All that a man does out of fear of hell and not out of love of God and of perfect life has no religious significance whatever, although in the past the motive of fear was utilized to the utmost for religious purposes. If hell exists and is a menace to me, disinterested love of God is for me impossible, and my actions are inspired not by striving for perfection but by the desire to avoid eternal torments. Belief in hell turns men into hedonists and utilitarians and destroys disinterested love of truth. The mystics who expressed consent to suffer the torments of hell out of love for God were actuated by a deeply moral feeling. St. Paul consented to be parted from Christ out of love for his brethren. We find the same motive in the mysticism of the Quietists and of Fénélon, condemned by the Roman Catholic hedonism and utilitarianism. Particularly striking was the case of Marie des Vallées, who consented to suffer in hell for the sake of saving those possessed by Satan and doomed to perdition.[1] Mystics always rose above utilitarian

[1] Emile Dermengem, *La vie admirable et les révélations de Marie des Vallées.*

and hedonistic considerations connected with the vulgarized idea of hell. Fear of perdition and a longing for salvation and eternal bliss are by no means mystical motives. The ideas of everlasting bliss and everlasting torments, salvation and perdition are exoteric ideas, a revelation of the divine life refracted in the herd-mind. A religion adapted to the herd-mind always contains a utilitarian element. Only mysticism which rises to the heights of disinterestedness is free from it. Salvation from eternal perdition is not the last word of truth, it is merely a utilitarian and vulgarized version of the truth about seeking the Kingdom of God, the love of God, perfect life and deification. It does not in any way solve the problem of hell or blunt its poignancy.

Thus speaks one of the voices in the soul's dialogue with itself. But the other voice begins to speak, making our attitude to hell hopelessly contradictory. We cannot admit the reality of hell, our moral consciousness rebels against it, and we cannot simply deny it, for that would mean sacrificing unquestionable values. It is easy enough to deny hell if one denies freedom and personality. There is no hell if personality is not eternal and if man is not free, but can be forced to be good and to enter paradise. The idea of hell is ontologically connected with freedom and personality, and not with justice and retribution. Paradoxical as it sounds, hell is the moral postulate of man's spiritual freedom. Hell is necessary not to ensure the triumph of justice and retribution to the wicked, but to save man from being forced to be good and compulsorily installed in heaven. In a certain sense man has a moral right to hell—the right freely to prefer hell to heaven. This sums up the moral dialectic of hell.

The justification of hell on the grounds of justice, such as we find in St. Thomas Aquinas and Dante, is particularly revolting and lacking in spiritual depth. It is the idea of freedom and not of justice that dialectically presupposes hell. Hell is admissible in the sense that a man may want it and prefer it to paradise ; he may feel better there than in heaven. The idea of hell is the expression of an acute and intense experience of the indestructible nature of personality. Eternal perdition means that personality remains self-contained, indissoluble and absolutely isolated. Hell consists precisely in the fact that the self does not want to give it up. The pantheistic mergence of personality in God cancels, of course, the idea of hell, but it also cancels the idea of personality. Such is the ontological basis of the idea of hell. Every moral valuation is the beginning of it, for it is the starting point of the division into two realms, one of which is that of hell. The problem is how to avoid hell without giving up valuation and distinction. Men like St. Augustine and Dante are inspired by the idea of the division which prepares hell. But to struggle against hell does not mean to abandon the struggle against evil : on the contrary, it means pursuing it to the end. The question is whether hell is a good thing, as its " good " champions believe.

In its inner dialogue about hell the soul takes up now the objective and now the subjective point of view, looking at the problem alternately from within and from without. It is this that leads to contradictions. One can look at hell from the human and from the divine point of view. And if one looks at it from the point of view of God and objectifies it, it is incomprehensible, inadmissible and revolting. It is impossible to be reconciled to the thought that God could have created the world and man if He foresaw hell, that He could have predetermined it for the sake of justice, or that He tolerates it as a special diabolical realm of being side by side with His Own Kingdom. From the divine point of view it means that creation is a failure. The idea of an objectified hell as a special sphere of eternal life is altogether intolerable, unthinkable and, indeed, incompatible with faith in God. A God who deliberately allows the existence of eternal torments is not God at all but is more like the devil. Hell as a place of retribution for the wicked, which is a comfort to the good, is a fairy tale ; there is not a shadow of reality about it ; it is borrowed from our everyday existence with its rewards and punishments. The idea of an eternal hell as a rightful retribution for holding false and heretical beliefs is one of the most hideous and contemptible products of the triumphant herd-mind. From the objective point of view, from the point of view of God, there cannot be any hell. To admit hell would be to deny God.

But everything is changed the moment we take up the subjective point of view, the point of view of man. Another voice begins to speak then, and hell becomes comprehensible, for it is given in human experience. Man's moral revolt begins only when hell is objectified and affirmed as having its source and, as it were, its being in God, instead of in man. Hell belongs entirely to the subjective and not to the objective sphere ; it exists in the subject and not in the object, in man and not in God. There is no hell as an objective realm of being ; such a conception is utterly godless and is Manichean rather than Christian. Metaphysical theories of hell are therefore absolutely impossible and inadmissible. All attempts to conceive of hell as objective justly rouse our indignation and opposition.

Unthinkable as a realm of objective being, hell exists in the subjective sphere and is a part of human experience. Hell, like heaven, is merely a symbol of man's spiritual life. The experience of hell means complete self-centredness, inability to enter into objective being, self-absorption to which eternity is closed and nothing but bad infinity left. Eternal hell is a vicious and self-contradictory combination of words. Hell is a denial of eternity, impossibility to have a part in it and to enter eternal life. There can be no diabolical eternity—the only eternity is that of the Kingdom of God and there is no other reality on a level with it.

But the bad infinity of torments may exist in the self-contained subjective realm. In his own inner life a man may feel that his pain is endless, and this experience gives rise to the idea of an everlasting hell. In our life on earth it is given us to experience torments that appear to us to go on for ever, that are not for a moment, for an hour or a day, but seem to last an infinity. It is only such torments that are really terrifying and suggestive of hell. But their infinity has nothing to do with eternity and has no objective reality. It is due to the subject shutting himself up in his self-centred suffering and being unable to escape from it into objective reality. Objectively this infinity may last a moment, an hour, or a day, but it receives the name of everlasting hell. The experience of unending torments is that of being unable to escape from one's self-centred agony. There is no hell anywhere except in the illusory and utterly unreal sphere of egocentric subjectivity powerless to enter eternity.

Hell is not eternity at all but endless duration in time. The torments of hell are temporal, for they are in the " bad infinity " of time ; they do not mean abiding in an eternity different from the eternity of the Kingdom of God. In hell are those who remain in time and do not pass into eternity, those who remain in the subjective closed-in sphere and do not enter the objective realm of the Kingdom of God. In itself hell is illusory, phantasmagorical and unreal, but it may be the greatest psychological subjective reality for the individual. Hell is a phantasm, a nightmare which cannot be eternal but may be experienced by man as endless. Phantasms created by human passions plunge the self into hell. Passions weave the illusory web of dreams and nightmares from which man cannot wake in eternity, but which for that very reason cannot be eternal. There is nothing objectively real in those nightmares. It is not God's objective justice that dooms man to the experience of them, but man's irrational freedom which draws him to pre-existential non-being. After the experience of living in God's world, that non-being proves to be of the nature of hell.

The creature can feel the torments of hell only in so far as the image of God has not been completely dimmed in it, in so far as the divine light still shines in the darkness of evil phantasms. If the image and likeness of God become completely dimmed and the divine light ceases to shine, the torments of hell will cease and there will be a final return to non-being. Final perdition can only be thought of as non-being which no longer knows any suffering. The torments of hell are not inflicted on man by God but by man himself, by means of the idea of God. The divine light is the source of torments as a reminder of man's true calling. The struggle against the powers of hell is the struggle to make man's consciousness so clear, strong and complete that he can wake up in eternity from the nightmare which seems to last an infinite time. The phantasms of hell mean the loss of the wholeness of personality and of the synthesizing power of consciousness, but the disintegrated shreds of personality go on existing and dreaming, and the broken up personal consciousness goes on functioning. These dissevered fragments of personality experience absolute loneliness.

Liberation from the nightmare of hell and the painful dreams which are a state between being and non-being consists either in the victory of the complete consciousness (or one might say of super consciousness), the return to true being and transition to eternity, or the final annihilation of the disintegrated consciousness and transition to utter non-being. Man passes from the subconscious through consciousness to the superconscious. Wholeness and fullness are attained only in superconscious life. Our "conscious" life from birth to death contains menacing dreamlike states which anticipate the nightmare of hell. Those states are created by sinful passions, and in them consciousness is broken up and distorted by the unenlightened and unregenerated subconscious. But human life contains other dreams and visions which are an anticipation of paradise. They gave us glimpses of superconscious life in which the subconscious is transfigured and sublimated.

The existence of hell as a subjective realm depends upon the correlation between subconsciousness, consciousness and superconsciousness. Struggle against hell consists in awakening superconsciousness, i.e. the spiritual life. If there is no spiritual life, the relation between consciousness and the subconscious gives rise to evil dreams and nightmares. Consciousness as such does not imply that the wholeness of personality has been attained, but it is only by attaining such wholeness that we can combat the disintegrated fragments of consciousness which drag us down to hell. Wholeness of personality disappears in hell in consequence of self-absorption, self-centredness and evil isolation, i.e. of the impotence to love and to attain superconscious wholeness. We know all this and can study it in the experience of our own life which passes in the intermediate stratum of consciousness. In the disintegration of personality we slide downwards to dreams and nightmares. Final awakening is attained through spiritual sobriety which leads to the light of superconsciousness. Spiritual sobriety and ecstatic illumination equally testify to the attainment of wholeness which makes a return to the illusory semi-existence of hell impossble. The primary, unconscious, elementary wholeness disappears once consciousness has dawned. After passing through consciousness with its inner dividedness the self can move either upwards, to the heaven of superconsciousness, or downwards into hell in which fragments of consciousness are still preserved. Pain and suffering are connected with consciousness, and consciousness cannot be completely destroyed. The very origin of consciousness involves disruption, and consciousness suffers because it cannot be whole. But the dividedness of consciousness may become complete disintegration, and then the pain and suffering will increase. Pain ceases when either superconscious wholeness or utter non-being is attained.

The daylight, waking consciousness is not so sharply divided from the dreaming, dark unconscious as is commonly supposed. In the ancient world, at the dawn of history, the division between them was still less marked, and man mistook " dreams " for " realities ". It was under those conditions that the myth-making process took place. The idea of hell became distinct only in the Christian era, but it originated in profound antiquity. At first it was not definitely associated with the idea of punitive justice. Hades, the subterranean realm of shadows and semi-existence, was the sad destiny of all mortals. Ancient Greeks knew no salvation from that fate. The existence after death was connected with the chthonic, subterranean gods. This was the beginning of the nightmares of hell, woven out of the images of the dark underworld and the painful dreams of semi-existence. The Greeks, whose conception of life was essentially tragic, were resigned to the melancholy fate of mortals. The terrible thing was that men did not die completely but were doomed to a semi-existence and semi-consciousness, similar to a painful dream from which one cannot awake. The Greek aristocracy built up an Olympus above the twilight realm of the underworld. It was in the Mysteries that the ancient Greeks sought victory over death and the attainment of true immortality. But the Greek mind had not elaborated the conception of the two camps—of the " good " and the " wicked "—of the struggle between two world-principles and of the final defeat of Satan, pushed back into hell.

Religiously moral dualism is characteristic of Persian thought and is particularly marked in Manicheism. It cannot be denied that the Hebrew eschatological theories were framed under Persian influences and that the Christian conception of the devil and his kingdom has a Persian source. Strictly speaking, Christian thought has never completely freed itself from Manichean elements. When the conception of hell became crystallized, it gave expression to the ancient instinct of vengeance, transferring it from time into eternity. The element of vengeance enters into Dante's conception of hell, and we can well understand Feodorov's antipathy to Dante, whom he regarded as a genius of vengeance.

Hell appeared to the human mind in two forms : either as the final doom of mankind in general, for there is no salvation and no one can enter the Divine Kingdom which is for the gods alone, or as the triumph of retributive justice reserved for the wicked after the salvation of the good has been made manifest. The original image of hell is the sad dream of sinful humanity which does not know salvation and can neither live in eternity nor completely die. The second image is created by those who having learned about salvation and regard themselves as " good ", relegating the " wicked " to hell. It is impossible to suppose that hell is created by God ; it is created by the devil, it is created by human sin. But the dreadful thing is that hell is created not only by the " wicked" and by evil but to a far greater extent by the " virtuous " and by " good " itself for the " wicked " and for evil. The " wicked " create hell for themselves, but the " good " create hell for others. For centuries the " good " who found salvation affirmed and strengthened the idea of hell. It was a powerful influence in Christian thought, inspired not by a Christian, not by a Gospel idea of justice. The first Greek teachers of the Church were the least guilty of building up and perpetuating the idea of hell. That evil work of the " good " was done chiefly in Western Christian thought, beginning with St. Augustine and culminating in the writings of St. Thomas Aquinas and Dante.[1] The conception of hell created by the good for the " wicked " is triumphant in all catechisms and in all official courses of theology. It is based upon Gospel texts which are taken literally, without any consideration for the metaphorical language of the Gospel or any understanding of its symbolism. It is only the new Christian consciousness that is worried by the Gospel words about hell ; the old rejoiced in them.

All the antinomies connected with the problem of freedom and necessity arise with reference to hell and indeed become more irreconcilable

[1] See Tixeront, *Histoire des dogmes dans l'antiquité chrétienne*. The author is a Roman Catholic, but he is very fair and admits that the idea of universal salvation was more natural to the East, and the idea of hell to the West.

and give rise to fresh difficulties. If out of pity and humanity we admit the necessity, i.e. the inevitability of universal salvation, we must deny the freedom of the creature. Origen's doctrine of apocatastasis contradicts his own doctrine of freedom. The salvation of the whole world, understood as the reinstatement of all in the condition prior to the Fall, is conceived as the result of an externally determined process independent of human liberty. All creatures will be compelled in the end to enter the Kingdom of God. Hell exists, but it is only temporal, i.e. strictly speaking it is a purgatory. A temporal hell is always merely a purgatory and has an educative significance.

In the inner dialogue of the soul about hell the voice of Origen always represents one of the disputants.[1] When Origen said that Christ will remain on the cross so long as a single creature remains in hell, he expressed an eternal truth. And yet we must admit that to regard salvation as predetermined is to rationalize the eschatological mystery. But is it possible to maintain the opposite and say that hell and perdition are predetermined in God's creation? That certainly is still less admissible. Origen is better than Calvin, there is more moral truth in Origen than in St. Augustine. The fundamental antinomy which confronts the mind perplexed by the problem of hell is this : human freedom is irreconcilable with a compulsory, predetermined salvation, but that same freedom rebels against the idea of hell as a predetermined doom. We cannot deny hell because this would be contrary to freedom, and we cannot admit it because freedom rises against it. Hell is the dark, irrational, meonic freedom which has crystallized into fate. Christian consciousness denies the existence of fate in the ancient Greek sense, for that is incompatible with God and human freedom. But the idea of hell is equivalent to that of fate. True, it will be said that hell is the fate of the " wicked " and that the " good " are free from it. Such an argument, however, is superficial. The freedom of the " wicked " is a fatal freedom and leads to their doom. Freedom which is usually contrasted with fate may degenerate into fate. The dark, evil freedom devoid of grace is the " fate " recognized by Christianity. The dark freedom which rejects grace may not want heaven ; it may prefer hell. This is frequently done by those who rebel against the idea of it. Thus free preference of hell to paradise proves to be the fate that hangs over creation.

[1] In the nineteenth century Jean Reynard defended a theory similar to that of Origen. See his book, *Ciel et terre*, which contains interesting thoughts about hell expressed, as usual with him, in the form of a dialogue between a theologian and a philosopher.

The antinomy of freedom and necessity exists not only for man and the created world but for God also. The impossibility of solving it has given rise to the doctrine of predestination. If God foresees, or rather, if He knows from all eternity whither the freedom with which He endowed the creature will lead it, He thereby predetermines some to salvation and others to perdition. This terrible doctrine ascribes the character of fate not to freedom but to God Himself. God is the fate of the creature, predetermining their salvation or perdition. The doctrine of predestination is, of course, a form of rationalizing the mystery of the last things, and the most revolting form of it. But in any case hell proves to be fated—whether it is preordained by God or is an inevitable consequence of human freedom. The antinomy remains insoluble and the inner dialogue of the soul, divided against itself by the painful efforts to solve the problem, continues. It may even be said that the effort to solve it is itself an experience of hell-fire.

The argument may be carried so far that God Himself will be found to deserve everlasting torments. This is precisely what is done by the most remarkable and profound writer of modern France, Marcel Jouhandeau. These are his striking words : " La mélancolie que je peux Lui donner est terrible : tous les Anges ne le consolent pas de moi. Et qui sait que Lui si ce n'est pas ' le péché de Dieu,' Son unique faiblesse, que de n'aimer, si, m'aimant, Dieu ne mérite pas de partager l'Enfer qu'Il me promet? L'Enfer n'est pas ailleurs qu'à la place la plus brulante du Cœur de Dieu,"[1] He raises here the inevitable question of God Himself suffering in hell if the creatures whom He loves will burn in its flames.

The idea of hell is that of an eternal doom, for in hell there is neither freedom nor grace which might lead out of it. It is absolutely fatal and irremediable. Freedom which leads to hell is recognized, but freedom which leads out of it is denied; there is a free entrance but no free exit. Thus God's conception of the world involves an element of dark fate, far more terrible than the fate of Greek mythology. This fatal element overshadows the Christian mind and conscience. Hell as a special ontological realm indicates either the failure of the divine plan or an element of fate deliberately included in it by God. It would be profoundly wrong to call that fate a triumph of divine justice, for there is no justice in punishing by eternal torments sins committed in time. Time and eternity are incommensurable. There is more justice in the doctrine of Karma and reincar-

[1] See his wonderful novel, *Monsieur Godeau intime*. It is a metaphysical book that deals with satanic depths. Many interesting reflections are also to be found in W. Blake's *Marriage of Heaven and Hell* and *First Books of Prophecy*.

nation, according to which deeds done in time are expiated in time and not in eternity, and man has other and wider experience than that between birth and death in this one life. Theosophical theory of reincarnation cannot be accepted by the Christian mind. But it is essential to recognize that man's final fate can only be settled after an infinitely greater experience in spiritual worlds than is possible in our short earthly life.

Hell is the final result of a certain tendency of the moral will and the moral consciousness of mankind. It may be willed and affirmed by those who never trouble about theological problems. Hell as an objective realm is the creation of moral will which sharply divides the world into two camps—of the " good " and the " wicked "—into two spheres which culminate in heaven and hell. The "wicked" are thrust into hell, and it is done in this life and in this time. I mean " morally thrust ", for physically they may be the masters. Hell is the result of the complete separation of the fate of the good who inherit bliss from the fate of the wicked who inherit eternal torments. Hell as an objective realm is pre-eminently the work of the good. It appears to them as the final expression of justice, a just retribution. I am speaking here of hell in the objective sense, for as subjective it is to be found within the life of the " good " themselves and is an experience known to them also. Human will which sharply divides the world into two parts imagines hell as an eternal prison house in which the " wicked " are isolated, so that they can do no more harm to the good. Such a conception is, of course, not divine but human through and through. It is the culmination of the life of our sinful world on this side of good and evil. The possibility of real victory over evil, i.e. of the regeneration of the wicked, is not even thought of, and, what is worse, the will is not directed towards that end but rather to its opposite. Evil must be isolated, punished and thrust into hell. The good comfort themselves with that idea. No one wants to think of saving the " wicked " and the devil. People do think of course, of saving sinners, because everyone is a sinner. But there comes a moment when sinners are numbered with the " wicked " in the camp of the devil, and then they are forsaken and relegated to hell.

This separation of the fate of the " good " from the fate of the " wicked " and the final judgment passed by the good over the wicked is the greatest perversion of a morality generally acknowledged to be very lofty. It is a mistake to imagine that hell as punishment and retribution endured for ever in some objective realm of being is the result of Divine judgment. This is an invention of those who consider themselves " good ". The human, all too human, idea of hell objectifies wretched

[Handwritten margin note:] Ah! Instead of making hell out to be the final consequences of a choice to throw away one's life to non-being, he makes hell out to be somewhat of another earth with a bit more agony. So why cannot hell have a hell for those who choose non-being and so on ad infinitum?

human judgment which has nothing in common with God's judgment. " True believers " send " heretics " to hell in accordance with human and not with Divine justice. God's judgment, for which every human soul and the whole creation is waiting, will probably have very little resemblance to the judgment of men. The last will be first, and the first last—which is beyond our comprehension. It is utterly inadmissible that men should usurp God's right to judge. God will judge the world, but He will judge the idea of hell too. His judgment lies beyond our distinctions between good and evil. This idea may perhaps have found a reflection in the doctrine of predestination.

Man's moral will ought never to aim at relegating any creature to hell or to demand this in the name of justice. It may be possible to admit hell for oneself, because it has a subjective and not an objective existence. I' may experience the torments of hell and believe that I deserve them. But it is impossible to admit hell for others or to be reconciled to it, if only because hell cannot be objectified and conceived as a real order of being. It is hard to understand the psychology of pious Christians who calmly accept the fact that their neighbours, friends and relatives will perhaps be damned. I cannot resign myself to the fact that the man with whom I am drinking tea is doomed to eternal torments. If people were morally more sensitive they would direct the whole of their moral will and spirit towards delivering from the torments of hell every being they had ever met in life. It is a mistake to think that this is what people do when they help to develop other men's moral virtues and to strengthen them in the true faith. The true moral change is a change of attitude towards the " wicked " and the doomed, a desire that they too should be saved, i.e. acceptance of their fate for oneself, and readiness to share it. This implies that I cannot seek salvation individually, by my solitary self, and make my way into the Kingdom of God relying on my own merits. Such an interpretation of salvation destroys the unity of the cosmos. Paradise is inpossible for me if the people I love, my friends or relatives or mere acquaintances, will be in hell—if Boehme is in hell as a " heretic ", Nietzsche as " an antichrist ", Goethe as a " pagan " and Pushkin as a sinner. Roman Catholics who cannot take a step in their theology without Aristotle are ready to admit with perfect complacency that, not being a Christian, Aristotle is burning in hell. All this kind of thing has become impossible for us, and that is a tremendous moral progress. If I owe so much to Aristotle or Nietzsche I must share their fate, take their torments upon myself and free them from hell. Moral consciousness began with God's question, " Cain, where is thy brother Abel? " It will end with another question on the part of God : "Abel, where is thy brother Cain? "

Hell is the state of the soul powerless to come out of itself, absolute self-centredness, dark and evil isolation, i.e. final inability to love. It means being engulfed in an agonizing moment which opens upon a yawning abyss of infinity, so that the moment becomes endless time. Hell creates and organizes the separation of the soul from God, from God's world and from other men. In hell the soul is separated from everyone and from everything, completely isolated and at the same time enslaved by everything and everyone. The distortion of the idea of hell in the human mind has led to its being identified with the fear of God's judgment and retribution. But hell is not God's action upon the soul, retributive and punitive as that action may be ; it is the absence of any action of God upon the soul, the soul's incapacity to open itself to God's influence and its complete severance from God. Hell is nothing other than complete separation from God. The horror of hell is not inspired by the thought that God's judgment will be stern and implacable. God is love and mercy, and to give one's fate to Him means to overcome the horror. The horror is to have my fate left in my own hands. It is not what God will do to me that is terrible, but what I will do to myself. What is terrible is the judgment passed by the soul upon itself, upon its own impotence to enter eternal life. Hell really means not that man falls into the hands of God but that he is finally abandoned to his own devices. Nothing is more terrible than one's own dark meonic freedom which prepares life in hell. The fear of God's judgment means that darkness cannot endure Divine light and love. God's judgment is simply the terrible light thrown upon darkness, love directed upon malice and hatred.

Every human soul is sinful and subject to darkness and cannot by its own power come into the light. The soul becomes inclined to pass into the twilight dreamland of semi-existence. Its own free efforts cannot bring it to true and real being. The very essence of Christianity is bound up with this. " The Son of man is not come to destroy men's lives, but to save them." " I came not to judge the world, but to save the world." The coming of Christ is salvation from the hell which man prepares for himself. The coming of Christ is the turning point for the soul of man which begins to build up the Kingdom of God instead of building up hell. Without Christ, the Redeemer and Saviour, the Kingdom of God is unattainable for man. Man's moral efforts do not bring him to it. If there is no Christ and no change of heart connected with Christ, hell in one form or another is inevitable, for man cannot help creating it. The essence of salvation is liberation from hell, to which the creature naturally gravitates.

The idea of hell must be completely freed from all associations with criminal law transferred to the heavenly world. Hell as a subjective realm, as the absorption of the soul in its own darkness, is the immanent result of sinful existence and not a transcendental punishment for sin. Hell is absorption in the immanent and the inpossibility of passing to the transcendental. The descent of the Son of God into hell can alone liberate man from it. Hell is the consequence of the natural world being closed to Divine intervention and to the descent of God into it. All Divine action in the world is directed towards freeing man from hell.

Hell will not come in eternity, it will remain in time. Hence it cannot be eternal. One of the voices that speaks in my soul tells me that all are doomed to hell, because all more or less doom themselves to it. But this is reckoning without Christ. And the other voice in me says that all must be saved, that man's freedom must be enlightened from within, without any violence being done to it—and that comes through Christ and is salvation. In the spiritual world we cannot think of the devil as outside the human soul, he is immanent in it and means that it is abandoned to itself. Christ frees the soul from the devil. Unless one adopts the Manichean point of view, the devil must be regarded as a higher spirit, God's creature, and his fall can only be explained by meonic freedom. The problem of satanism is at bottom the problem of that abysmal, irrational freedom.

The idea of hell has been turned into an instrument of intimidation, of religious and moral terrorism. But there is no real horror of the anticipation of hell in these intimidations. The real horror is not in the threats of a transcendental Divine judgment and retribution, but in the immanent working out of human destiny from which all Divine action has been excluded. Paradoxically it might be said that the horror of hell possesses man when he submits his final destiny to his own judgment and not to that of God. The most pitiless tribunal is that of one's own conscience ; it brings with it torments of hell, division, loss of wholeness, a fragmentary existence. God's judgment is an outpouring of grace upon the creature. It establishes true realities and makes them all subordinate to the highest, not in a legal but in an ontological sense.

There was a time when the intimidating idea of hell retained the herdman within the church ; but now this idea can only hinder people from entering the church. Human consciousness has changed. It is clear to us now that we cannot seek the Kingdom of God and the perfect life out of fear of hell ; that such fear is a morbid emotion robbing our life of moral significance and preventing us from reaching perfection or working for the Kingdom of God. The fear of hell used as a spur to the religious life is a partial experience of hell, entrance into the moment in which hell is revealed. Therefore those who make religious life dependent upon the fear of damnation actually thrust the soul into hell.

Hell is immanent and subjective through and through, there is nothing transcendental and ontologically real about it. It is the state of being utterly closed in, of having no hope of breaking through to anything transcendent and of escaping from oneself. Hell is the experience of hopelessness, and such an experience is entirely subjective. The rise of hope is a way out.

A higher and maturer consciousness cannot accept the old-fashioned idea of hell ; but a too light-hearted, sentimentally optimistic rejection of it is equally untenable. Hell unquestionably exists, it is revealed to us in experience, it may be our own lot. But it belongs to time and therefore is temporal. Everything that is in time is temporal. The victory of eternity over time, i.e. the bringing-in of the temporal into eternity, is victory over hell and its powers. Hell is an aeon or an aeon of aeons, as it says in the Gospel, but not eternity. Only those are in hell who have not entered eternity but have remained in time. It is impossible, however, to remain in time for ever : one can only remain in time for a time. The perspective of a bad infinity is not an ontological reality, but a phantasm and a subjective illusion. There is something hideous and morally revolting in the idea of eternal torments as a just retribution for the crimes and sins of a short moment of life. Eternal damnation as the result of things done in a short period of time is one of the most disgusting of human nightmares. The doctrine of reincarnation, which has obvious advantages, involves, however, another nightmare—the nightmare of endless incarnations, of infinite wanderings along dark passages ; it finds the solution of man's destiny in the cosmos and not in God. But one thing is unquestionably true : after death the soul goes on living on other planes of being, just as it had lived on other planes before birth. The life in our world between birth and death is merely a small fragment of the human destiny, incomprehensible when regarded by itself, apart from the eternal destiny of man.

The idea of hell is particularly revolting when it is interpreted in a legalistic sense. Such an interpretation is common and vulgar and must be completely banished from religious ethics, philosophy and theology. The idea of hell must be entirely freed from all utilitarian considerations, and only then can the light of knowledge be shed upon it. It will then be clear to us that there may be a psychology of hell, but there can be no ontology of it. The problem of hell is completely irrational, and there is no way of rationalizing it. The doctrine of apocatastasis is also too rationalistic—quite as rationalistic as the doctrine of eternal damnation—and it does not interpret the cosmic process creatively. Calvin's doctrine of predestination is a *reductio ad absurdum* of the idea of eternal torments in hell, and this is its merit. It is a rationalistic doctrine, although it admits that God's decisions and judgment are absolutely irrational. According to that doctrine God Himself creates hell, which must be the case if God has endowed the creature with freedom and foresaw the results of it.

Man is haunted by the horror of death, but this is not the greatest horror. The greatest horror of all is the horror of hell. When it gains possession of the soul man is ready to seek salvation from hell in eternal death. But the horror of death is the horror of passing through pain, through the last agony, through dissolution ; it lies on this side of life. On the other side of life there is nothing of that. Death is terrible as the hardest and most painful fact of life. Passing through the experience of death appears to us like passing through the torments of hell. Hell is continual dying, the last agony which never ends. When the human mind is ready to seek escape from the horror of hell in death, it thinks of death which will be the end of everything, and not of an endless death. To seek deliverance from the horror of hell in death is a sign of decadence and an illusion. The struggle against the horror of hell is possible only in and through Christ. Faith in Christ and in Christ's resurrection is faith in victory over hell. The belief in an eternal hell is in the last resort unbelief in the power of Christ and faith in the power of the devil. Herein lies the fundamental contradiction of Christian theology. Manicheism was denounced as a wicked heresy, but Manichean elements penetrated into Christianity. Christians believed in the power of the devil as well as in the power of God and of Christ. Not infrequently they believed in the power of the devil more than in the power of Christ. The devil has taken the place of the evil god of the Manicheans, and it has not been settled whether God or the devil will have the last word. Manicheism is a metaphysical error but there is moral depth in it and an acute consciousness of the problem of evil which is too easily disposed of by rationalistic theology.

One of the proposed solutions of the terrible difficulties involved in the problem of hell is to acknowledge it as the triumph of the Divine justice and therefore as good. But this is a revolting consolation. Victory over the dark forces of hell is not a question of God's mercy and forgiveness, which is infinite, but of the way in which God can conquer the fathomless freedom of the creature that has turned away from Him and come to hate Him. The kingdom of the devil is not reality but non-being, the realm of dark meonic freedom, the illusory subjective realm. A man who withdraws into that realm no longer belongs to himself but to the dark powers of non-being. Victory over meonic freedom is impossible for God, since that freedom is not created by Him and is rooted in non-being ; it is equally impossible for man, since man has become the slave of that dark freedom and is not free in his freedom. It is possible only for the God-man Christ Who descends into the abysmal darkness of meonic freedom, and in Whom there is perfect union and interaction between the human and the Divine. Christ alone can conquer the horror of hell as a manifestation of the creature's freedom. Apart from Christ the tragic antinomy of freedom and necessity is insoluble, and in virtue of freedom hell remains a necessity. The horror of it means that the soul withdraws from Christ, and His image in it grows dim. The salvation from hell is open to all in Christ the Saviour.

N. Feodorov expressed a bold and startling idea of raising all the dead. But his idea must be carried further and deeper. Not only must all the dead be saved from death and raised to life again, but all must be saved and liberated from hell. This is the last and final demand of ethics. Direct all the power of your spirit to freeing everyone from hell. Do not build up hell by your will and actions, but do your utmost to destroy it. Do not create hell by thrusting the " wicked " into it. Do not imagine the Kingdom of God in too human a way as the victory of the " good " over the " wicked ", and the isolation of the " good " in a place of light and of the " wicked " in a place of darkness. Not to do so presupposes a very radical change in moral actions and valuations. The moral will must be directed in the first place towards universal salvation. This is an absolute moral truth and it does not depend upon this or that metaphysical conception of salvation and perdition. Do not create hell for anyone either in this world or in the next, get rid of the instincts of vengeance which assume lofty and idealistic forms and are projected into eternity. As immanent in experience and as a consequence of the dark freedom that has to be lived through, hell exists, anyway, but we must not create it as a place of retribution in which the " wicked " are to be segregated from " the good ". The Kingdom of God, in any case, lies beyond our " good " and " evil ", and we must not increase the nightmare of our sinful life on this side of the distinction. The " good " must take upon themselves the fate of the " wicked ", share their destiny and thus further their liberation. I may create hell for myself and, alas, I do too much to create it. But I must not create hell for others, not for a single living being. Let the " good " cease being lofty, idealistic avengers. The Emperor Justinian demanded once that the church should condemn Origen for his doctrine of universal salvation. Justinian was not content with there being temporal torments in this world, he wanted eternal torments in the next. It is time we stopped following the Emperor Justinian, but went against him. Let " the good " no longer interfere with saving the " wicked " from hell.

I have already quoted Gogol's words, " It is sad that one does not see any good in goodness ". These words express the deepest problem of ethics. There is very little good in goodness, and this is why hell is being prepared on all sides. The responsibility of good for evil, of " the good " for " the wicked ", is a new problem for ethics. It is unjust to lay the whole responsibility upon " evil " and the " wicked ". They have come into being because " the good " were bad and had not enough good in them. Both the " wicked " and the " good " will have to give an answer to God, but His judgment will be different from the human. Our distinction between good and evil may prove to be a confusion. The " good " will have to answer for having created hell, for having been satisfied with their own righteousness, for having ascribed a lofty character to their vindictive instincts, for having prevented the " wicked " from rising up and for speeding them on the way to perdition by condemning them. Such must be the conclusion of the new religious psychology and ethics.

The problem of hell is an ultimate mystery that cannot be rationalized. But the conception of eternal torments as the triumph of divine justice, holding as it does a place of honour in dogmatic theology, is a denial of the mystery and an attempt to rationalize it. Eschatology must be free both from pessimism and from optimism born of rationalization. All rationalistic eschatologies are a horrible nightmare. The idea of everlasting torments in hell is a nightmare, and so is the idea of endless reincarnations, of the disappearance of personality in the divine being, and even the idea of inevitable universal salvation. This is because they all violate the mystery by rationalizing it. We cannot and must not construct any rationalistic doctrine of hell, whether optimistic and pessimistic. But we can and must believe that the power of hell has been vanquished by Christ, and that the final word belongs to God and to the Divine meaning. The conception of hell deals not with the ultimate but with the penultimate realities. Mystical and apophatic knowledge of God has nothing to say about hell. Hell disappears in the fathomless and inexpressible depth of the Godhead (*Gottheit*). It belongs to cataphatic and rationalistic theology. Even if the knowledge that there shall be no hell is withheld - from me, I do know, at any rate, that there ought to be no hell and that I must do my utmost to save and free everyone from it. I must not isolate myself in the work of salvation and forget my neighbours doomed to perdition. We must not abandon to the devil greater and greater stretches of existence but must win them back for God. Hell is not a triumph for God—it is the triumph of the devil and of non-being.

CHAPTER THREE

Paradise. Beyond Good and Evil

MAN is tormented by the presentiment of hell. But deep down in his heart lives the memory and the dream of paradise—and the dream and the memory seem to be one. Our life passes between paradise and hell. We are exiles from paradise, but we have not yet come to hell. In the midst of our world which is so completely unlike heaven, we think of paradise in the past, at the beginning, and in the future, at the end. The earliest past and the final future come together in the idea of paradise. The myth of the golden age in the pagan world was a myth of paradise. Pagan mythological consciousness knows the golden age in the past but has no Messianic expectation of the paradise to come. Only the ancient Israel had that expectation. Mythology is always concerned with the past, and Messianism with the future. The biblical story of paradise as the original state of man and nature is a myth (in the realistic sense of the word). But the prophecies, the expectation of the coming Messiah and of the Kingdom of God, are Messianic. The Bible combines mythology and Messianism.

The cosmic process starts from paradise and begins with the exile from it. But on earth man not merely recalls the lost paradise ; he is also capable of experiencing moments of heavenly bliss through the contemplation of God, truth and beauty, through love and creative ecstasy. Paradise exists not merely in man's memories, dreams and creative imagination. It is preserved in the beauty of nature, in the sunlight, the shining stars, the blue sky, the virgin snow of the mountain peaks, the seas and the rivers, the forests and cornfields, the precious stones and flowers and the splendour of the animal world. The culture of ancient Greece and its plastic beauty was a glimpse of paradise in the history of human civilization. The cosmic process began with paradise and is going on towards paradise—but towards hell also. Man recalls paradise in the past, at the source of the world life, he dreams of paradise in the future, at the end of things, and at the same time with horror he anticipates hell. Paradise, at the beginning, paradise and hell at the end. Hell seems to be the only gain made in the cosmic process. Hell is the new reality to be revealed at the end of cosmic life. Paradise is not new, it is a return to what has been. But how sad will be the return to paradise of one part of mankind, when the other will have gone to perdition ! Such appears to be the result of eating the fruit of the tree of knowledge.

Life in paradise was all of a piece and there was nothing outside it so long as there was no distinction between good and evil. When that distinction was made, life was split into two, and hell appeared beside paradise. Such was the price of freedom—of the freedom of knowing good and evil and of choosing between them. The memory and the dream of paradise are poisoned by the terrible anticipation of hell, whether for oneself or for others. Freedom was bought at the price of hell. If it had not been for freedom, life in paradise would have gone on for ever, without any dark clouds over it. Man is perpetually haunted by the dream of re-creating paradisaical life in its integrity, not darkened by the fatal consequences of spiritual freedom. That dream lies at the basis of all utopias of a heaven on earth. Man was banished from the Garden of Eden because his freedom proved fatal. Could he not return to it if he renounced freedom? Could he not avoid hell by renouncing freedom? The dialectics of freedom and paradise have been worked out by Dostoevsky with the force of genius.[1] *The Dream of a Ridiculous Man, Versilov's Dream* and *The Legend of the Grand Inquisitor* deal with the problem of paradise which tormented Dostoevsky. He could not be reconciled either to a paradise which had not yet passed through the trial of freedom or to the paradise which, after all man's trials, will be established compulsorily, without regard to the freedom of the human spirit. He can only accept a paradise that has passed through freedom and been freely chosen by man. A compulsory paradise in the past and in the future inspired Dostoevsky with horror and seemed to him a lure of the antichrist. Christ means, first and foremost, freedom. This throws a new light upon the myth of the Fall. The lure of the devil is not freedom, as has often been thought, but the rejection of freedom for the sake of bliss mechanically forced upon man. This brings us to the ultimate mystery of the Fall, which cannot be solved rationally and coincides with the mystery of man's and all creation's ultimate destiny. God willed the freedom of the creature and based His idea of creation upon freedom. Man's creative vocation is connected with freedom. Hence our conception of the Fall is bound to be irrational and contradictory. The Fall is a manifestation and trial of man's freedom, a way out of the original, pre-conscious, natural paradise in which spiritual freedom was as yet unknown, and at the same time the Fall is the loss of freedom and subjection to the lower natural elements. This was when the knot of the cosmic life was tied. The Fall proved to be necessary, since

[1] See my book, *Mirosozertasnie Dostoevskago* (Dostoevsky's conception of life).

freedom was necessary for the realization of the higher meaning of creation. But " necessity of freedom " is a contradiction and a paradox. We are not able to solve this contradiction in thought, we can only live it out in the experience of life. The Fall is a violation of Meaning and a falling away from it, and yet we must recognize meaning in the Fall, the meaning of transition from the original paradise in which freedom is unknown to a paradise in which there is a knowledge of freedom.

It is therefore impossible to speak of returning to the original paradisaical state. We neither can nor ought to return to it. A return would mean that the cosmic process has been useless and therefore meaningless. The paradise at the end of the cosmic process is quite different from the paradise at its beginning. It comes after all the trials and with the knowledge of freedom. It may be said indeed to be the paradise after hell, after the experience of evil and a free rejection of hell. The temptation of returning to the primeval pre-cosmic non-being is freely overcome by entities which conform to God's conception of being. Paradise, in which there is as yet no awareness of man's creative vocation and the highest idea of man is not yet realized, is replaced by a paradise in which his vocation and idea are revealed to the full. In other words, the natural paradise is replaced by the spiritual. In his original paradisaical state man knows nothing of the coming of the God-man, but the paradise at the end of the cosmic process will be the Kingdom of Christ. The first paradise knows nothing of the Divine Humanity which is a positive result of the cosmic process.

But within the cosmic process man in his pain and suffering continually dreams of returning to the lost paradise and regaining his original innocence and wholeness. He is ready to renounce knowledge, which appears to him to be the result of the inner dividedness and the loss of wholeness. He is prepared to flee from the agonies of " culture " to the joy and bliss of " nature ". Every time, however, he experiences a sinful disappointment in his dreams and desires, for not only " culture " but "nature " too proves to be affected by original sin. There is only one way open to him —that of being faithful to the end to the idea of " man " and entering the kingdom of the spirit, which transfigured nature will enter also. The knowledge of good and evil involves the loss of paradisaical wholeness, but the way of knowledge must be trodden to the end. Once man has entered the path of discriminating between good and evil, knowledge as such is not evil.[1] Knowledge has evil for its object, but itself is not evil. And through knowledge man's creative vocation is realized. This is the

[1] This is the chief point of difference between L. Shestov and me.

justification of " culture " against the attacks made upon it by the champions of " nature ". Man is bound to follow the path of tragedy and heroism. The return to the original wholeness, to paradisaical " nature ", means forsaking that path. A reflection of the lost paradise is preserved in the primeval beauty of nature, and man finds his way to it through artistic contemplation which is a creative transfiguration of the everyday world. There is a reflection of the lost paradise in art and poetry, and in them man participates in heavenly bliss through creative ecstasy, i.e. through creative ascent to higher realms. There is a reflection of paradise in Pushkin's poetry which overcomes the " heaviness " of the world. Pushkin's art is neither Christian nor Pagan—it is paradisaical. But in it, too, paradise is reached through human creativeness, through following the way of man and not through returning to primeval nature. And it is the same with everything.

The so-called moral life is not heavenly, and paradise is not the triumph of " the good ". The good and the moral life are always to some extent poisoned by judgment, division, constant rejection of " evil " and " the wicked ". In the realm of " the good " there is no divine liberation, lightness, wholeness and radiance. Paradise means cessation of care, escape from Heidegger's world of anxiety, and acquisition of spiritual wholeness. But moral life is weighed down by care, by the anxiety of struggling against evil, and there is division in it—the division of mankind into the good and the wicked. Heaven conceived as a correlative to hell would be the kingdom of the good, opposed to the kingdom of evil. There could be no wholeness in that kingdom and it would be poisoned by the proximity of hell with the everlasting torments of the wicked. The idea of an eternal realm of bliss by the side of an eternal hell is one of the most monstrous human inventions—an evil invention of " the good ". We live in a world of sin, on this side of good and evil, and it is extremely difficult for us to conceive of heaven. We transfer to it the categories of our sinful life, our distinctions between good and evil. But paradise lies beyond good and evil and therefore is not exclusively the kingdom of " the good " in our sense of the term. We come nearer to it when we think of it as beauty. The transfiguration and regeneration of the world is beauty and not goodness. Paradise is theosis, deification of the creature. The good is relative to an untransfigured and an unregenerate world. Beauty alone is liberation from the burden of care ; goodness is not yet free from care. An eternal life on the other side of death, in which there would be a division into heaven and hell, the realm of the good and the realm of the wicked, would be weighed down by care and give man no peace, no perfect wholeness or perfect joy. The tragic process of struggle against hell would be bound to begin in any case. Hell cannot help attacking heaven, for it is its nature to seek expansion. The idea of hell as a final triumph of God's truth and justice is untenable and cannot reassure those who are in heaven. Hell is bound to be a torment to heaven, and heaven cannot exist beside it.

We have to think of paradise in negative terms. All positive conceptions of it lead to insoluble contradictions, for we transfer the categories of this life to the life beyond. The main antinomy with regard to paradise is that man passionately dreams of heavenly bliss and at the same time fears it, imagining that it will be dull, monotonous, fixed and unchangeable. This antinomy is connected with the paradox of time and eternity. We transfer to eternity ideas which only have meaning with reference to time. It is impossible to think of perfection, fullness and wholeness as being in time. The thought of perfection in time is painfully boring and seems to imply complacency and the end of all creative movement. This is why all utopias of an earthly paradise are so dull and false. It is false to transfer perfection from eternity into time. Perfection, fullness and wholeness are not realizable in time, for they indicate the end of time, victory over it and entrance into eternity. Time implies imperfection, incompleteness and disruption. Perfection transferred into time is always finite, while perfection in eternity is positive infinity. Paradise in our time, on earth, would be the end of the creative process of life, of infinite striving, and consequently would mean boredom. But people have managed to ascribe the same character to the heavenly life in the world beyond. We think in time and project paradise into the future ; hence it appears to us as a standstill, as the cessation of infinite striving, movement, and creativeness, as the attainment of complete satisfaction. It is as though in heaven there would be no more freedom. And like Dostoevsky's hero " with a reactionary and ironical expression " we are ready to let paradise go to the devil, so that we could live according to our own sweet will. Man dreams of paradise and fears it, and returns to the tragic freedom of cosmic life. World-order and harmony to which personal freedom is sacrificed are unendurable.

But paradise is not in the future, is not in time, but in eternity. Eternity is attained in the actual moment, it comes in the present—not in the present which is a part of the broken up time, but in the present which is an escape from time. Eternity is not a cessation of movement and of creative life ; it is creative life of a different order, it is movement which is not spatial and temporal but inward, symbolized not by a straight line but by a circle, i.e. it is an inner mystery play, a mystery play of the spirit which embraces the whole tragedy of the cosmic life. We must think of paradise as containing not less but more life than our sinful world, not less but more movement—though it is movement of the spirit and not of nature and is not based upon the continuity of time. It is impossible to think of perfection as the absence of creative dynamism. In the perfect, heavenly life there is no anxiety, care, longing and restlessness born of time, but there is in it a creative movement of its own. Paradise proves to be a paradox for man, for it is as impossible to conceive infinity in time with its longing, restlessness and pain as to conceive perfection wthout dynamism and movement. In experiencing that paradox we remiain on this side and do not break through to the beyond. We transfer the agonizing difficulties of our world to the world beyond. But paradise can only be conceived apophatically as lying beyond our time and all that is connected with it, and beyond good and evil. .

A foretaste of paradise is given us in ecstasy, in which time, as we know it, is rent asunder, the distinction between good and evil disappears, all sense of heaviness is gone and there is a feeling of final liberation. The ecstasy of creative inspiration, of love, of contemplating the divine light, transfers us for a moment to heaven, and those moments are no longer in time. But after a moment of eternity we find ourselves in the continuing time once more ; everything grows heavy, sinks down and falls prey to the cares and anxieties of everyday life.

In trying to think of the last things we are confronted with the paradox of time and eternity which vitiates all our eschatological theories. This paradox is felt with particular acuteness in the expectations of the millennium. The chiliastic idea is the expression of the human dream of bliss and happiness, of the Messianic feast and a paradise which is not only in heaven but on earth also, both in eternity and in our historical time. In the idea of the millennium eternity passes over into time and time enters eternity. Man has always hoped that at the end of the cosmic process the Kingdom of God will be revealed, divine righteousness will be realized and the saints will reign on earth. It is the hope that the positive result of the cosmic process will be revealed in some intermediary sphere between time and eternity ; it will no longer be in time and not as yet in eternity. This is the essential difficulty of interpreting the Apocalypse. The language of eternity has to be translated into the language of time. Completely to deny the chiliastic idea is to deny the paradox itself and to transfer everything into eternity, leaving on this side of it, in time, the non-divine world banished from paradise. But the paradox is also denied by those who think of the Kingdom of God in sensuous terms on our earth and in our time.

The Christian revelation is, first and foremost, a message of the Kingdom of God. The quest of that Kingdom is the essence of Christianity. But the idea of it is extremely difficult to interpret and leads to irreconcilable contradictions. The Kingdom of God cannot be thought of as existing in time ; it is the end of time, the end of the world, a new heaven and a new earth. But if the Kingdom of God is out of time and in eternity, it cannot be referred entirely to the end of the world, for that end is in time. The Kingdom of God comes not only at the end of time but at every moment. A moment may lead us from time into eternity. The Kingdom of God or eternity is not separated from me by the length of time which is to pass before the end of the world. There are two ways to eternity—through the depth of the moment and through the end of time and of the world. The Kingdom of God cometh not with observation. We think of it as the Heavenly Kingdom, but it is possible on earth too, for earth may also be regenerated and inherit eternity. We cannot draw a dividing line between that new earth and earth as we know it. The idea of an earthly paradise is a utopia and a false hope. But in a deeper sense we may think of heaven on earth ; we can enter eternity, we can experience ecstasy, contemplate God and have joy and light. An eschatological interpretation of the Kingdom of God is the only true one. But the paradox of eschatological consciousness is that the end is both put off to an indefinite time in the future and is near to every moment of life. There is an eschatology within the process of life. Apocalypse is not merely the revelation of the end of the world and of history. It is also the revelation of the end within the world and the historical process, within human life and every moment of life.

It is particularly important to rise above a passive interpretation of the Apocalypse as the expectation of the end and of the Last Judgment. It is possible to interpret it actively as a call to creative activity, to heroic effort and achievement. The end depends to a certain extent on man, and the nature of it will be determined by man's activity. The image of the Heavenly Jerusalem descending from heaven to earth is one of the ways of picturing it. The New Jerusalem is built up, partly at any rate, by man, by his freedom, efforts and creativeness. Man actively creates heaven and hell. They are expressions of his spiritual life and are revealed in the depths of the spirit. Only the weak consciousness vitiated by sin projects heaven and hell into the outer world and transfers them to an objective sphere, similar to that of nature. A deeper and more integral consciousness holds heaven and hell within the spirit, i.e. ceases passively to dream of paradise and to feel a passive horror of hell, projecting them into a future time. God's Judgment takes place every moment and is the voice of eternity in time. The idea of heaven, like that of hell, must therefore be completely freed from all utilitarian considerations. The Kingdom of God is not a reward but the attainment of perfection, deification, beauty and spiritual wholeness.

The idea of paradise is based upon the supposition that perfection involves bliss, that the perfect, the beautiful, the righteous, the holy are in a state of blessedness. Life in God is bliss. The idea of the bliss of the righteous is the source of hedonism. Hedonism was heavenly before it became earthly. " Man is born to happiness " is the contention of the earthly hedonism ; " man is created for bliss " is the assertion of the heavenly hedonism. Pain, misery, suffering are the result of sin. There was bliss in the Garden of Eden before the Fall. Blissful, blessed, is the same as righteous, holy, obedient to God. The new paradise to which the righteous will return will be a state of bliss. The identity of righteousness and bliss is the identity of the subjective and the objective, i.e. wholeness. We who live in a world of sin are ruled by its laws and bear its stain, have difficulty in grasping this. We regard heavenly bliss with suspicion. In a sinful world tragedy, suffering, dissatisfaction are a sign of a higher and more perfect state. The idea that happiness is the end of life and a criterion of good and evil is the invention of those who hold the lowest moral theories—hedonism, eudaimonism and utilitarianism. We rightly consider the pursuit of happiness a snare and a delusion. There can be no lasting happiness in our world, though there may be moments of joy and even of bliss as an escape from this life and communion with another, free world in which there are no cares and burdens. And indeed man never does strive for happiness—he strives for objective goods and values the attainment of which may bring happiness. The idea that happiness is the end of life is the product of reflection and self-analysis.

Still more important for the question we are considering is the fact that people who do not suffer, but are too happy, contented and at peace, make us suspect that they are shallow, limited in their ideas, self-satisfied and indifferent to the sorrows of others. The bliss of paradise in our sinful world seems to us reprehensible. Thus aestheticism is a pretension to attain paradise in the midst of sin. We find it difficult to transfer ourselves to a plane of being where bliss is the expression of righteousness and perfection. We are confronted with an ethical and psychological paradox. The bliss of paradise, which, in spite of all, we do experience at rare moments of life, is the attainment of wholeness, completeness, divine-like perfection. And at the same time the state of bliss troubles us as a halt in the movement of the spirit, as a cessation of the infinite seeking and striving, as self-sufficiency and indifference to the sorrows of others and to the existence of hell.

The bliss of paradise means eating of the tree of life and ignorance of good and evil. but we feed from the tree of knowledge, live by the distinction between good and evil and transfer it to that new paradise which will appear at the end of the cosmic process. This is the ontological difference between the paradise at the beginning and at the end of the world process. The paradise at the beginning is the original wholeness which is free from the poison of consciousness, the poison of knowing good and evil and of distinguishing between them. To that paradise there is no returning. And that paradise knows nothing of freedom which we value so greatly as the expression of our highest dignity. The paradise at the end presupposes that man has already passed through the acuteness and division of consciousness, through freedom and the knowledge of good and evil. That paradise signifies a new wholeness and completeness after the division and disruption. But it troubles us because its correlate is hell. What is to be done with evil, which is the consequence of the division of consciousness and the trial of freedom? How can we enjoy bliss in paradise if there exist torments of hell for the wicked, if evil is not really conquered but has a kingdom of its own? If paradise at the beginning of the cosmic life cannot be accepted by us because freedom has not been tried in it, paradise at the end of the cosmic life cannot be accepted because freedom has already been tried and has given rise to evil. This is the fundamental problem of ethics in its eschatological aspect. Ethics is faced with this problem but cannot solve it. The idea of perfection connected with bliss both attracts and repels us. It repels us because we think of bliss and perfection as finite while they are infinite, i.e. we rationalize things that are not susceptible of rationalization and think cataphatically instead of thinking apophatically.

For Christian consciousness paradise is the Kingdom of Christ and is unthinkable apart from Christ. But this changes everything. The cross and the crucifixion enter into the bliss of paradise. The Son of God and the Son of man descends into hell to free those who suffer there. The mystery of the cross solves the chief contradiction of paradise and freedom. To conquer evil the Good must crucify itself. The Good appears in a new aspect : it does not condemn " the wicked " to eternal torments but suffers upon the cross. The " good " do not relegate the " wicked " to hell and enjoy their own triumph but descend with Christ into hell in order to free them. This liberation from hell cannot, however, be an act of violence towards the "wicked" who are there. This is the extraordinary difficulty of the problem. It cannot be solved by human and natural means ; it can only be solved through the God-man and grace. Neither God nor man can do violence to the wicked and compel them to be good and happy in paradise. But the God-man in Whom grace and freedom are mysteriously combined knows the mystery of liberating the wicked.

We find it difficult to conceive this and have to fall back upon *docta ignorantia*. The wicked cannot be made "good" in our sense of the term, which has arisen after the Fall and the division into good and evil. The wicked and those who are in hell can only be won by the transcendent good, i.e. brought to the Kingdom of Heaven which lies beyond good and evil and is free both from our good and from our evil. Paradise conceived as the kingdom of the good and goodness in our sense cannot be accepted by the moral consciousness and may be positively repellent to it. It is supposed to belong to the world beyond, but its nature is of this world and conformable to our categories.

The Kingdom of God is not the kingdom of our good but of the transcendent good, in which the results and the trials of freedom assume other forms than they do in this world. This implies quite a different morality in this life, a revaluation of values. Eschatology throws back a reflected light upon the whole of our life. Ethics becomes a teaching about the transcendent good and the ways to the Kingdom of God ; it acquires a prophetic character and rises above the hard and fast determinations of the law. But it was the revaluation of values and the desire to rise beyond good and evil that wrecked Nietzsche, who had something of the unenlightened prophetism. Nietzsche transferred to the realm beyond good and evil the evil which is on this side, and that shows that he really never reached the world beyond.

The morality of the transcendent good does not by any means imply indifference to good and evil or toleration of evil. It demands more and not less. A morality based upon relegating the wicked to hell is a minimum and not a maximum morality ; it renounces victory over evil, it gives up the idea of enlightening and liberating the wicked ; it confines itself to distinctions and valuations and does not lead to any actual change and transfiguration of reality. Religious morality based upon the idea of personal salvation is a " minimum morality ", a morality of transcendental egoism. It invites man to settle down comfortably while other people and the world are in misery ; it denies that everyone is responsible for everyone else and rejects the essential oneness of the created world. In the realm of the spirit there is no such thing as a self-contained and isolated personality. The morality of personal salvation leads to a distortion of the idea of paradise and of the Divine Kingdom. True heavenly bliss is impossible for me if I isolate myself from the world-whole and care about myself only. It is impossible for the good alone who demand a privileged position for themselves. The Fall involved the world-soul and man as a microcosm, and it is only as a microcosm that he can be saved, together with the world-soul. The separation of man from man and of man from the cosmos is the result of original sin, and it is impossible to transfer this result of sin to the work of salvation and to make the Kingdom of God in the image of the sinful world. Salvation is the reunion of man with man and with the cosmos through reunion with God. Hence there can be no individual salvation or salvation of the elect. Crucifixion, pain and tragedy will go on in the world until all mankind and the whole world are saved, transfigured and regenerated. And if it cannot be attained in our world-aeon, there will be other aeons in which the work of salvation and transfiguration will be continued. That work is not limited to our earthly life. My salvation is bound up with that not only of other men but also of animals, plants, minerals, of every blade of grass—all must be transfigured and brought into the Kingdom of God. And this depends upon my creative efforts.

Thus the province of ethics is the whole world. Man is the supreme centre of the cosmic life ; it fell through him, and through him it must rise. Man cannot raise himself only. The idea of the Divine Kingdom is incompatible with religious or moral individualism, with an exclusive concern for personal salvation. To affirm the supreme value of personality does not mean to be concerned with personal salvation ; it means to recognize that man has the highest creative vocation in the life of the world. The least admissible form of aristocracy is the aristocracy of salvation. There may be an aristocracy of knowledge, of beauty, of refinement, of the fine flower of life—but there cannot be one of salvation.

There are two different kinds of good—the good in the conditions of our sinful world that judges and makes valuations and is on this side of the distinction between good and evil and the good which is the attainment of the highest quality of life, the good on the other side of the distinction, which does not judge or make valuations but radiates light. The first kind of good has no relation to the heavenly life ; it is the good of purgatory, and it dies together with sin. When that good is projected into eternity, it creates hell. Hell is precisely the transference of the life on this side into eternity. The second kind of good is heavenly ; it is above and beyond our distinction between good and evil and does not admit of the existence of hell beside it. It is a mistake to think that only the first kind of good may serve as a guide in our life here, and that the second kind can have no guiding significance. On the contrary, it leads to a revaluation of values and to a higher moral level ; it springs not from indifference to evil but from a deep and painful experience of the problem that evil presents. The first kind of good does not solve the problem of evil.

As a rule ethics does not know what to do with evil ; it judges and condemns it, but is powerless to conquer it and indeed does not want to do so. Hence ethics knows nothing about either heaven or hell, it knows only the purgatory. Our task is to build up a system of ethics in which the heavenly good is recognized and therefore the problem of hell is faced. The ethics of creativeness belongs to the heavenly realm, though it knows the torments of hell also. Paradise is the ecstatic creative flight into infinity, rising above the heaviness, dividedness and limitations of the world. This creative flight is beyond Judgment based upon the distinction between good and evil—it is above good. Love is above good and is the beginning of the heavenly life, though it is darkened by suffering born of sin. The ethics of creativeness must be in a sense chiliastic and directed towards the aeon which lies between time and eternity, between this world and the world beyond, in which the hard-set limitations of our existence are melted down. This is what happens in all creative inspiration.

Heavenly life must be interpreted dynamically and not statically. This is the difference between the paradise at the end and at the beginning. When we dream of flying, we dream of the heavenly life. It is winged and not fettered to earth, not immobile. Heavenly life is in the first place victory over the nightmare of disruption in time. Time is the nightmare and torment of our life in this world. We are drawn towards the past in memory and towards the future in imagination. Through memory the past abides in the present, and through imagination the future enters the present. This is the paradox of time. We seek the eternal present as the victory over the death-bringing flow of time, and in order to do so we constantly leave the present for the past and the future, as though the eternal present could be captured in that way. Hence, living in time we are doomed never to live in the present. The striving towards the future, characteristic of our world-aeon, brings about a quickening of time and makes it impossible to dwell in the present for contemplating the eternal.

But heavenly life is in the eternal present and means victory over the torment of time. Modern civilization is the opposite of heavenly life. Its speeding up of time and its striving for the future are not a flight towards eternity ; on the contrary, they enslave man to the death-bringing time, so that one begins to understand the torment of insatiable everlasting longing. This aeon moves towards a catastrophe ; it cannot last for ever, it is self-destructive. There will come another aeon in which the bad quickening of time and the bad striving for the future will be replaced by a creative flight into infinity and eternity.

There are two typical answers to the question of man's vocation. One is that man is called to contemplation and the other that he is called to action. But it is a mistake to oppose contemplation to action as though they were mutually exclusive. Man is called to creative activity, he is not merely a spectator—even though it be of divine beauty. Creativeness is action. It presupposes overcoming difficulties and there is an element of labour in it. But it also includes moments of contemplation which may be called heavenly, moments of rest when difficulties and labour vanish and the self is in communion with the divine. Contemplation is the highest state, it is an end in itself and cannot be a means. But contemplation is also creativeness, spiritual activity which overcomes anxiety and difficulties.

The last eschatological problem of ethics is the most painful of all— the problem of the meaning of evil. Attempts are made to solve it monistically and dualistically. The dualistic solution of it lies entirely on this side of the distinction between good and evil engendered by the Fall and consists in projecting that distinction into eternity as heaven and hell. Evil is thus relegated to a special order of being and proves to be utterly meaningless ; but it confirms the existence of meaning, since it receives its punishment. The monistic solution does not want to perpetuate hell as the kingdom of evil beside the kingdom of good or paradise, and in principle evil is subordinated to the good, either as a part of the good which, owing to the limitations of our consciousness, appears to us as evil, or as insufficiently revealed good, or as an illusion. Knowledge of evil invariably implies a question as to its meaning. The dualistic solution sees the meaning of evil in the fact that evil is tormented by the triumph of the good. The monistic solution sees the meaning of evil in the fact that it is a part of the good and is subordinate to the good as a whole. But in truth, in the first case evil is meaningless, and the world in which it came into being cannot be justified. In the second case evil is simply said not to exist and the problem of it is not really recognized.

Paradise. Beyond Good and Evil

The dualistic and the monistic modes of thought are equally invalid and merely show the insolubly paradoxical character of the problem of evil. The paradox is that evil is meaningless, is the absence and violation of Meaning and yet must have a positive significance if Meaning, i.e. God, is to have the last word. It is impossible to find a way out of the dilemma by adopting one of the diametrically opposite assertions. We must recognize both that evil is meaningless and that it has meaning. Rational theology which regards itself as orthodox has no solution to offer. If evil is pure non-sense and violation of the Meaning of the world, and if it is crowned by eternal hell, something essentially unmeaning forms part of God's conception of the world, and creation is a failure. But if evil has a positive meaning and does not result in everlasting hell, if it will be turned to account in heaven, struggle against evil becomes difficult, for evil proves to be an unrealized form of the good.

Attempts have been made to solve the difficulty by means of the traditional doctrine of the freedom of will. But as we have seen, this merely throws the difficulty further back and raises the question as to the source of freedom. The positive meaning of evil lies in the fact that it is a trial of freedom and that freedom, the highest quality of the creature, presupposes the possibility of evil. Life in paradise which does not know evil, i.e. does not know freedom, does not satisfy man who bears the image and likeness of God. Man seeks a paradise in which freedom will have been tried to the end. But a trial of freedom gives rise to evil, and therefore a heavenly life that has passed through the trial of freedom is a life that knows the positive meaning of evil.

Freedom springs from an abysmal, pre-existential source, and the darkness that comes from that source must be enlightened and transfigured by the divine light, the Logos. The genesis of evil shows that we must both recognize its positive significance, which will be turned to account in heavenly life, and condemn it, waging an unwearying struggle against it. The positive meaning of evil lies solely in the enrichment of life brought about by the heroic struggle against it and the victory over it. That struggle and victory, however, mean not the relegation of evil to a special realm of being but an actual and final conquest of it, i.e. its transfiguration and redemption. This is the fundamental paradox of ethics, which has both an esoteric and an exoteric aspect. Ethics inevitably passes into eschatology and is resolved into it. Its last word is theosis, deification, attained through man's freedom and creativeness which enrich the divine life itself.

The main position of an ethics which recognizes the paradox of good and evil may be formulated as follows : act as though you could hear the

297

Divine call to participate through free and creative activity in the Divine work; cultivate in yourself a pure and original conscience, discipline your personality, struggle with evil in yourself and around you—not in order to relegate the wicked to hell and create a kingdom of evil, but to conquer evil and to further a creative regeneration of the wicked.